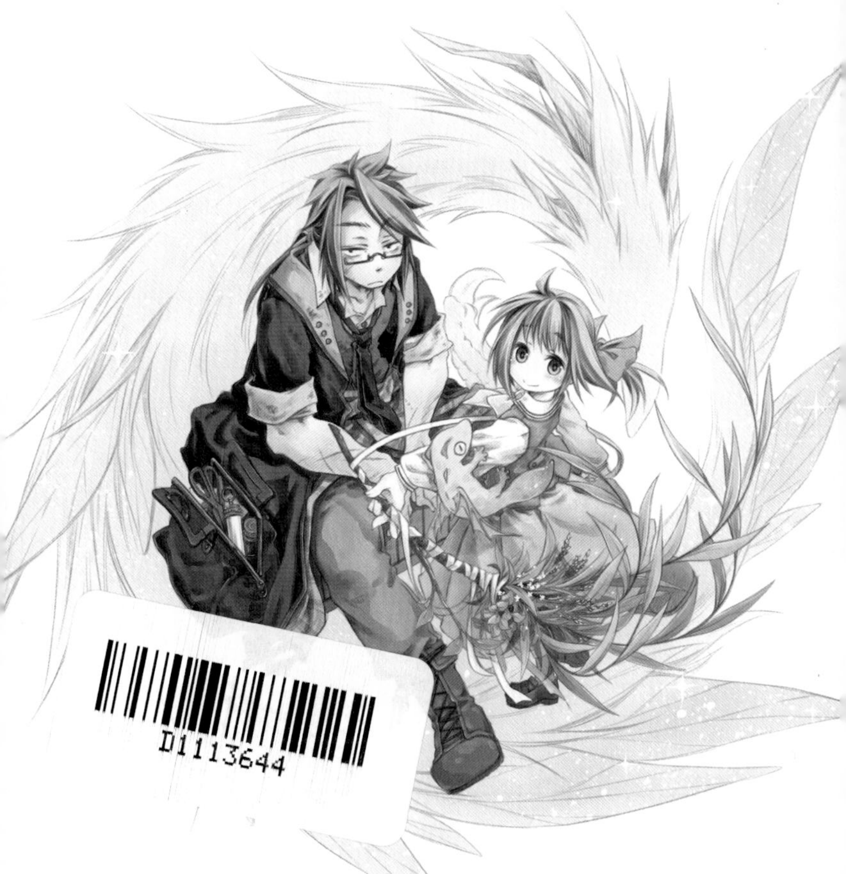

How to Treat Magical Beasts
Mine and Master's Medical Journal

1

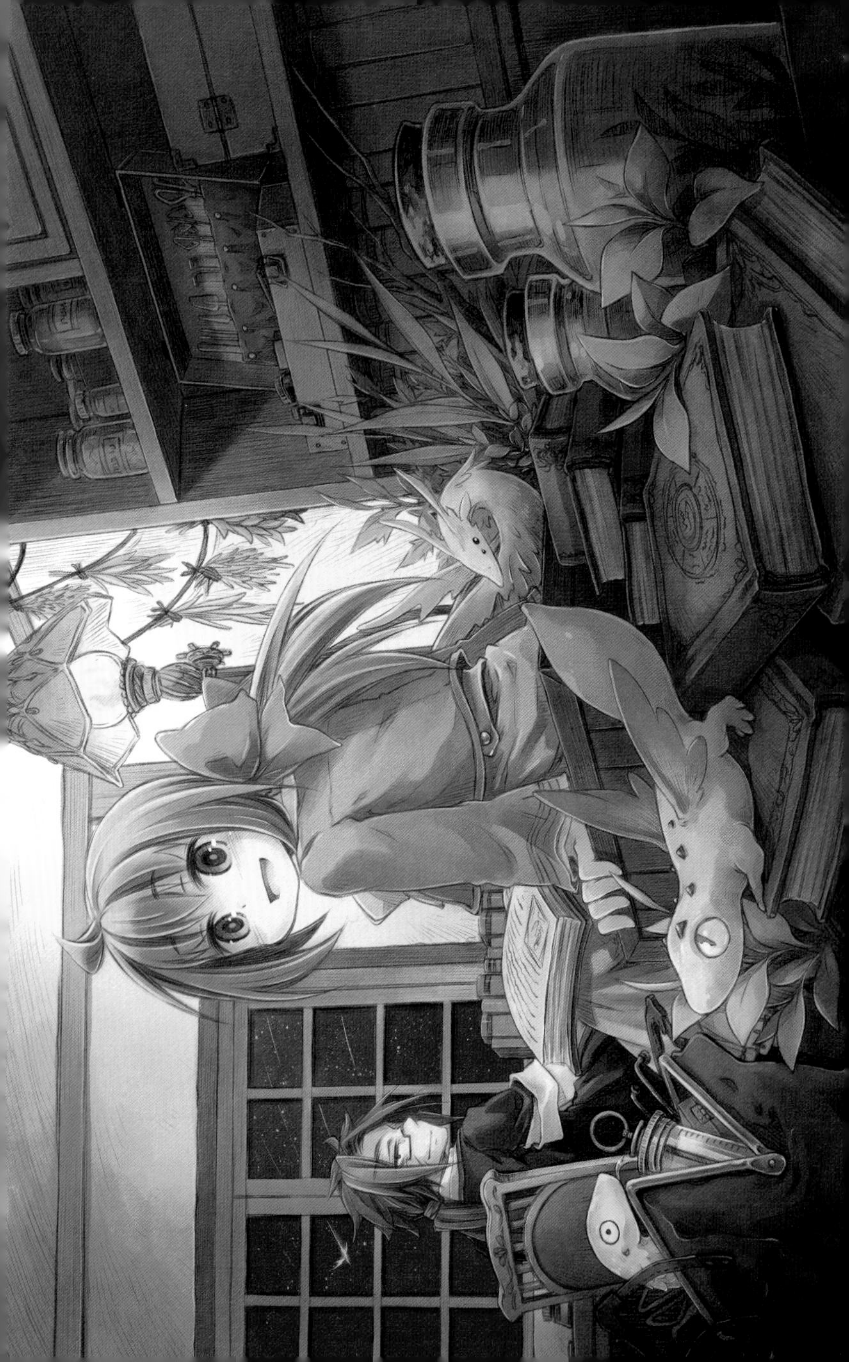

SEVEN SEAS ENTERTAINMENT PRESENTS

How to Treat Magical Beasts
Mine and Master's Medical Journal

story and art by KAZIYA   VOLUME 1

TRANSLATION
Angela Liu

ADAPTATION
Jaymee Goh

LETTERING AND RETOUCH
Annaliese Christman

COVER DESIGN
KC Fabellon

PROOFREADER
Danielle King
Brett Hallahan

EDITOR
Jenn Grunigen

PRODUCTION ASSISTANT
CK Russell

PRODUCTION MANAGER
Lissa Pattillo

EDITOR-IN-CHIEF
Adam Arnold

PUBLISHER
Jason DeAngelis

WATASHI TO SENSEI NO GENJUU SHINRYOUROKU VOL. 1
© Kaziya 2017
Originally published in Japan in 2017 by MAG Garden Corporation, Tokyo.
English translation rights arranged through TOHAN CORPORATION, Tokyo.

Seven Seas books may be purchased in bulk for promotional, educational, or
business use. Please contact your local bookseller or the Macmillan Corporate
and Premium Sales Department at 1-800-221-7945, extension 5442, or by
e-mail at MacmillanSpecialMarkets@macmillan.com.

Seven Seas and the Seven Seas logo are trademarks of
Seven Seas Entertainment, LLC. All rights reserved.

ISBN: 978-1-626928-90-9

Printed in Canada

First Printing: May 2018

10 9 8 7 6 5 4 3 2 1

FOLLOW US ONLINE: *www.sevenseasentertainment.com*

READING DIRECTIONS

This book reads from *right to left*, Japanese style.
If this is your first time reading manga, you start
reading from the top right panel on each page and
take it from there. If you get lost, just follow the
numbered diagram here. It may seem backwards at
first, but you'll get the hang of it! Have fun!!

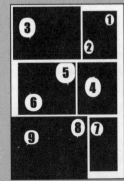

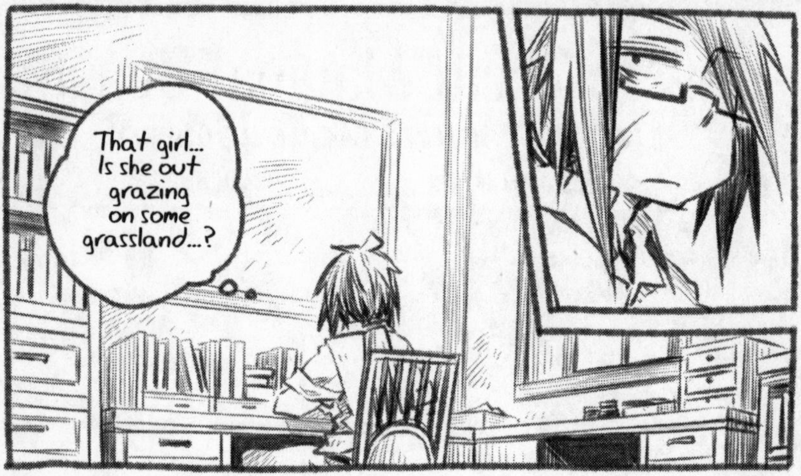
That girl... Is she out grazing on some grassland...?

Thank you for reading!!

There are some artistic liberties taken in some parts of the story, but I hope you enjoy the story itself.

Please watch out for me in the next volume, as well!!

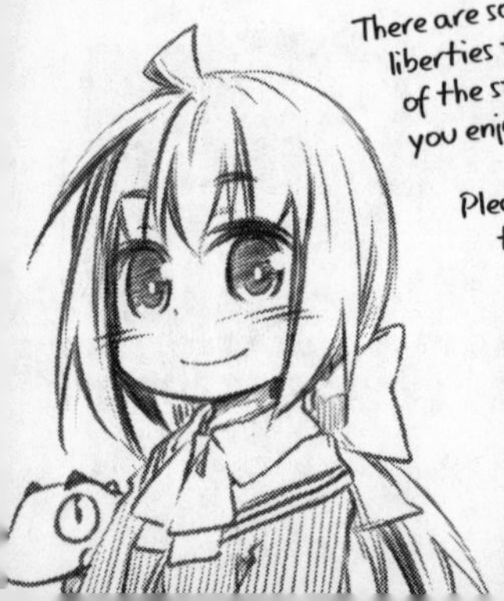

How to Treat Magical Beasts: Mine and Master's Medical Journal Official Twitter

Follow us!

https://twitter.com/genjuushinryou

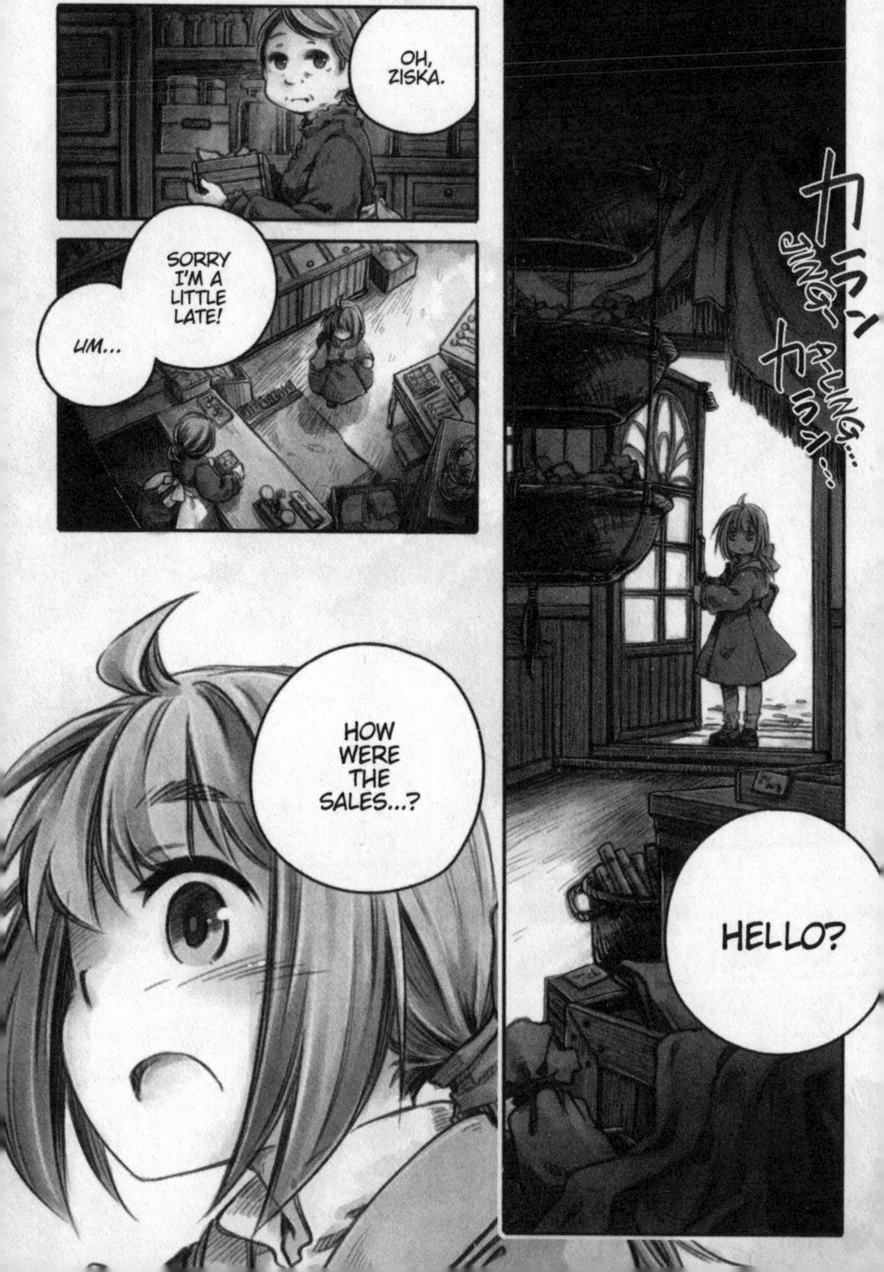
カラン カラン…
JINGA-LING...
HELLO?
OH, ZISKA.
SORRY I'M A LITTLE LATE!
UM...
HOW WERE THE SALES...?

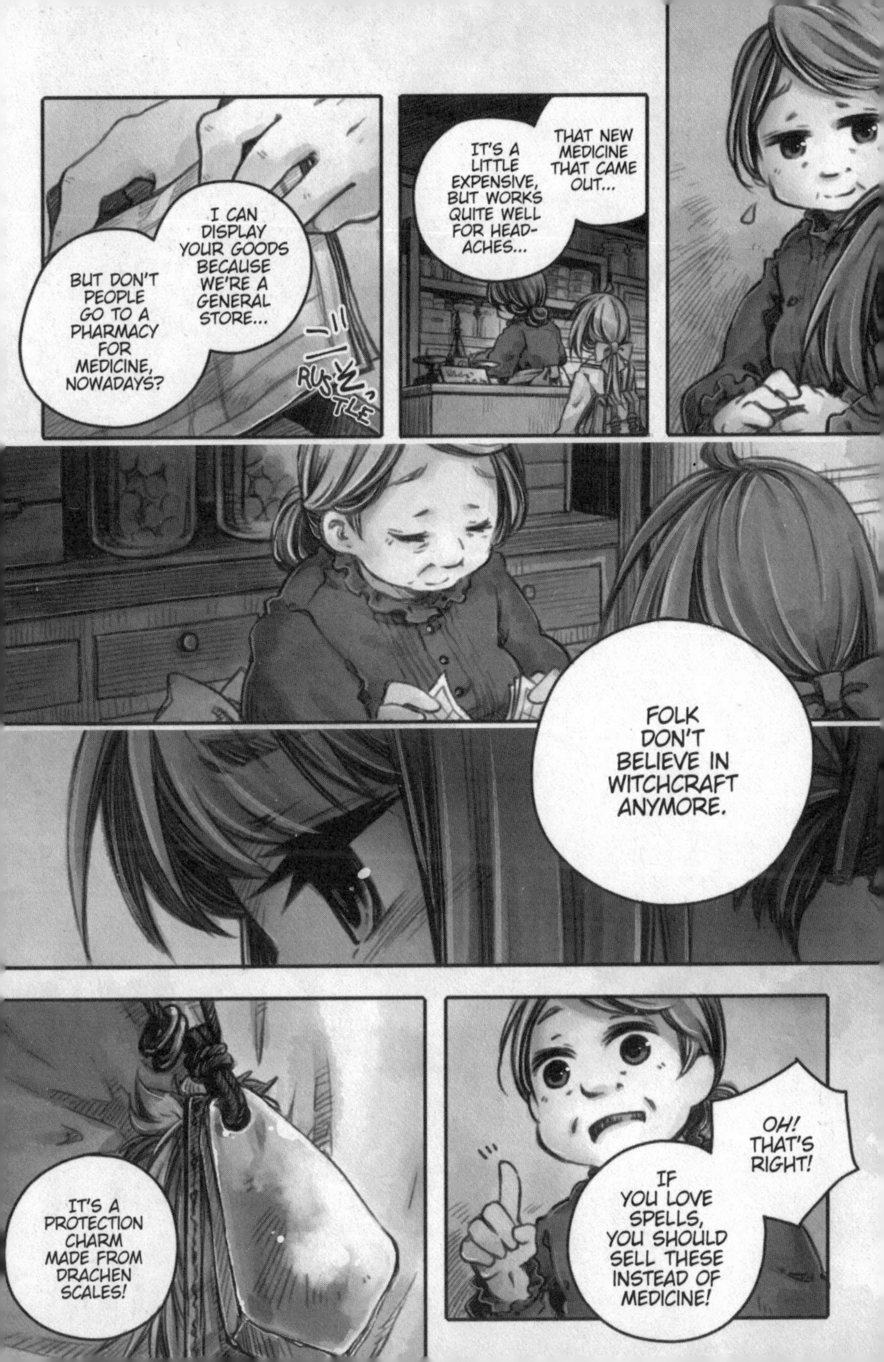
THAT NEW MEDICINE THAT CAME OUT...
IT'S A LITTLE EXPENSIVE, BUT WORKS QUITE WELL FOR HEAD-ACHES...
I CAN DISPLAY YOUR GOODS BECAUSE WE'RE A GENERAL STORE...
BUT DON'T PEOPLE GO TO A PHARMACY FOR MEDICINE, NOWADAYS?
RUSTLE
FOLK DON'T BELIEVE IN WITCHCRAFT ANYMORE.
OH! THAT'S RIGHT!
IF YOU LOVE SPELLS, YOU SHOULD SELL THESE INSTEAD OF MEDICINE!
IT'S A PROTECTION CHARM MADE FROM DRACHEN SCALES!

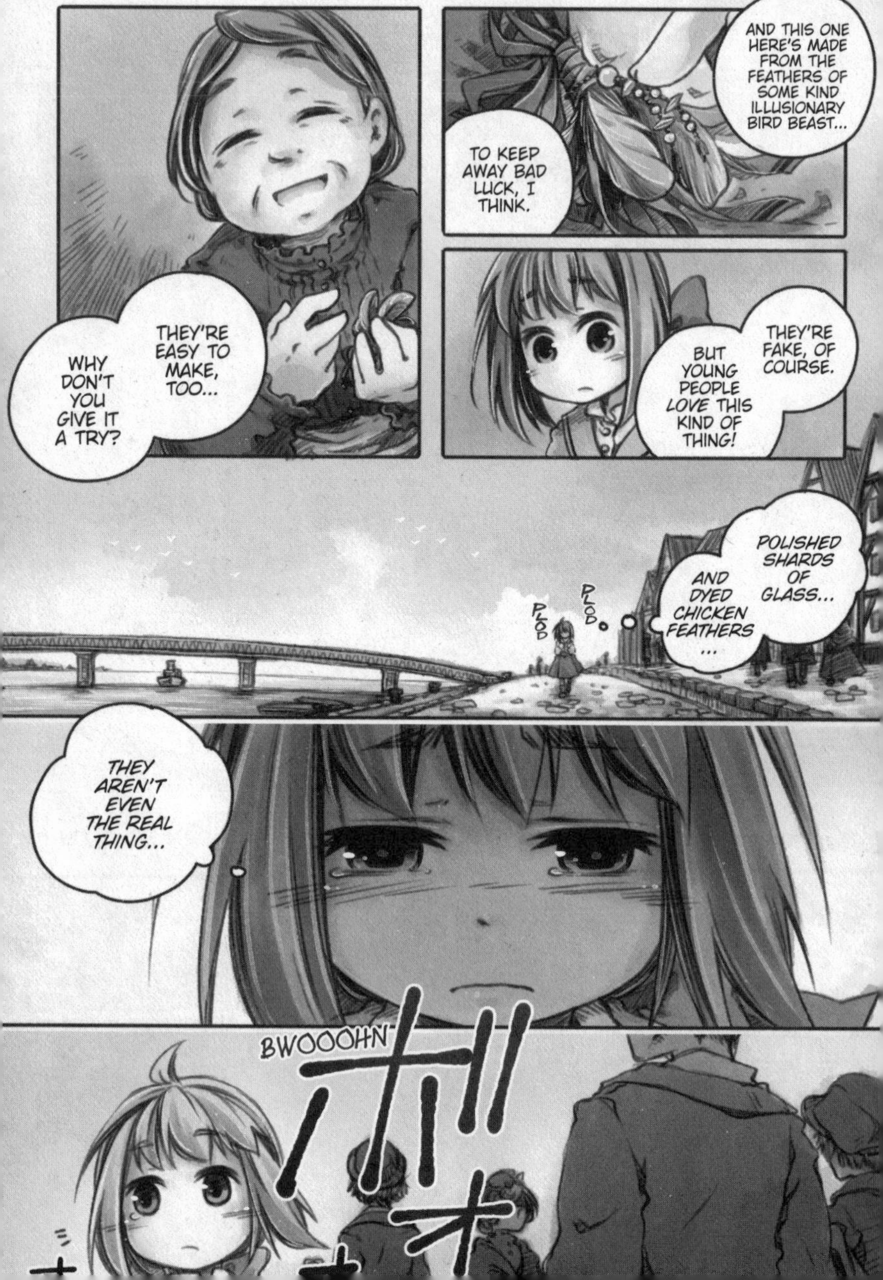
AND THIS ONE HERE'S MADE FROM THE FEATHERS OF SOME KIND ILLUSIONARY BIRD BEAST...
TO KEEP AWAY BAD LUCK, I THINK.
THEY'RE FAKE, OF COURSE.
BUT YOUNG PEOPLE LOVE THIS KIND OF THING!
THEY'RE EASY TO MAKE, TOO...
WHY DON'T YOU GIVE IT A TRY?
PLOD
PLOD
POLISHED SHARDS OF GLASS...
AND DYED CHICKEN FEATHERS...
THEY AREN'T EVEN THE REAL THING...
BWOOOHN

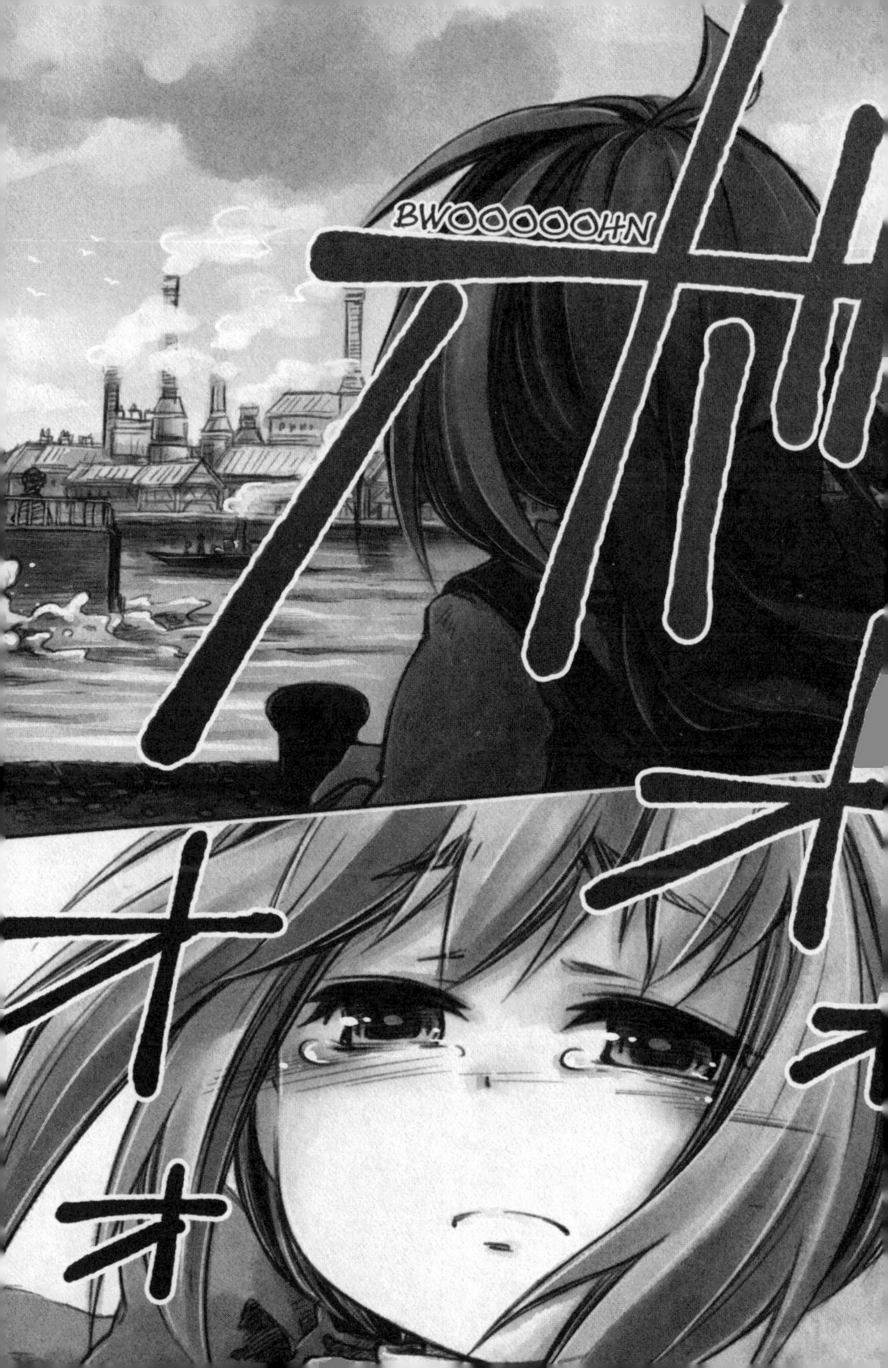
BWOOOOOHN
ボォォォ

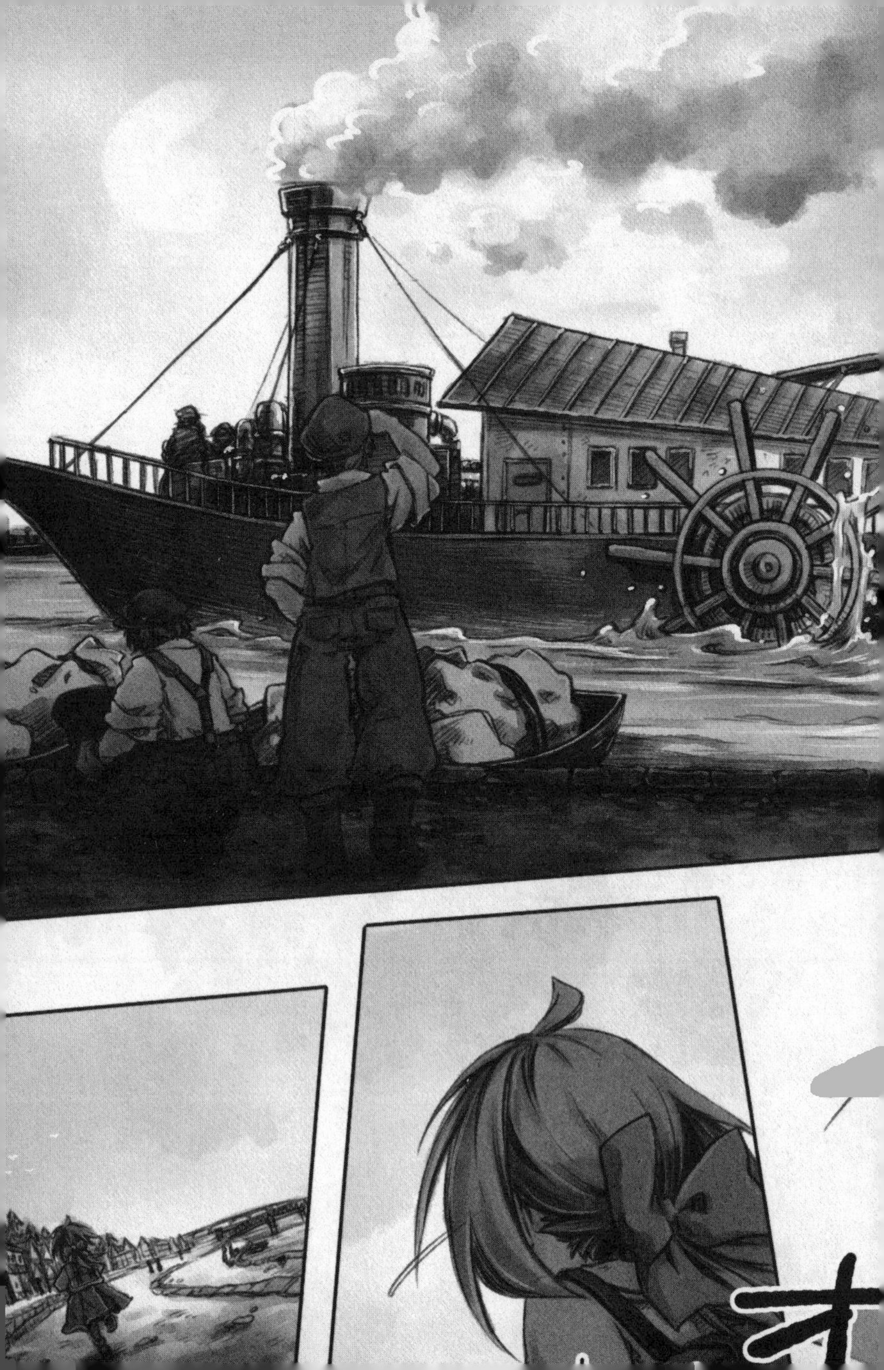

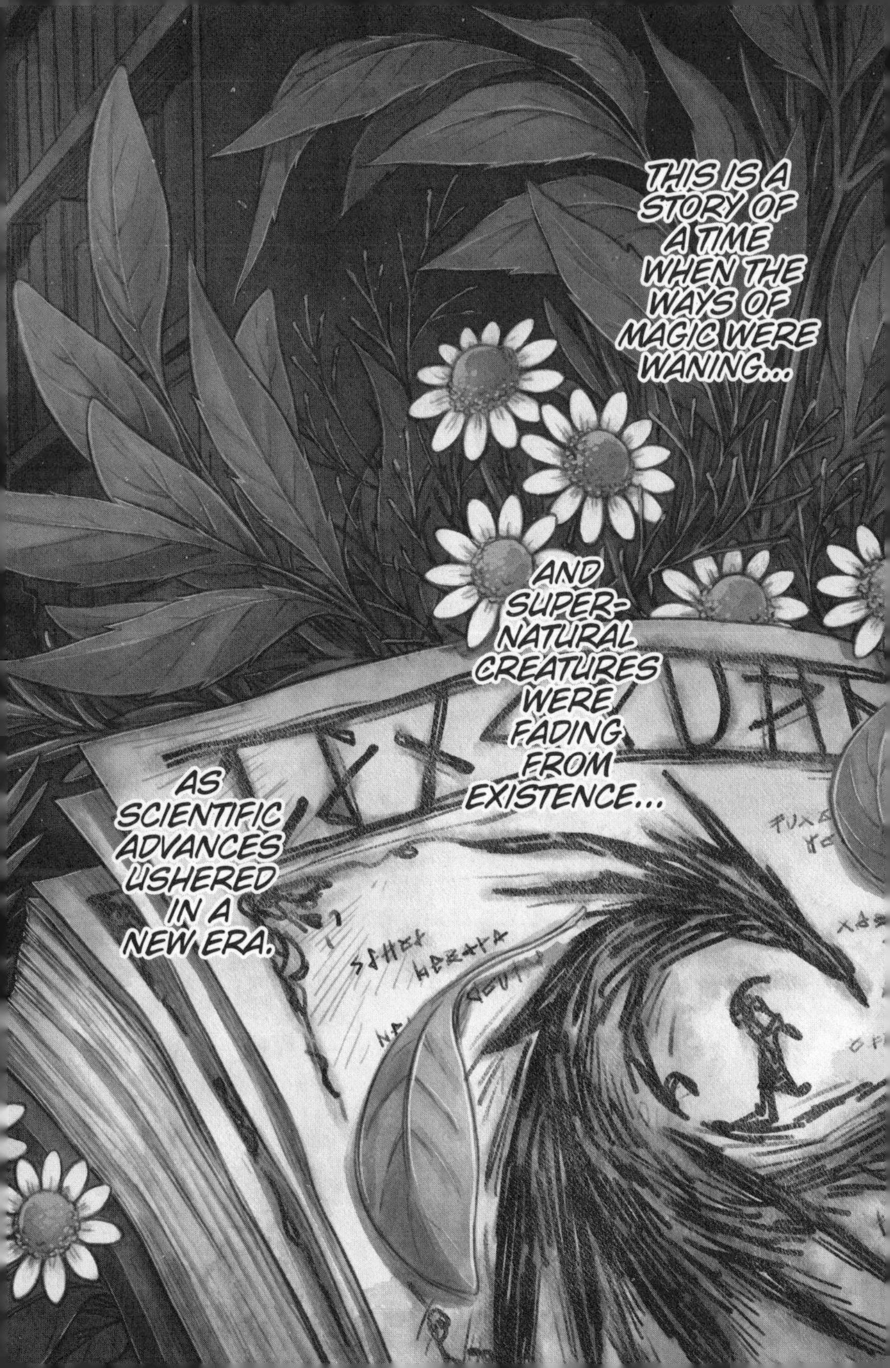
THIS IS A STORY OF A TIME WHEN THE WAYS OF MAGIC WERE WANING...
AND SUPER-NATURAL CREATURES WERE FADING FROM EXISTENCE...
AS SCIENTIFIC ADVANCES USHERED IN A NEW ERA.

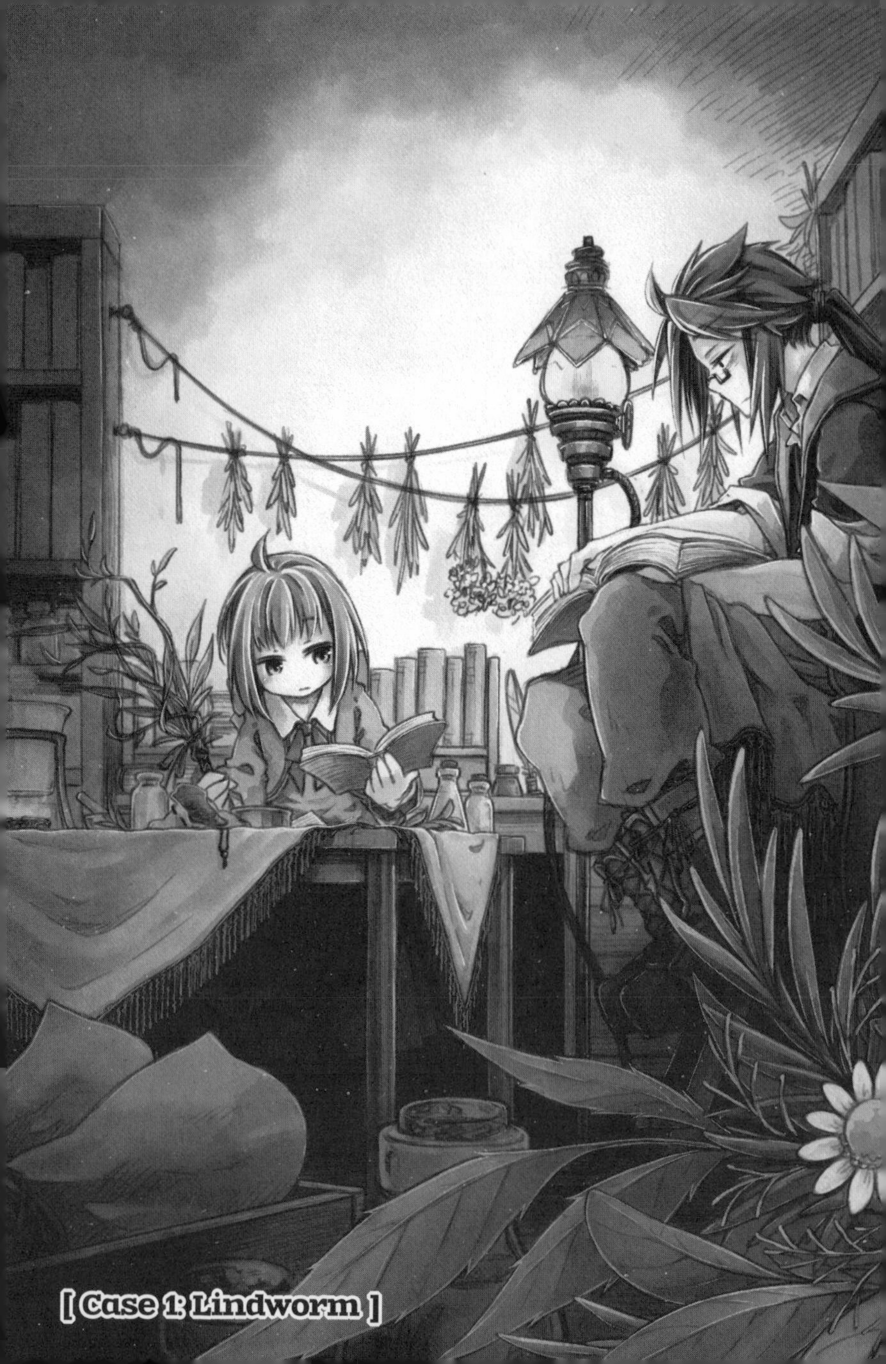
[Case 1: Lindworm]

There's a **puk** hiding in every chapter! Try to find them all!!

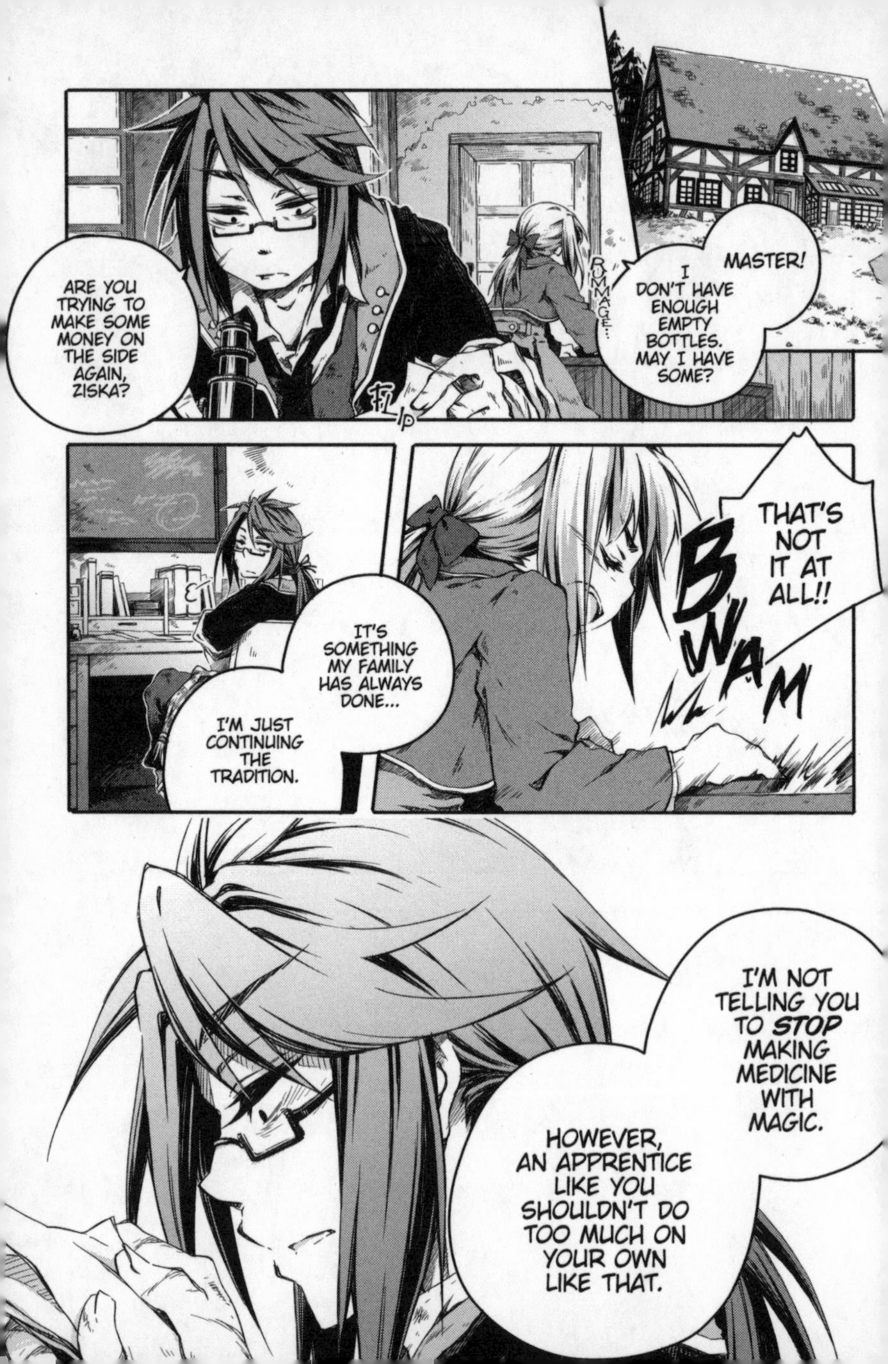
MASTER!
I DON'T HAVE ENOUGH EMPTY BOTTLES. MAY I HAVE SOME?
RUMMAGE...
ARE YOU TRYING TO MAKE SOME MONEY ON THE SIDE AGAIN, ZISKA?
FLIP
THAT'S NOT IT AT ALL!!
BWAM
IT'S SOMETHING MY FAMILY HAS ALWAYS DONE...
I'M JUST CONTINUING THE TRADITION.
I'M NOT TELLING YOU TO *STOP* MAKING MEDICINE WITH MAGIC.
HOWEVER, AN APPRENTICE LIKE YOU SHOULDN'T DO TOO MUCH ON YOUR OWN LIKE THAT.

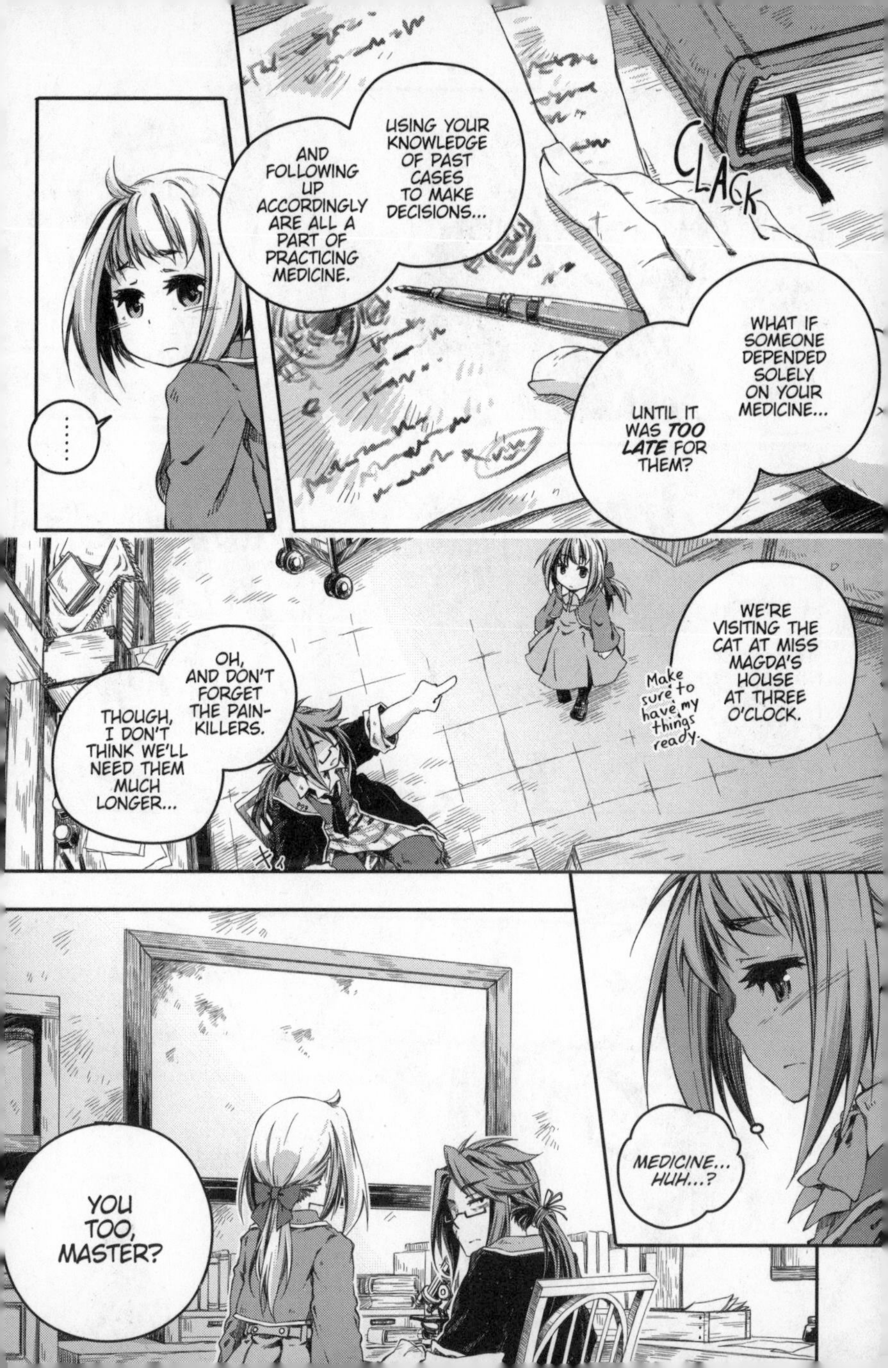
USING YOUR KNOWLEDGE OF PAST CASES TO MAKE DECISIONS...
AND FOLLOWING UP ACCORDINGLY ARE ALL A PART OF PRACTICING MEDICINE.
CLACK
WHAT IF SOMEONE DEPENDED SOLELY ON YOUR MEDICINE...
UNTIL IT WAS ***TOO LATE*** FOR THEM?
......
WE'RE VISITING THE CAT AT MISS MAGDA'S HOUSE AT THREE O'CLOCK.
Make sure to have my things ready.
OH, AND DON'T FORGET THE PAIN-KILLERS.
THOUGH, I DON'T THINK WE'LL NEED THEM MUCH LONGER...
MEDICINE... HUH...?
YOU TOO, MASTER?

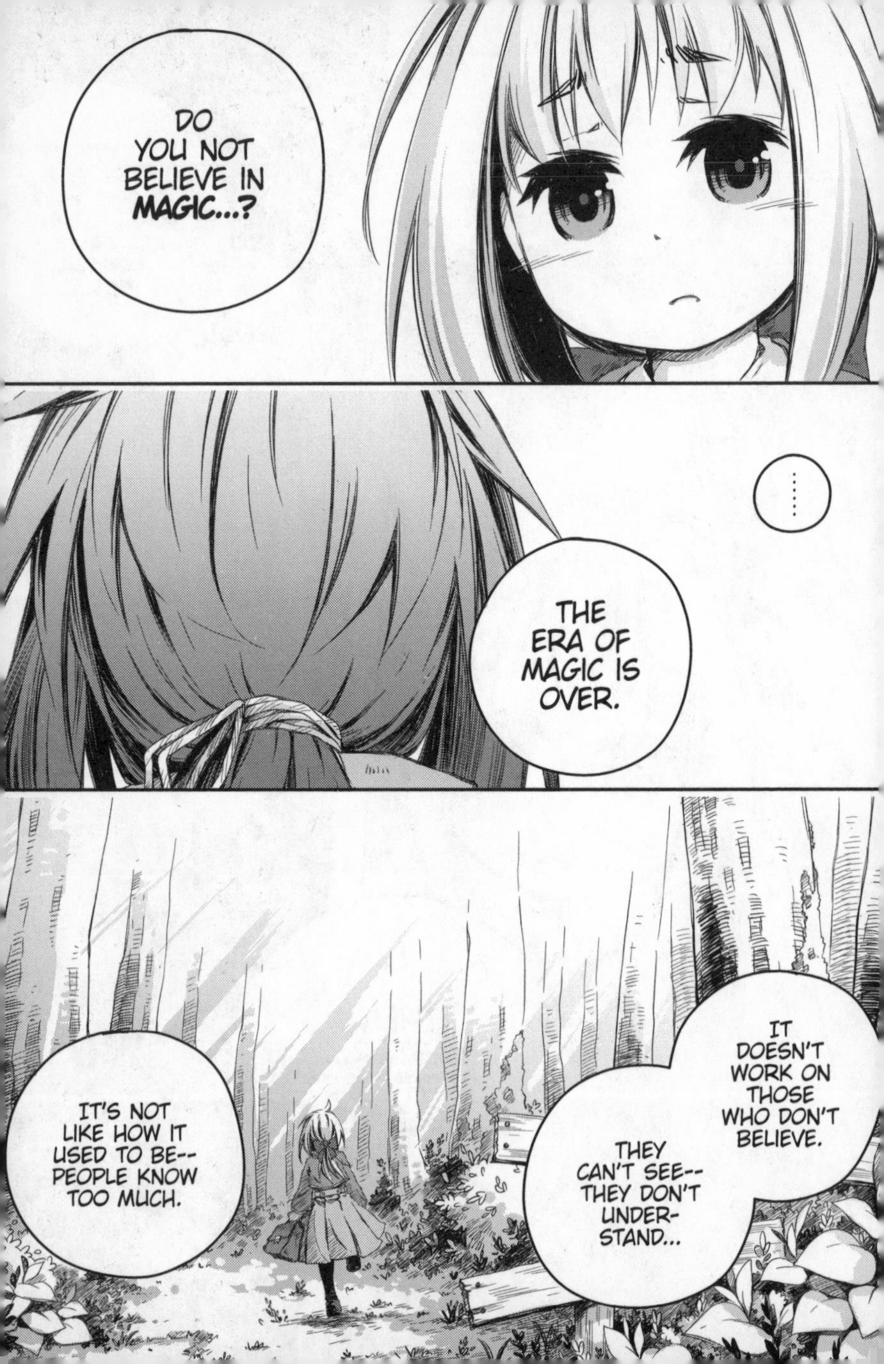
DO YOU NOT BELIEVE IN MAGIC...?
......
THE ERA OF MAGIC IS OVER.
IT DOESN'T WORK ON THOSE WHO DON'T BELIEVE.
THEY CAN'T SEE-- THEY DON'T UNDER-STAND...
IT'S NOT LIKE HOW IT USED TO BE-- PEOPLE KNOW TOO MUCH.

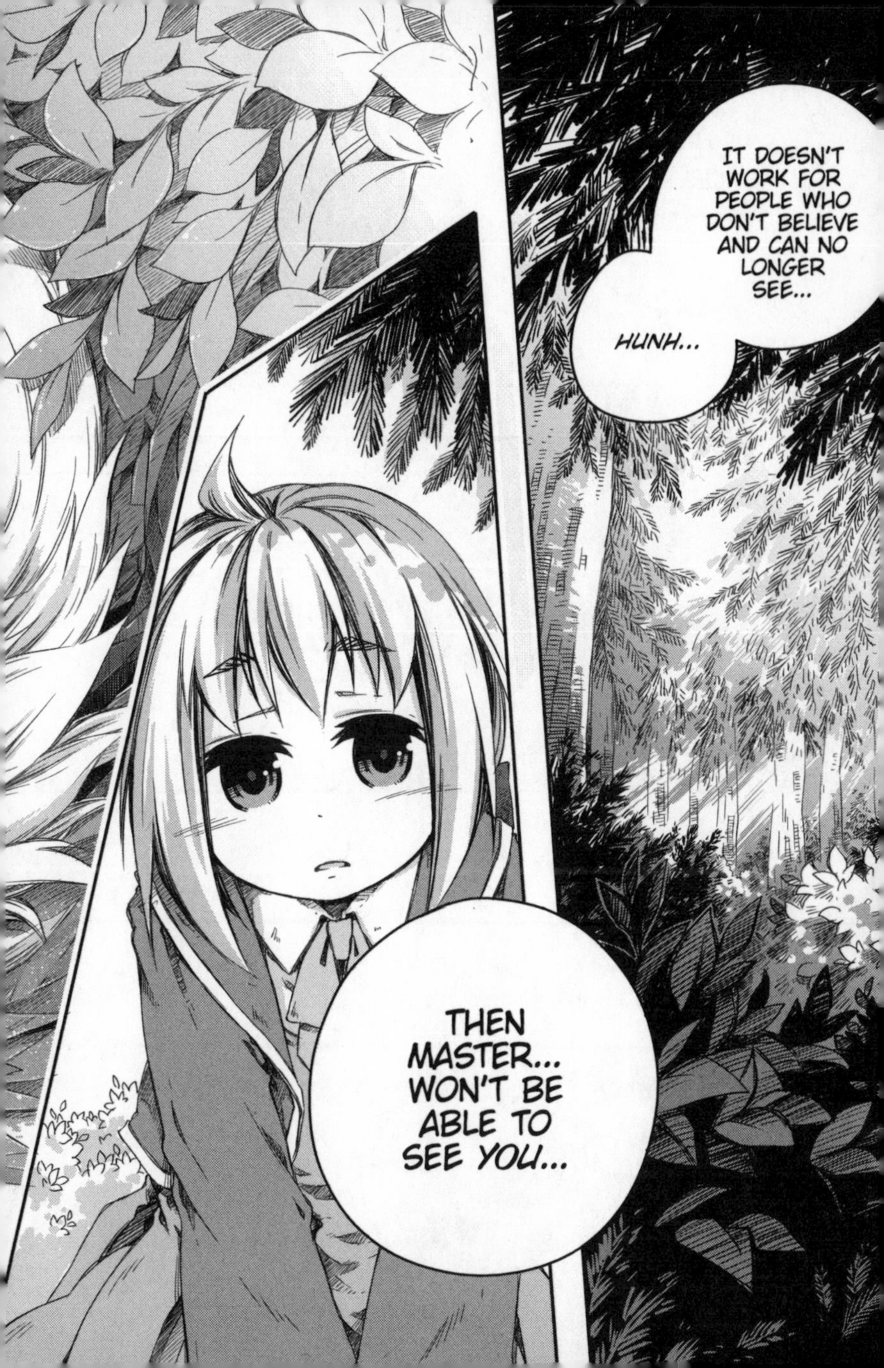
IT DOESN'T WORK FOR PEOPLE WHO DON'T BELIEVE AND CAN NO LONGER SEE...
HUNH...
THEN MASTER... WON'T BE ABLE TO SEE YOU...

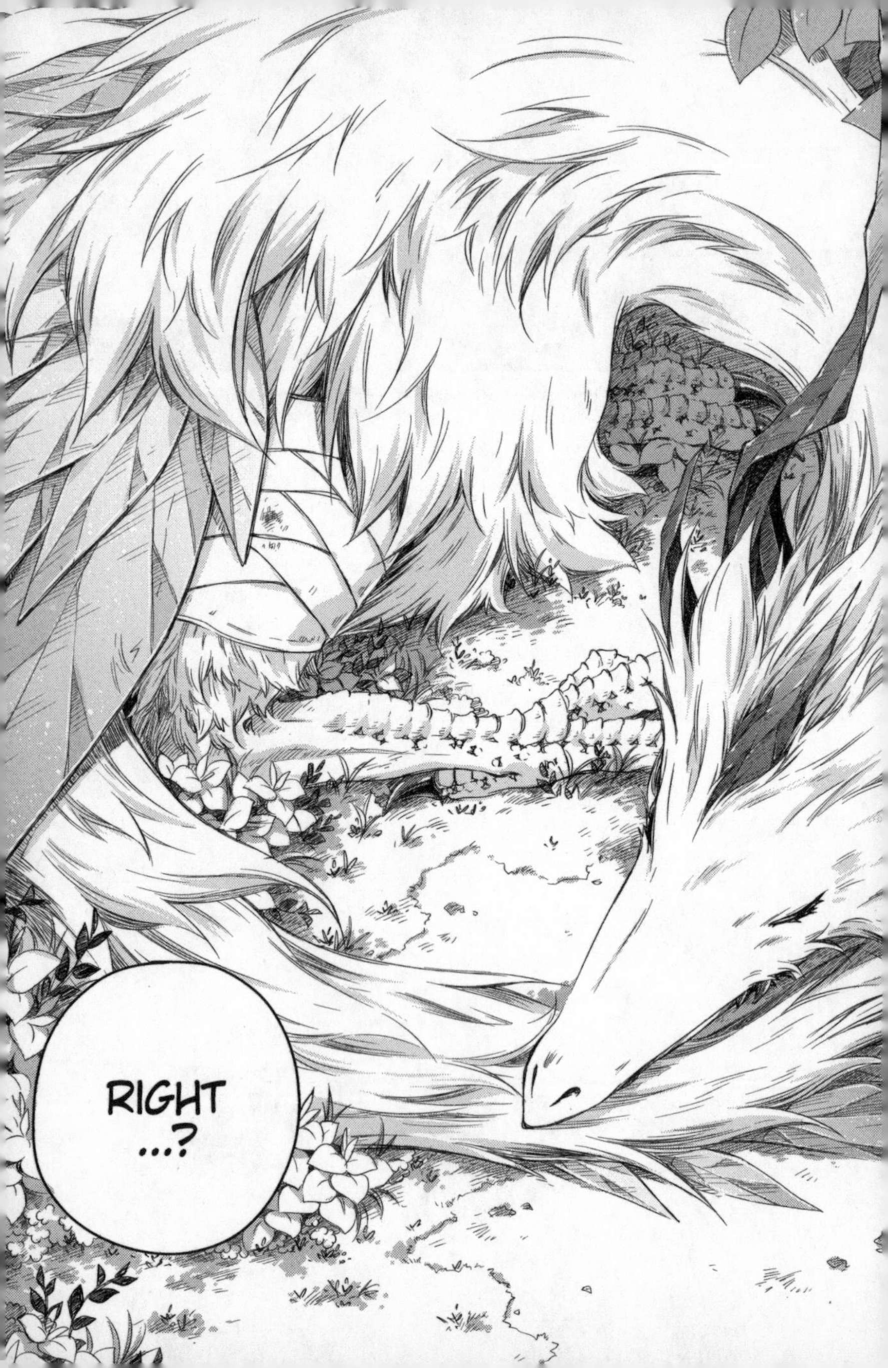
RIGHT ...?

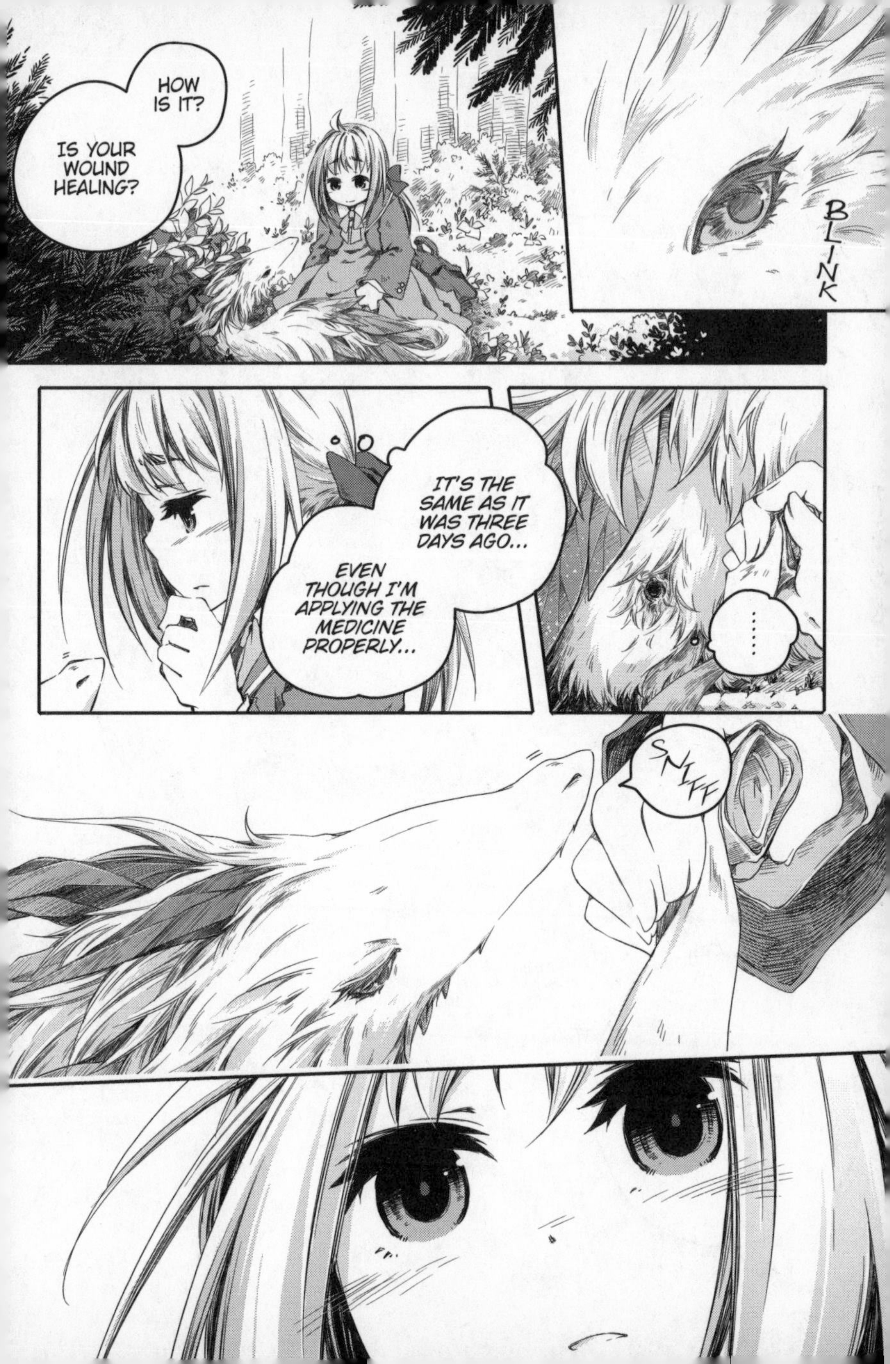
BLINK
HOW IS IT?
IS YOUR WOUND HEALING?
......
IT'S THE SAME AS IT WAS THREE DAYS AGO...
EVEN THOUGH I'M APPLYING THE MEDICINE PROPERLY...
SNIFF

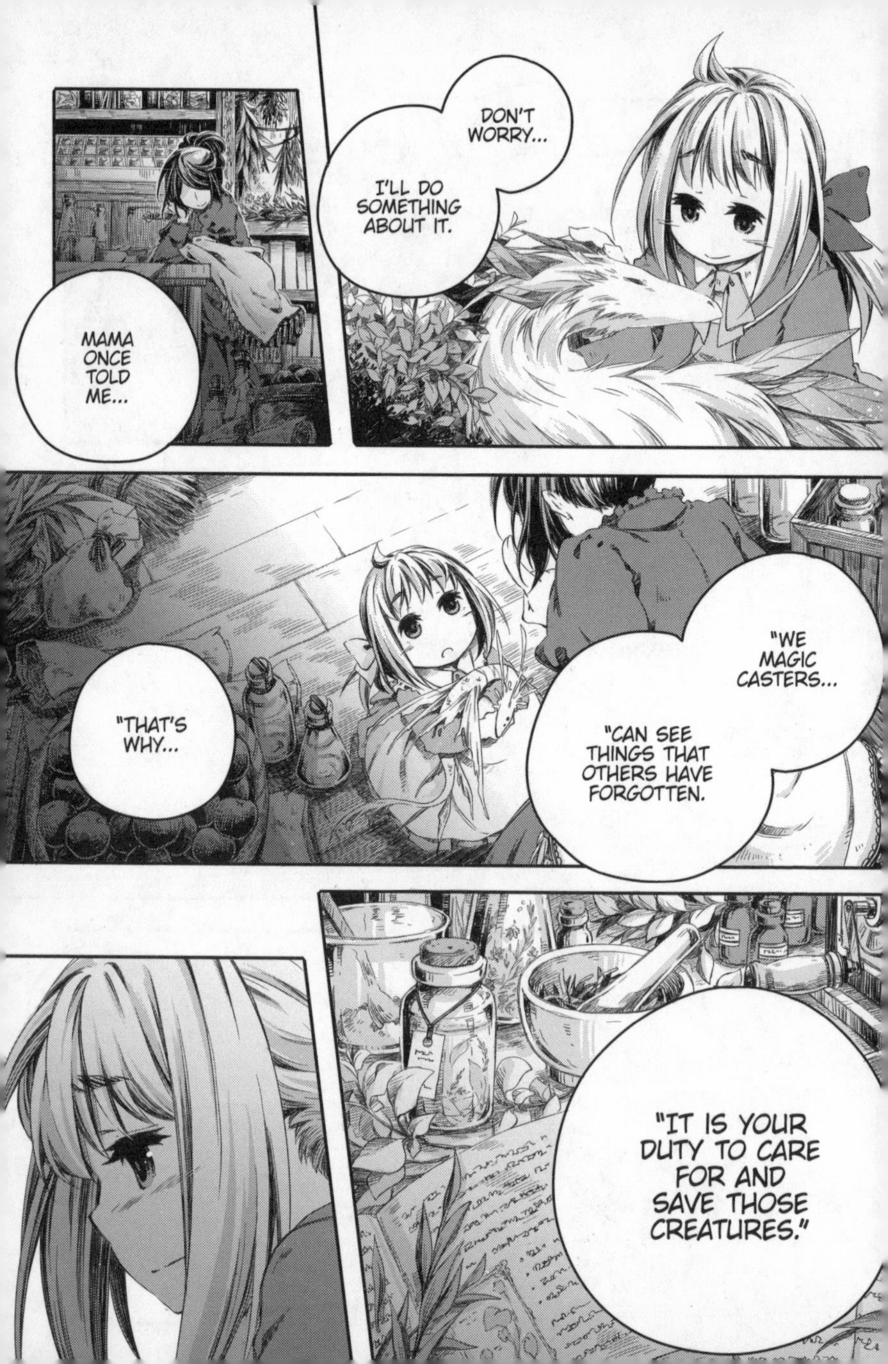
DON'T WORRY...
I'LL DO SOMETHING ABOUT IT.
MAMA ONCE TOLD ME...
"WE MAGIC CASTERS...
"CAN SEE THINGS THAT OTHERS HAVE FORGOTTEN.
"THAT'S WHY...
"IT IS YOUR DUTY TO CARE FOR AND SAVE THOSE CREATURES."

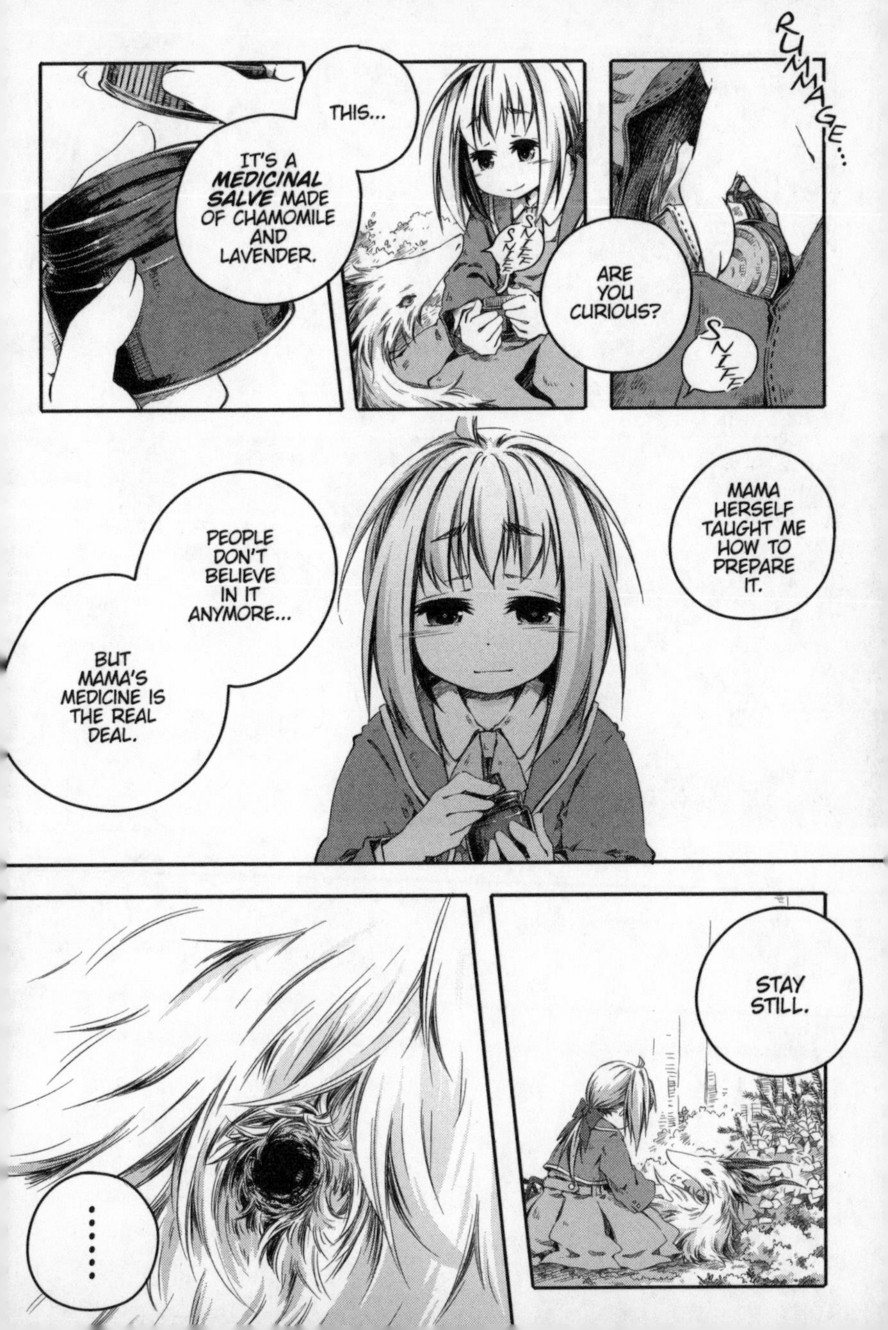
RUMMAGE...
SNIFF
ARE YOU CURIOUS?
SNIFF SNIFF
THIS...
IT'S A MEDICINAL SALVE MADE OF CHAMOMILE AND LAVENDER.
MAMA HERSELF TAUGHT ME HOW TO PREPARE IT.
PEOPLE DON'T BELIEVE IN IT ANYMORE...
BUT MAMA'S MEDICINE IS THE REAL DEAL.
STAY STILL.
......

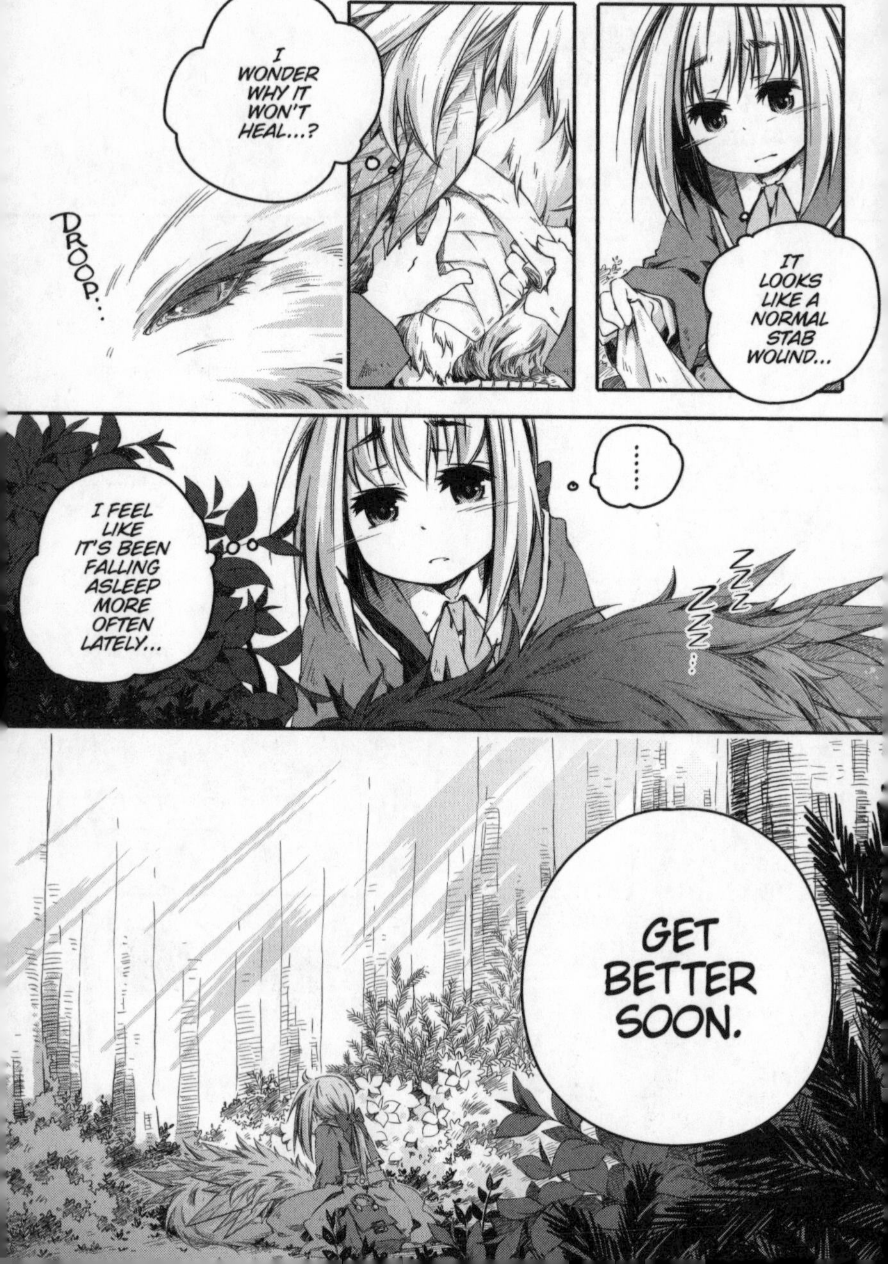

IT LOOKS LIKE A NORMAL STAB WOUND...
I WONDER WHY IT WON'T HEAL...?
DROOP...
......
I FEEL LIKE IT'S BEEN FALLING ASLEEP MORE OFTEN LATELY...
ZZZ ZZZ...
GET BETTER SOON.

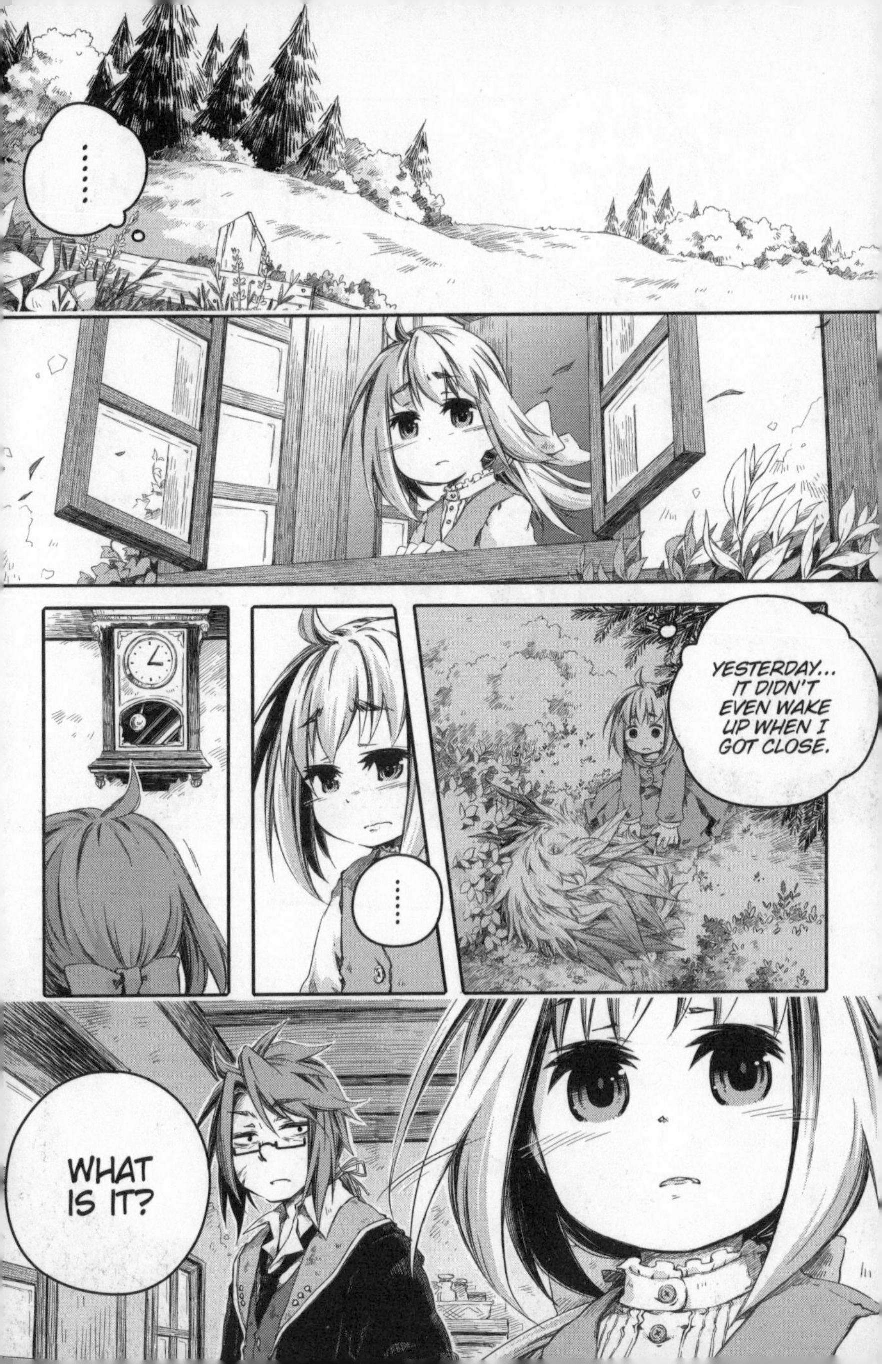
......
YESTERDAY... IT DIDN'T EVEN WAKE UP WHEN I GOT CLOSE.
......
WHAT IS IT?

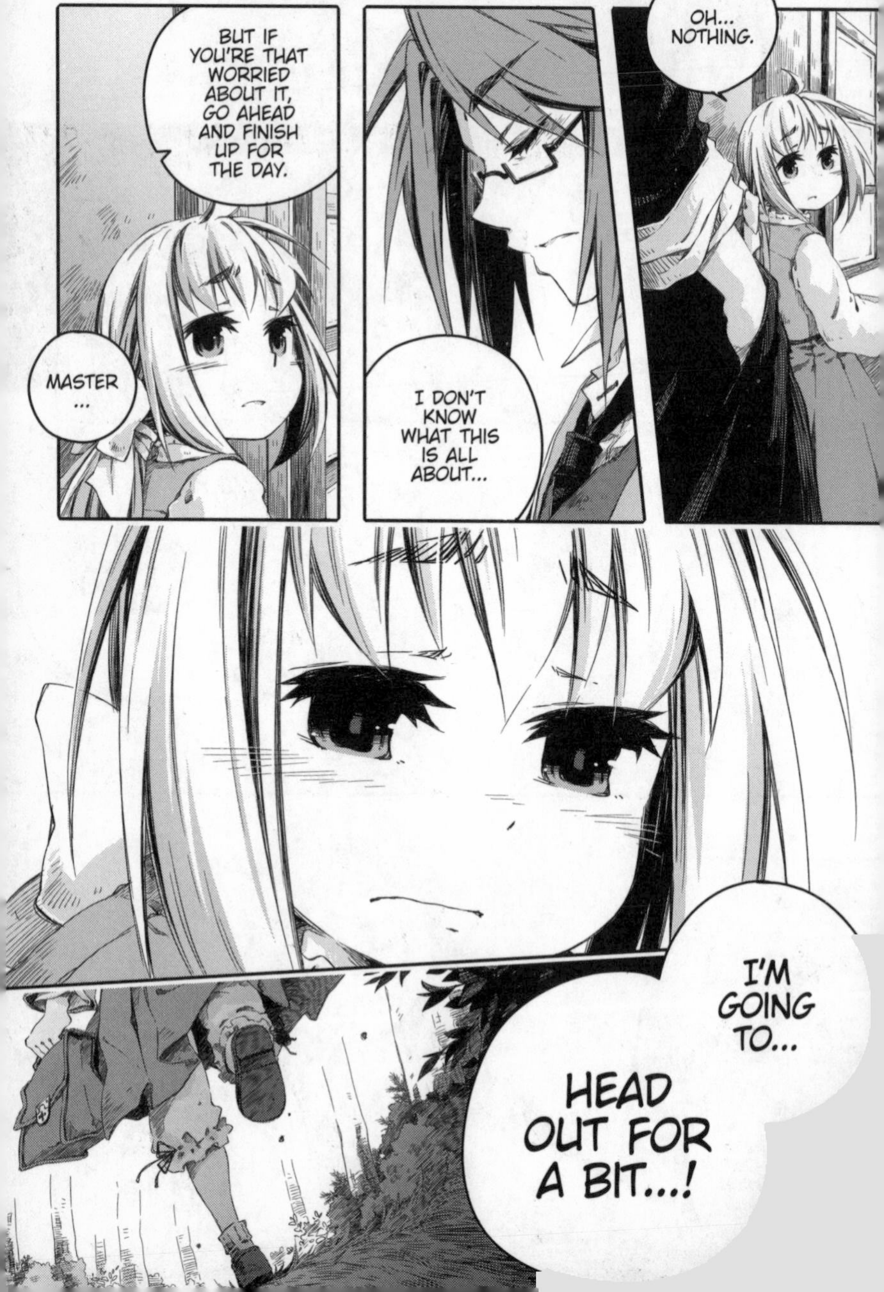
OH... NOTHING.
I DON'T KNOW WHAT THIS IS ALL ABOUT...
BUT IF YOU'RE THAT WORRIED ABOUT IT, GO AHEAD AND FINISH UP FOR THE DAY.
MASTER ...
I'M GOING TO...
HEAD OUT FOR A BIT...!

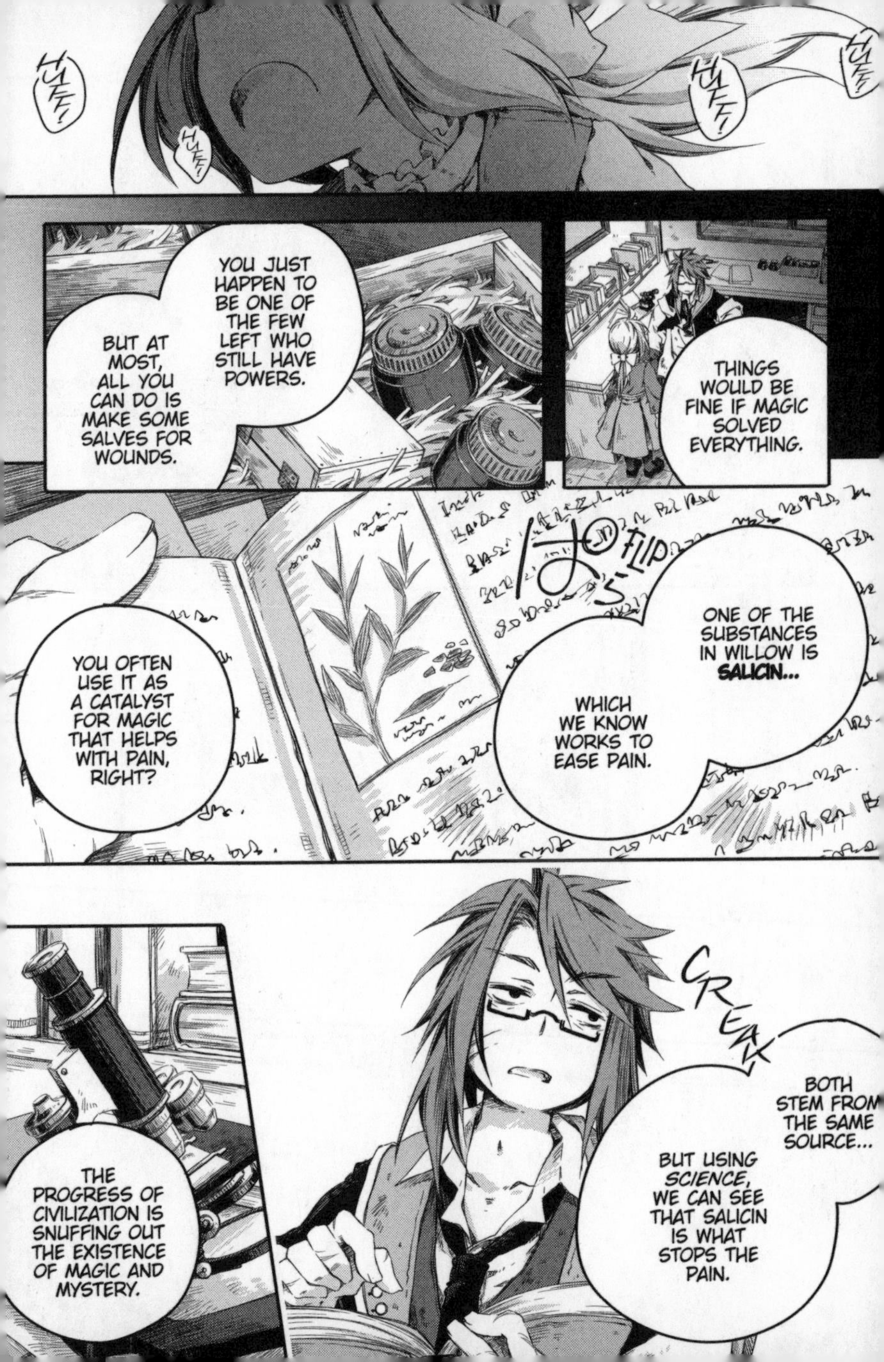
HUFF!
HUFF!
HUFF!
HUFF!
THINGS WOULD BE FINE IF MAGIC SOLVED EVERYTHING.
YOU JUST HAPPEN TO BE ONE OF THE FEW LEFT WHO STILL HAVE POWERS.
BUT AT MOST, ALL YOU CAN DO IS MAKE SOME SALVES FOR WOUNDS.
FLIP
ONE OF THE SUBSTANCES IN WILLOW IS **SALICIN...**
WHICH WE KNOW WORKS TO EASE PAIN.
YOU OFTEN USE IT AS A CATALYST FOR MAGIC THAT HELPS WITH PAIN, RIGHT?
CREAK
BOTH STEM FROM THE SAME SOURCE...
BUT USING *SCIENCE*, WE CAN SEE THAT SALICIN IS WHAT STOPS THE PAIN.
THE PROGRESS OF CIVILIZATION IS SNUFFING OUT THE EXISTENCE OF MAGIC AND MYSTERY.

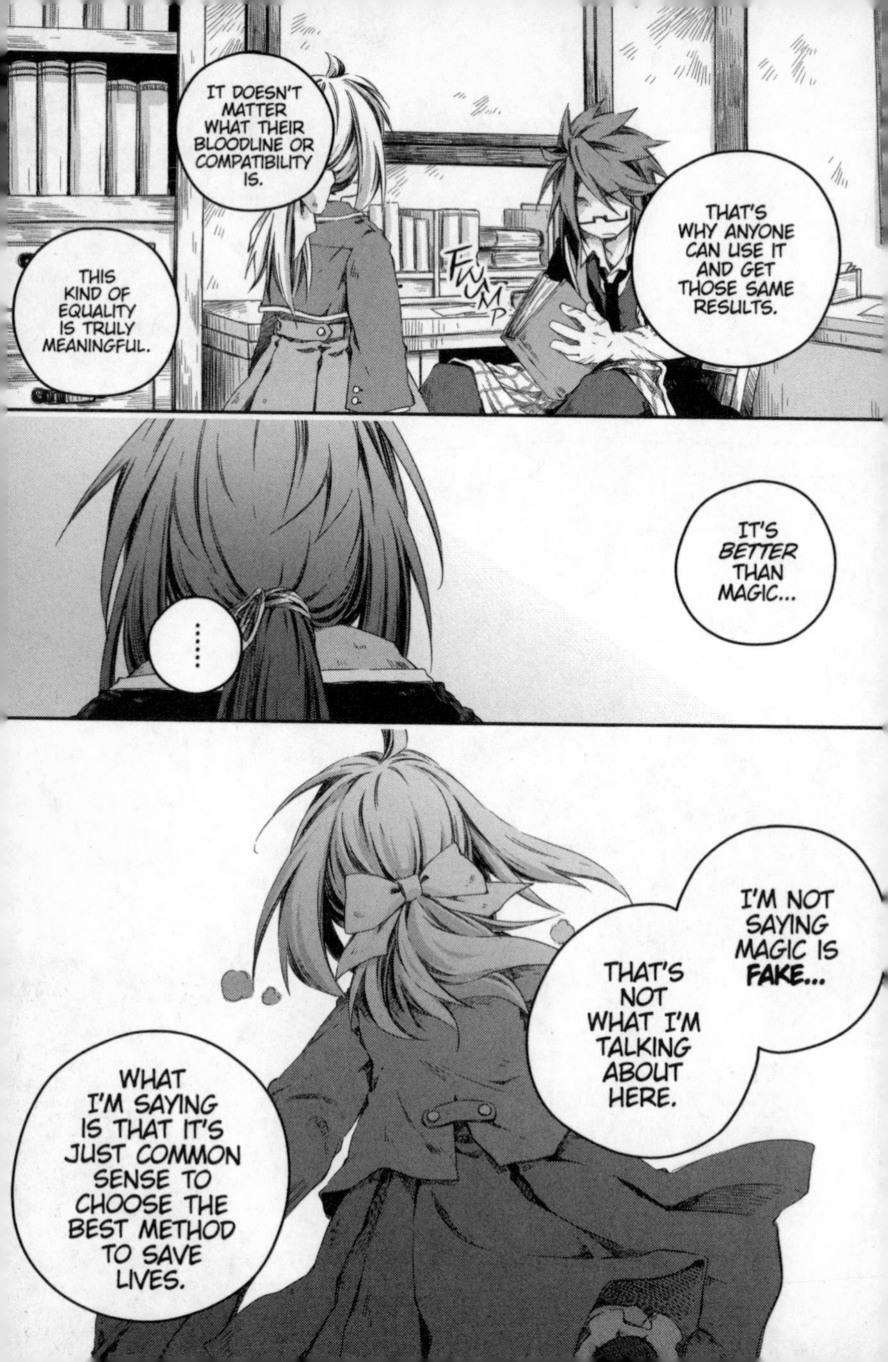
IT DOESN'T MATTER WHAT THEIR BLOODLINE OR COMPATIBILITY IS.
THAT'S WHY ANYONE CAN USE IT AND GET THOSE SAME RESULTS.
FWUMP
THIS KIND OF EQUALITY IS TRULY MEANINGFUL.
IT'S *BETTER* THAN MAGIC...
......
I'M NOT SAYING MAGIC IS **FAKE...**
THAT'S NOT WHAT I'M TALKING ABOUT HERE.
WHAT I'M SAYING IS THAT IT'S JUST COMMON SENSE TO CHOOSE THE BEST METHOD TO SAVE LIVES.

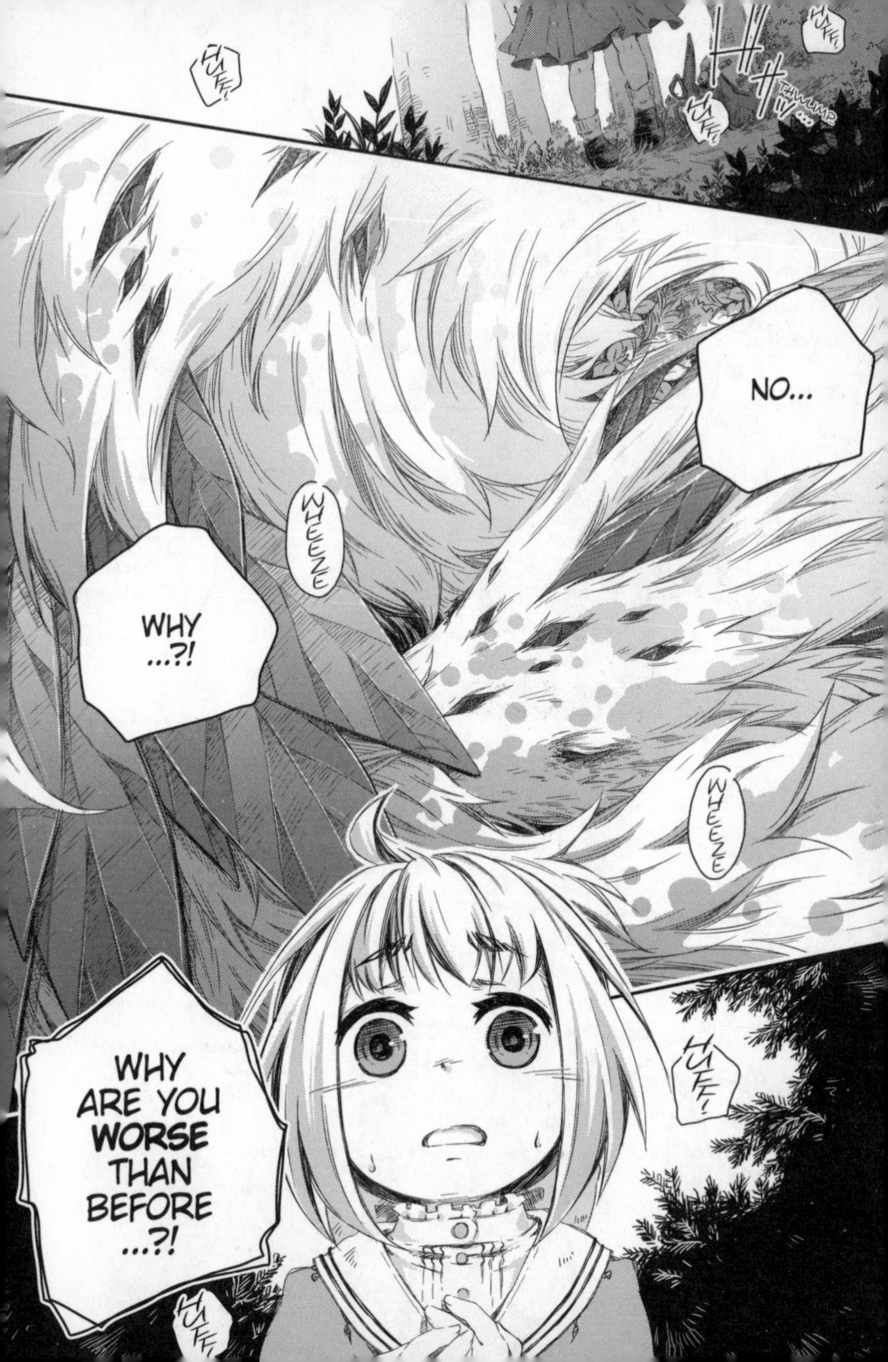
HUFF!
THWUMP...
HUFF!
HUFF!
NO...
WHEEZE
WHY ...?!
WHEEZE
HUFF!
WHY ARE YOU **WORSE** THAN BEFORE ...?!
HUFF!

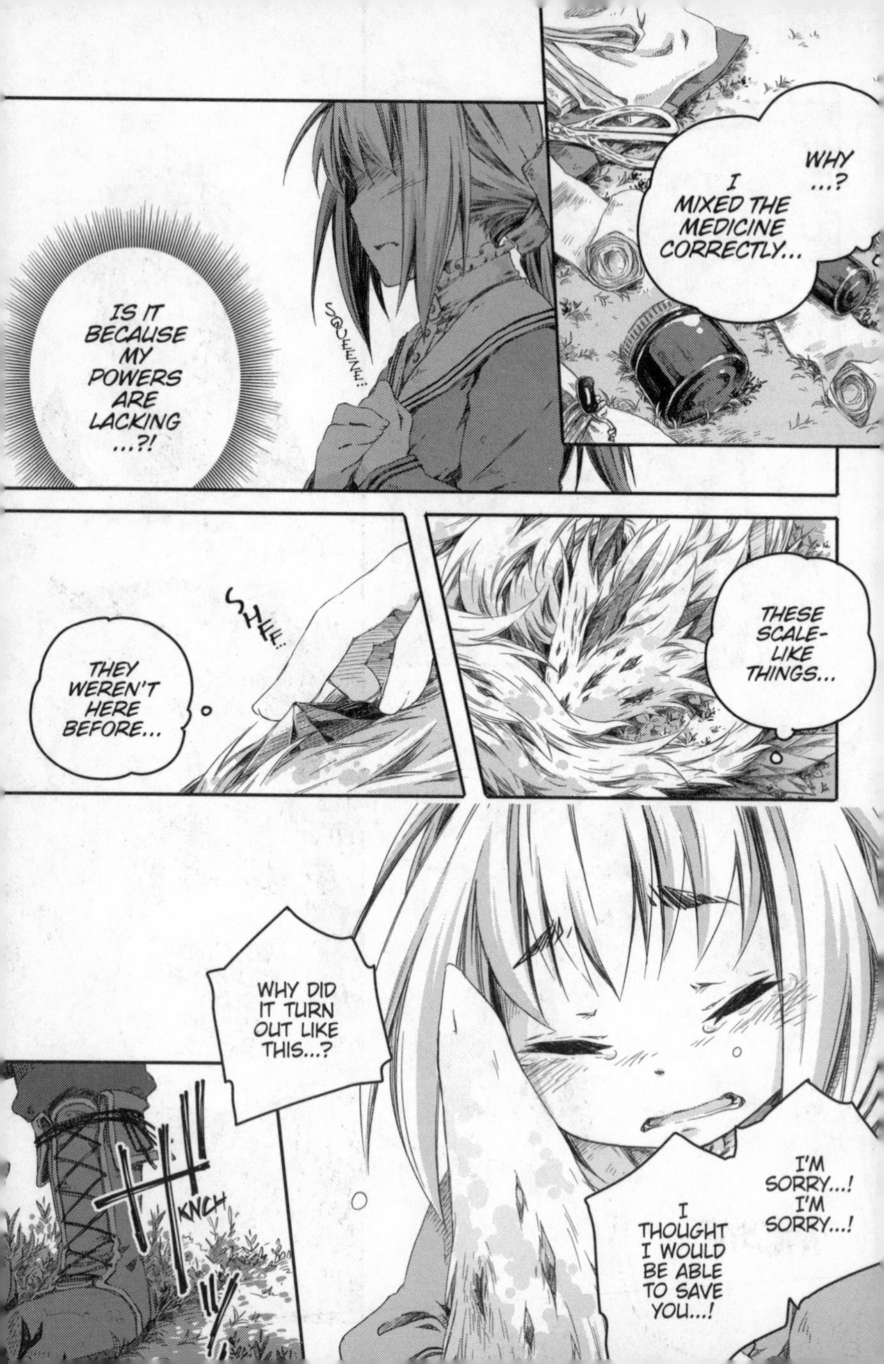
WHY ...? I MIXED THE MEDICINE CORRECTLY...
SQUEEZE...
IS IT BECAUSE MY POWERS ARE LACKING ...?!
THESE SCALE-LIKE THINGS...
SHFF...
THEY WEREN'T HERE BEFORE...
WHY DID IT TURN OUT LIKE THIS...?
I'M SORRY...! I'M SORRY...!
I THOUGHT I WOULD BE ABLE TO SAVE YOU...!
KNCH

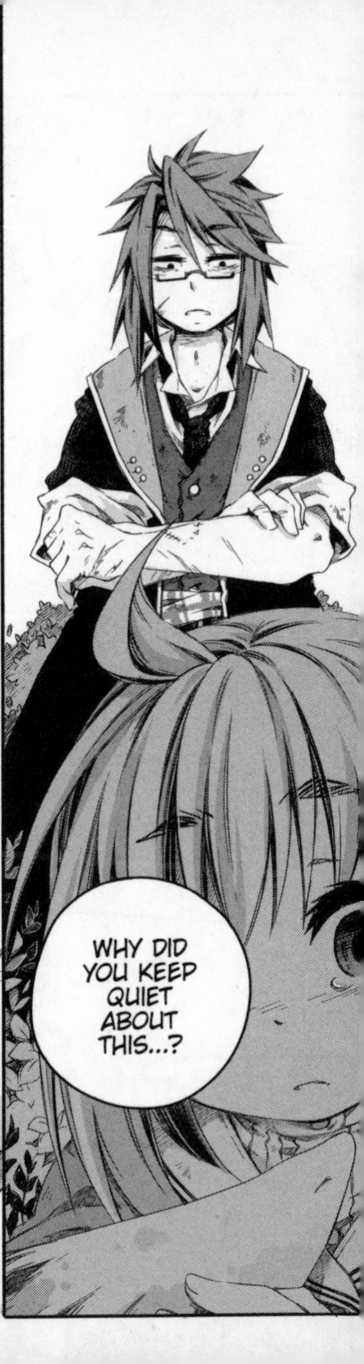
WHY DID YOU KEEP QUIET ABOUT THIS...?

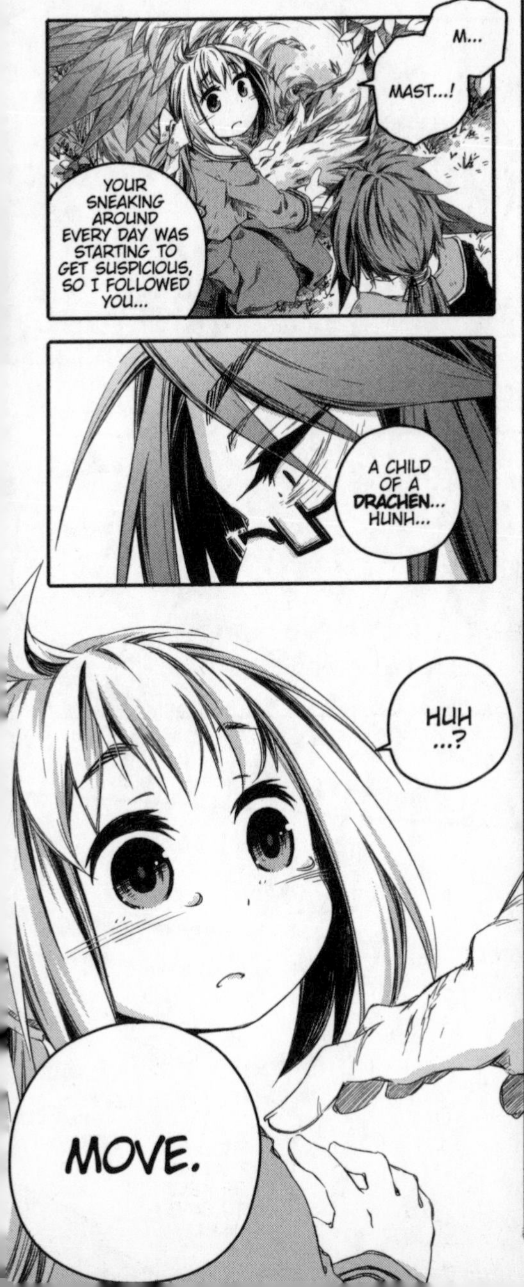
M...
MAST...!
YOUR SNEAKING AROUND EVERY DAY WAS STARTING TO GET SUSPICIOUS, SO I FOLLOWED YOU...
A CHILD OF A **DRACHEN**... HUNH...
HUH ...?
MOVE.

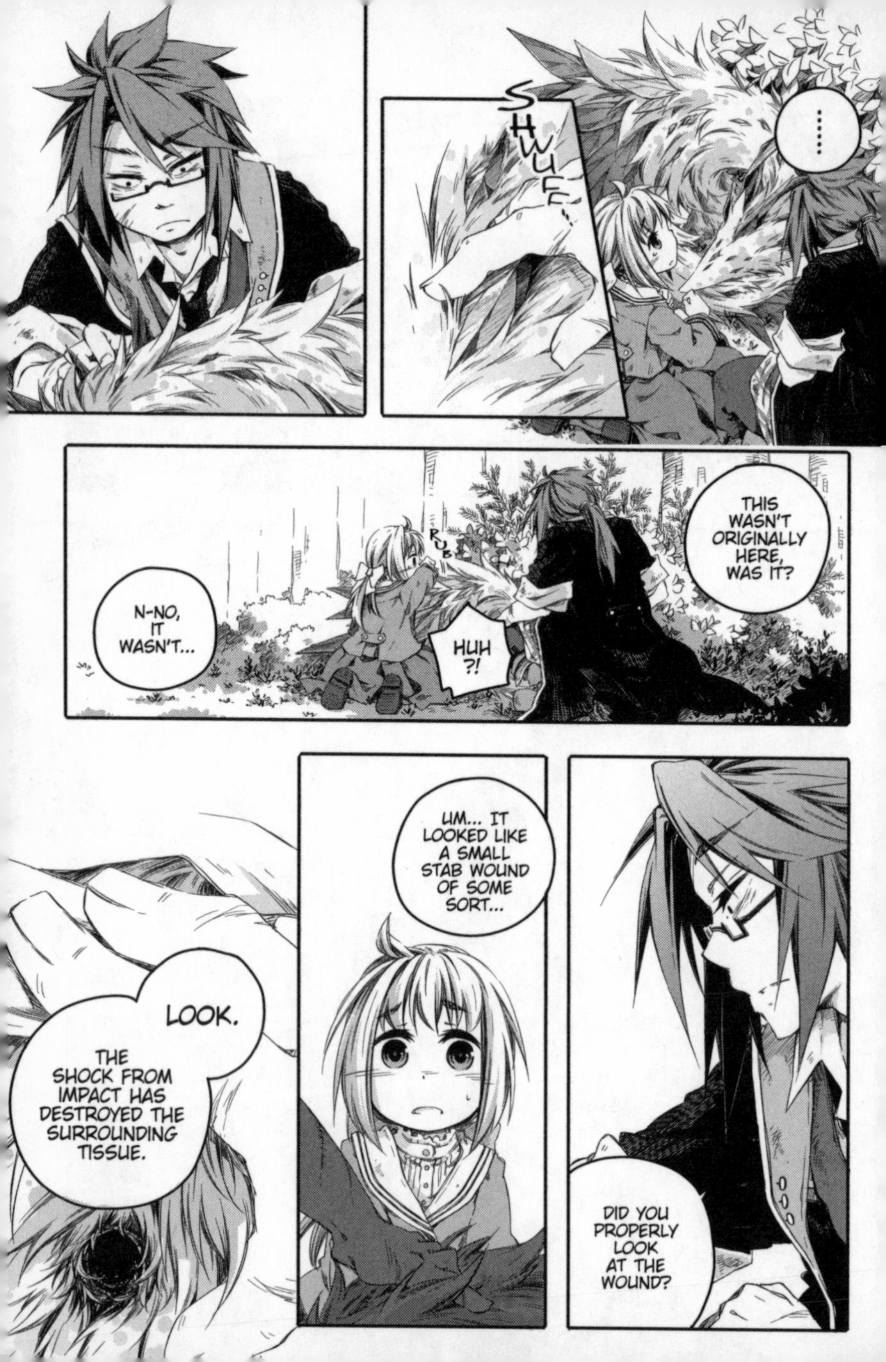
……
SHWUFF...
THIS WASN'T ORIGINALLY HERE, WAS IT?
RUB
HUH ?!
N-NO, IT WASN'T...
DID YOU PROPERLY LOOK AT THE WOUND?
UM... IT LOOKED LIKE A SMALL STAB WOUND OF SOME SORT...
LOOK.
THE SHOCK FROM IMPACT HAS DESTROYED THE SURROUNDING TISSUE.

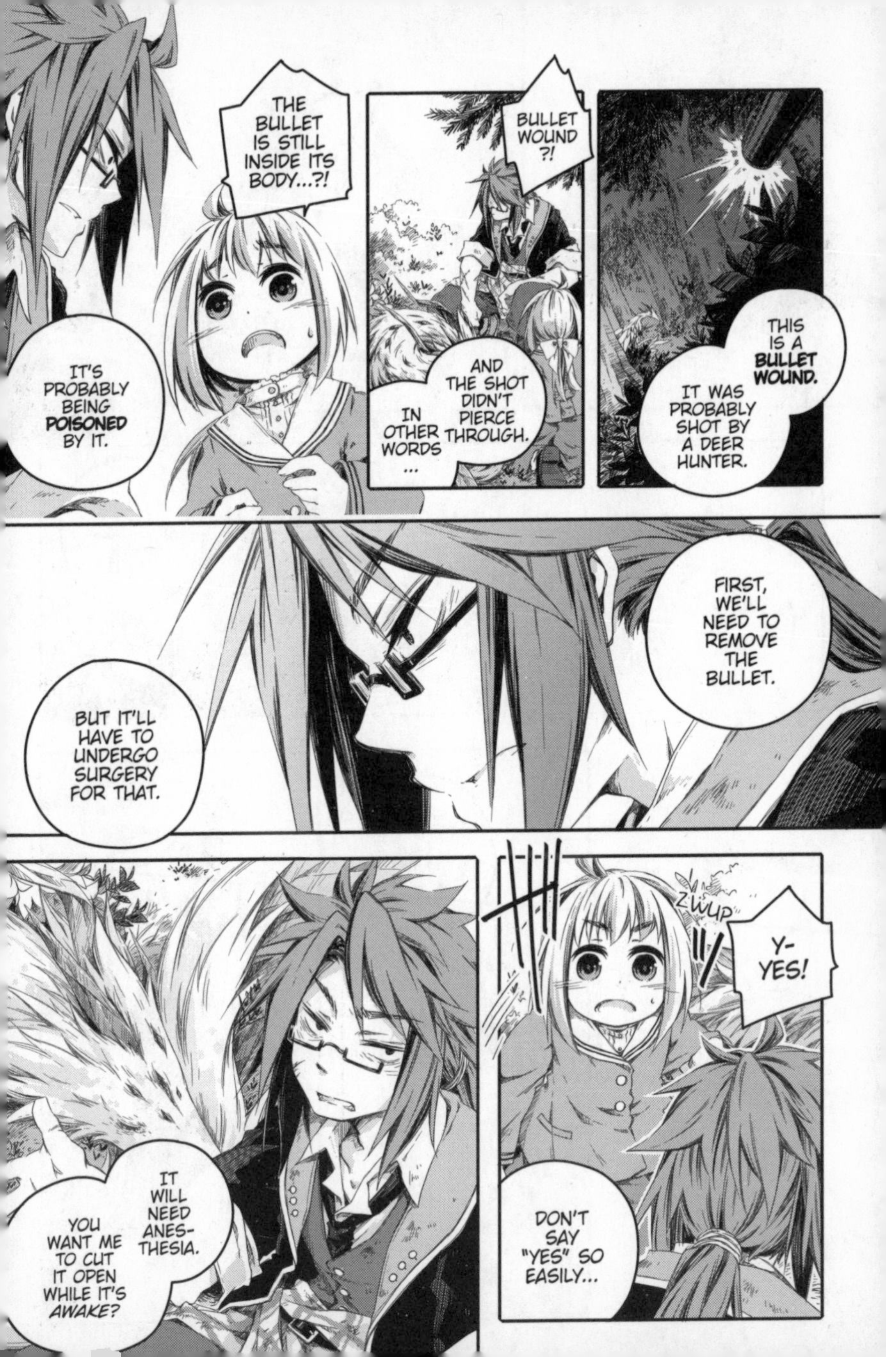
THIS IS A BULLET WOUND.
IT WAS PROBABLY SHOT BY A DEER HUNTER.
BULLET WOUND?!
AND THE SHOT DIDN'T PIERCE THROUGH.
IN OTHER WORDS...
THE BULLET IS STILL INSIDE ITS BODY...?!
IT'S PROBABLY BEING POISONED BY IT.
FIRST, WE'LL NEED TO REMOVE THE BULLET.
BUT IT'LL HAVE TO UNDERGO SURGERY FOR THAT.
ZWUP
Y-YES!
DON'T SAY "YES" SO EASILY...
IT WILL NEED ANES-THESIA.
YOU WANT ME TO CUT IT OPEN WHILE IT'S AWAKE?

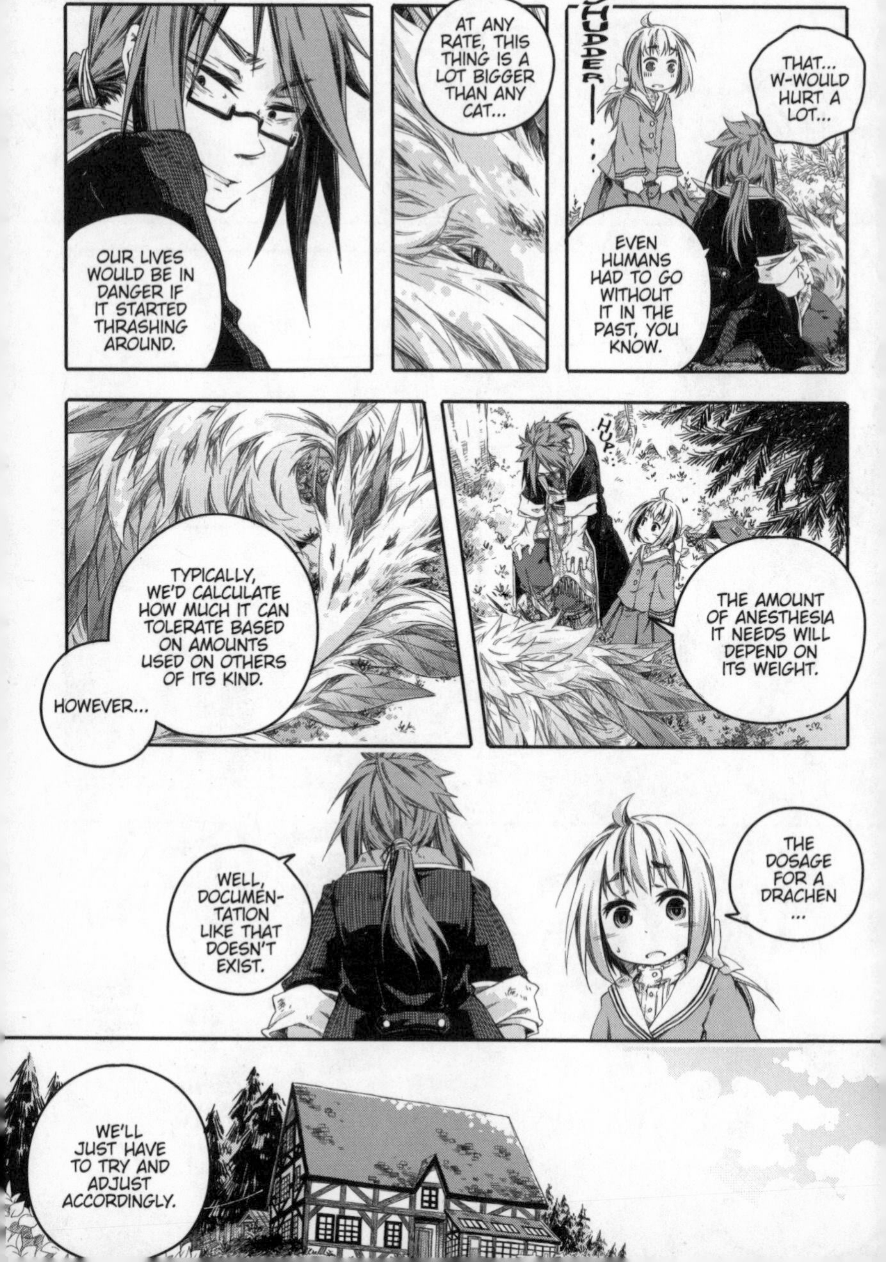
SHUDDER...
THAT... W-WOULD HURT A LOT...
EVEN HUMANS HAD TO GO WITHOUT IT IN THE PAST, YOU KNOW.
AT ANY RATE, THIS THING IS A LOT BIGGER THAN ANY CAT...
OUR LIVES WOULD BE IN DANGER IF IT STARTED THRASHING AROUND.
HUP...
THE AMOUNT OF ANESTHESIA IT NEEDS WILL DEPEND ON ITS WEIGHT.
TYPICALLY, WE'D CALCULATE HOW MUCH IT CAN TOLERATE BASED ON AMOUNTS USED ON OTHERS OF ITS KIND.
HOWEVER...
THE DOSAGE FOR A DRACHEN ...
WELL, DOCUMENTATION LIKE THAT DOESN'T EXIST.
WE'LL JUST HAVE TO TRY AND ADJUST ACCORDINGLY.

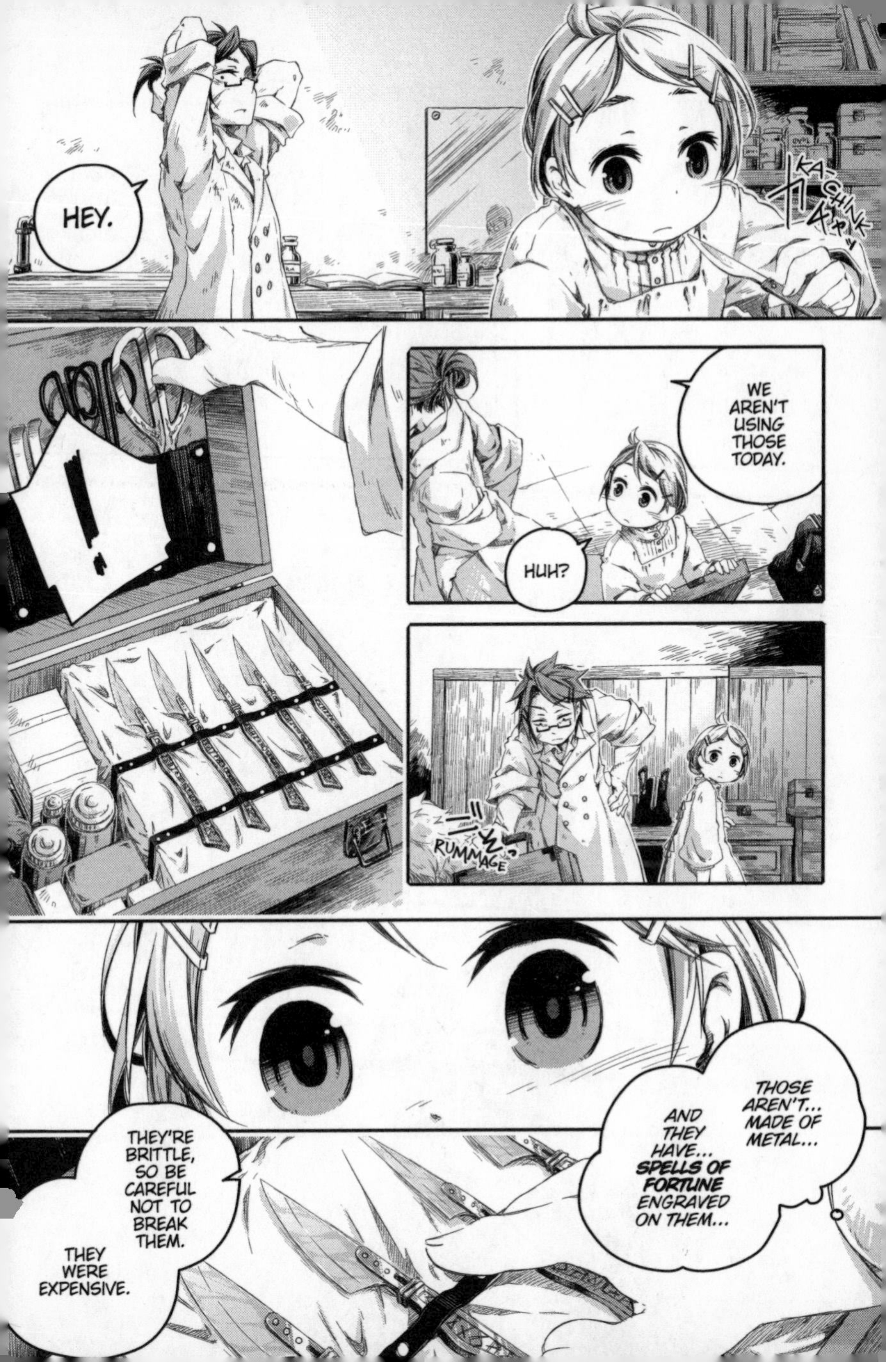
KA-CHINK
HEY.
WE AREN'T USING THOSE TODAY.
HUH?
RUMMAGE
!
THOSE AREN'T... MADE OF METAL...
AND THEY HAVE... **SPELLS OF FORTUNE** ENGRAVED ON THEM...
THEY'RE BRITTLE, SO BE CAREFUL NOT TO BREAK THEM.
THEY WERE EXPENSIVE.

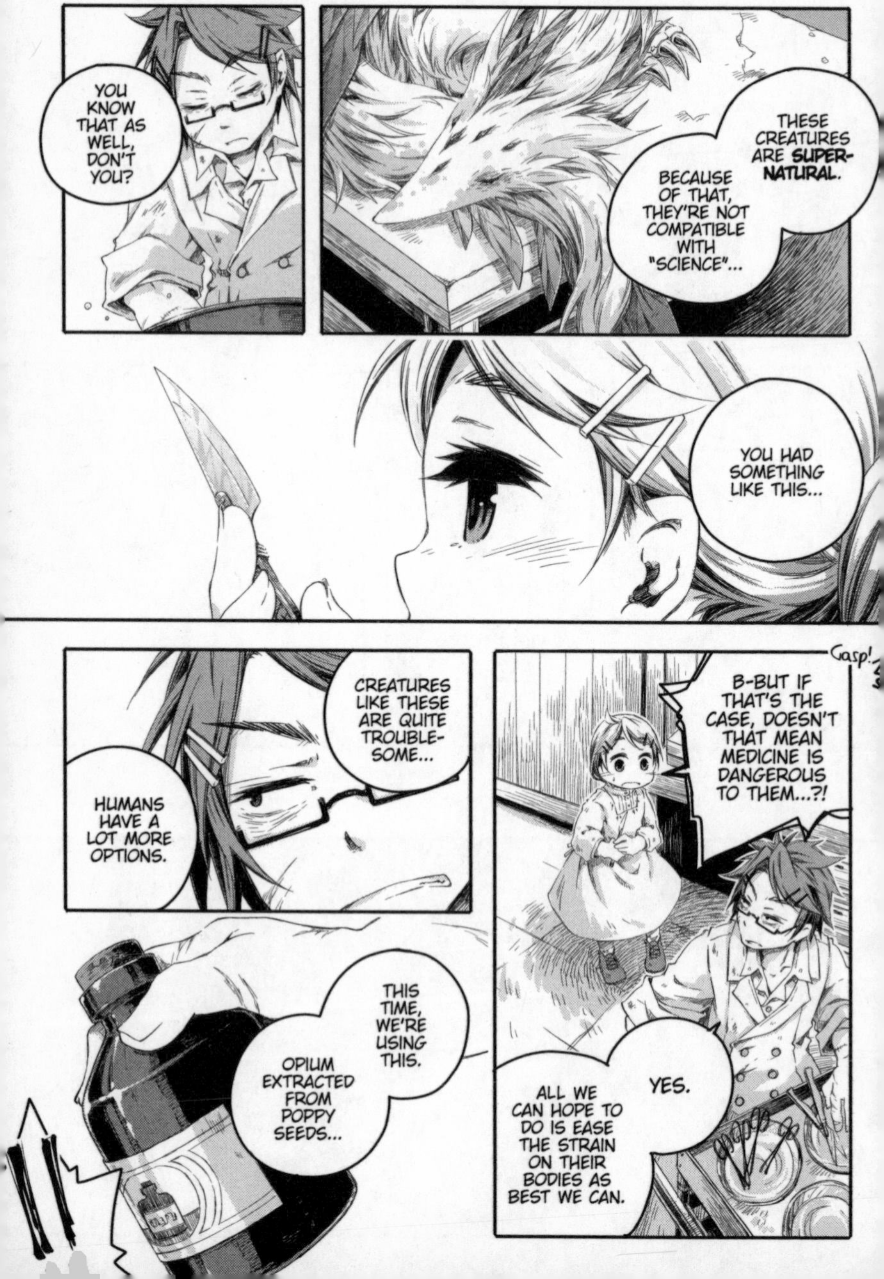
THESE CREATURES ARE **SUPER-NATURAL.**
BECAUSE OF THAT, THEY'RE NOT COMPATIBLE WITH "SCIENCE"...
YOU KNOW THAT AS WELL, DON'T YOU?
YOU HAD SOMETHING LIKE THIS...
Gasp!
B-BUT IF THAT'S THE CASE, DOESN'T THAT MEAN MEDICINE IS DANGEROUS TO THEM...?!
YES.
ALL WE CAN HOPE TO DO IS EASE THE STRAIN ON THEIR BODIES AS BEST WE CAN.
CREATURES LIKE THESE ARE QUITE TROUBLE-SOME...
HUMANS HAVE A LOT MORE OPTIONS.
THIS TIME, WE'RE USING THIS.
OPIUM EXTRACTED FROM POPPY SEEDS...

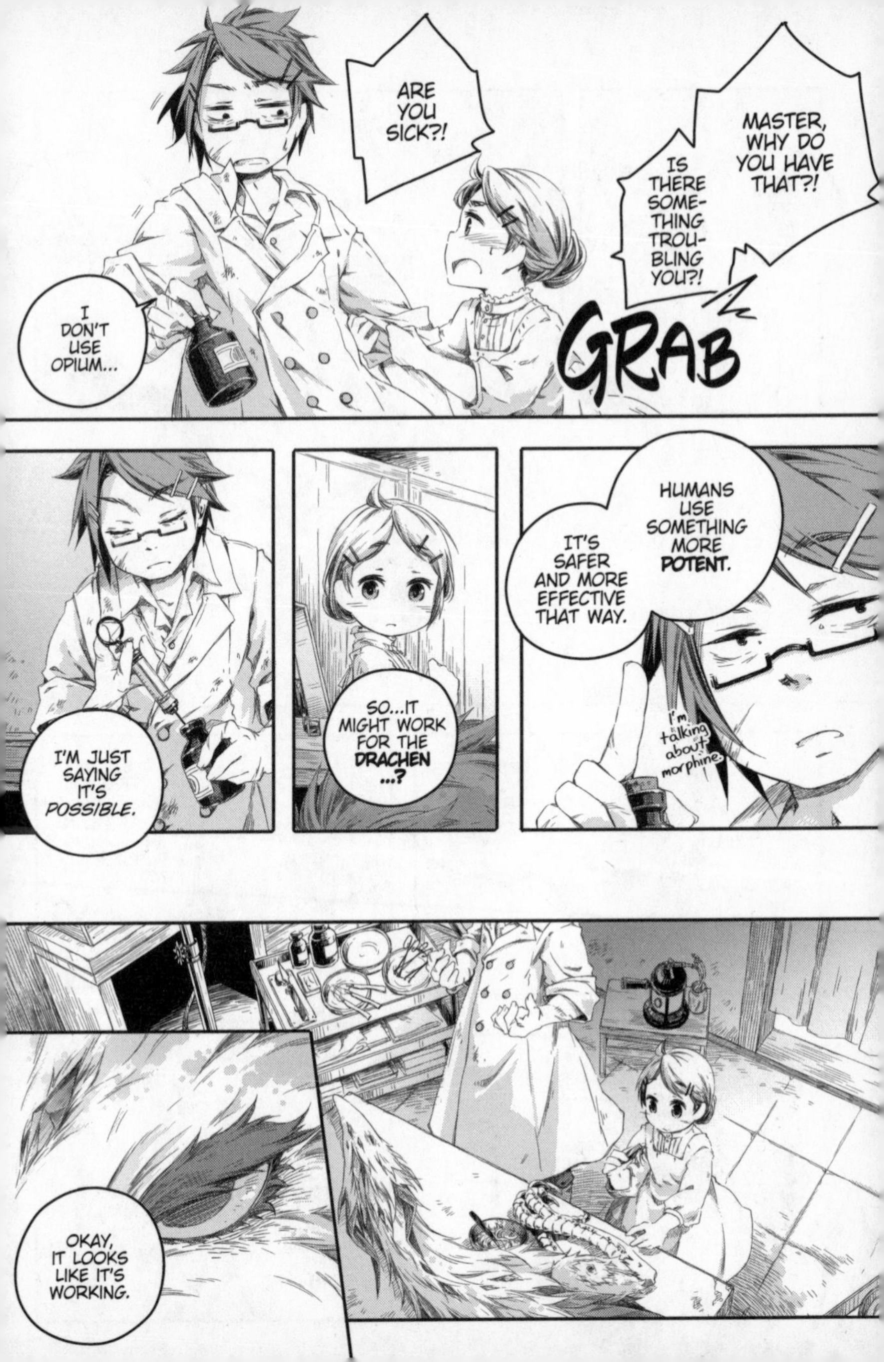
MASTER, WHY DO YOU HAVE THAT?!
IS THERE SOMETHING TROUBLING YOU?!
GRAB
ARE YOU SICK?!
I DON'T USE OPIUM...
HUMANS USE SOMETHING MORE POTENT.
IT'S SAFER AND MORE EFFECTIVE THAT WAY.
I'm talking about morphine.
SO...IT MIGHT WORK FOR THE DRACHEN...?
I'M JUST SAYING IT'S POSSIBLE.
OKAY, IT LOOKS LIKE IT'S WORKING.

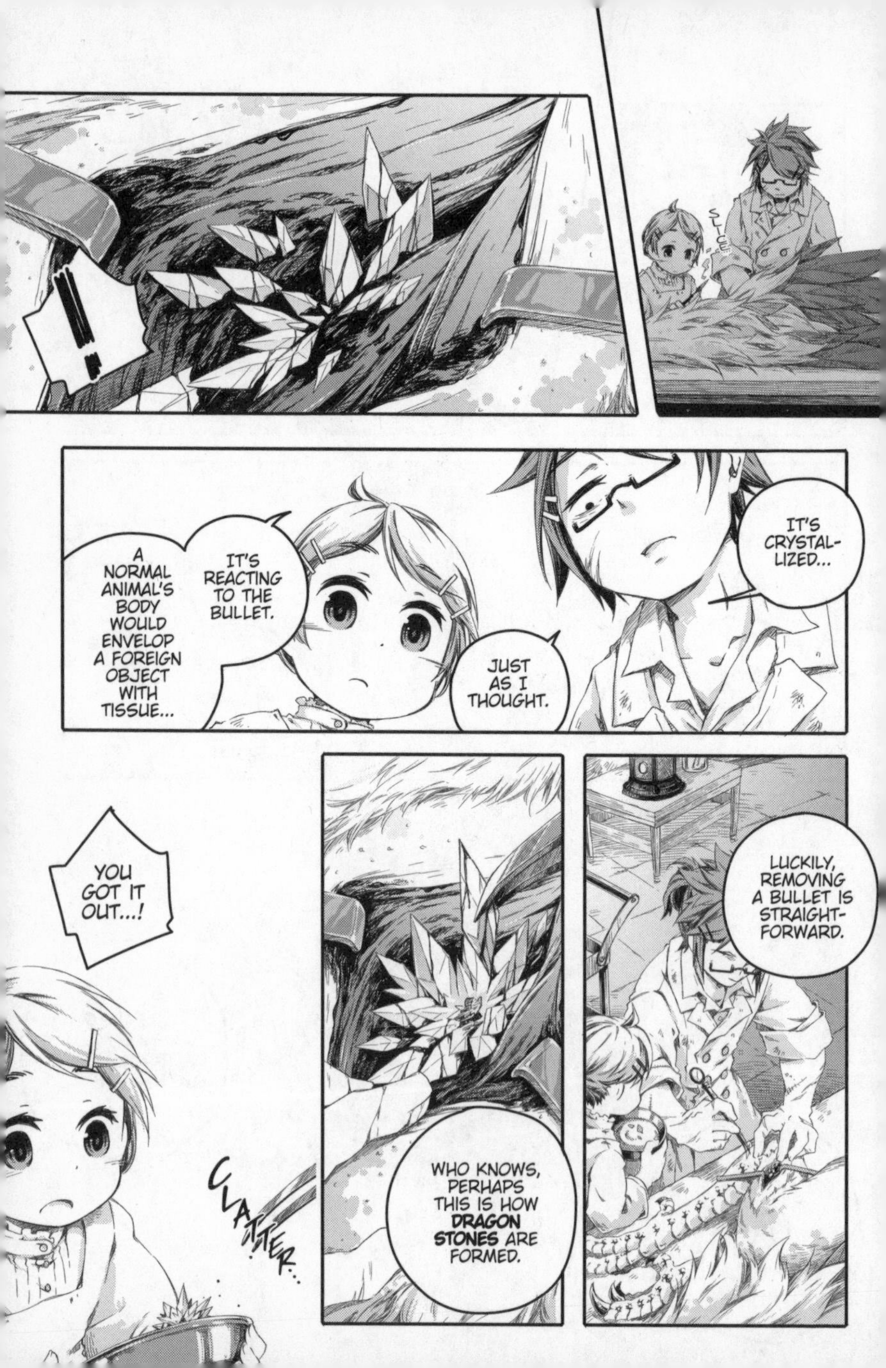
SLICE...
IT'S CRYSTAL-LIZED...
JUST AS I THOUGHT.
IT'S REACTING TO THE BULLET.
A NORMAL ANIMAL'S BODY WOULD ENVELOP A FOREIGN OBJECT WITH TISSUE...
LUCKILY, REMOVING A BULLET IS STRAIGHT-FORWARD.
WHO KNOWS, PERHAPS THIS IS HOW **DRAGON STONES** ARE FORMED.
YOU GOT IT OUT...!
CLATTER...

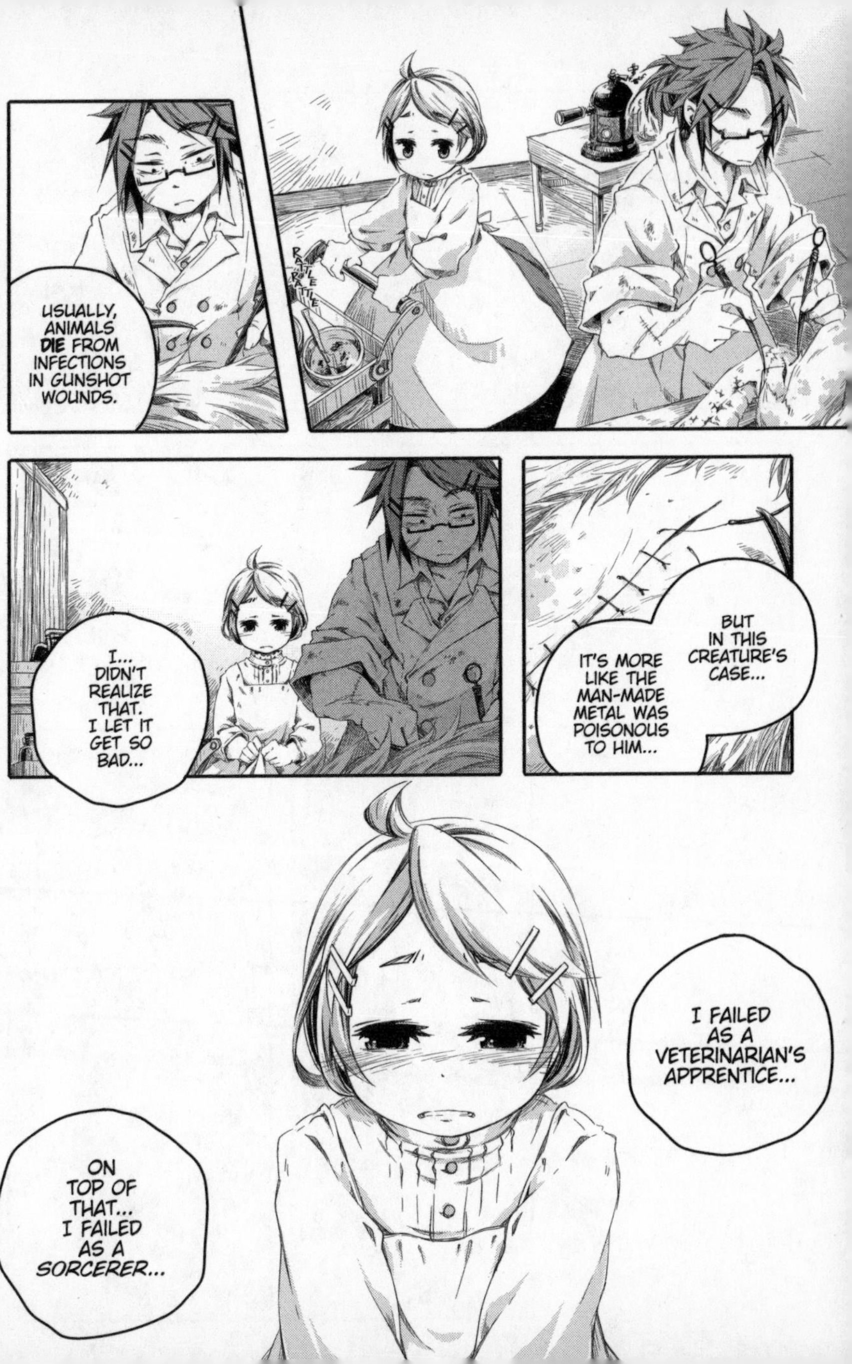
RATTLE RATTLE
USUALLY, ANIMALS DIE FROM INFECTIONS IN GUNSHOT WOUNDS.
BUT IN THIS CREATURE'S CASE...
IT'S MORE LIKE THE MAN-MADE METAL WAS POISONOUS TO HIM...
I... DIDN'T REALIZE THAT. I LET IT GET SO BAD...
I FAILED AS A VETERINARIAN'S APPRENTICE...
ON TOP OF THAT... I FAILED AS A SORCERER...

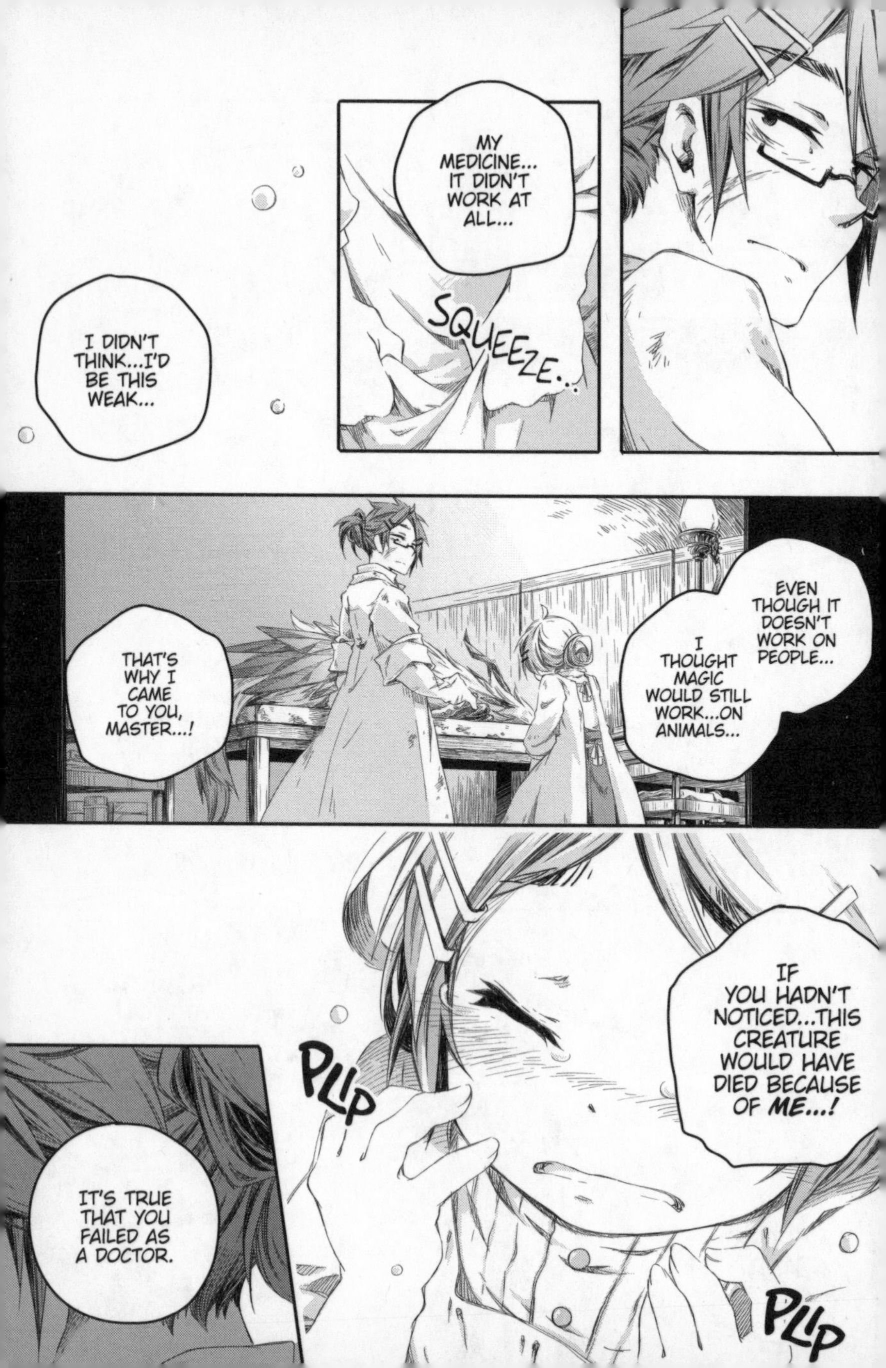
MY MEDICINE... IT DIDN'T WORK AT ALL...
SQUEEZE...
I DIDN'T THINK...I'D BE THIS WEAK...
EVEN THOUGH IT DOESN'T WORK ON PEOPLE...
I THOUGHT MAGIC WOULD STILL WORK...ON ANIMALS...
THAT'S WHY I CAME TO YOU, MASTER...!
IF YOU HADN'T NOTICED...THIS CREATURE WOULD HAVE DIED BECAUSE OF **ME...!**
PLIP
PLIP
IT'S TRUE THAT YOU FAILED AS A DOCTOR.

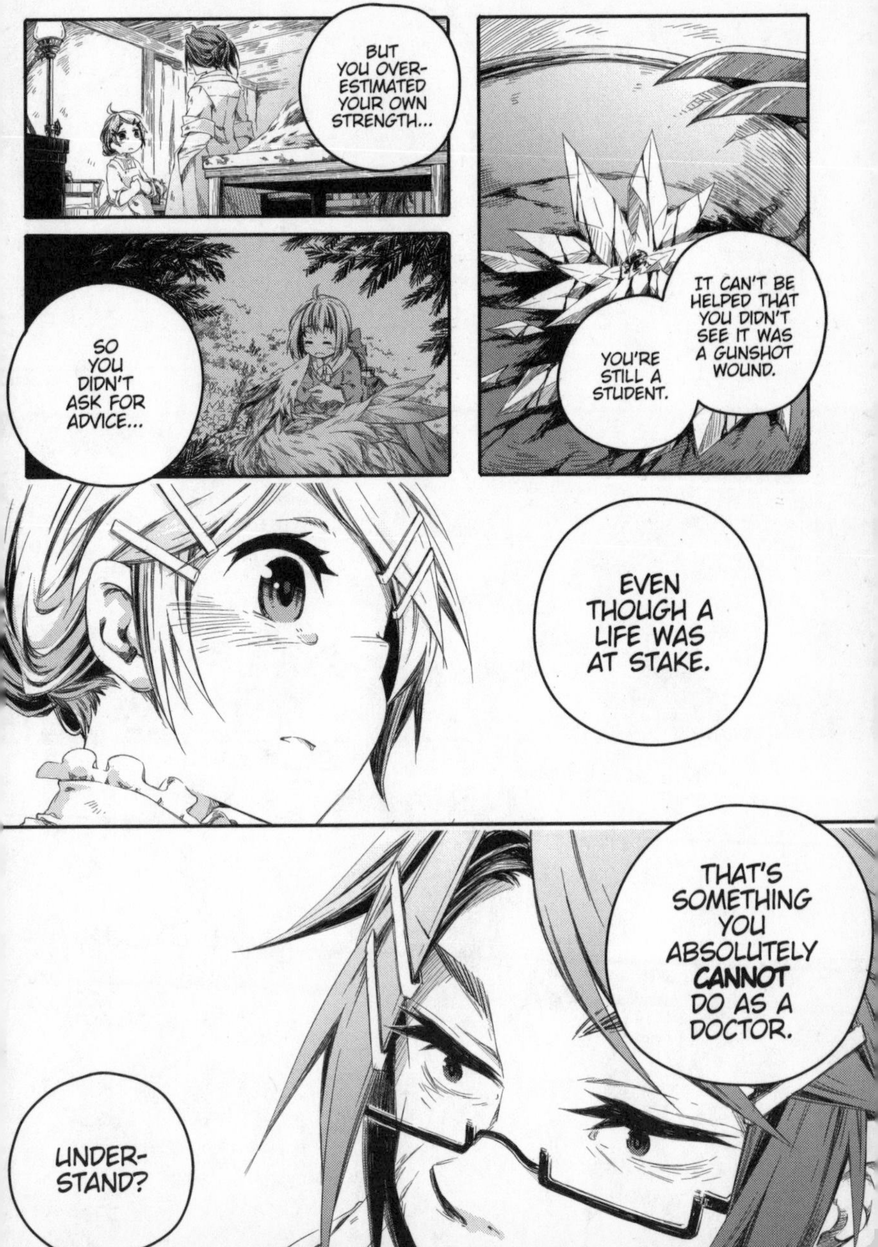
IT CAN'T BE HELPED THAT YOU DIDN'T SEE IT WAS A GUNSHOT WOUND.
YOU'RE STILL A STUDENT.
BUT YOU OVER-ESTIMATED YOUR OWN STRENGTH...
SO YOU DIDN'T ASK FOR ADVICE...
EVEN THOUGH A LIFE WAS AT STAKE.
THAT'S SOMETHING YOU ABSOLUTELY **CANNOT** DO AS A DOCTOR.
UNDER-STAND?

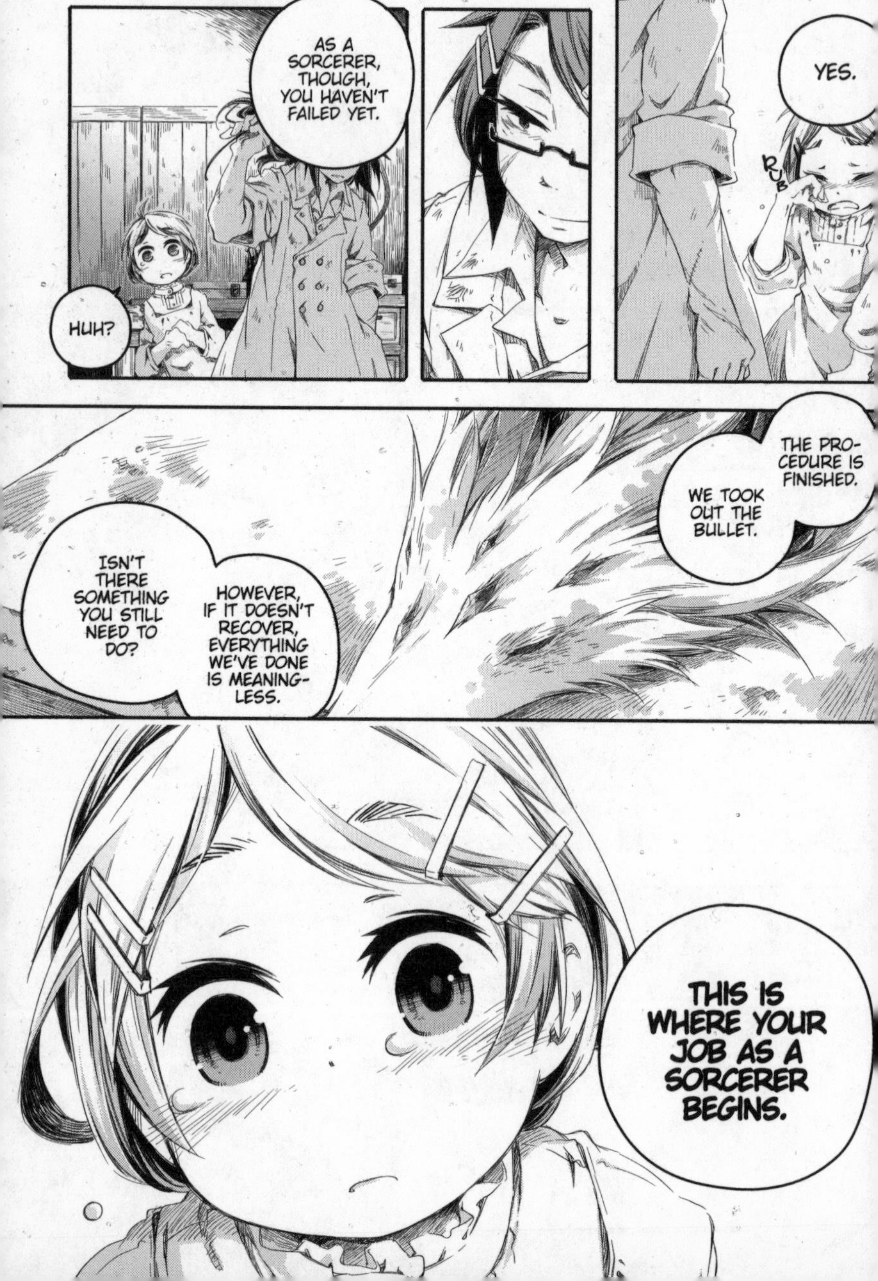
YES.
RUB
AS A SORCERER, THOUGH, YOU HAVEN'T FAILED YET.
HUH?
THE PRO-CEDURE IS FINISHED.
WE TOOK OUT THE BULLET.
HOWEVER, IF IT DOESN'T RECOVER, EVERYTHING WE'VE DONE IS MEANING-LESS.
ISN'T THERE SOMETHING YOU STILL NEED TO DO?
THIS IS WHERE YOUR JOB AS A SORCERER BEGINS.

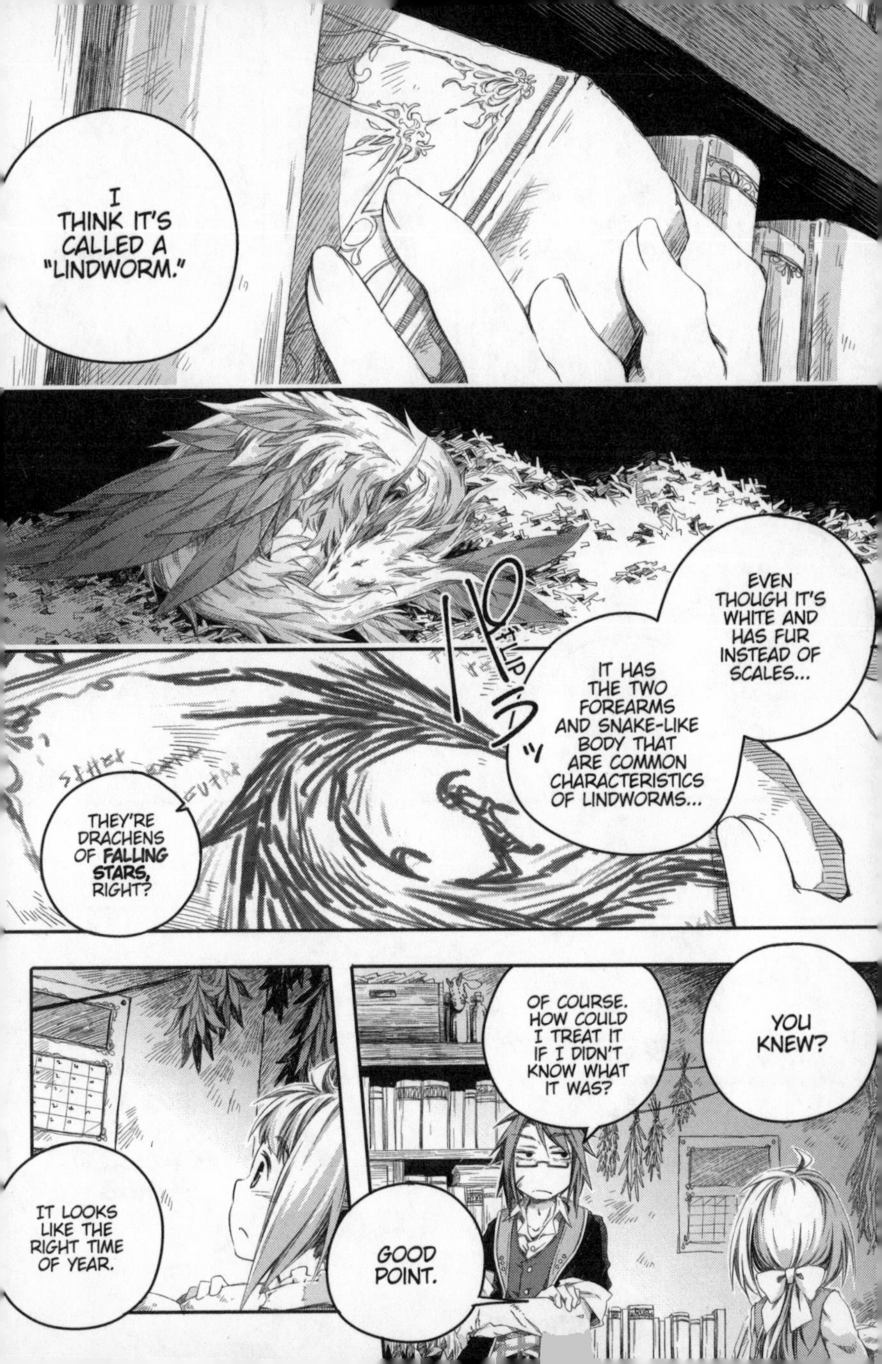

I THINK IT'S CALLED A "LINDWORM."
EVEN THOUGH IT'S WHITE AND HAS FUR INSTEAD OF SCALES...
IT HAS THE TWO FOREARMS AND SNAKE-LIKE BODY THAT ARE COMMON CHARACTERISTICS OF LINDWORMS...
FLIP
THEY'RE DRACHENS OF **FALLING STARS,** RIGHT?
YOU KNEW?
OF COURSE. HOW COULD I TREAT IT IF I DIDN'T KNOW WHAT IT WAS?
GOOD POINT.
IT LOOKS LIKE THE RIGHT TIME OF YEAR.

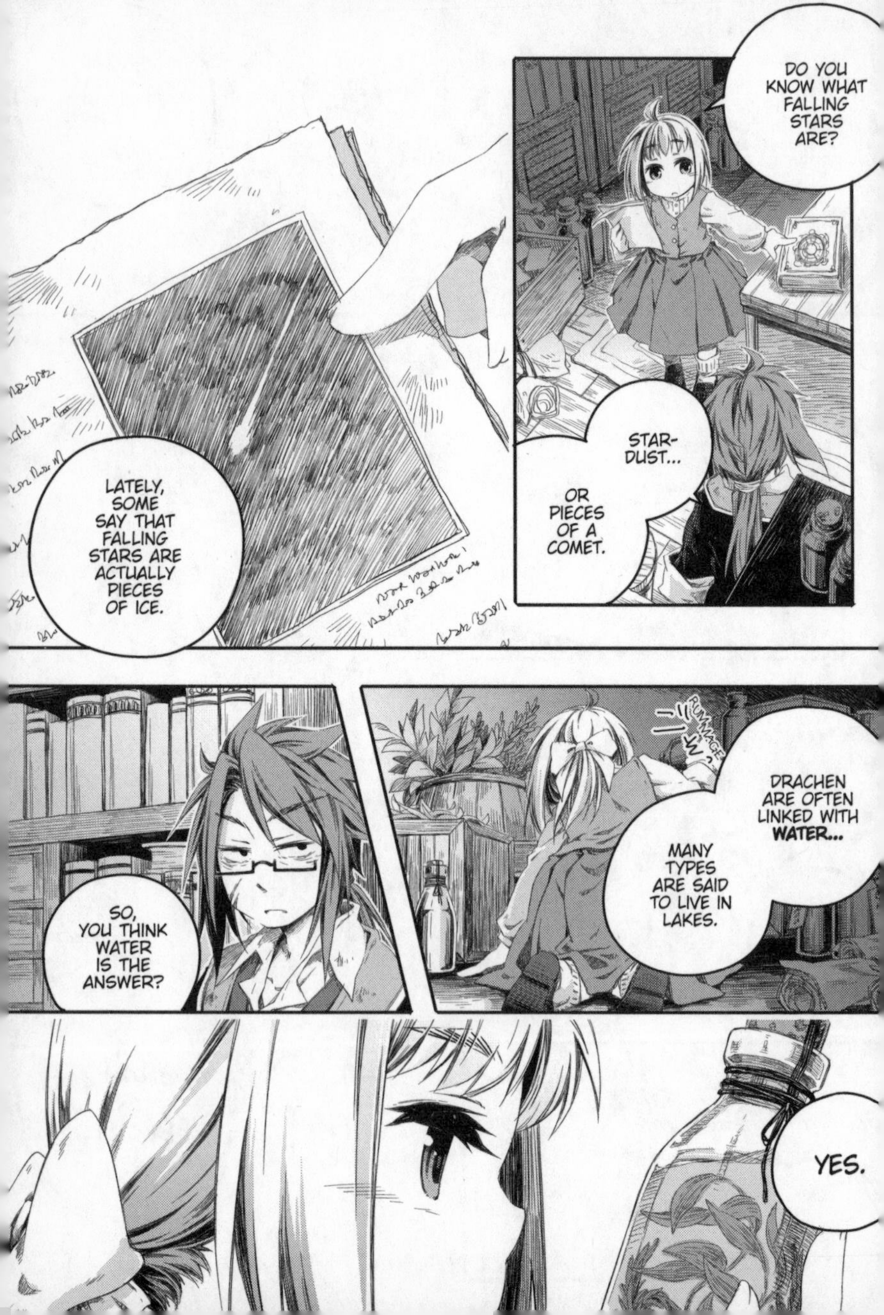
DO YOU KNOW WHAT FALLING STARS ARE?
STAR-DUST...
OR PIECES OF A COMET.
LATELY, SOME SAY THAT FALLING STARS ARE ACTUALLY PIECES OF ICE.
RUMMAGE
DRACHEN ARE OFTEN LINKED WITH WATER...
MANY TYPES ARE SAID TO LIVE IN LAKES.
SO, YOU THINK WATER IS THE ANSWER?
YES.

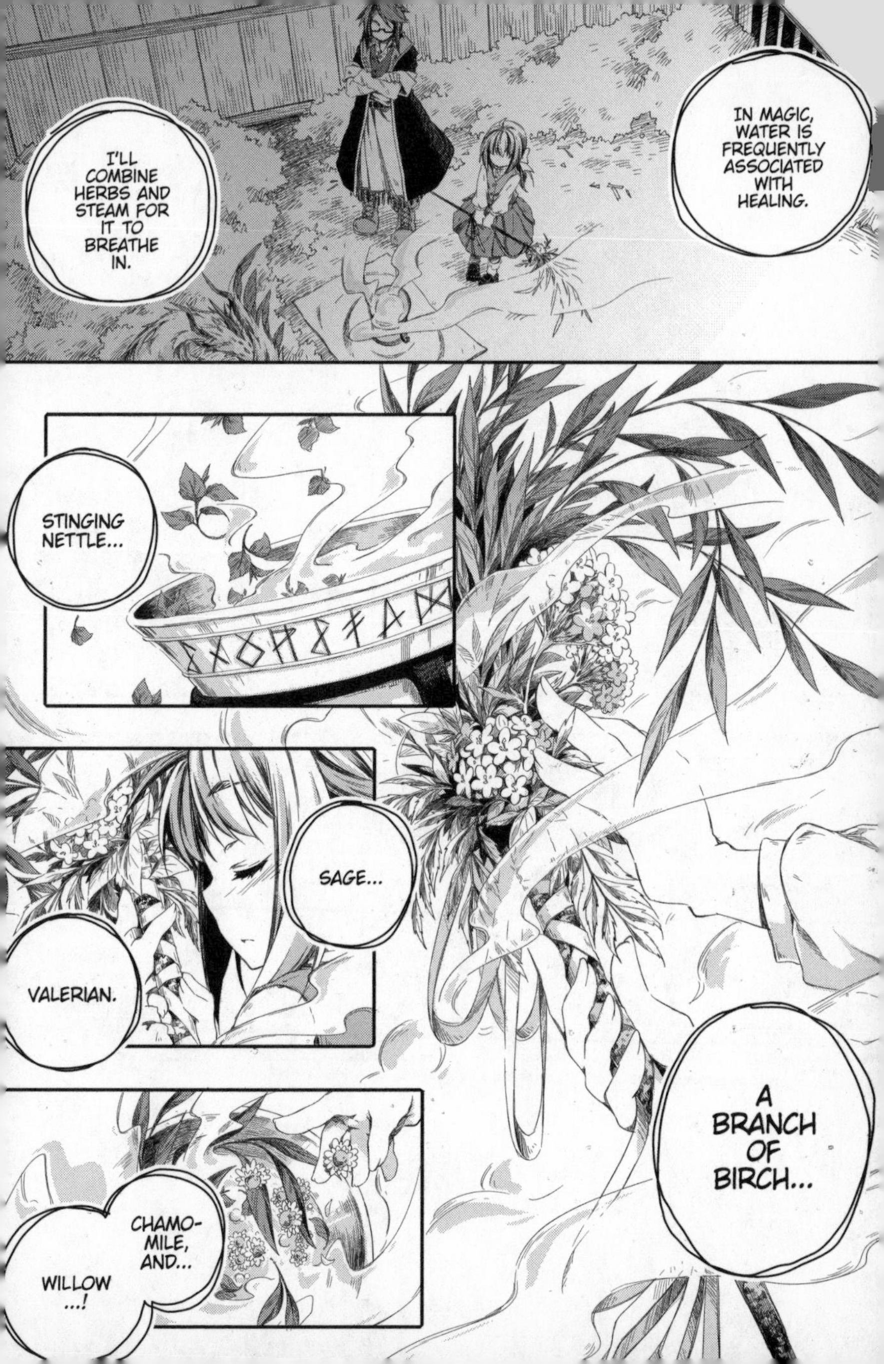
IN MAGIC, WATER IS FREQUENTLY ASSOCIATED WITH HEALING.
I'LL COMBINE HERBS AND STEAM FOR IT TO BREATHE IN.
A BRANCH OF BIRCH...
STINGING NETTLE...
SAGE...
VALERIAN.
CHAMO-MILE, AND...
WILLOW ...!

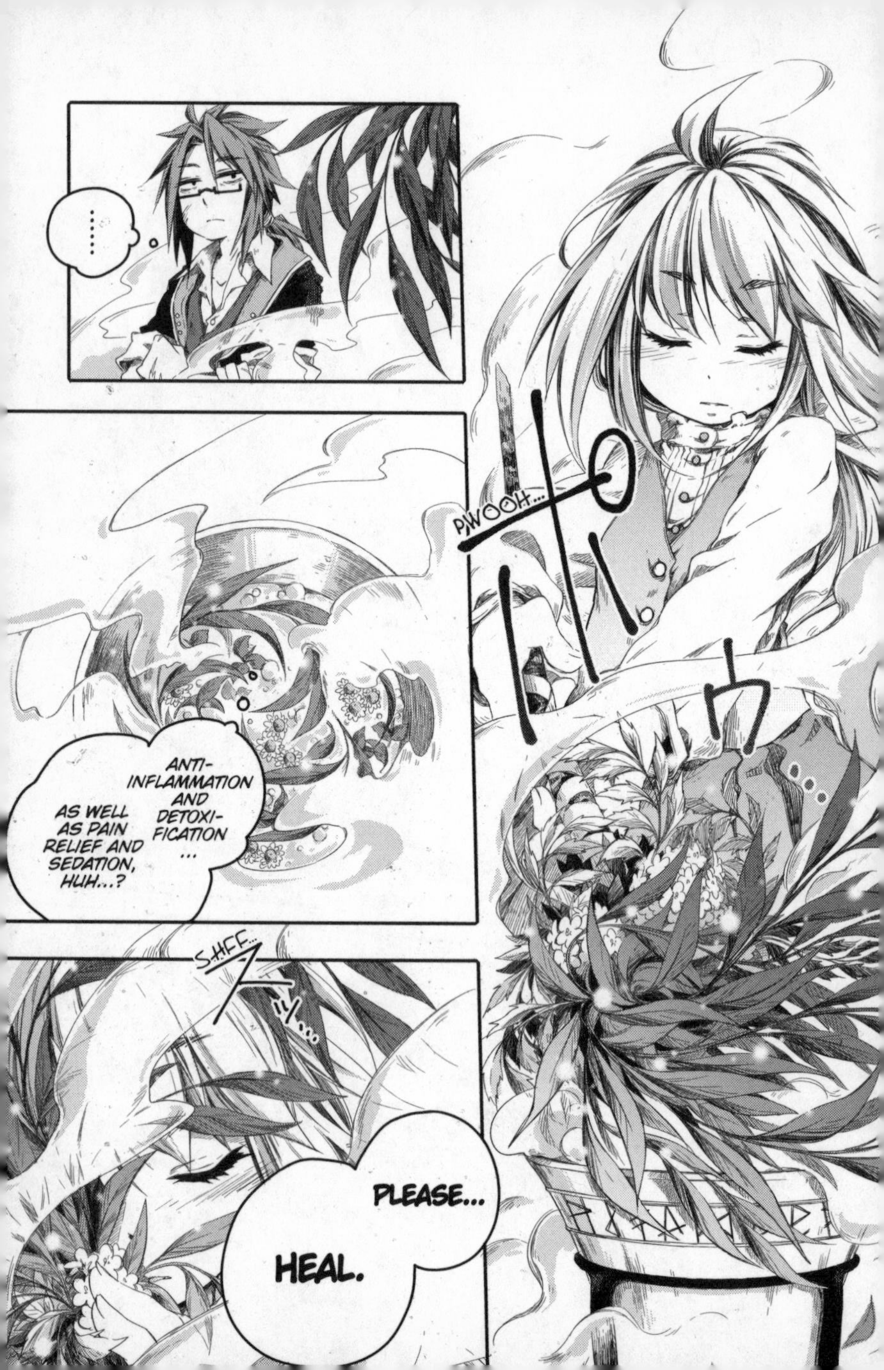
PWOOH...
......
ANTI-INFLAMMATION AND DETOXIFICATION...
AS WELL AS PAIN RELIEF AND SEDATION, HUH...?
SHFF...
PLEASE...
HEAL.

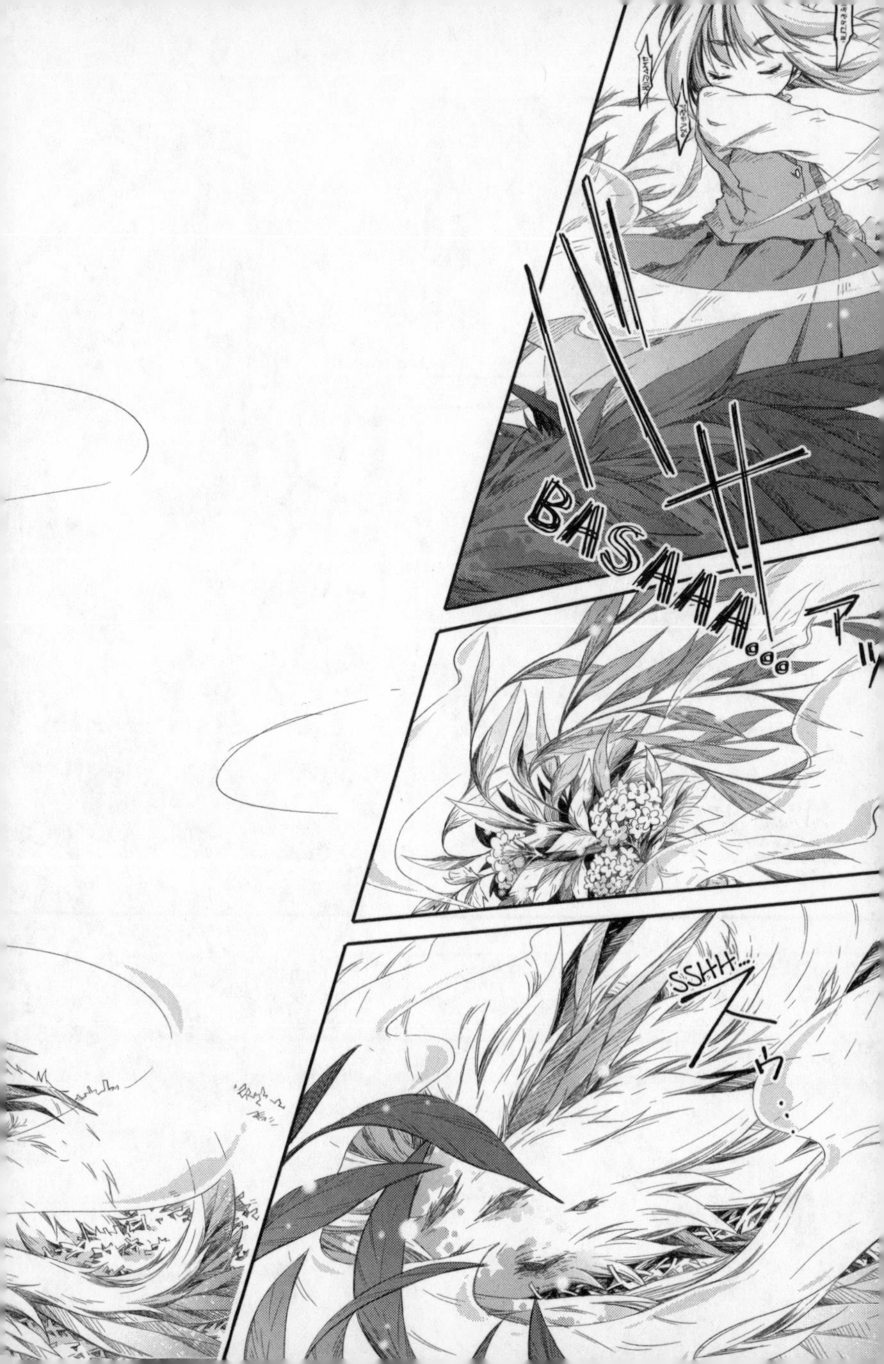
BASAAA...
SSHH...

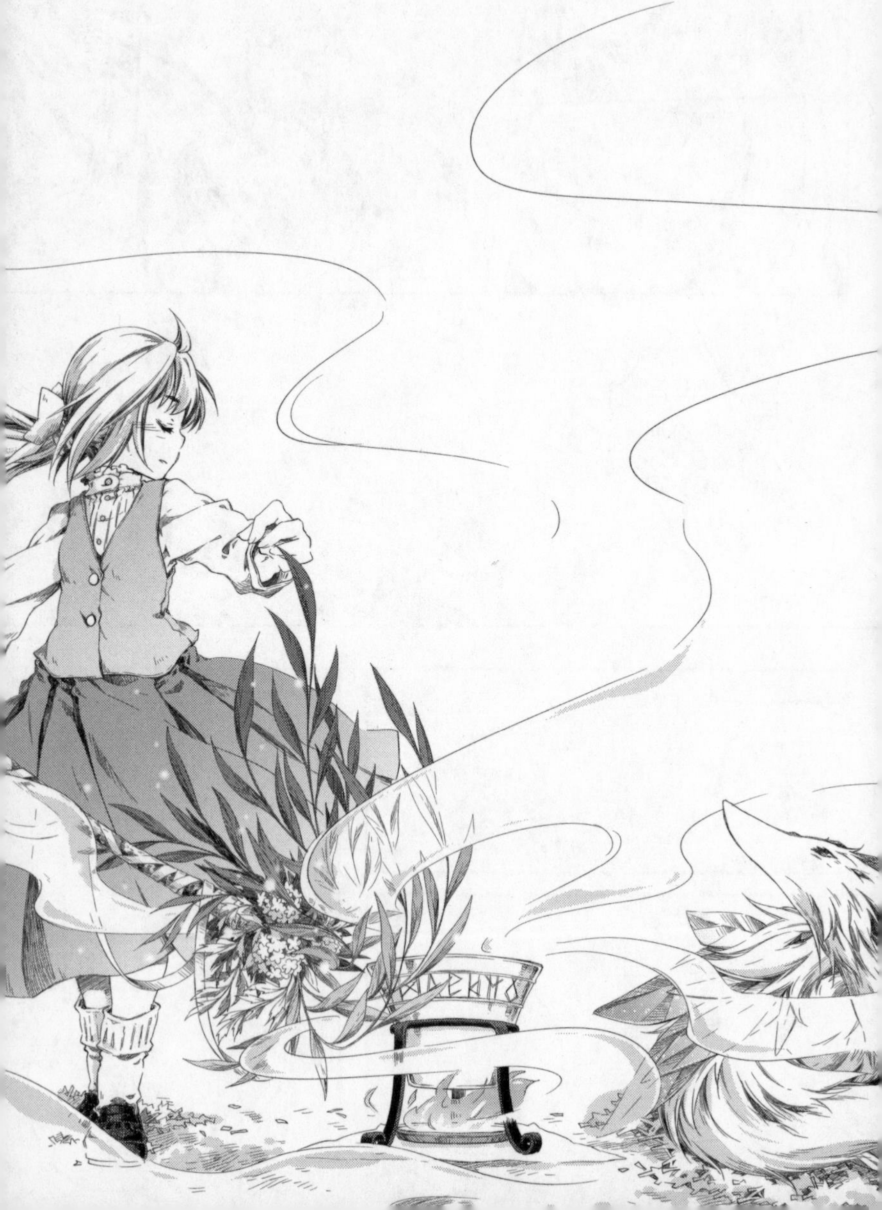

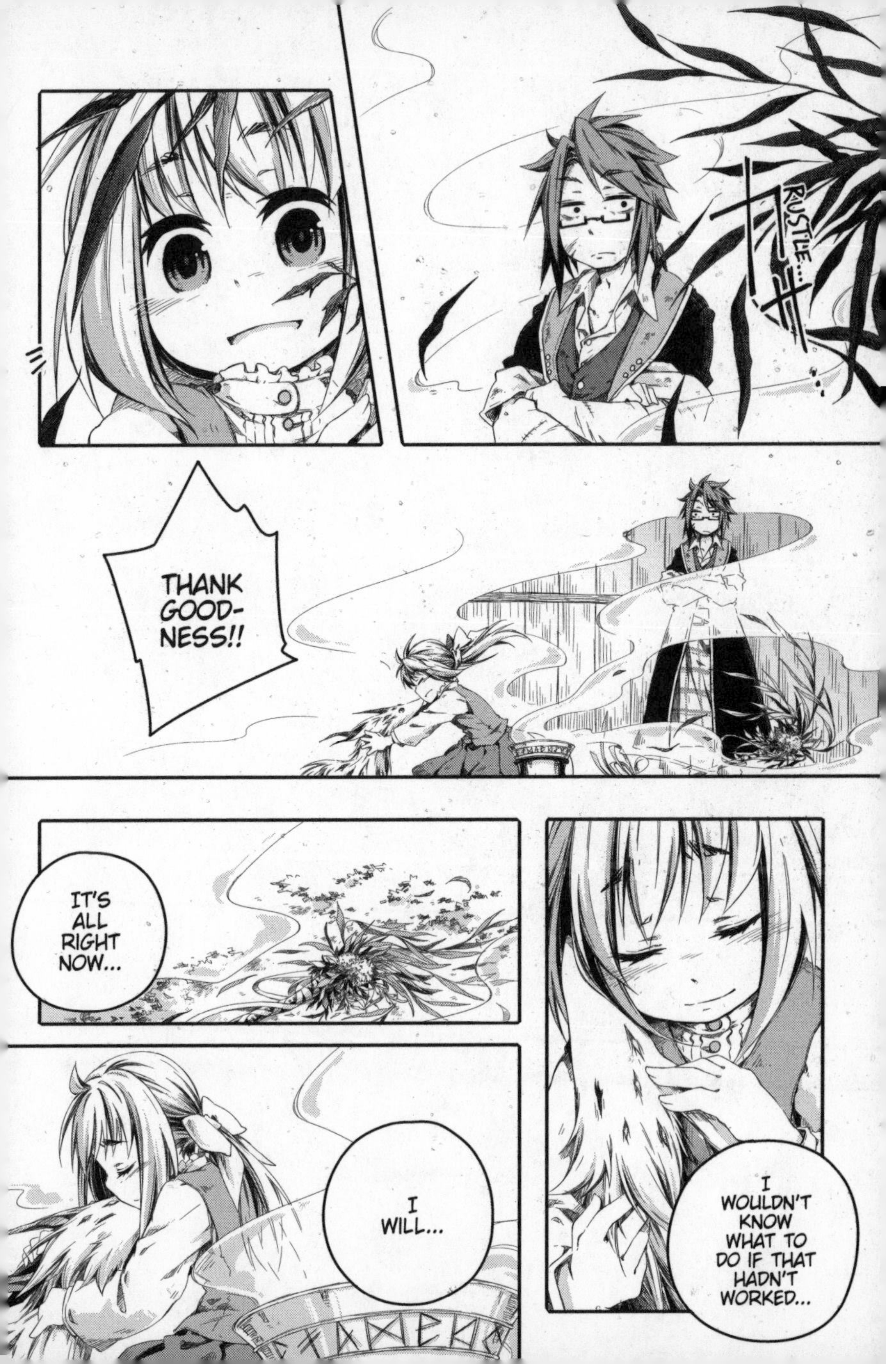

RUSTLE...
THANK GOOD-NESS!!
I WOULDN'T KNOW WHAT TO DO IF THAT HADN'T WORKED...
IT'S ALL RIGHT NOW...
I WILL...

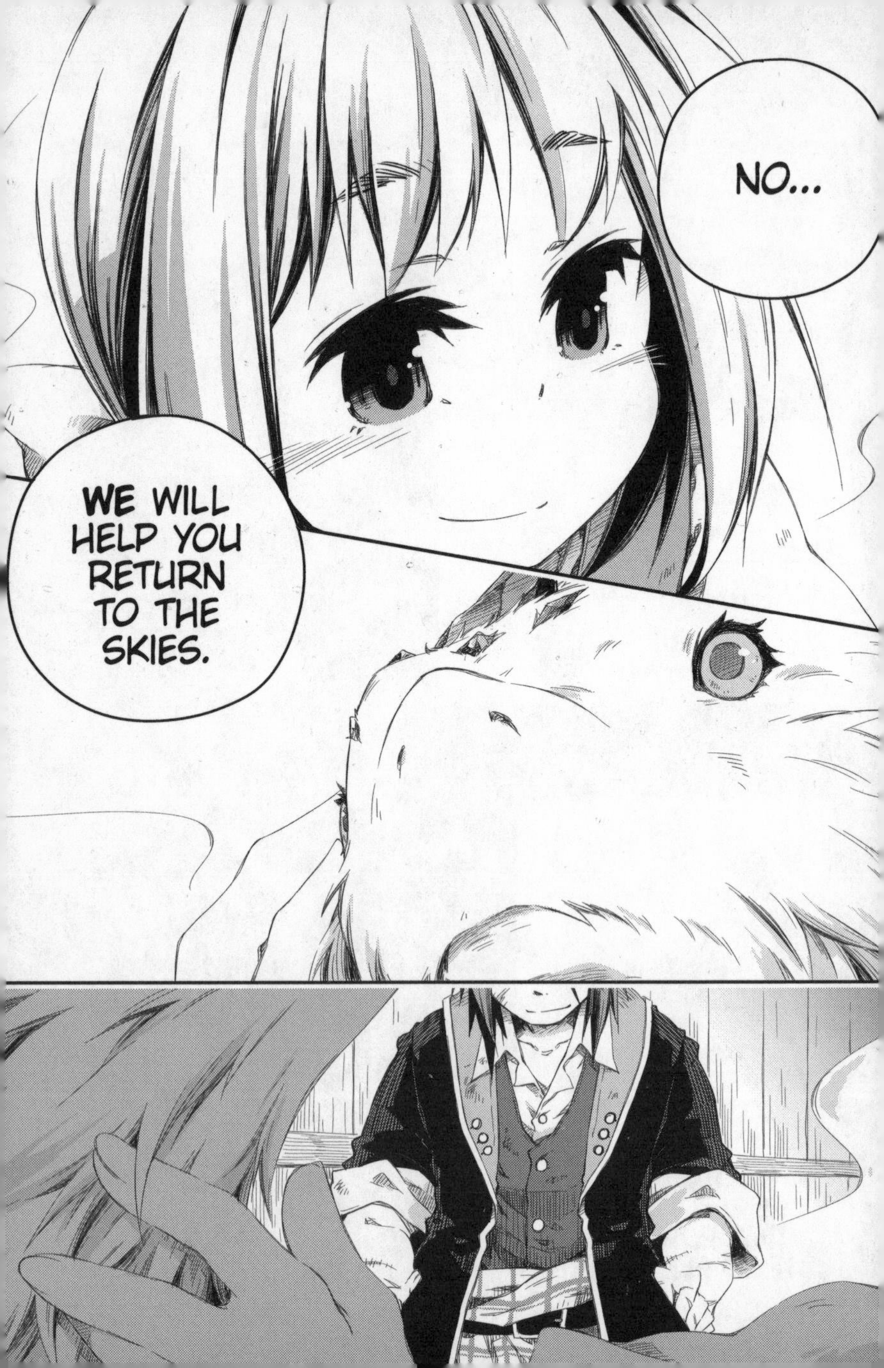
NO...
WE WILL HELP YOU RETURN TO THE SKIES.

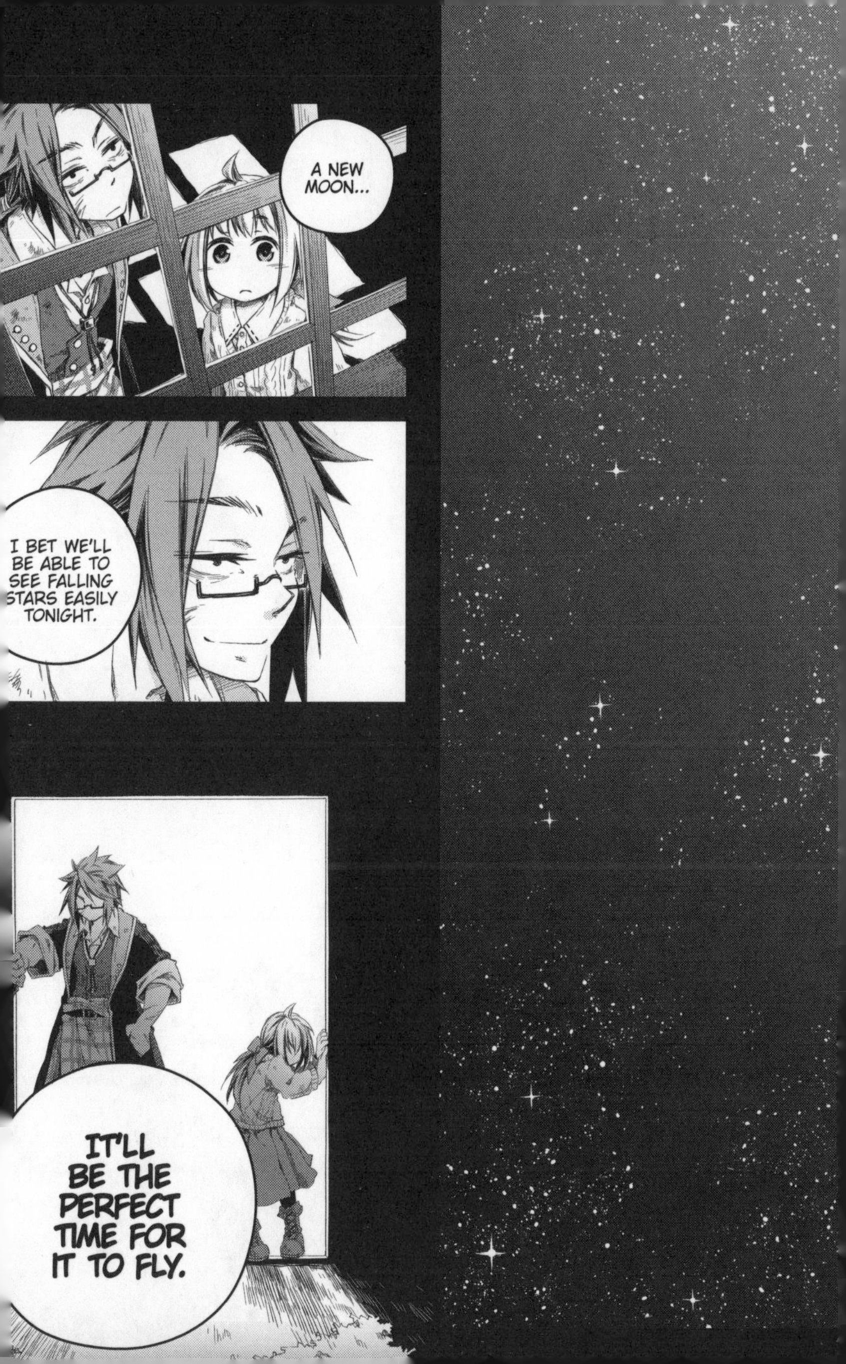
A NEW MOON...
I BET WE'LL BE ABLE TO SEE FALLING STARS EASILY TONIGHT.
IT'LL BE THE PERFECT TIME FOR IT TO FLY.

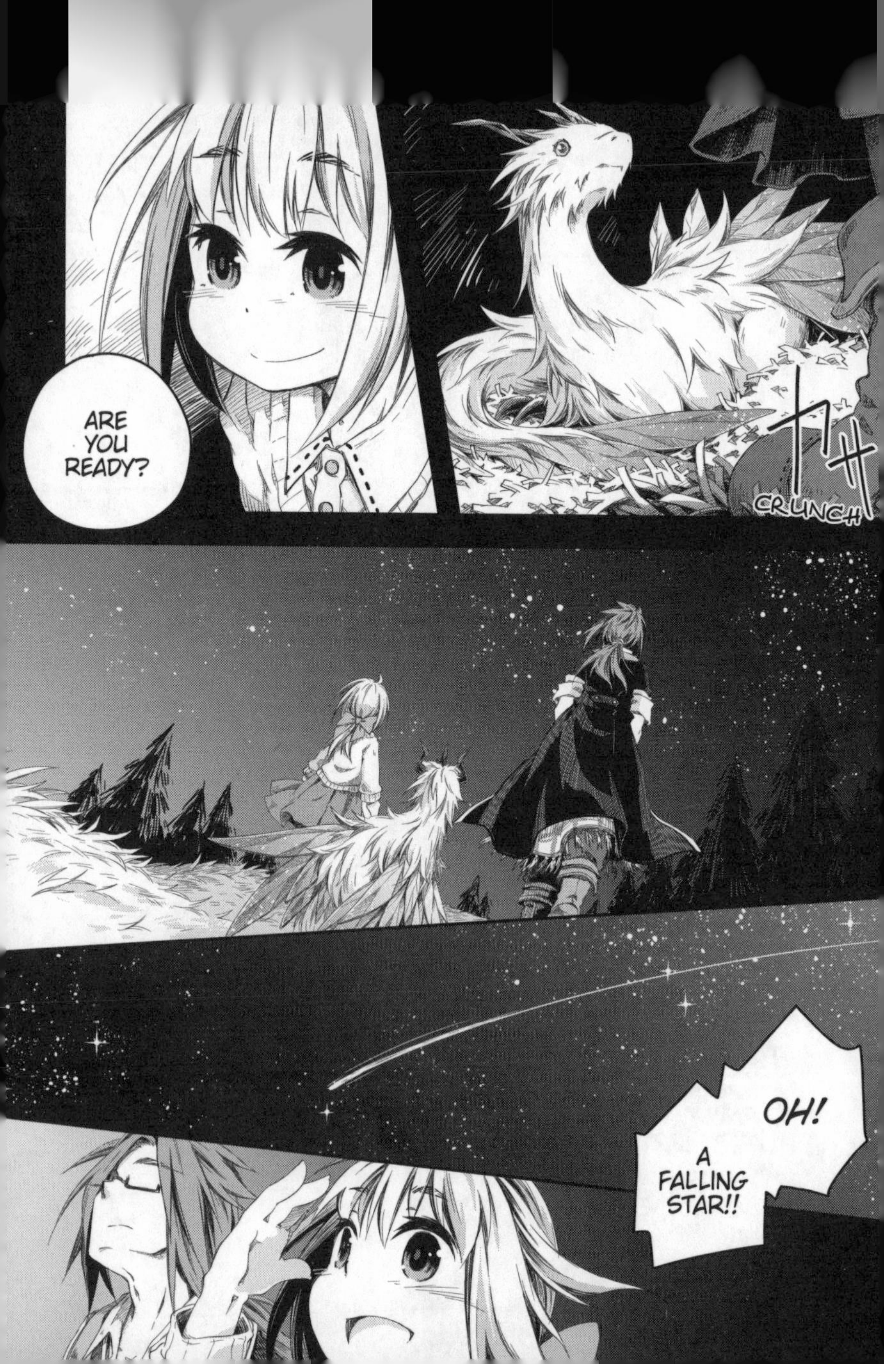

CRUNCH
ARE YOU READY?
OH!
A FALLING STAR!!

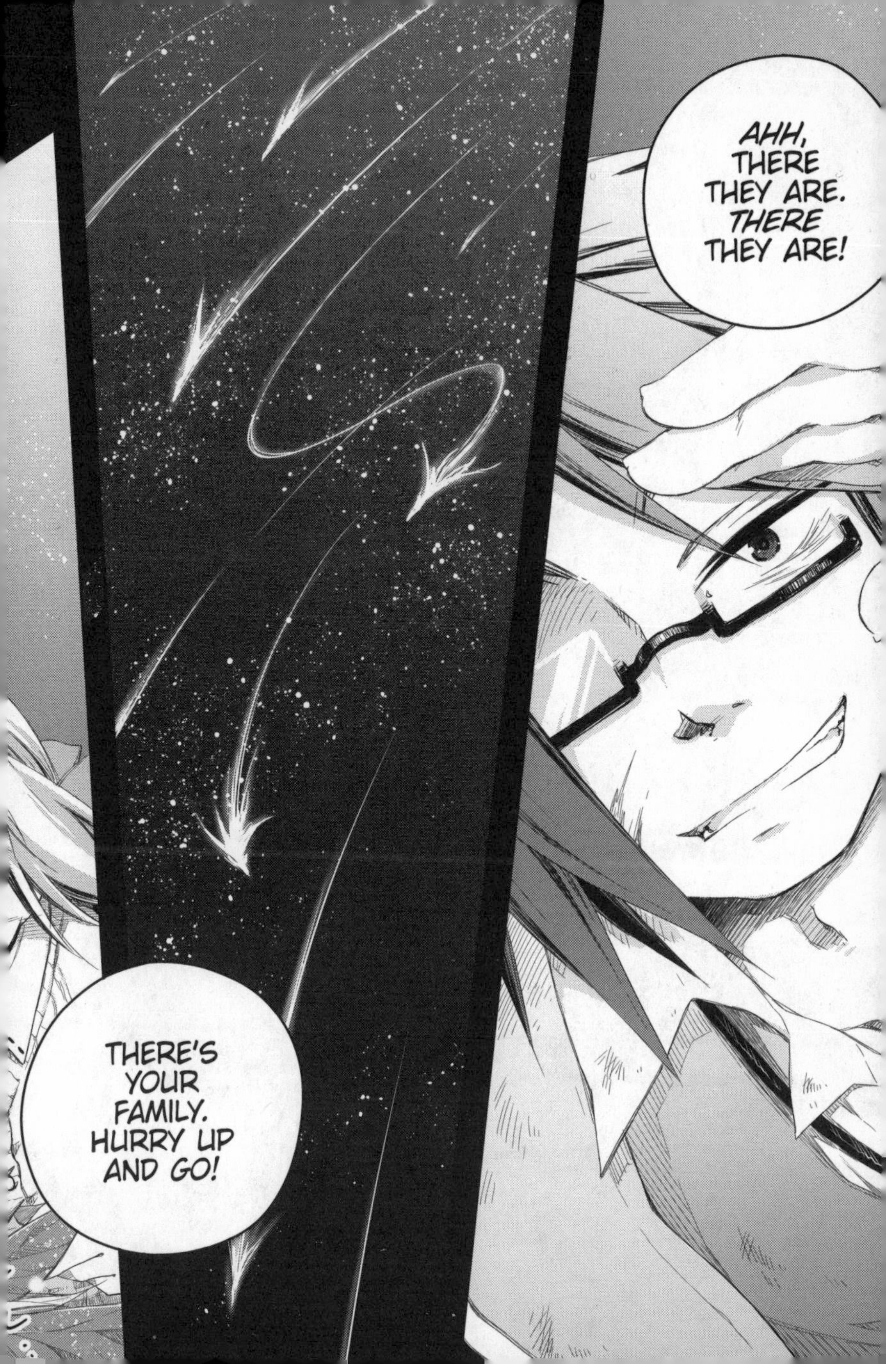
AHH, THERE THEY ARE. THERE THEY ARE!
THERE'S YOUR FAMILY. HURRY UP AND GO!

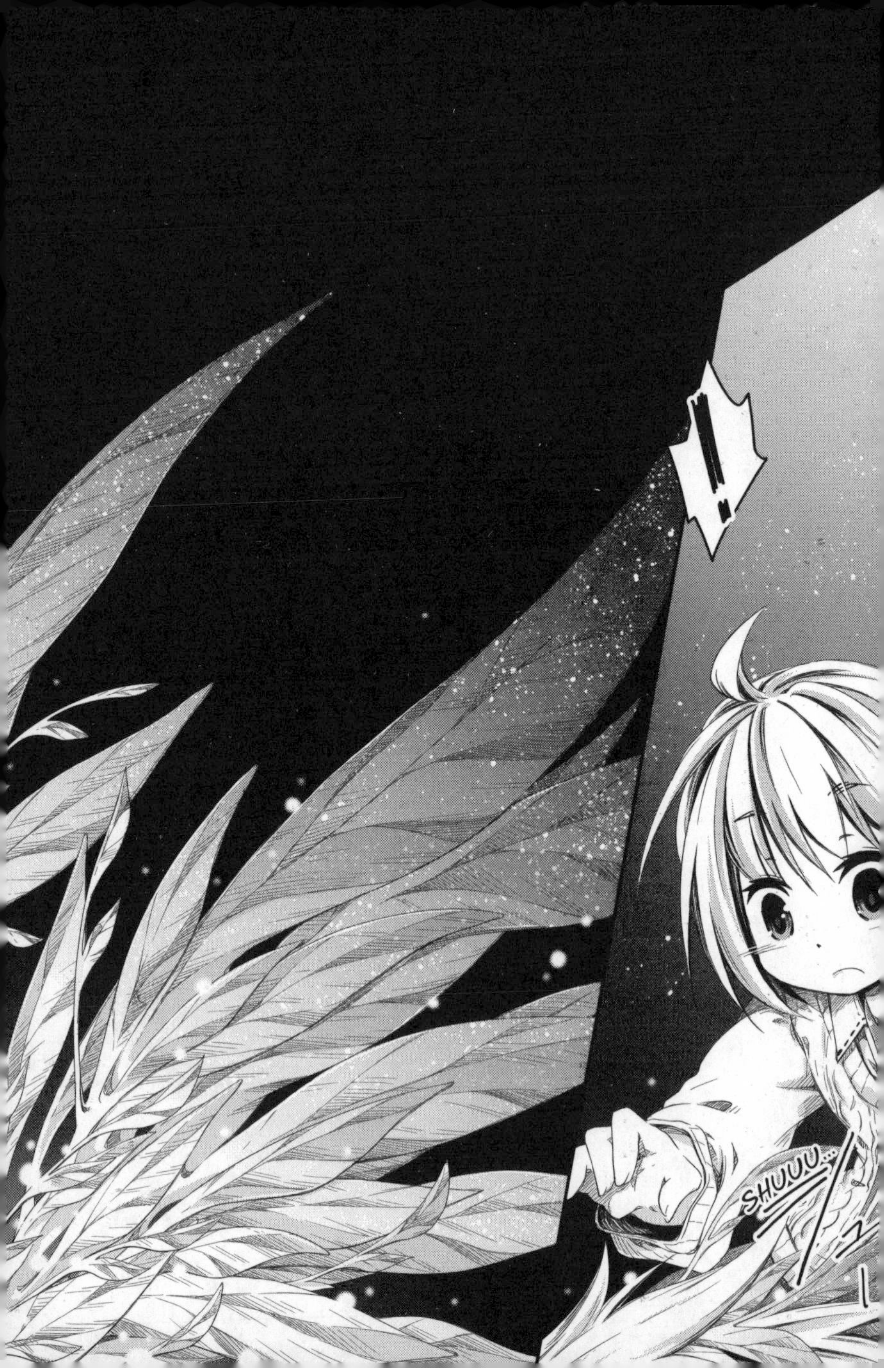
!!
SHUUU...

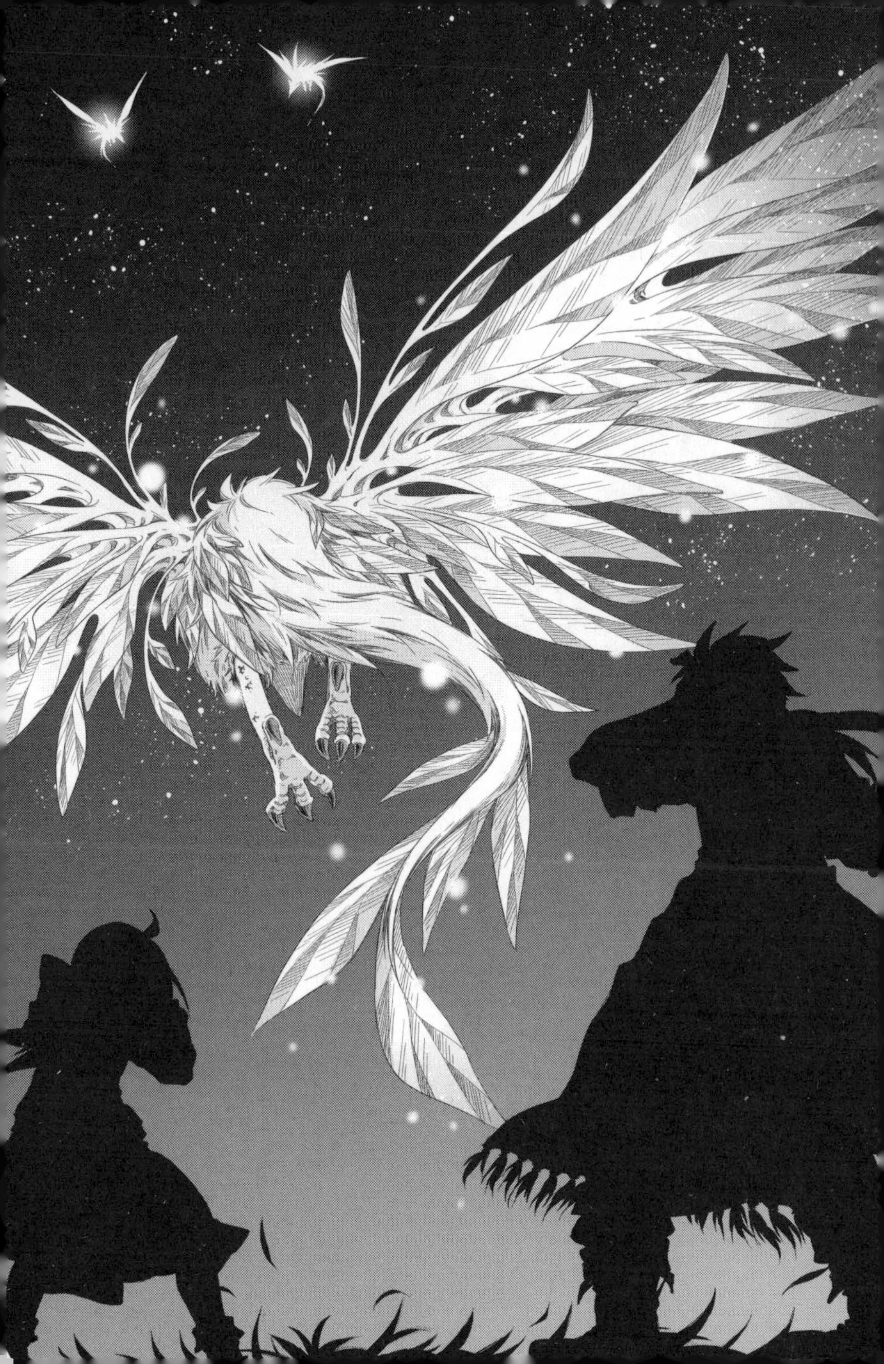

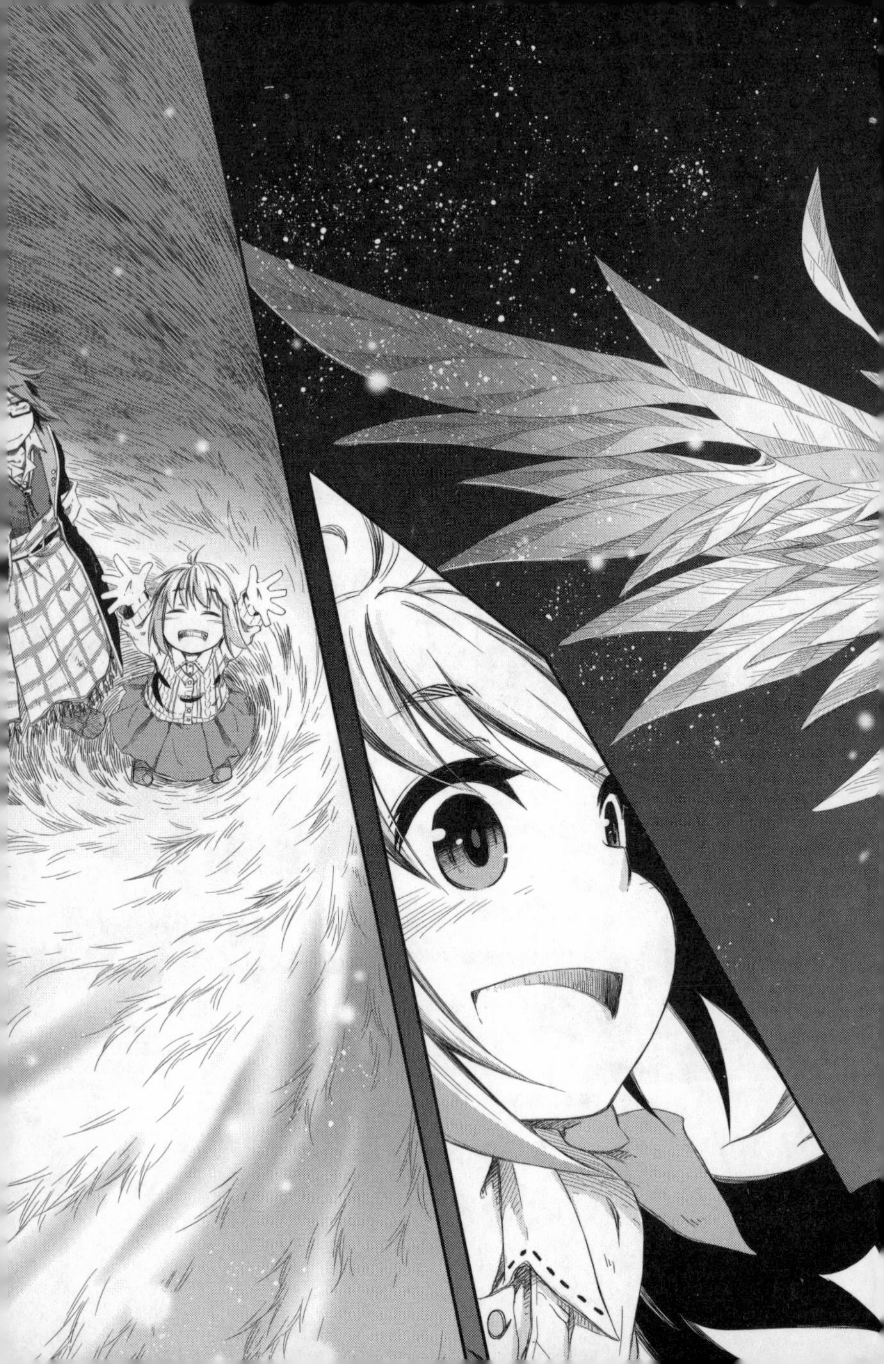

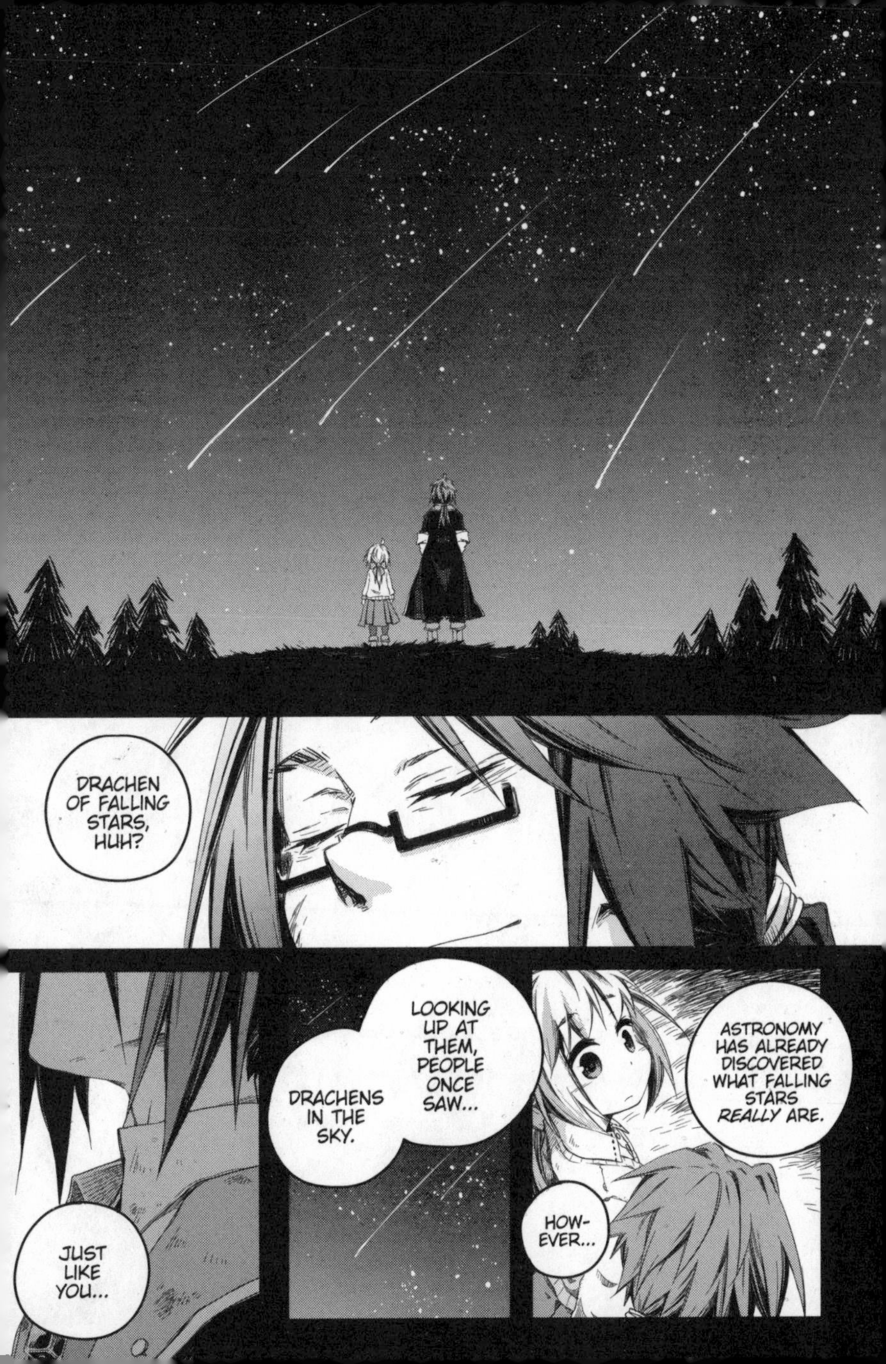
DRACHEN OF FALLING STARS, HUH?
ASTRONOMY HAS ALREADY DISCOVERED WHAT FALLING STARS *REALLY* ARE.
HOW-EVER...
LOOKING UP AT THEM, PEOPLE ONCE SAW...
DRACHENS IN THE SKY.
JUST LIKE YOU...

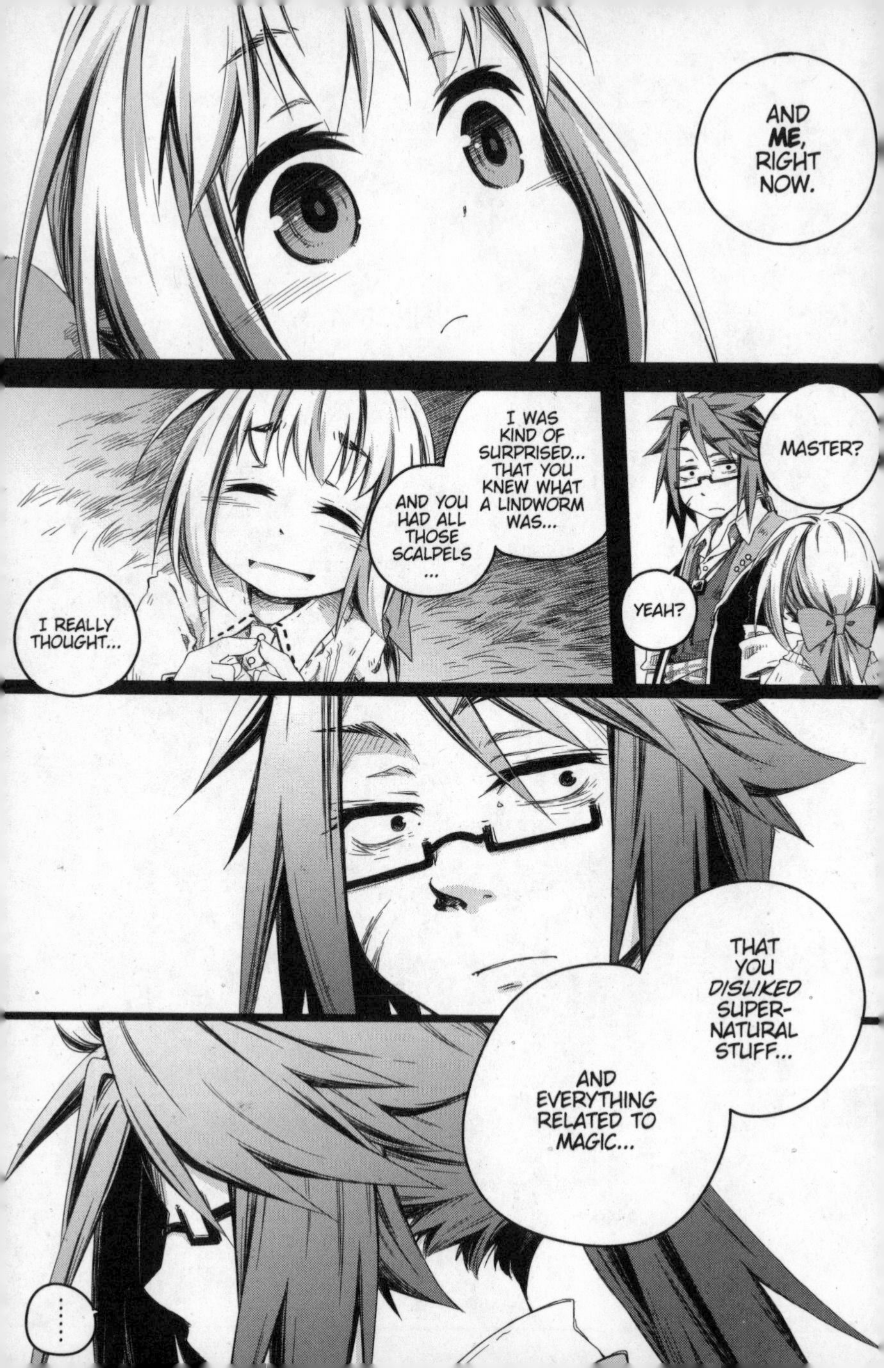
AND **ME**, RIGHT NOW.
MASTER?
YEAH?
I WAS KIND OF SURPRISED... THAT YOU KNEW WHAT A LINDWORM WAS...
AND YOU HAD ALL THOSE SCALPELS ...
I REALLY THOUGHT...
THAT YOU *DISLIKED* SUPER-NATURAL STUFF...
AND EVERYTHING RELATED TO MAGIC...
......

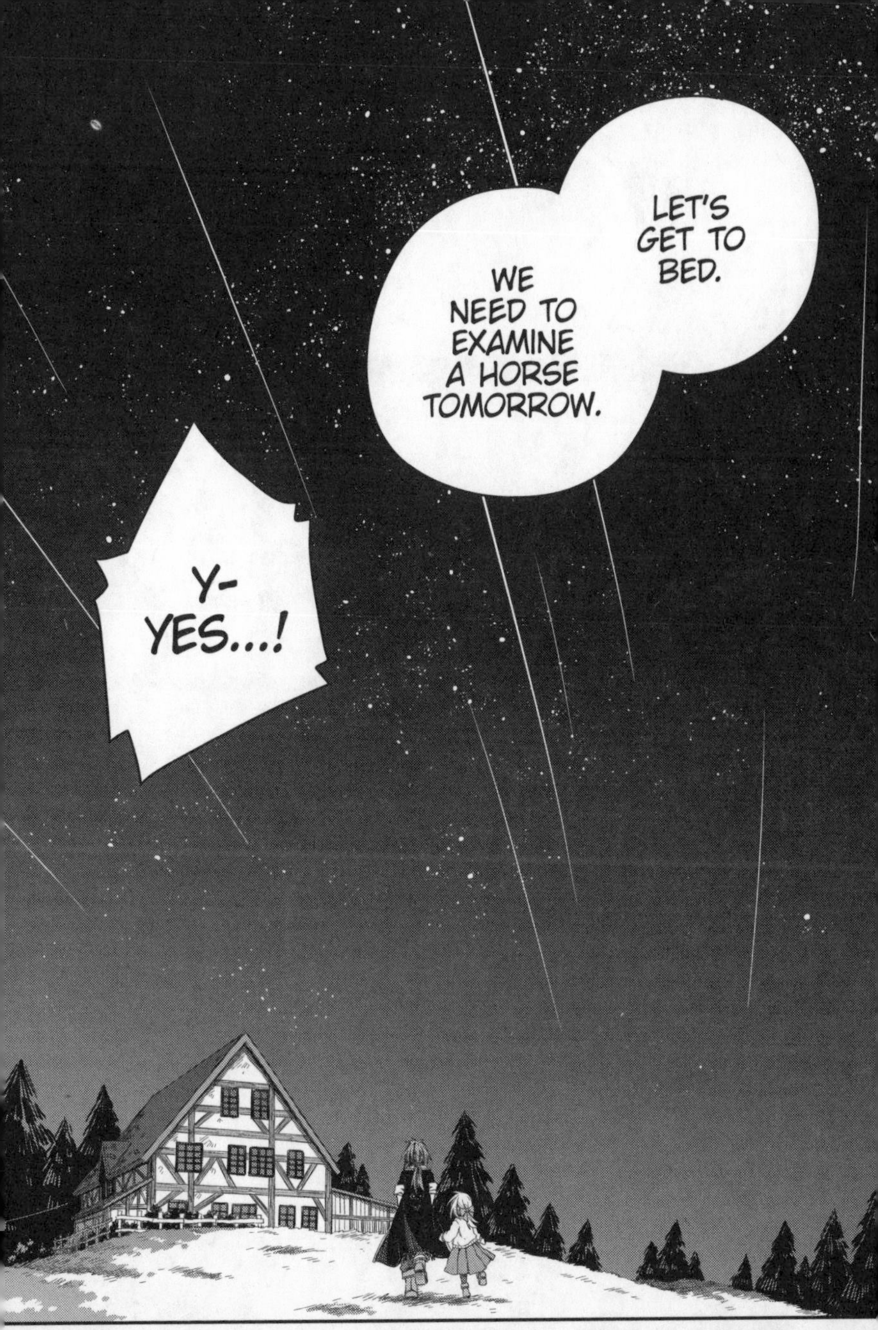
LET'S GET TO BED.
WE NEED TO EXAMINE A HORSE TOMORROW.
Y-YES...!

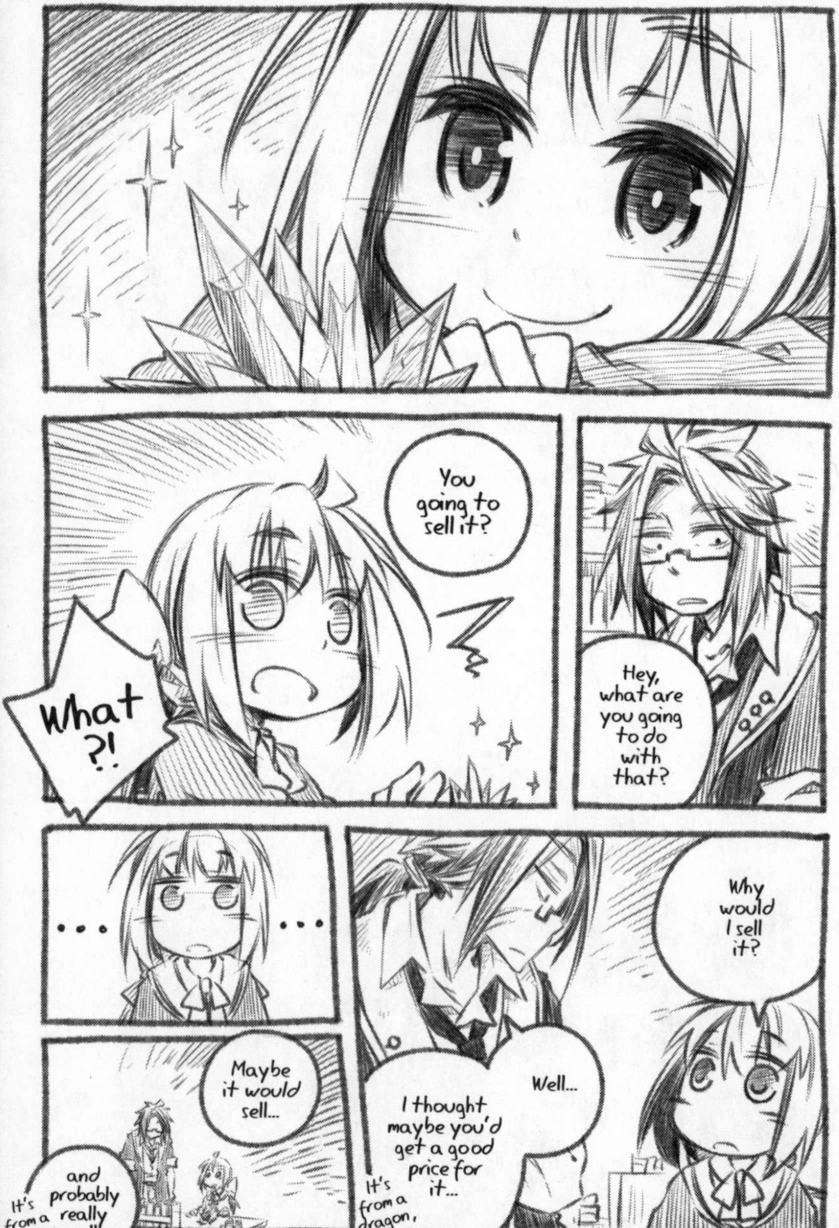
Hey, what are you going to do with that?
You going to sell it?
What ?!
Why would I sell it?
Well...
I thought maybe you'd get a good price for it...
It's from a dragon, after all.
... ...
Maybe it would sell...
and probably really well!
It's from a dragon, after all...

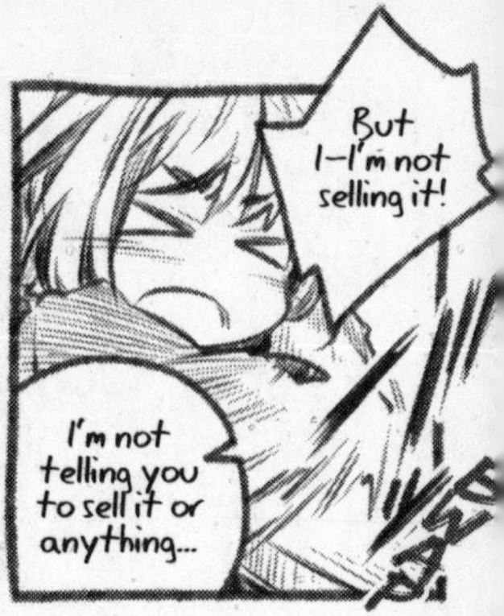
But I-I'm not selling it!
I'm not telling you to sell it or anything...
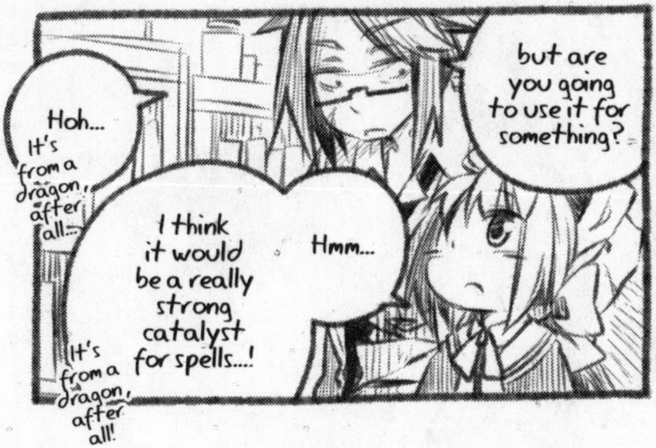
but are you going to use it for something?
Hoh... It's from a dragon, after all...
Hmm...
I think it would be a really strong catalyst for spells...!
It's from a dragon, after all!
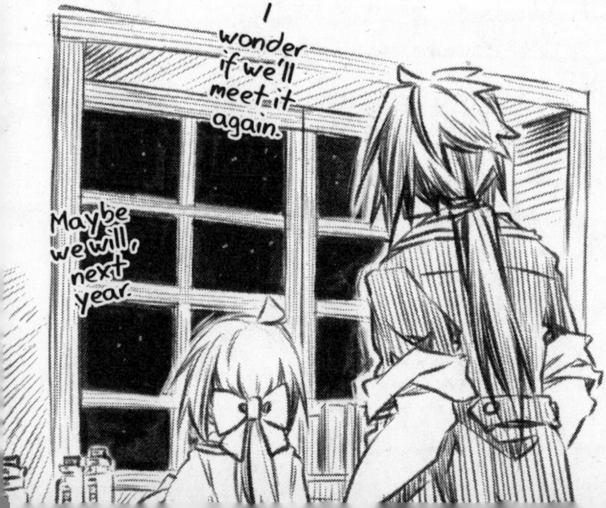
I wonder if we'll meet it again.
Maybe we will, next year.

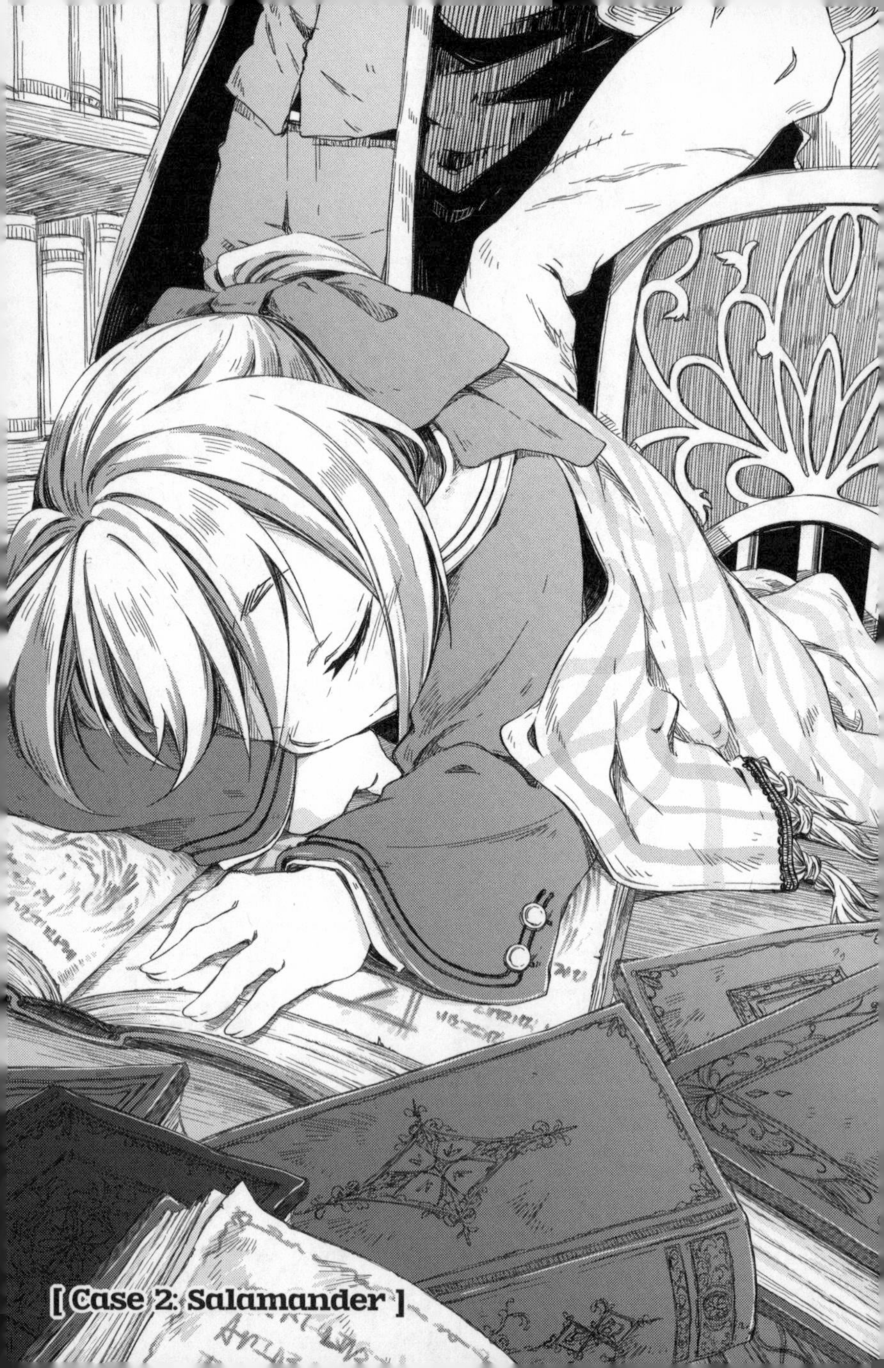

[Case 2: Salamander]

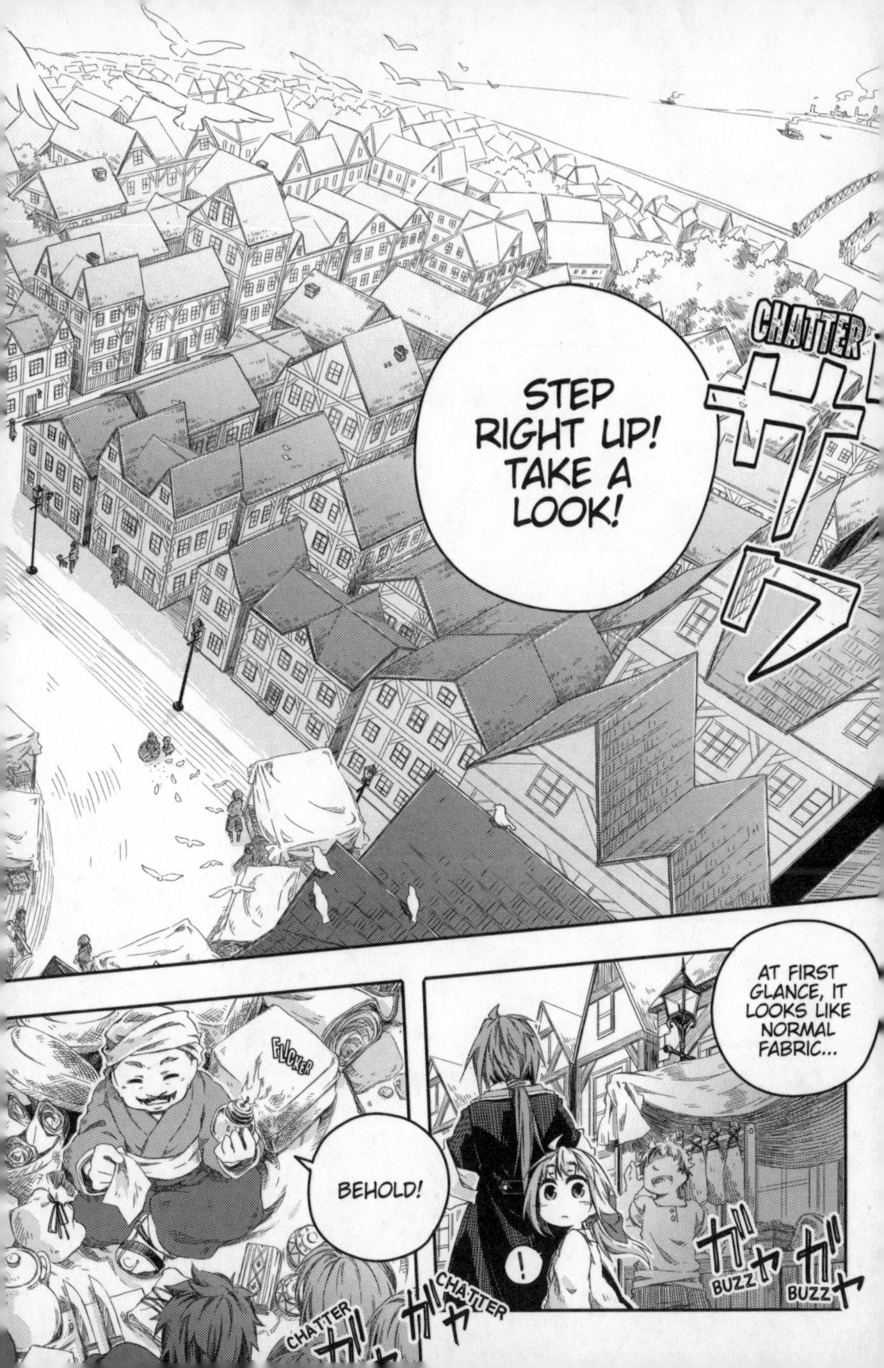
CHATTER
STEP RIGHT UP! TAKE A LOOK!
AT FIRST GLANCE, IT LOOKS LIKE NORMAL FABRIC...
BUZZ
BUZZ
!
FLICKER
BEHOLD!
CHATTER
CHATTER

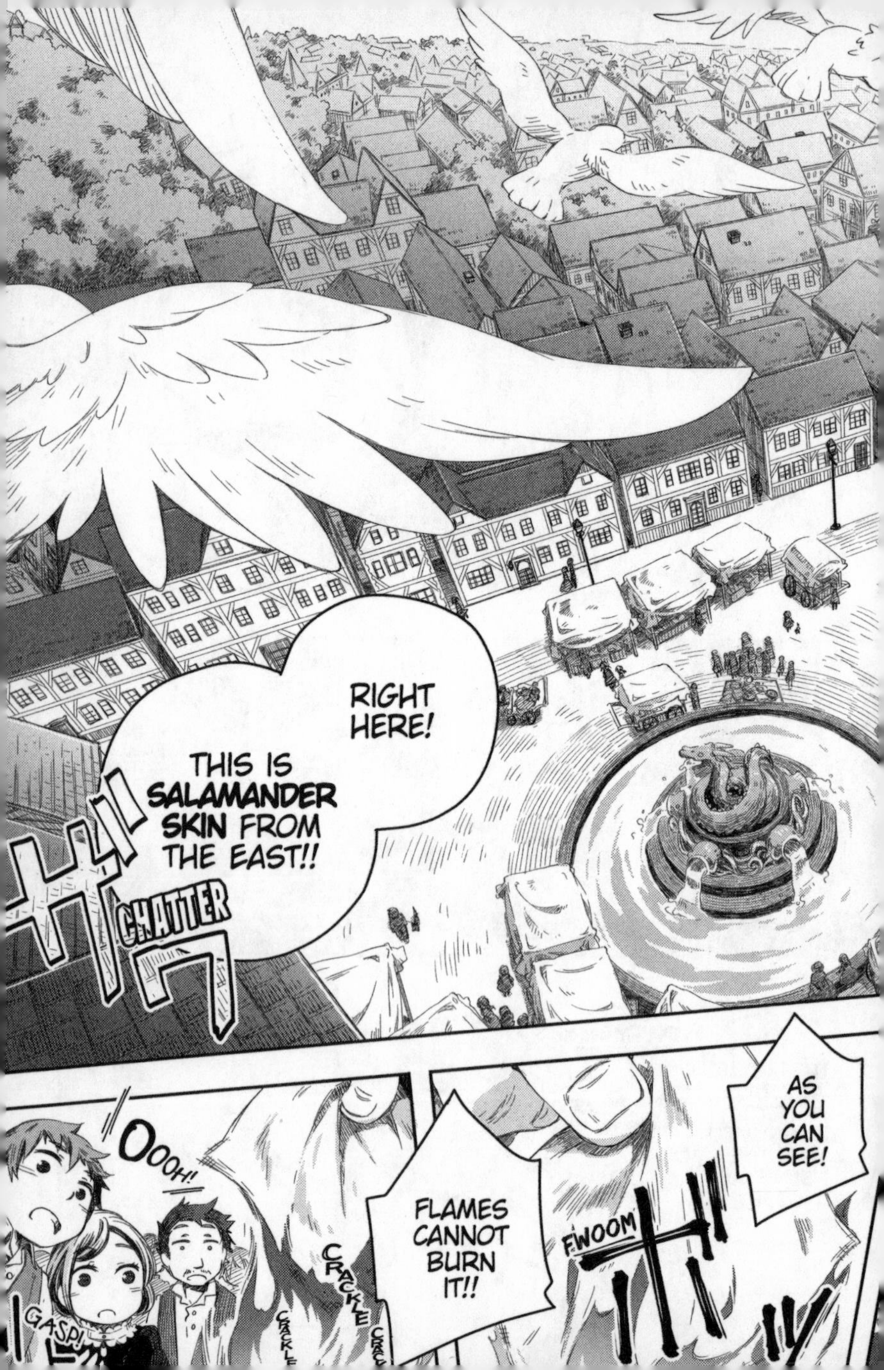
RIGHT HERE!
THIS IS SALAMANDER SKIN FROM THE EAST!!
CHATTER
AS YOU CAN SEE!
FLAMES CANNOT BURN IT!!
FWOOM
CRACKLE
CRACKLE
OOOH!
GASP!

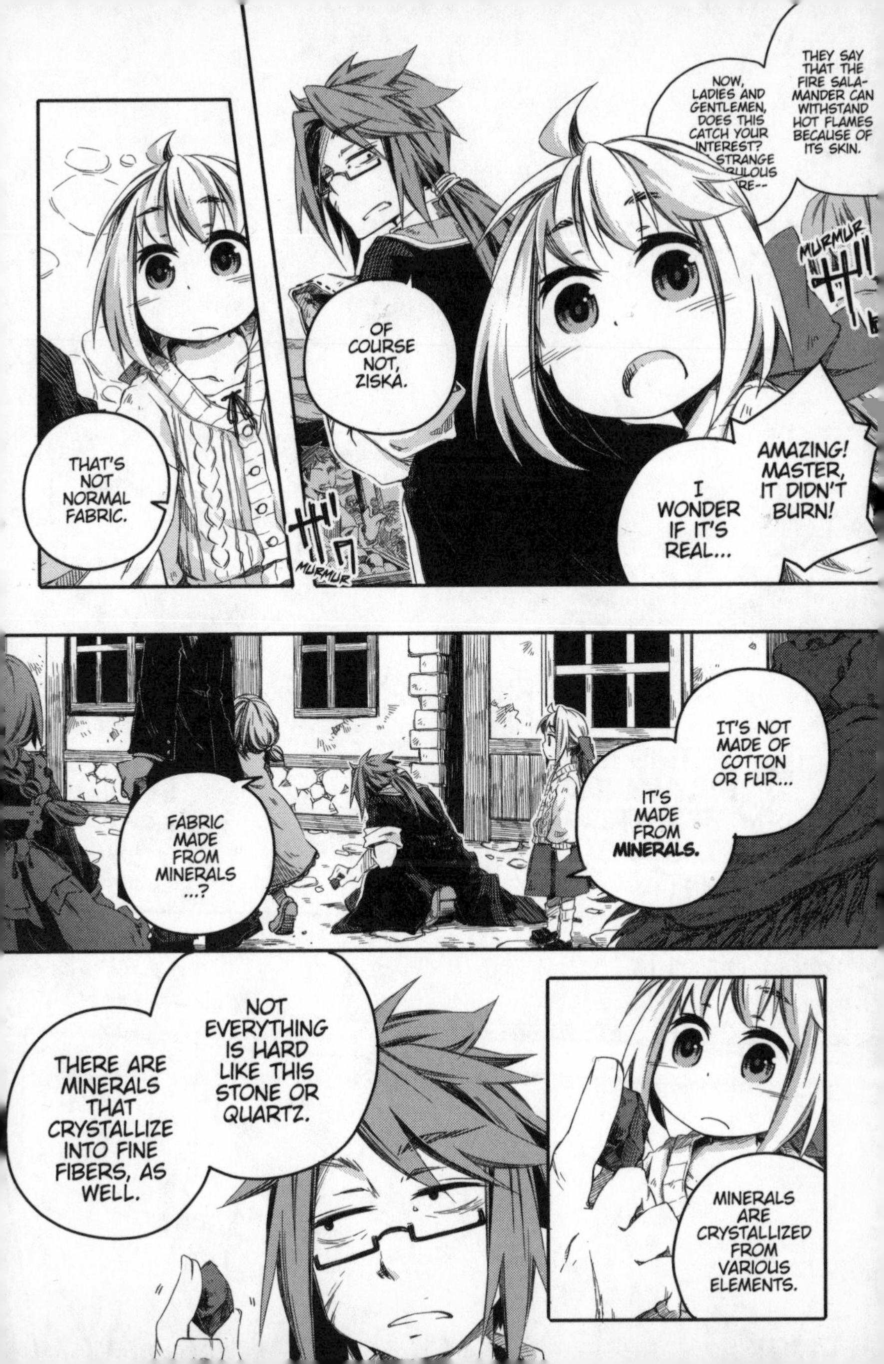
THEY SAY THAT THE FIRE SALAMANDER CAN WITHSTAND HOT FLAMES BECAUSE OF ITS SKIN.
NOW, LADIES AND GENTLEMEN, DOES THIS CATCH YOUR INTEREST?
MURMUR
AMAZING! MASTER, IT DIDN'T BURN!
I WONDER IF IT'S REAL...
MURMUR
OF COURSE NOT, ZISKA.
THAT'S NOT NORMAL FABRIC.
IT'S NOT MADE OF COTTON OR FUR...
IT'S MADE FROM MINERALS.
FABRIC MADE FROM MINERALS ...?
MINERALS ARE CRYSTALLIZED FROM VARIOUS ELEMENTS.
NOT EVERYTHING IS HARD LIKE THIS STONE OR QUARTZ.
THERE ARE MINERALS THAT CRYSTALLIZE INTO FINE FIBERS, AS WELL.

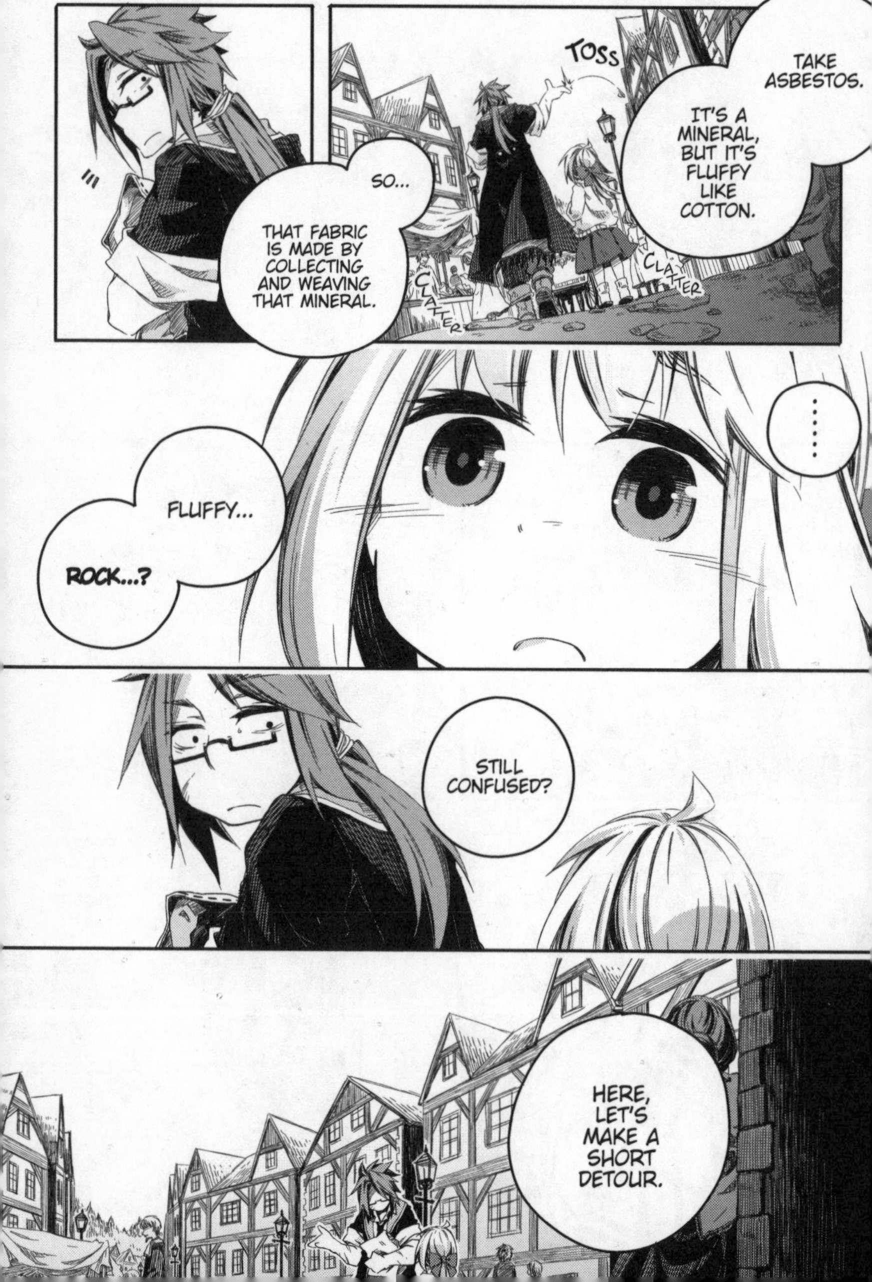
TAKE ASBESTOS.
IT'S A MINERAL, BUT IT'S FLUFFY LIKE COTTON.
TOSS
CLATTER
SO...
THAT FABRIC IS MADE BY COLLECTING AND WEAVING THAT MINERAL.
CLATTER
......
FLUFFY...
ROCK...?
STILL CONFUSED?
HERE, LET'S MAKE A SHORT DETOUR.

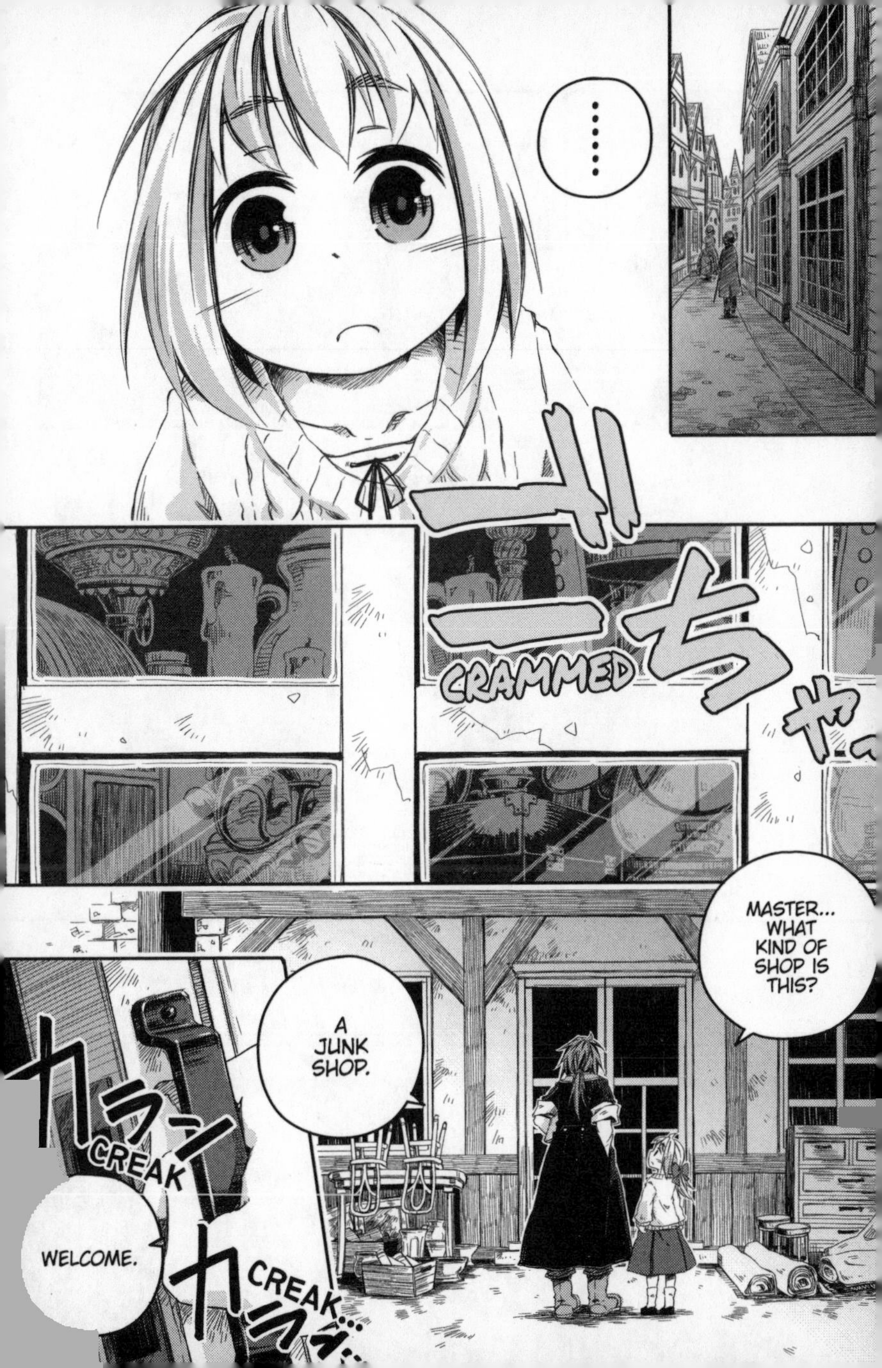
……
CRAMMED
MASTER... WHAT KIND OF SHOP IS THIS?
A JUNK SHOP.
CREAK
WELCOME.
CREAK

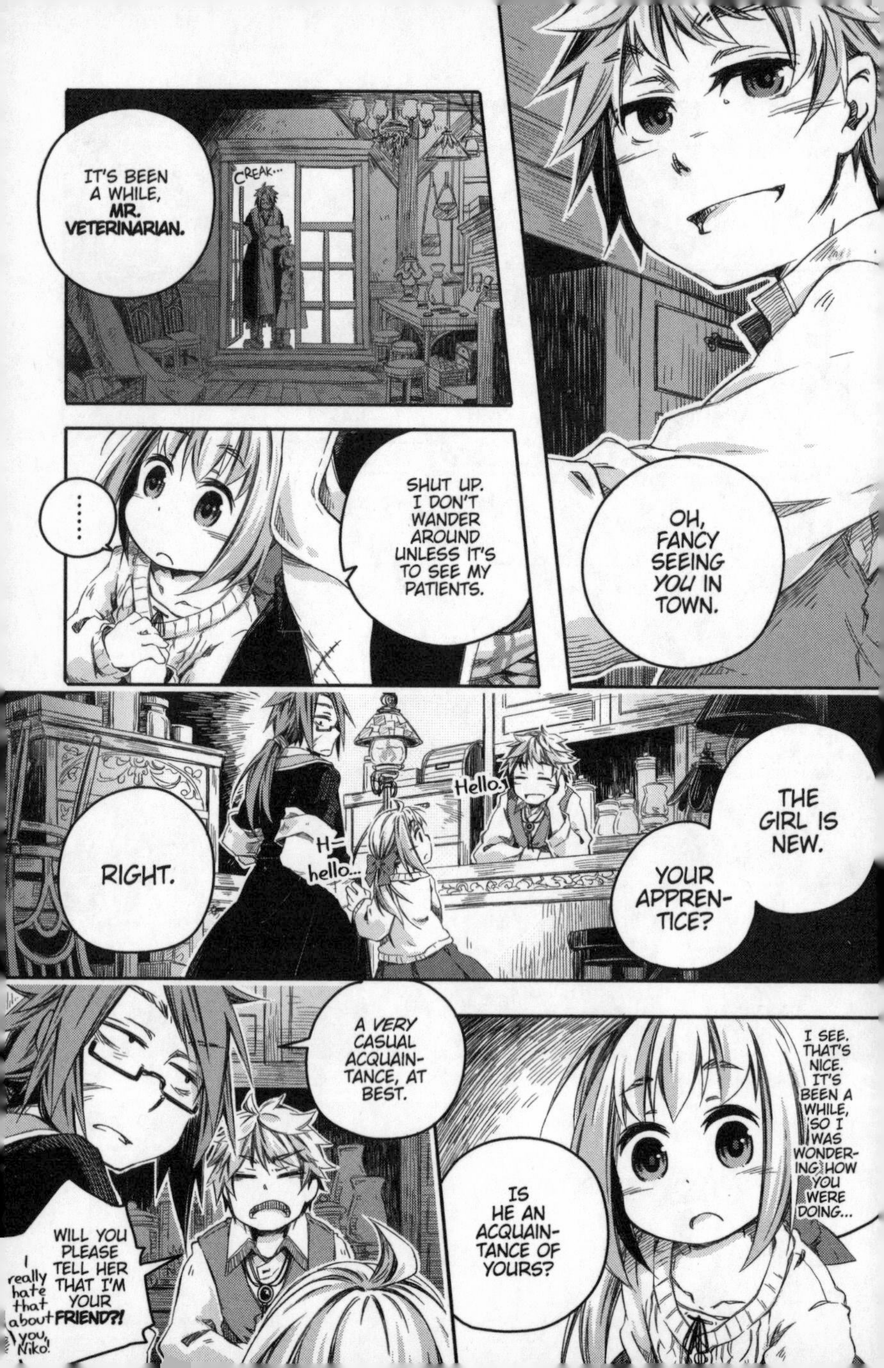
OH, FANCY SEEING *YOU* IN TOWN.
CREAK...
IT'S BEEN A WHILE, **MR. VETERINARIAN.**
SHUT UP. I DON'T WANDER AROUND UNLESS IT'S TO SEE MY PATIENTS.
......
THE GIRL IS NEW.
YOUR APPRENTICE?
Hello.
H-hello...
RIGHT.
I SEE. THAT'S NICE. IT'S BEEN A WHILE, SO I WAS WONDERING HOW YOU WERE DOING...
IS HE AN ACQUAINTANCE OF YOURS?
A *VERY* CASUAL ACQUAINTANCE, AT BEST.
WILL YOU PLEASE TELL HER THAT I'M YOUR **FRIEND?!**
I really hate that about you, Niko!

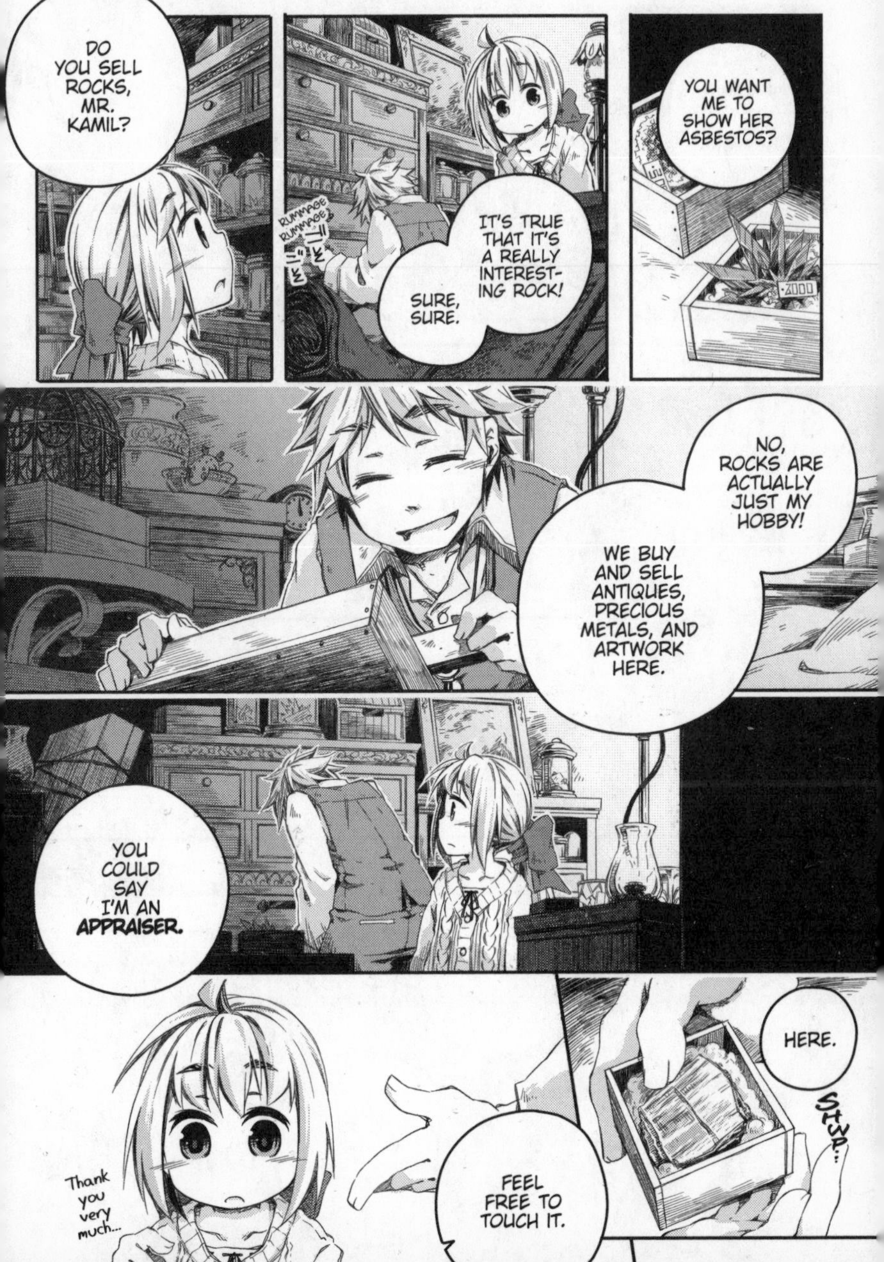
YOU WANT ME TO SHOW HER ASBESTOS?
IT'S TRUE THAT IT'S A REALLY INTEREST-ING ROCK!
SURE, SURE.
RUMMAGE RUMMAGE
DO YOU SELL ROCKS, MR. KAMIL?
NO, ROCKS ARE ACTUALLY JUST MY HOBBY!
WE BUY AND SELL ANTIQUES, PRECIOUS METALS, AND ARTWORK HERE.
YOU COULD SAY I'M AN **APPRAISER.**
HERE.
SHWP...
FEEL FREE TO TOUCH IT.
Thank you very much...

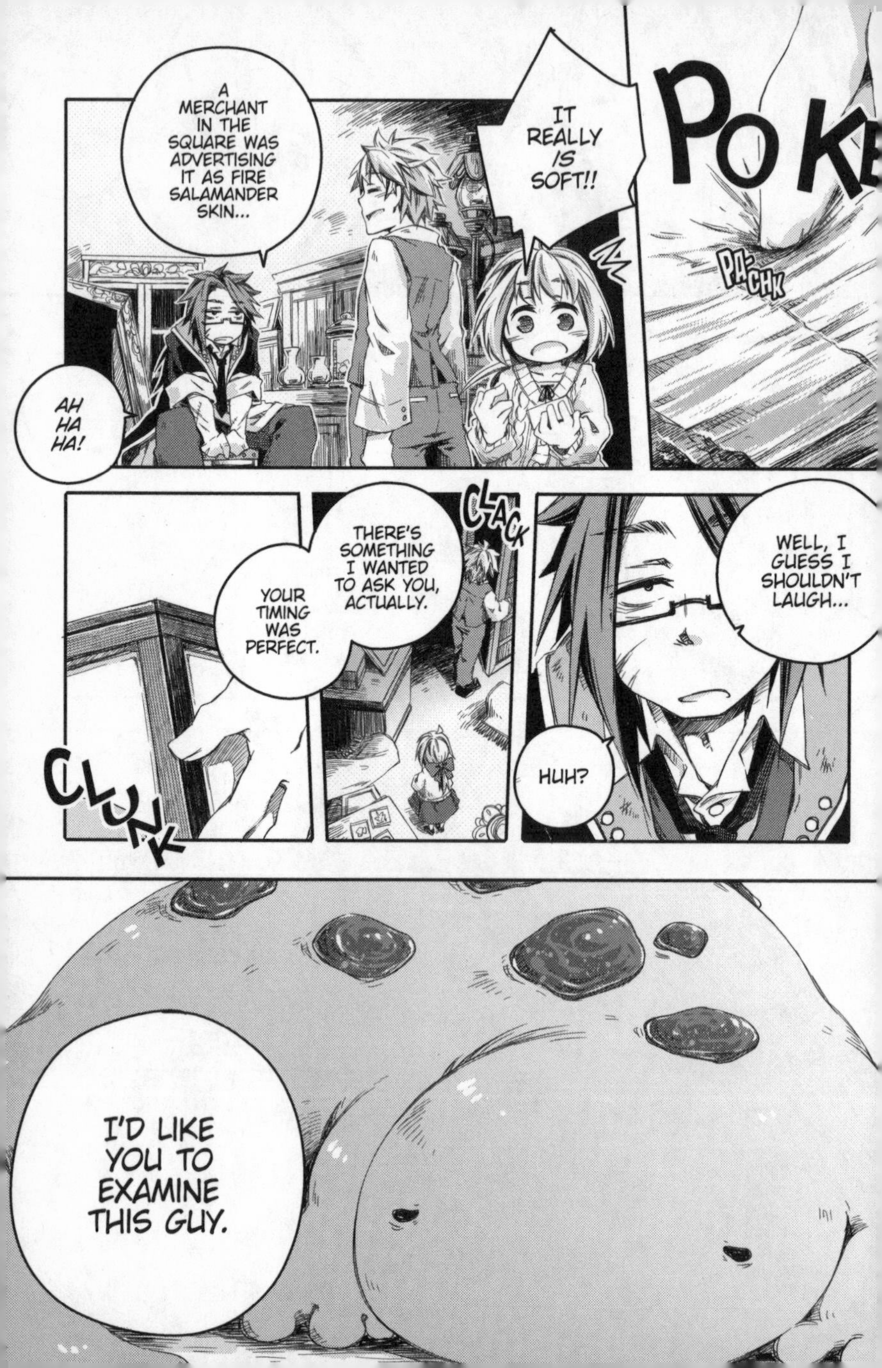
POKE
PA-CHK
IT REALLY IS SOFT!!
A MERCHANT IN THE SQUARE WAS ADVERTISING IT AS FIRE SALAMANDER SKIN...
AH HA HA!
WELL, I GUESS I SHOULDN'T LAUGH...
HUH?
CLACK
THERE'S SOMETHING I WANTED TO ASK YOU, ACTUALLY.
YOUR TIMING WAS PERFECT.
CLUNK
I'D LIKE YOU TO EXAMINE THIS GUY.

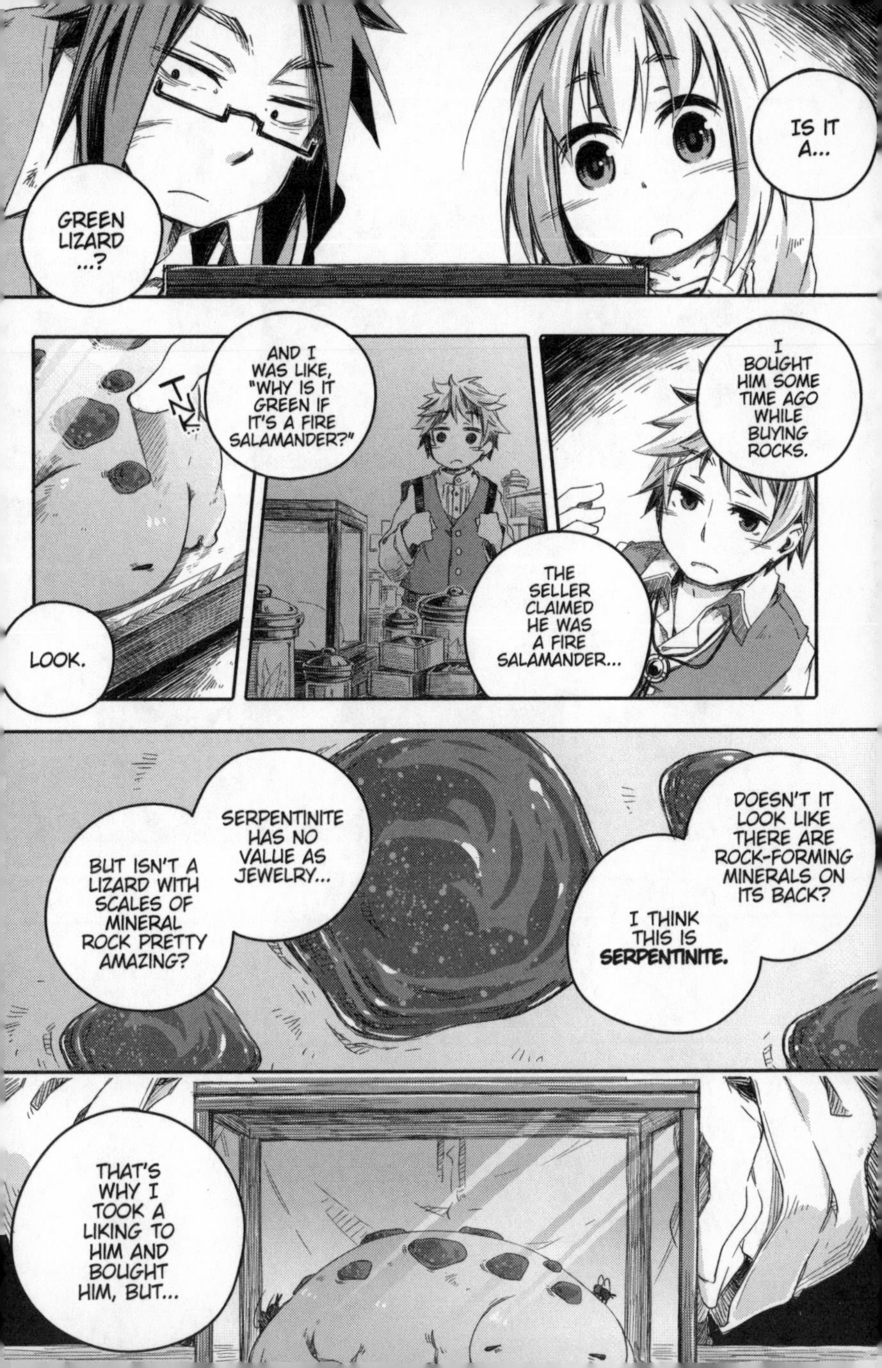
IS IT A...
GREEN LIZARD ...?
I BOUGHT HIM SOME TIME AGO WHILE BUYING ROCKS.
THE SELLER CLAIMED HE WAS A FIRE SALAMANDER...
AND I WAS LIKE, "WHY IS IT GREEN IF IT'S A FIRE SALAMANDER?"
TNK...
LOOK.
DOESN'T IT LOOK LIKE THERE ARE ROCK-FORMING MINERALS ON ITS BACK?
I THINK THIS IS **SERPENTINITE.**
SERPENTINITE HAS NO VALUE AS JEWELRY...
BUT ISN'T A LIZARD WITH SCALES OF MINERAL ROCK PRETTY AMAZING?
THAT'S WHY I TOOK A LIKING TO HIM AND BOUGHT HIM, BUT...

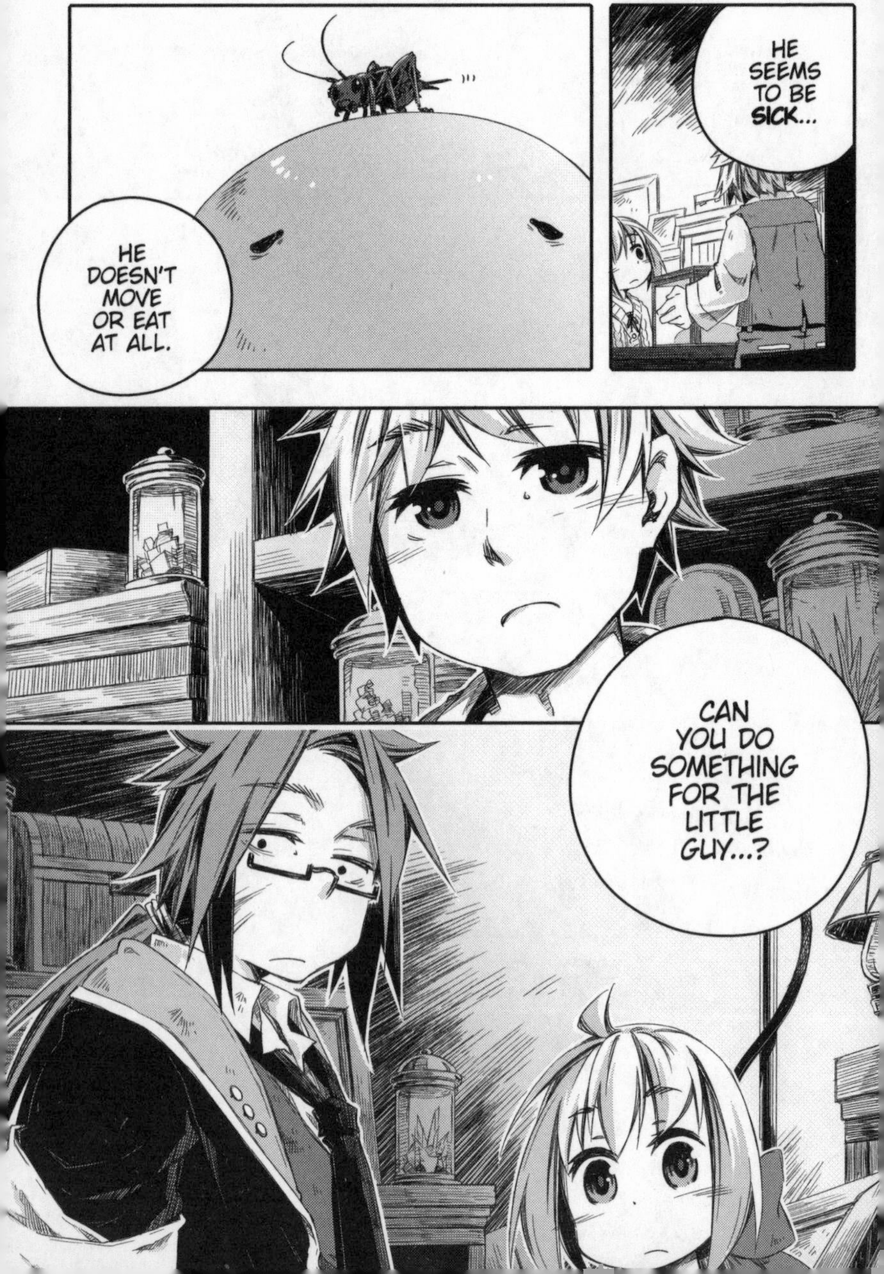
HE SEEMS TO BE SICK...
HE DOESN'T MOVE OR EAT AT ALL.
CAN YOU DO SOMETHING FOR THE LITTLE GUY...?

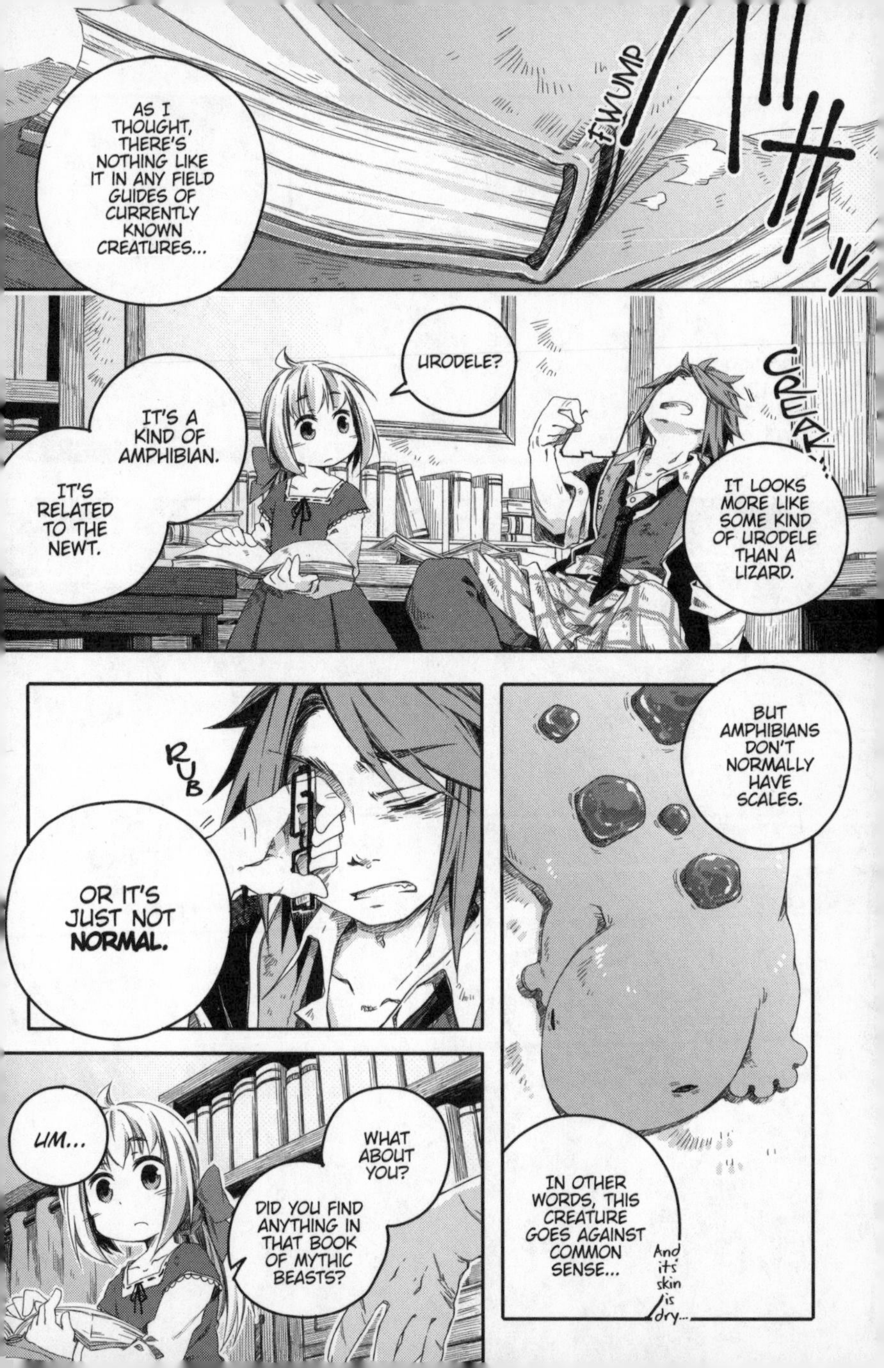
FWUMP
AS I THOUGHT, THERE'S NOTHING LIKE IT IN ANY FIELD GUIDES OF CURRENTLY KNOWN CREATURES...
CREAK...
IT LOOKS MORE LIKE SOME KIND OF URODELE THAN A LIZARD.
URODELE?
IT'S A KIND OF AMPHIBIAN.
IT'S RELATED TO THE NEWT.
BUT AMPHIBIANS DON'T NORMALLY HAVE SCALES.
IN OTHER WORDS, THIS CREATURE GOES AGAINST COMMON SENSE...
And its skin is dry...
RUB
OR IT'S JUST NOT NORMAL.
WHAT ABOUT YOU?
DID YOU FIND ANYTHING IN THAT BOOK OF MYTHIC BEASTS?
UM...

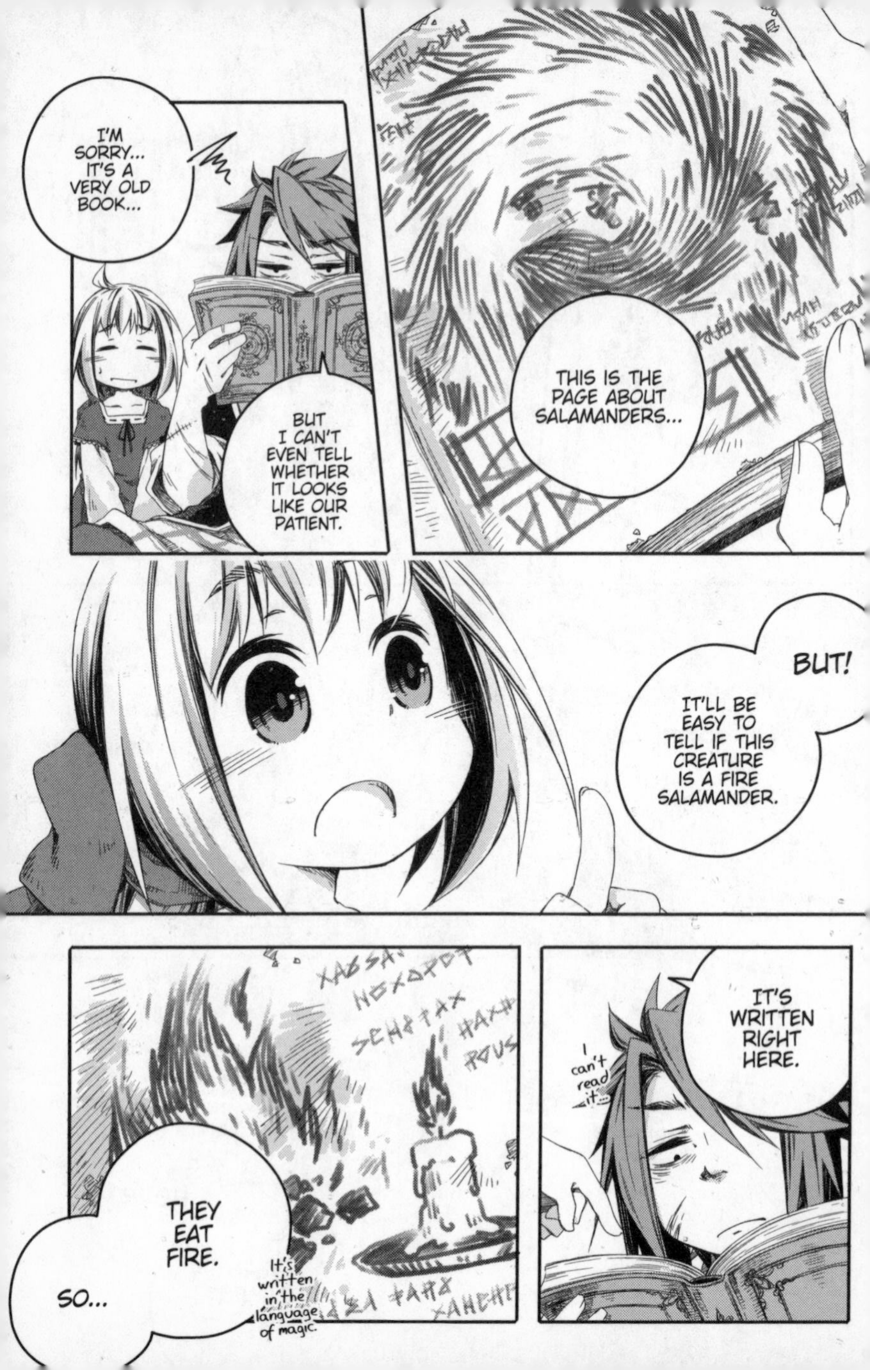
THIS IS THE PAGE ABOUT SALAMANDERS...
I'M SORRY... IT'S A VERY OLD BOOK...
BUT I CAN'T EVEN TELL WHETHER IT LOOKS LIKE OUR PATIENT.
BUT!
IT'LL BE EASY TO TELL IF THIS CREATURE IS A FIRE SALAMANDER.
IT'S WRITTEN RIGHT HERE.
I can't read it...
THEY EAT FIRE.
SO...
It's written in the language of magic.

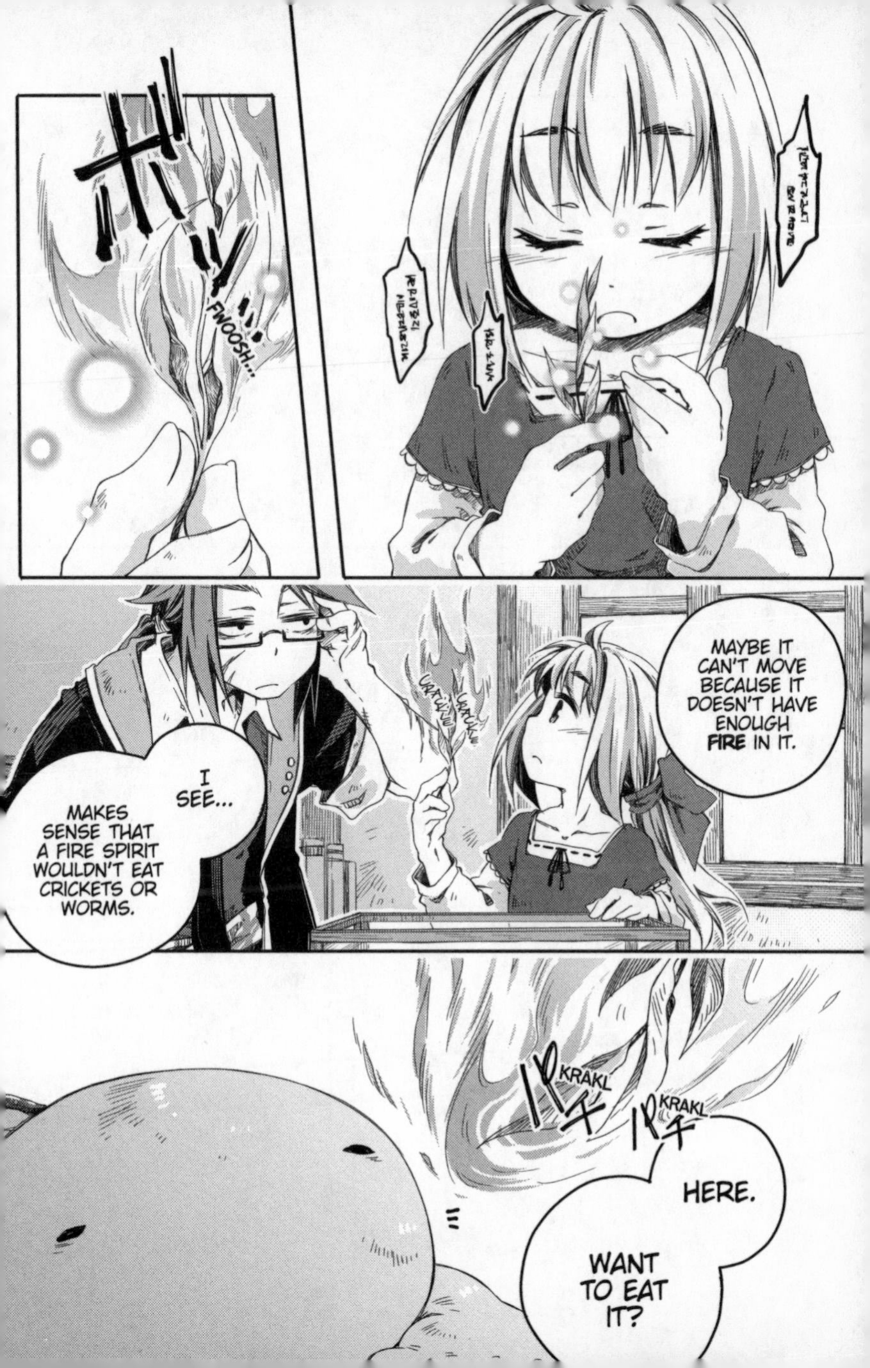
ボッ
FWOOSH...
CRACKLE
CRACKLE
MAYBE IT CAN'T MOVE BECAUSE IT DOESN'T HAVE ENOUGH **FIRE** IN IT.
I SEE...
MAKES SENSE THAT A FIRE SPIRIT WOULDN'T EAT CRICKETS OR WORMS.
パチ KRAKL
パチ KRAKL
HERE.
WANT TO EAT IT?

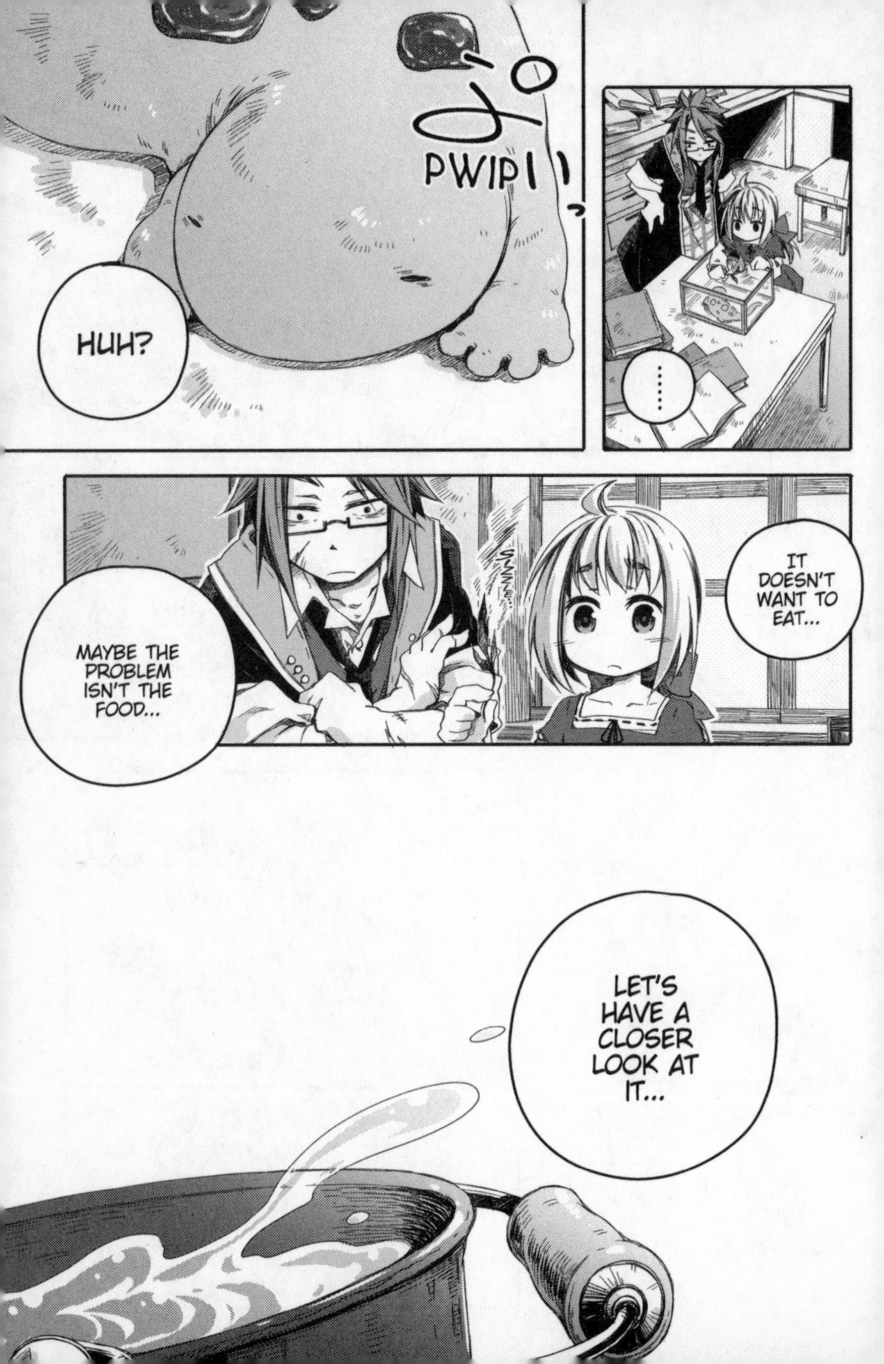
......
PWIP
HUH?
IT DOESN'T WANT TO EAT...
MAYBE THE PROBLEM ISN'T THE FOOD...
LET'S HAVE A CLOSER LOOK AT IT...

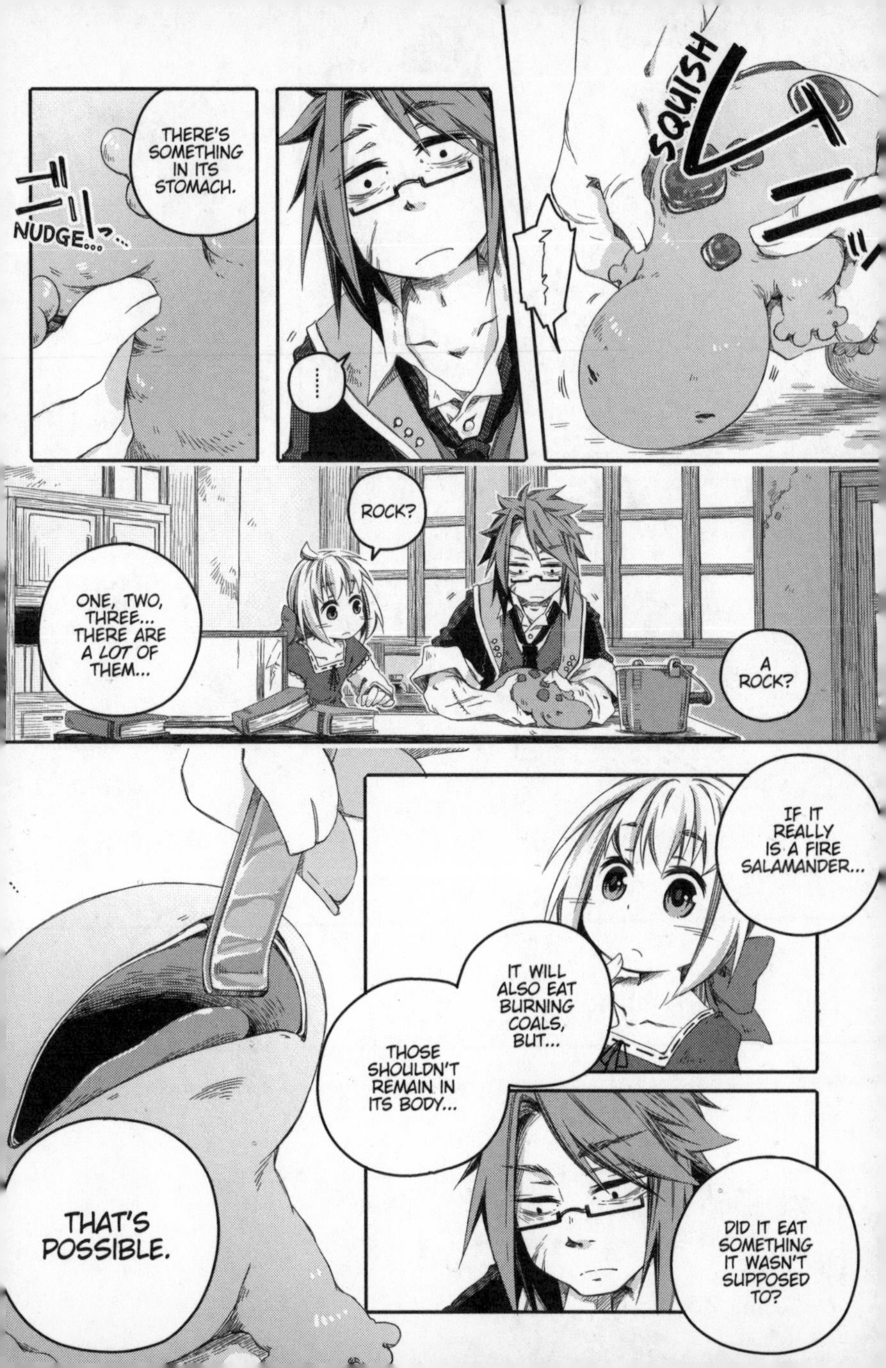
SQUISH
......
THERE'S SOMETHING IN ITS STOMACH.
NUDGE...
A ROCK?
ROCK?
ONE, TWO, THREE... THERE ARE A *LOT* OF THEM...
IF IT REALLY IS A FIRE SALAMANDER...
IT WILL ALSO EAT BURNING COALS, BUT...
THOSE SHOULDN'T REMAIN IN ITS BODY...
DID IT EAT SOMETHING IT WASN'T SUPPOSED TO?
THAT'S POSSIBLE.

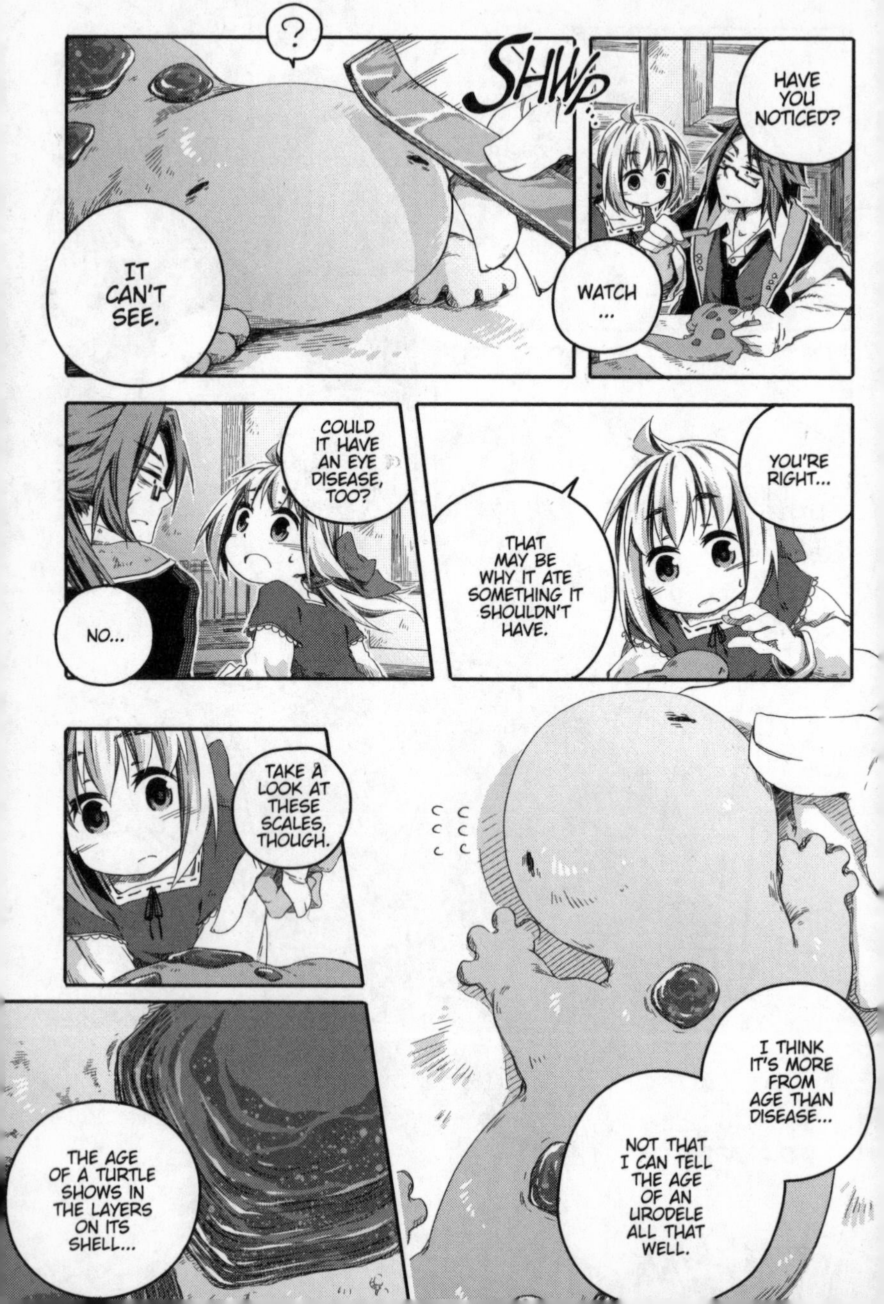
HAVE YOU NOTICED?
WATCH ...
SHWP
?
IT CAN'T SEE.
YOU'RE RIGHT...
THAT MAY BE WHY IT ATE SOMETHING IT SHOULDN'T HAVE.
COULD IT HAVE AN EYE DISEASE, TOO?
NO...
I THINK IT'S MORE FROM AGE THAN DISEASE...
NOT THAT I CAN TELL THE AGE OF AN URODELE ALL THAT WELL.
TAKE A LOOK AT THESE SCALES, THOUGH.
THE AGE OF A TURTLE SHOWS IN THE LAYERS ON ITS SHELL...

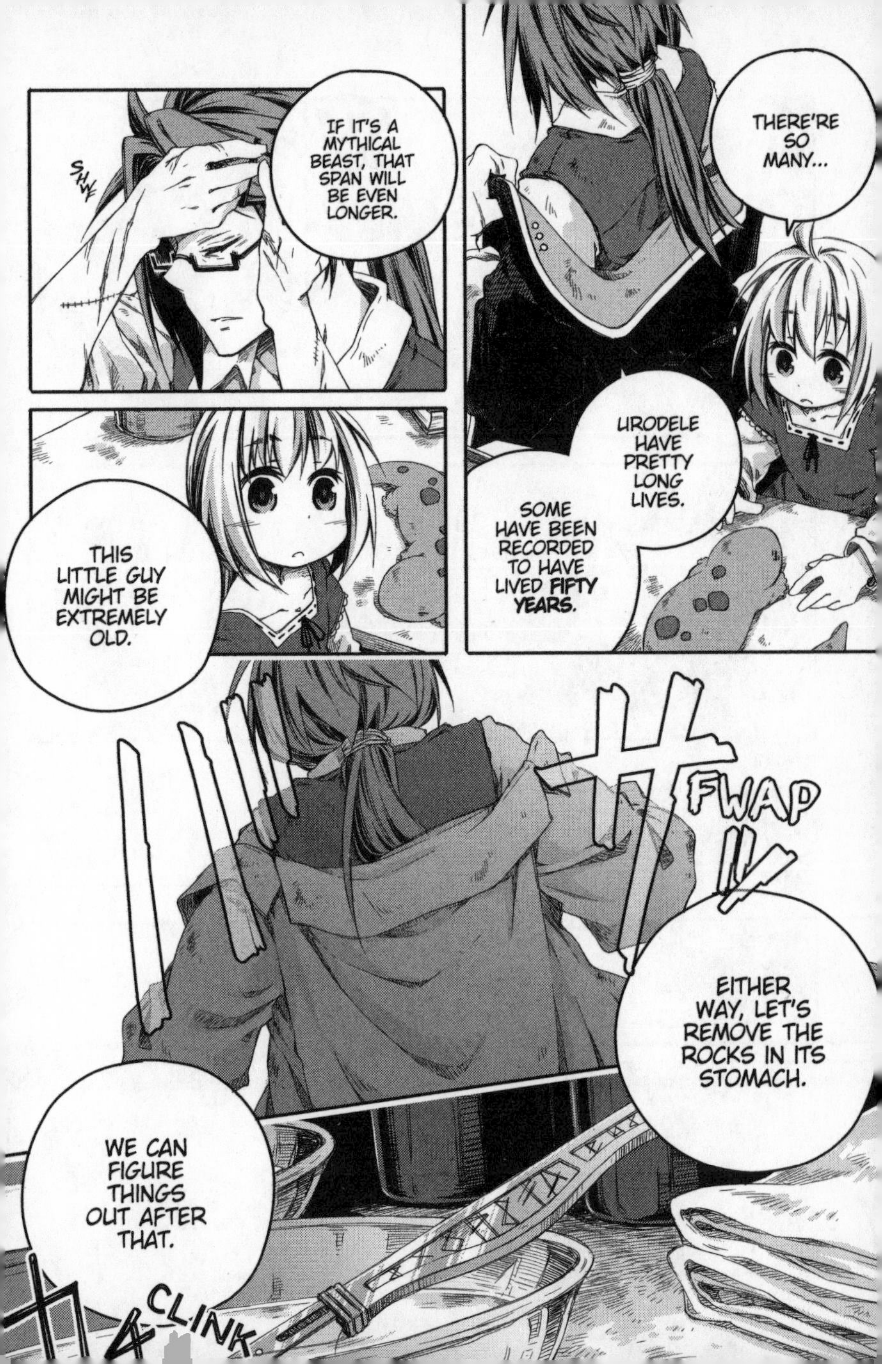
THERE'RE SO MANY...
URODELE HAVE PRETTY LONG LIVES.
SOME HAVE BEEN RECORDED TO HAVE LIVED **FIFTY YEARS.**
SHW
IF IT'S A MYTHICAL BEAST, THAT SPAN WILL BE EVEN LONGER.
THIS LITTLE GUY MIGHT BE EXTREMELY OLD.
FWAP
EITHER WAY, LET'S REMOVE THE ROCKS IN ITS STOMACH.
WE CAN FIGURE THINGS OUT AFTER THAT.
CLINK

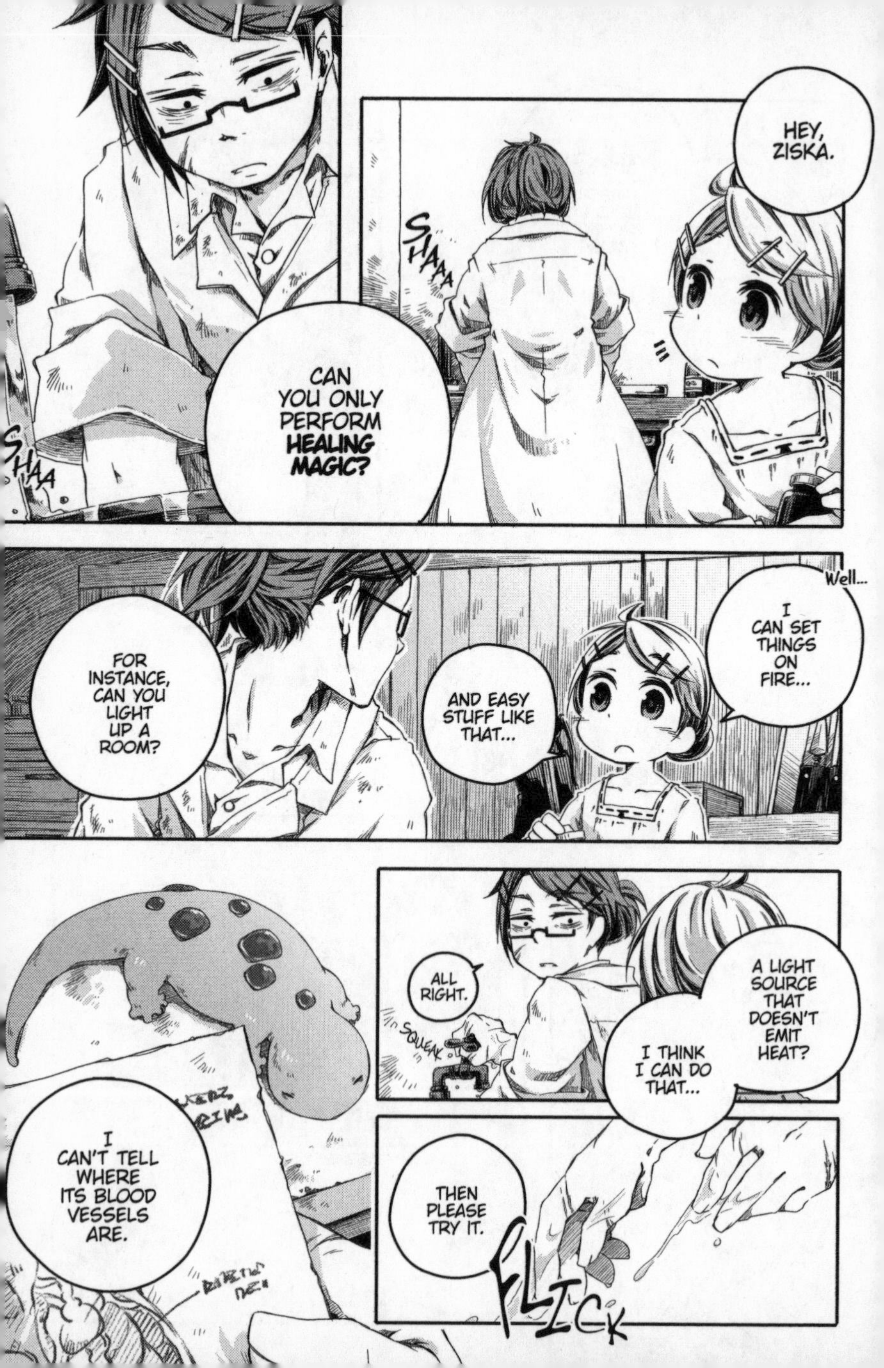
HEY, ZISKA.
SHAAA
CAN YOU ONLY PERFORM HEALING MAGIC?
SHAA
Well...
I CAN SET THINGS ON FIRE...
AND EASY STUFF LIKE THAT...
FOR INSTANCE, CAN YOU LIGHT UP A ROOM?
A LIGHT SOURCE THAT DOESN'T EMIT HEAT?
I THINK I CAN DO THAT...
ALL RIGHT.
SQUEAK
THEN PLEASE TRY IT.
FLICK
I CAN'T TELL WHERE ITS BLOOD VESSELS ARE.

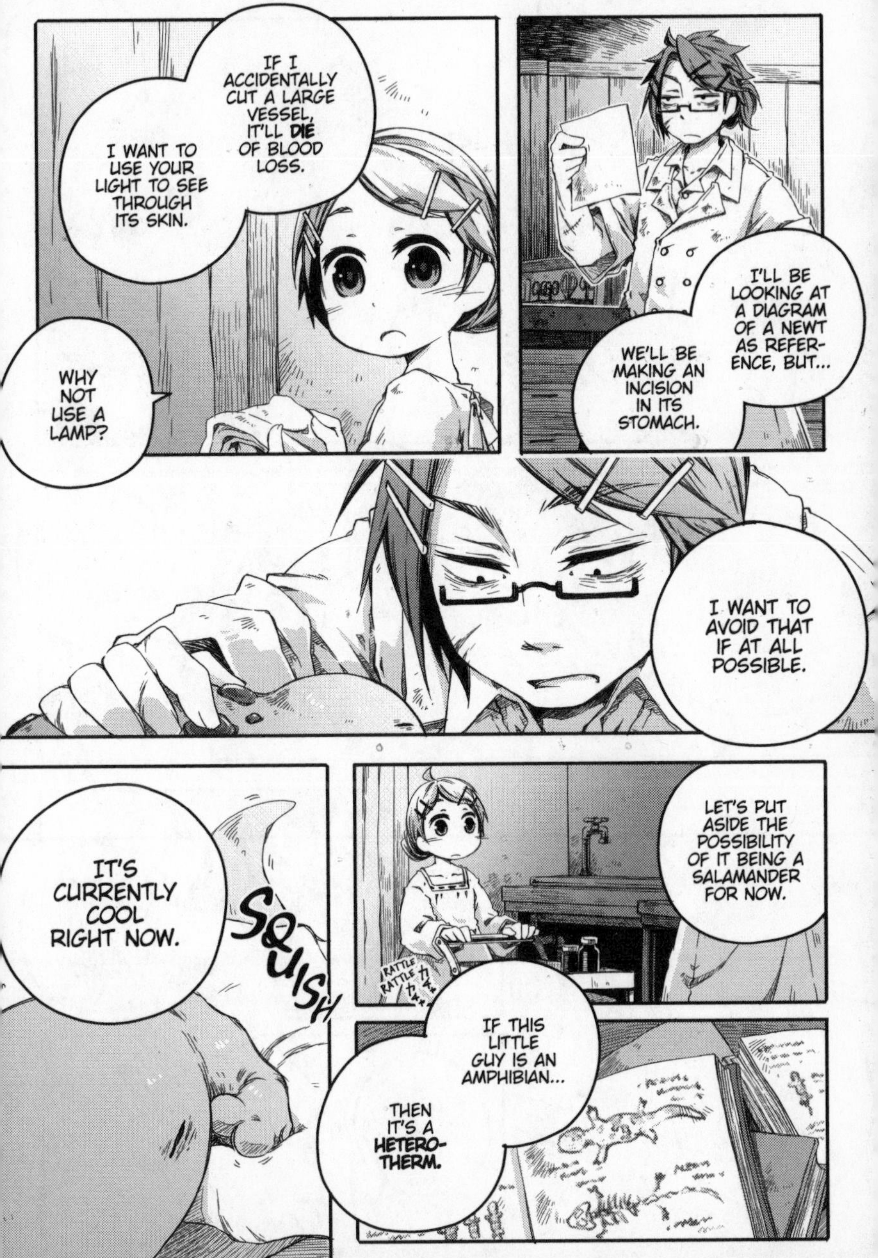
I'LL BE LOOKING AT A DIAGRAM OF A NEWT AS REFER-ENCE, BUT...
WE'LL BE MAKING AN INCISION IN ITS STOMACH.
IF I ACCIDENTALLY CUT A LARGE VESSEL, IT'LL **DIE** OF BLOOD LOSS.
I WANT TO USE YOUR LIGHT TO SEE THROUGH ITS SKIN.
WHY NOT USE A LAMP?
I WANT TO AVOID THAT IF AT ALL POSSIBLE.
LET'S PUT ASIDE THE POSSIBILITY OF IT BEING A SALAMANDER FOR NOW.
RATTLE RATTLE
IF THIS LITTLE GUY IS AN AMPHIBIAN...
THEN IT'S A **HETERO-THERM.**
SQUISH
IT'S CURRENTLY COOL RIGHT NOW.

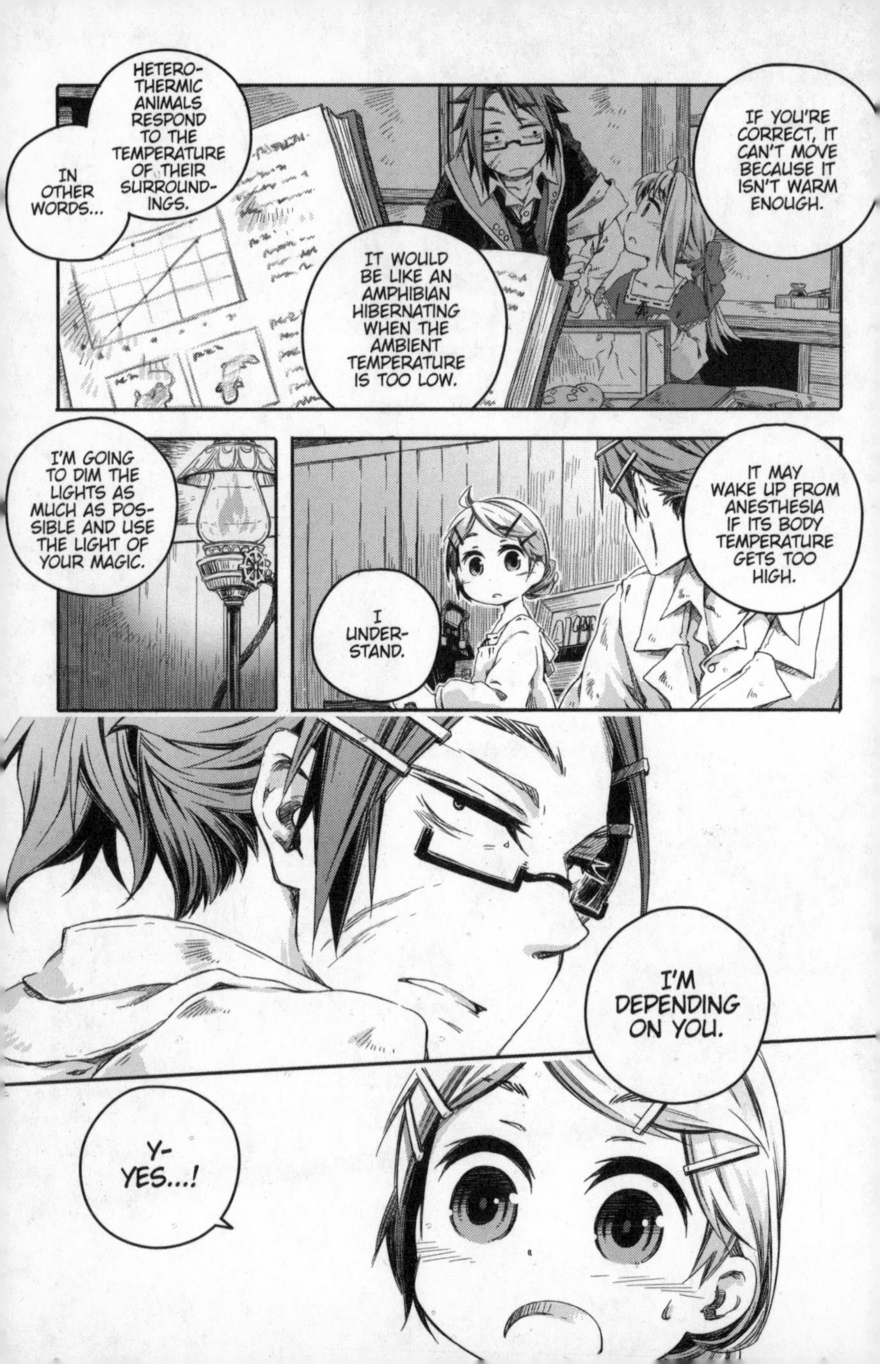
IF YOU'RE CORRECT, IT CAN'T MOVE BECAUSE IT ISN'T WARM ENOUGH.
IT WOULD BE LIKE AN AMPHIBIAN HIBERNATING WHEN THE AMBIENT TEMPERATURE IS TOO LOW.
HETERO-THERMIC ANIMALS RESPOND TO THE TEMPERATURE OF THEIR SURROUND-INGS.
IN OTHER WORDS...
IT MAY WAKE UP FROM ANESTHESIA IF ITS BODY TEMPERATURE GETS TOO HIGH.
I UNDER-STAND.
I'M GOING TO DIM THE LIGHTS AS MUCH AS POS-SIBLE AND USE THE LIGHT OF YOUR MAGIC.
I'M DEPENDING ON YOU.
Y-YES...!

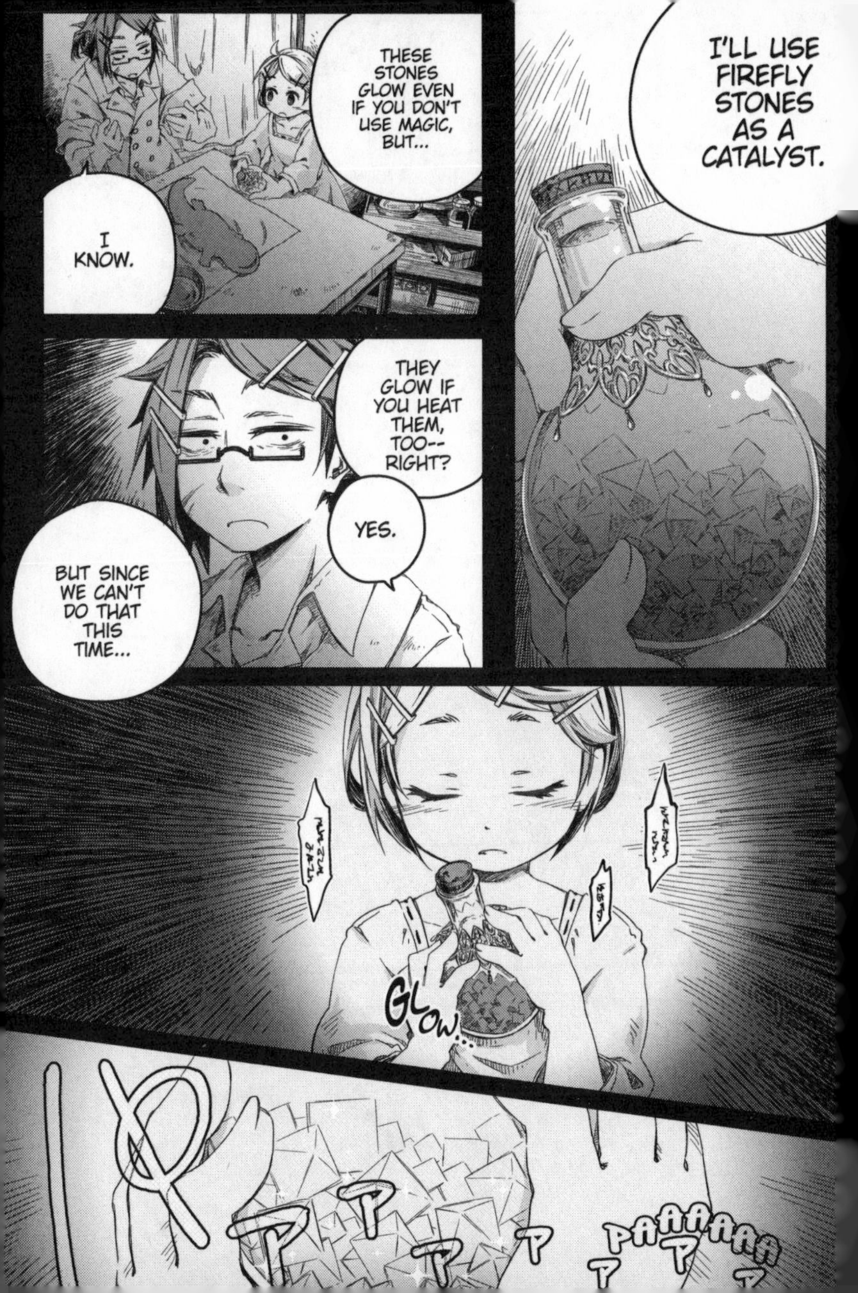
I'LL USE FIREFLY STONES AS A CATALYST.
THESE STONES GLOW EVEN IF YOU DON'T USE MAGIC, BUT...
I KNOW.
THEY GLOW IF YOU HEAT THEM, TOO--RIGHT?
YES.
BUT SINCE WE CAN'T DO THAT THIS TIME...
GLOW...
PAAAAAAA

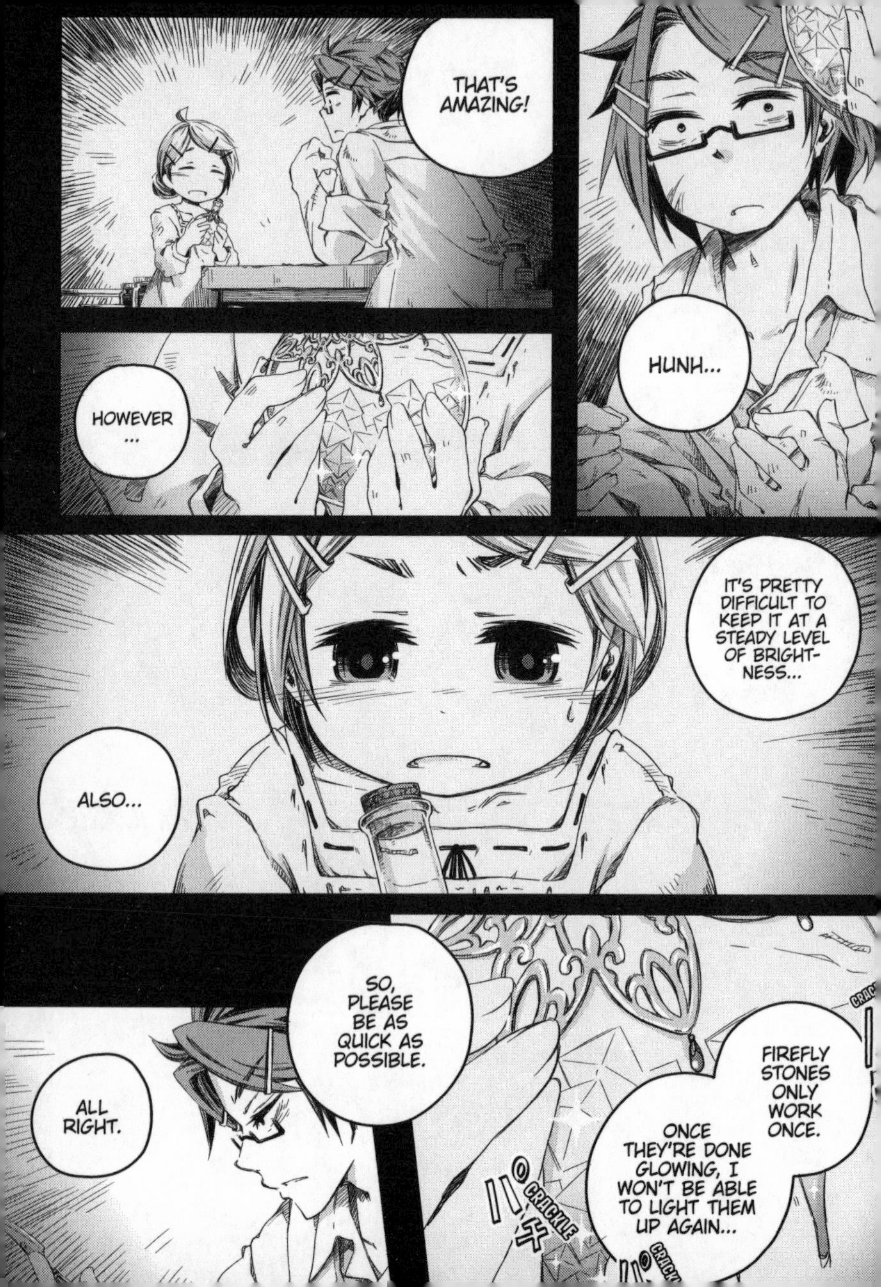
HUNH...
THAT'S AMAZING!
HOWEVER ...
IT'S PRETTY DIFFICULT TO KEEP IT AT A STEADY LEVEL OF BRIGHT-NESS...
ALSO...
FIREFLY STONES ONLY WORK ONCE.
ONCE THEY'RE DONE GLOWING, I WON'T BE ABLE TO LIGHT THEM UP AGAIN...
CRACKLE
SO, PLEASE BE AS QUICK AS POSSIBLE.
ALL RIGHT.

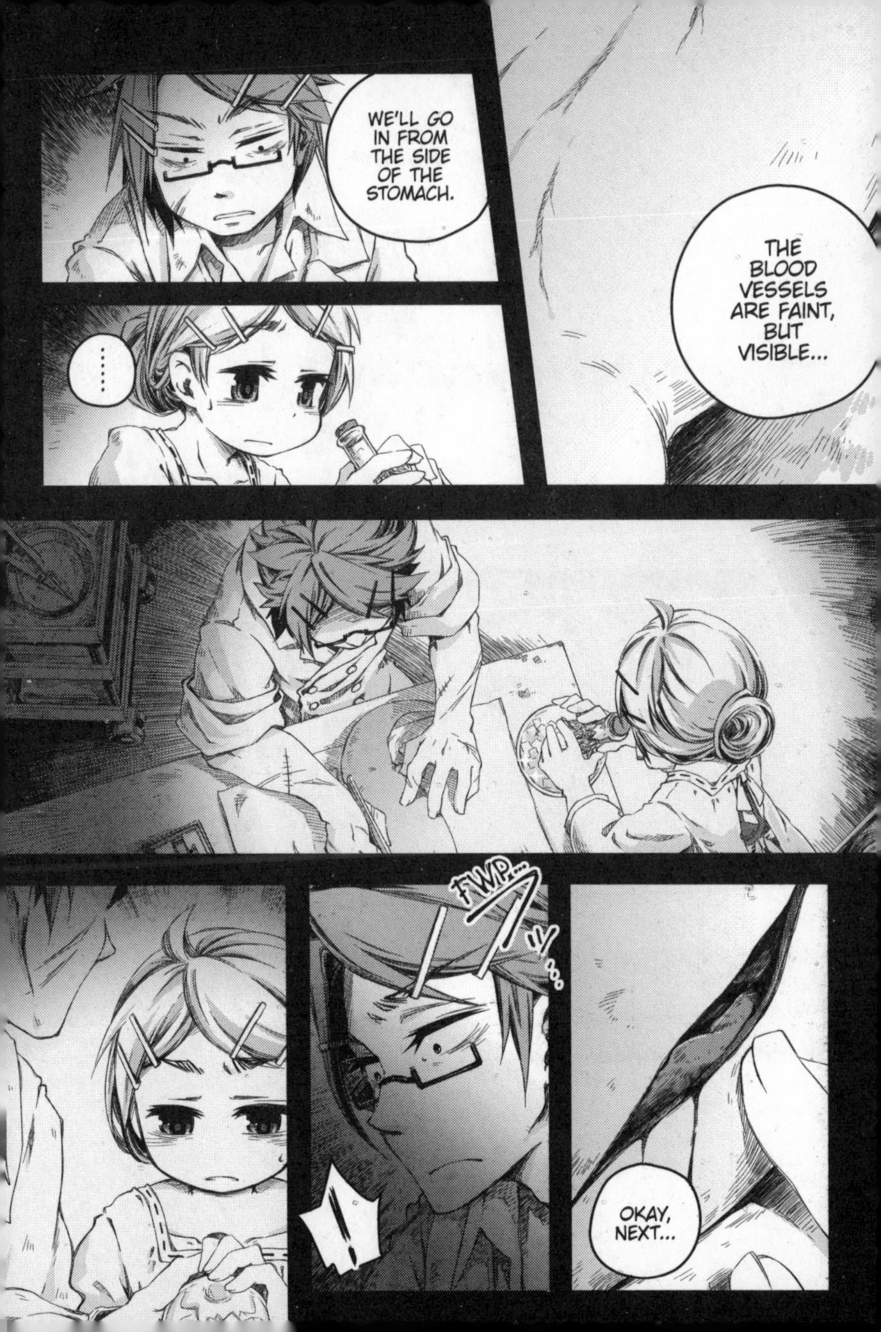
THE BLOOD VESSELS ARE FAINT, BUT VISIBLE...
WE'LL GO IN FROM THE SIDE OF THE STOMACH.
......
OKAY, NEXT...
FWP...
!

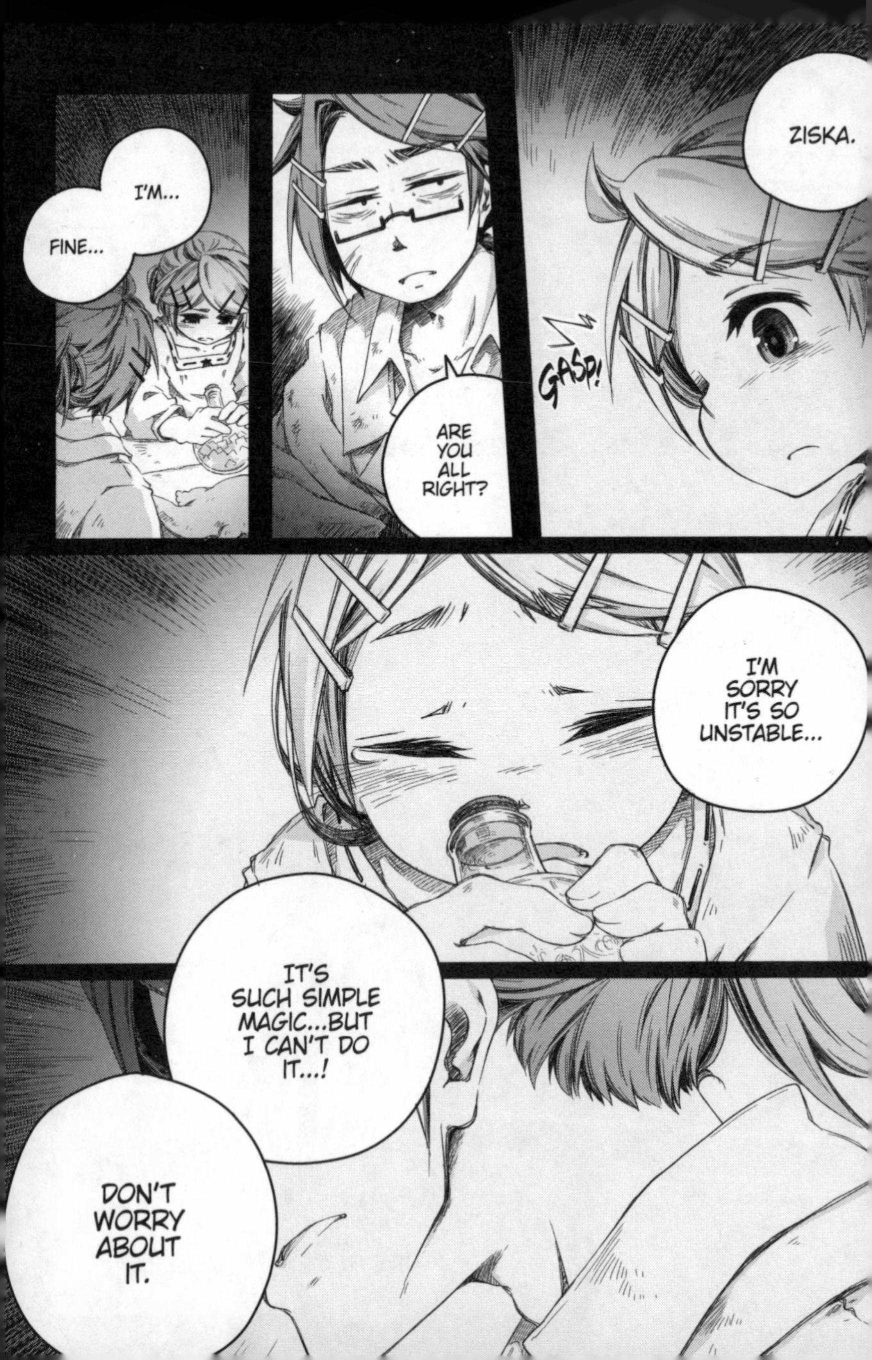
ZISKA.
GASP!
ARE YOU ALL RIGHT?
I'M... FINE...
I'M SORRY IT'S SO UNSTABLE...
IT'S SUCH SIMPLE MAGIC...BUT I CAN'T DO IT...!
DON'T WORRY ABOUT IT.

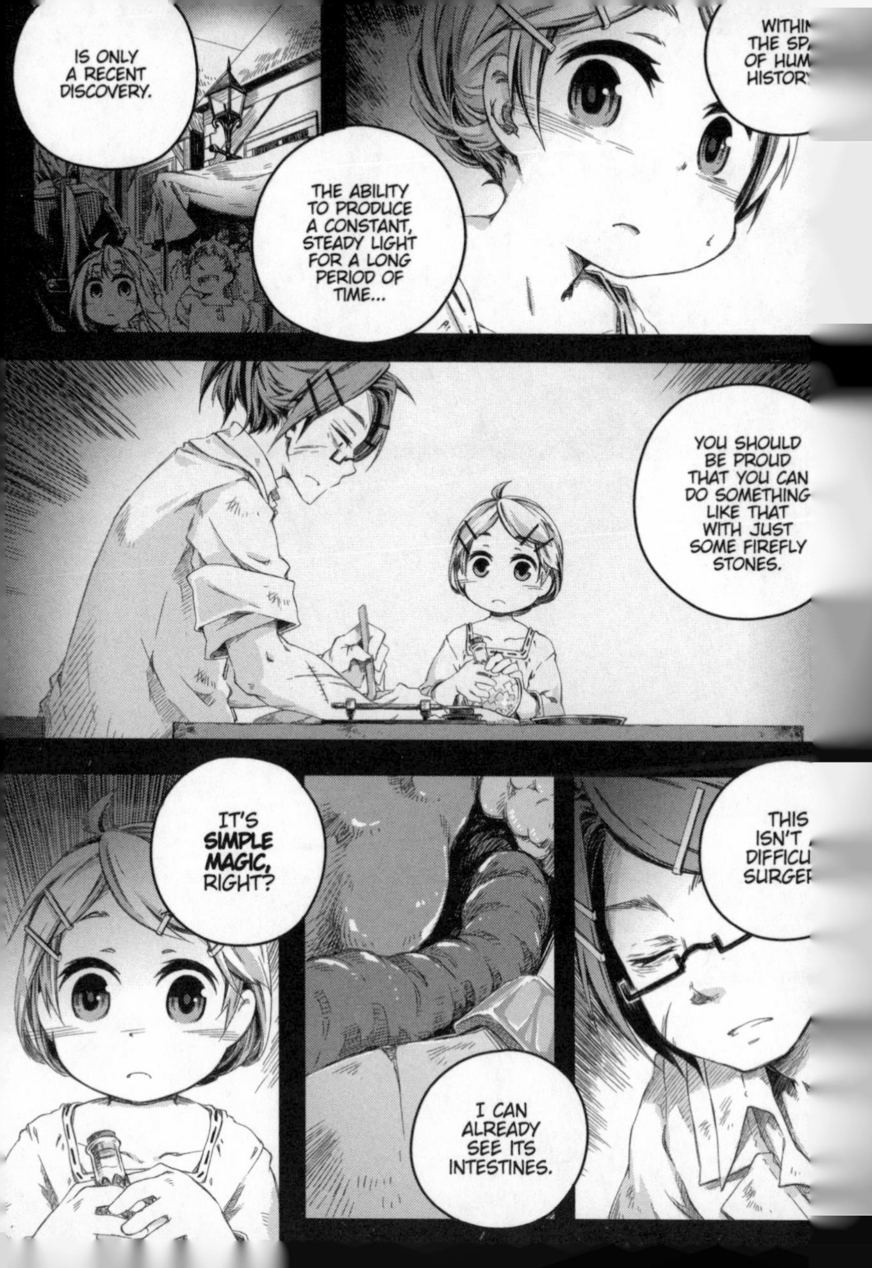
WITHIN THE SP OF HUM HISTORY
THE ABILITY TO PRODUCE A CONSTANT, STEADY LIGHT FOR A LONG PERIOD OF TIME...
IS ONLY A RECENT DISCOVERY.
YOU SHOULD BE PROUD THAT YOU CAN DO SOMETHING LIKE THAT WITH JUST SOME FIREFLY STONES.
THIS ISN'T DIFFICU SURGER
I CAN ALREADY SEE ITS INTESTINES.
IT'S **SIMPLE MAGIC,** RIGHT?

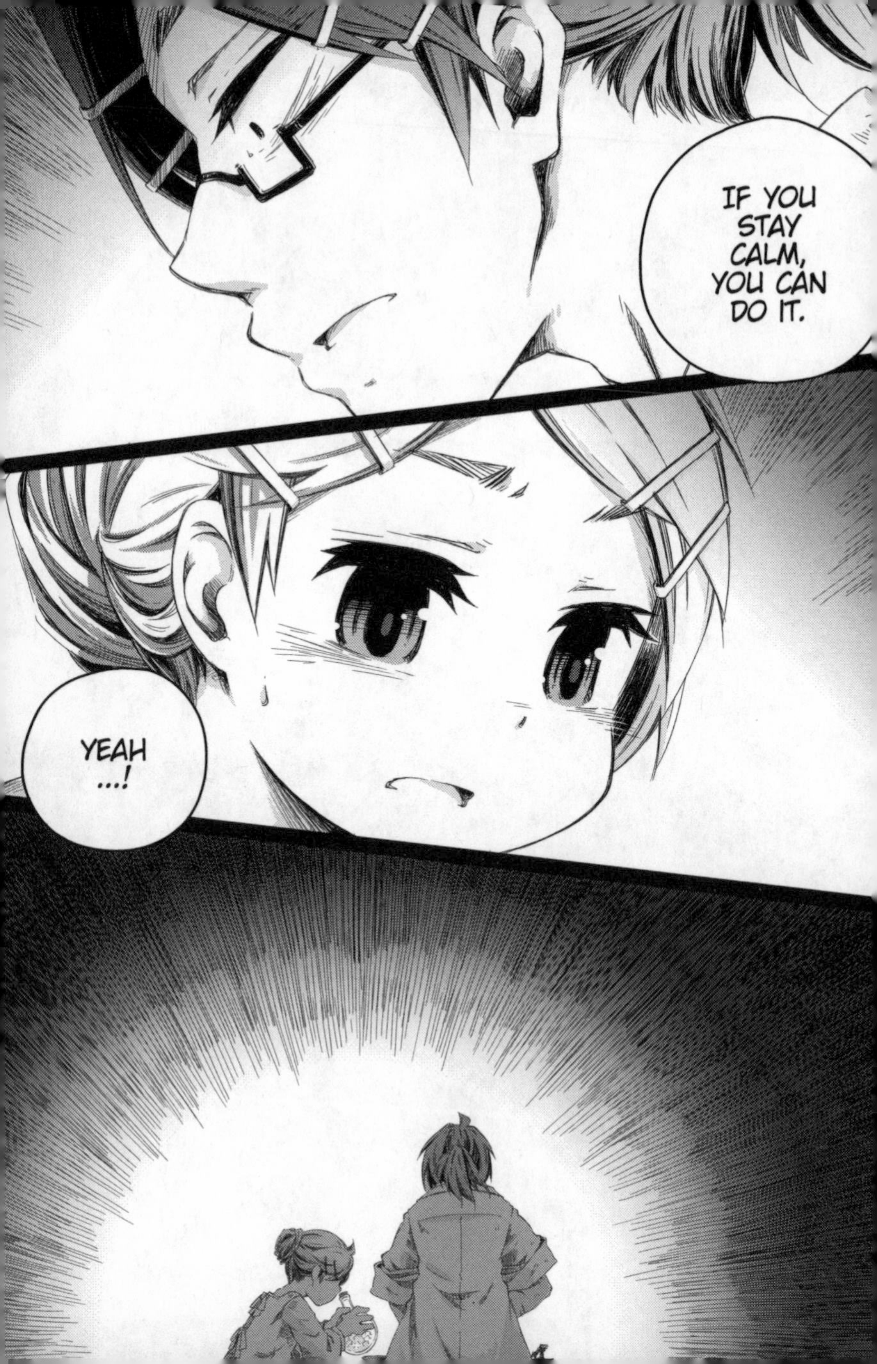
IF YOU STAY CALM, YOU CAN DO IT.
YEAH ...!

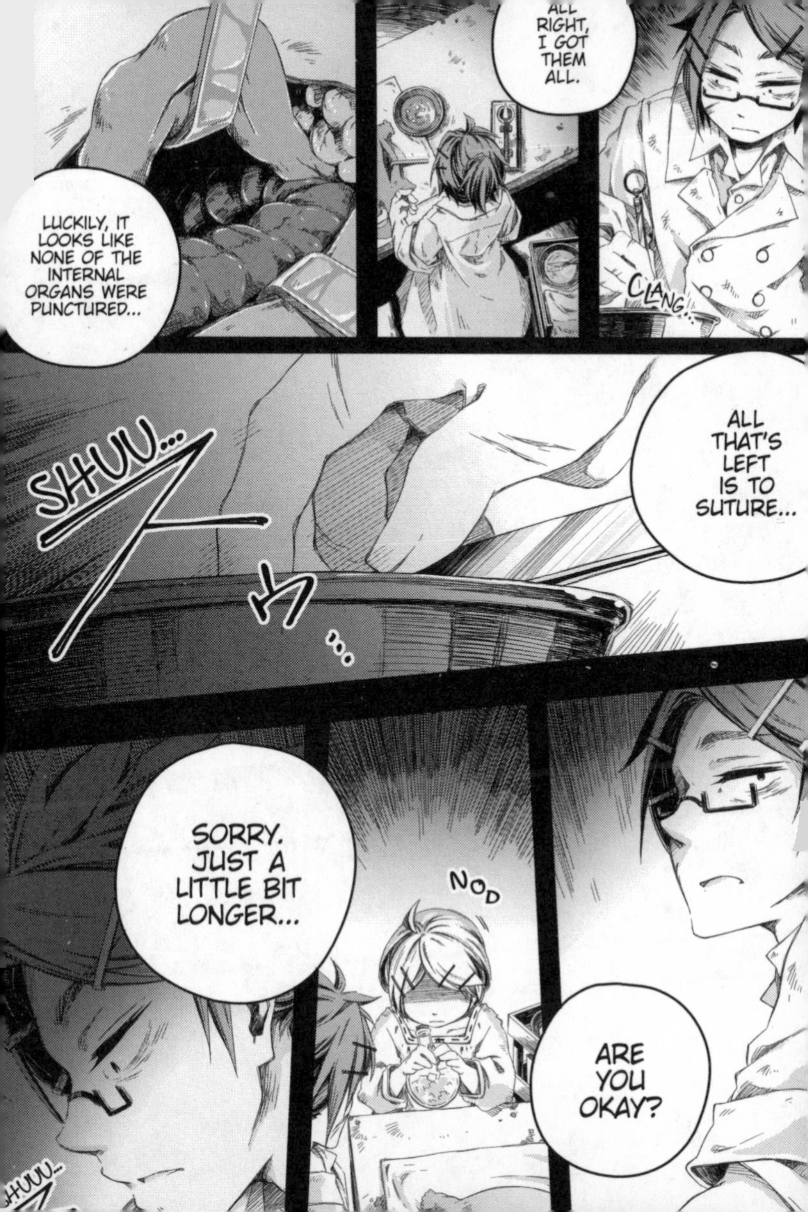
CLANG...
ALL RIGHT, I GOT THEM ALL.
LUCKILY, IT LOOKS LIKE NONE OF THE INTERNAL ORGANS WERE PUNCTURED...
ALL THAT'S LEFT IS TO SUTURE...
SHUU...
...
ARE YOU OKAY?
NOD
SORRY. JUST A LITTLE BIT LONGER...
SHUUU...

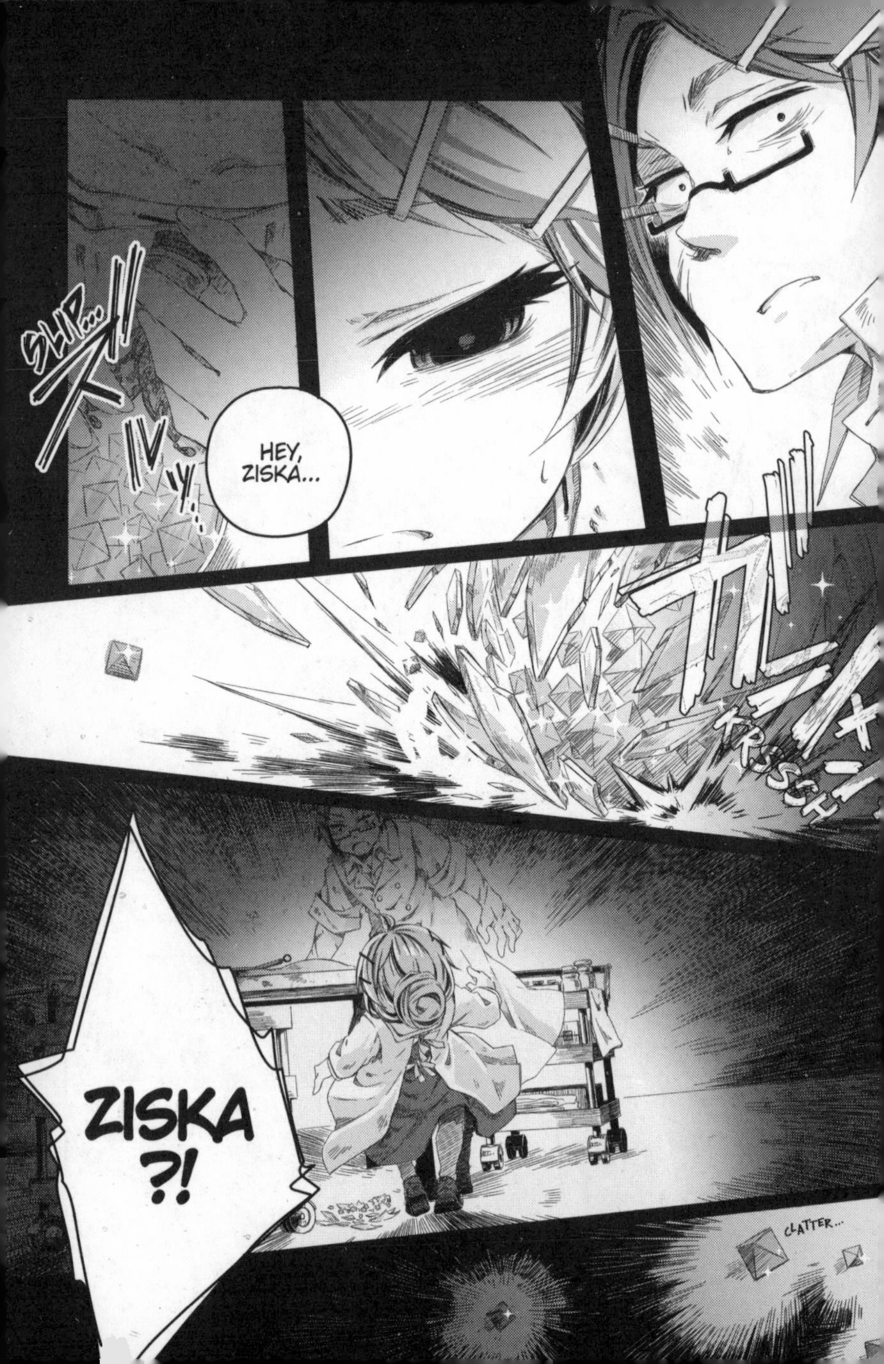
HEY, ZISKA...
SLIP...
KRSSH
ZISKA ?!
CLATTER...

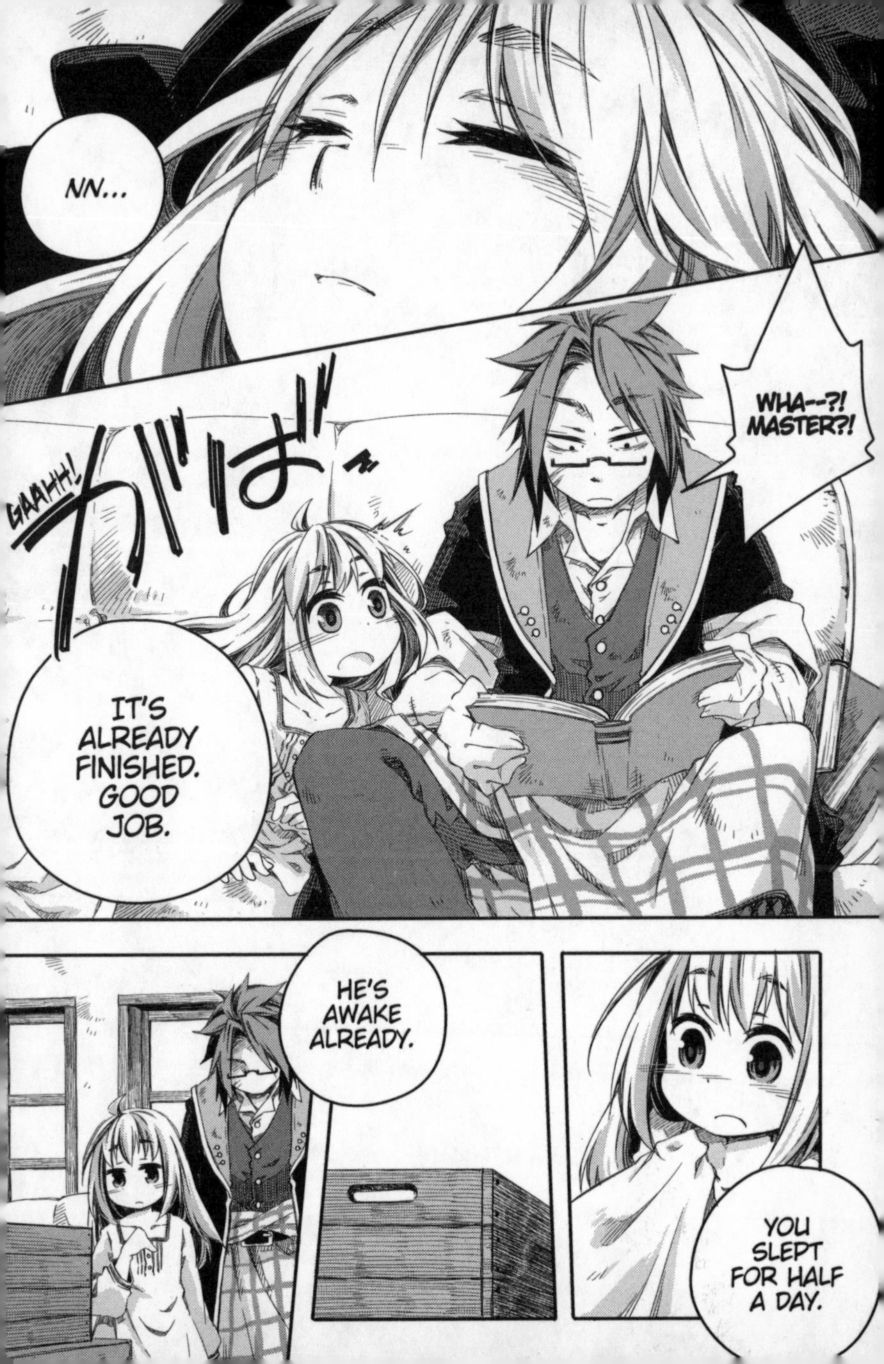
NN...
WHA--?! MASTER?!
GAAHH!
IT'S ALREADY FINISHED. GOOD JOB.
YOU SLEPT FOR HALF A DAY.
HE'S AWAKE ALREADY.

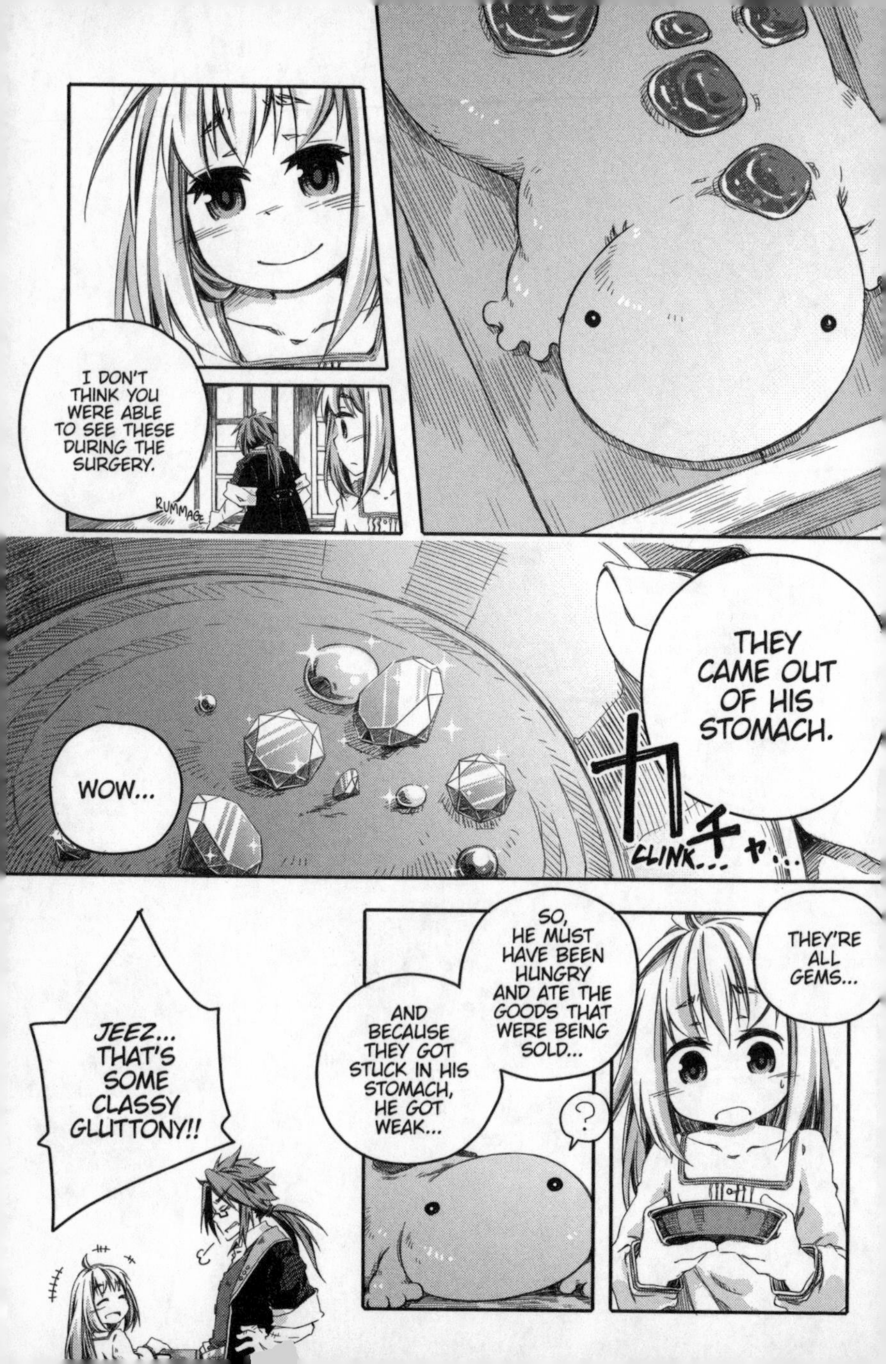
I DON'T THINK YOU WERE ABLE TO SEE THESE DURING THE SURGERY.
RUMMAGE
THEY CAME OUT OF HIS STOMACH.
カチャ
CLINK...
WOW...
THEY'RE ALL GEMS...
SO, HE MUST HAVE BEEN HUNGRY AND ATE THE GOODS THAT WERE BEING SOLD...
AND BECAUSE THEY GOT STUCK IN HIS STOMACH, HE GOT WEAK...
?
JEEZ... THAT'S SOME CLASSY GLUTTONY!!

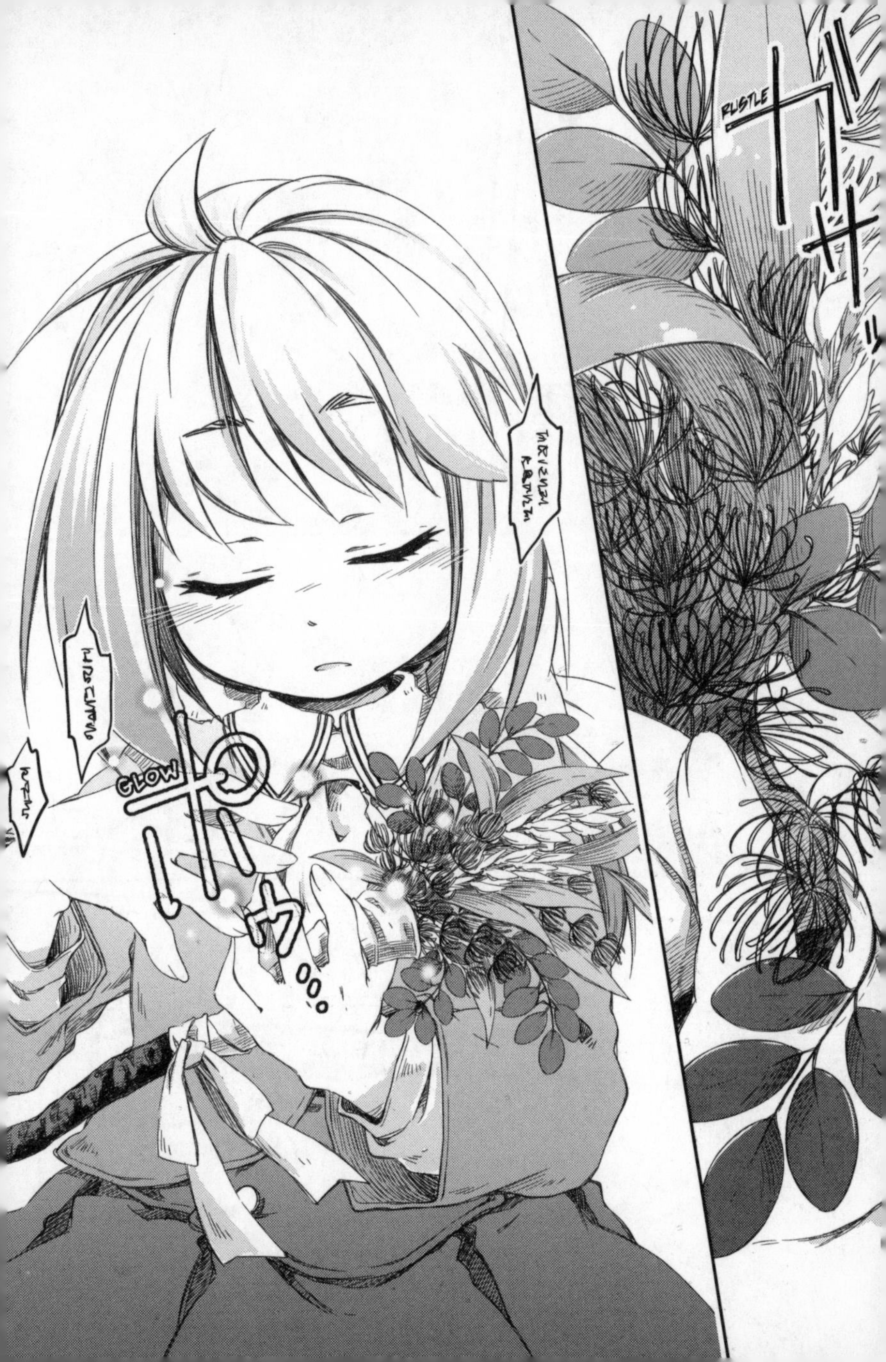
RUSTLE
GLOW

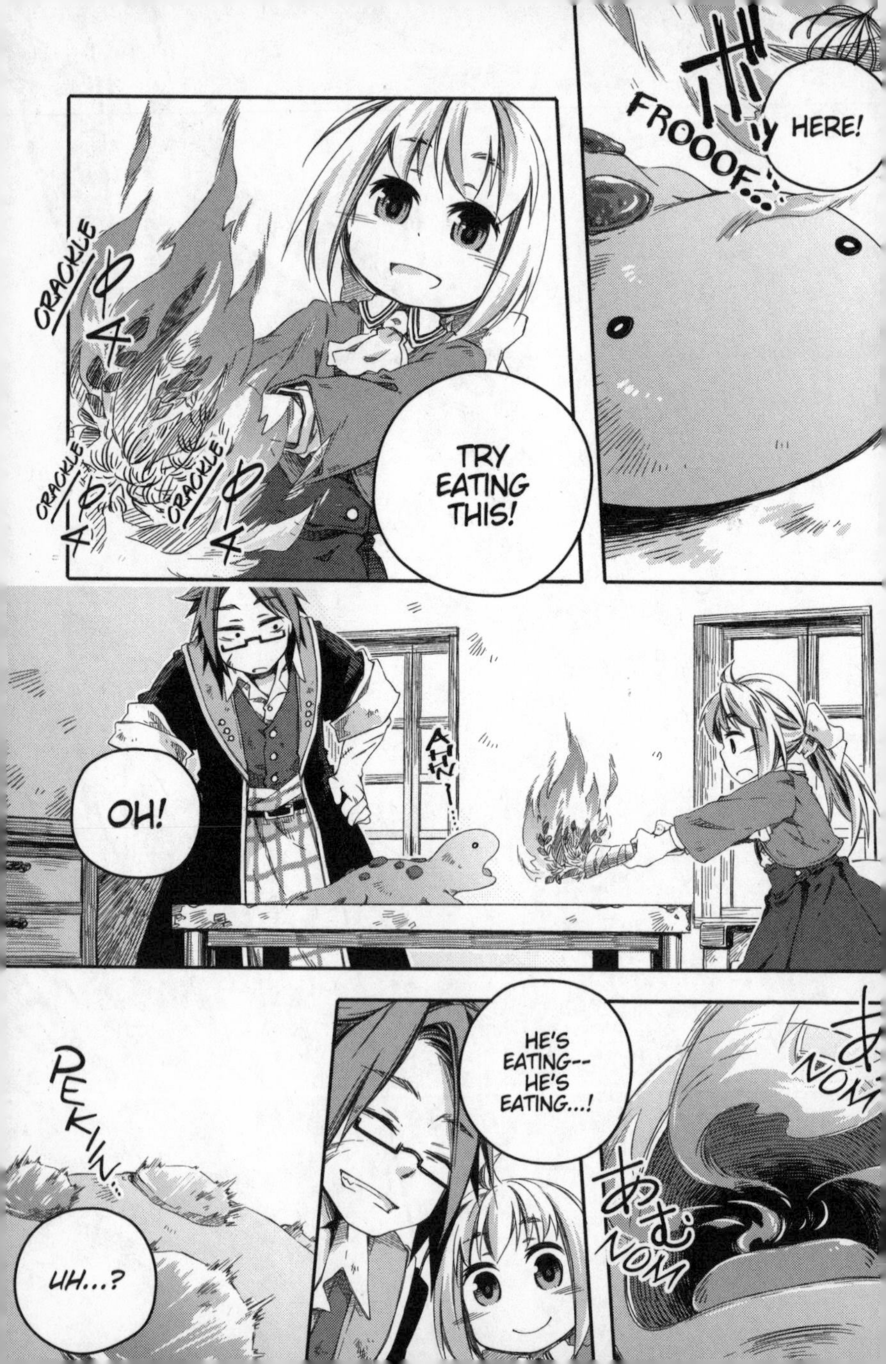
FROOOOF...!!
HERE!
TRY EATING THIS!
CRACKLE
CRACKLE
CRACKLE
OH!
AHN...
NOM
NOM
HE'S EATING-- HE'S EATING...!
PEKIN...
UH...?

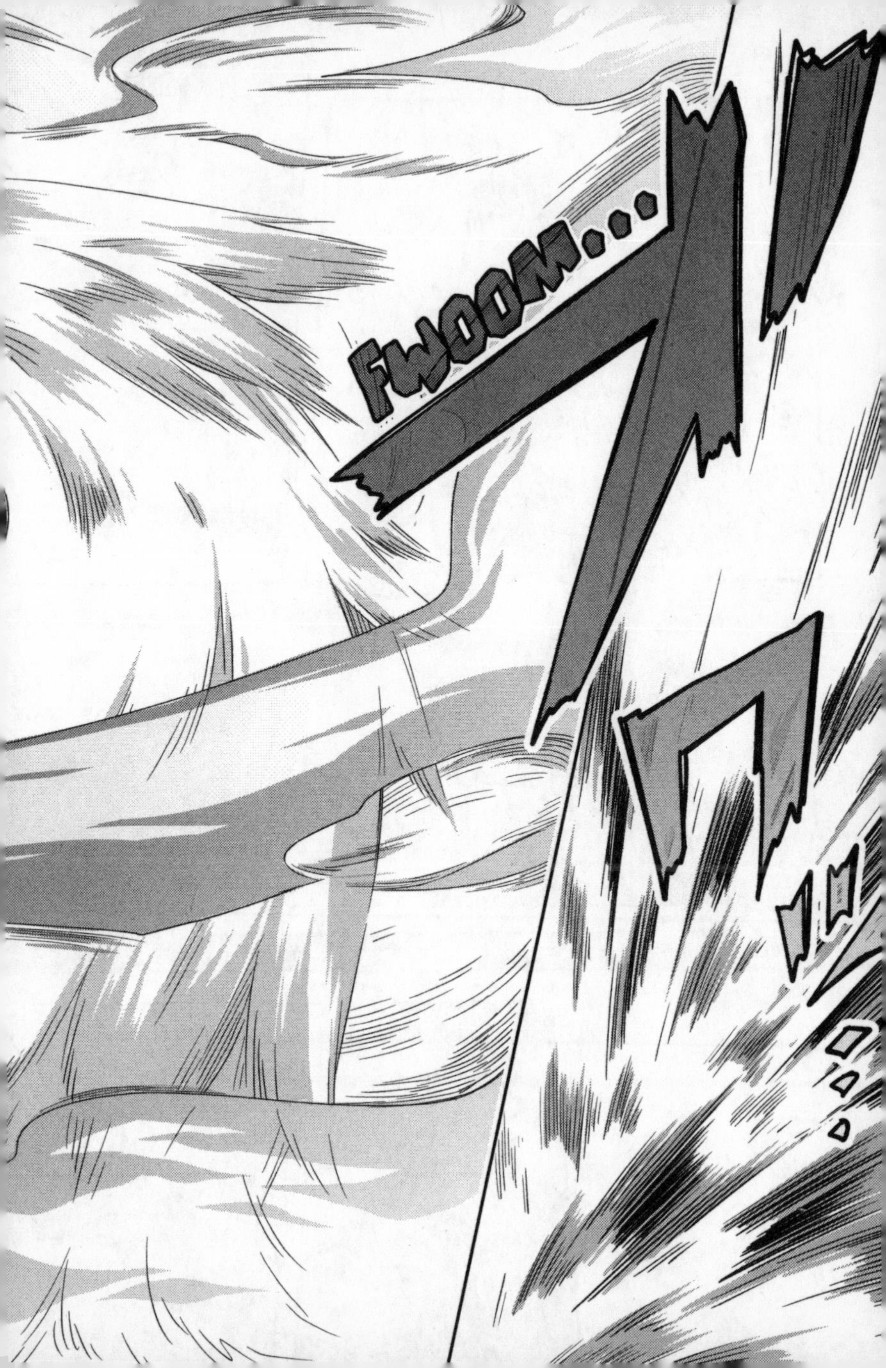
FWOOM...

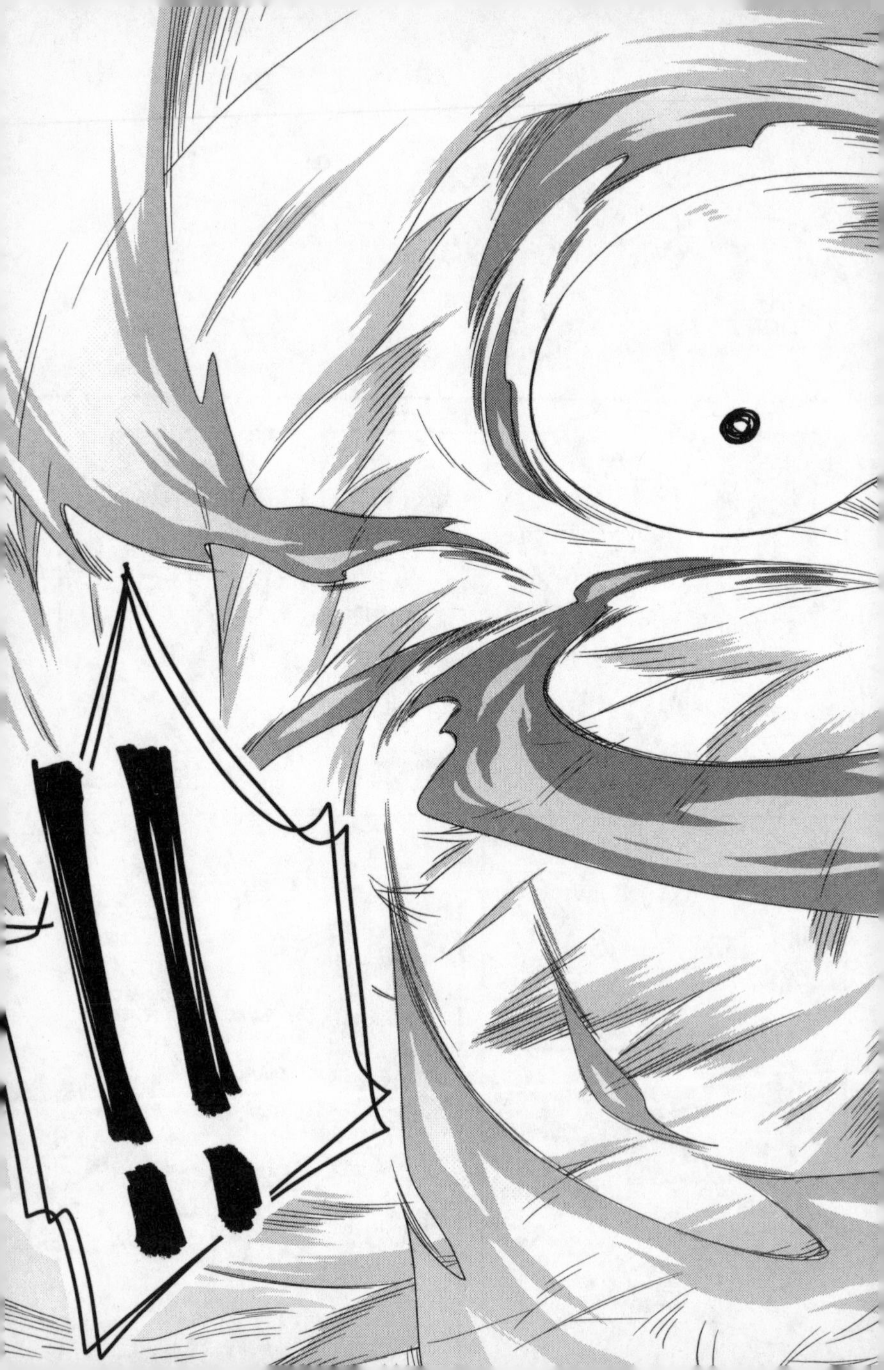
!!

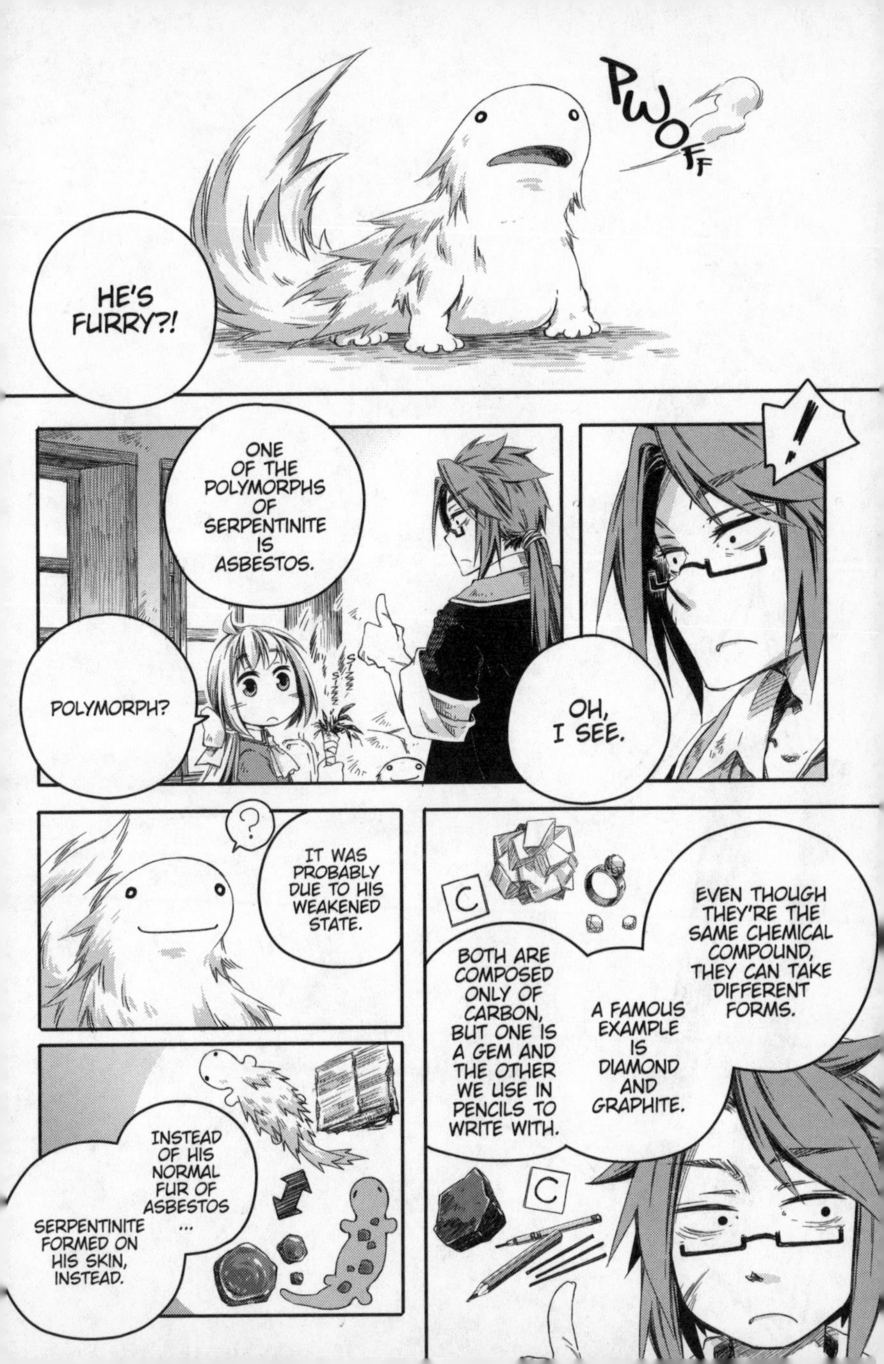
PWOFF
HE'S FURRY?!
!
OH, I SEE.
ONE OF THE POLYMORPHS OF SERPENTINITE IS ASBESTOS.
POLYMORPH?
EVEN THOUGH THEY'RE THE SAME CHEMICAL COMPOUND, THEY CAN TAKE DIFFERENT FORMS.
A FAMOUS EXAMPLE IS DIAMOND AND GRAPHITE.
BOTH ARE COMPOSED ONLY OF CARBON, BUT ONE IS A GEM AND THE OTHER WE USE IN PENCILS TO WRITE WITH.
C
C
?
IT WAS PROBABLY DUE TO HIS WEAKENED STATE.
INSTEAD OF HIS NORMAL FUR OF ASBESTOS ...
SERPENTINITE FORMED ON HIS SKIN, INSTEAD.

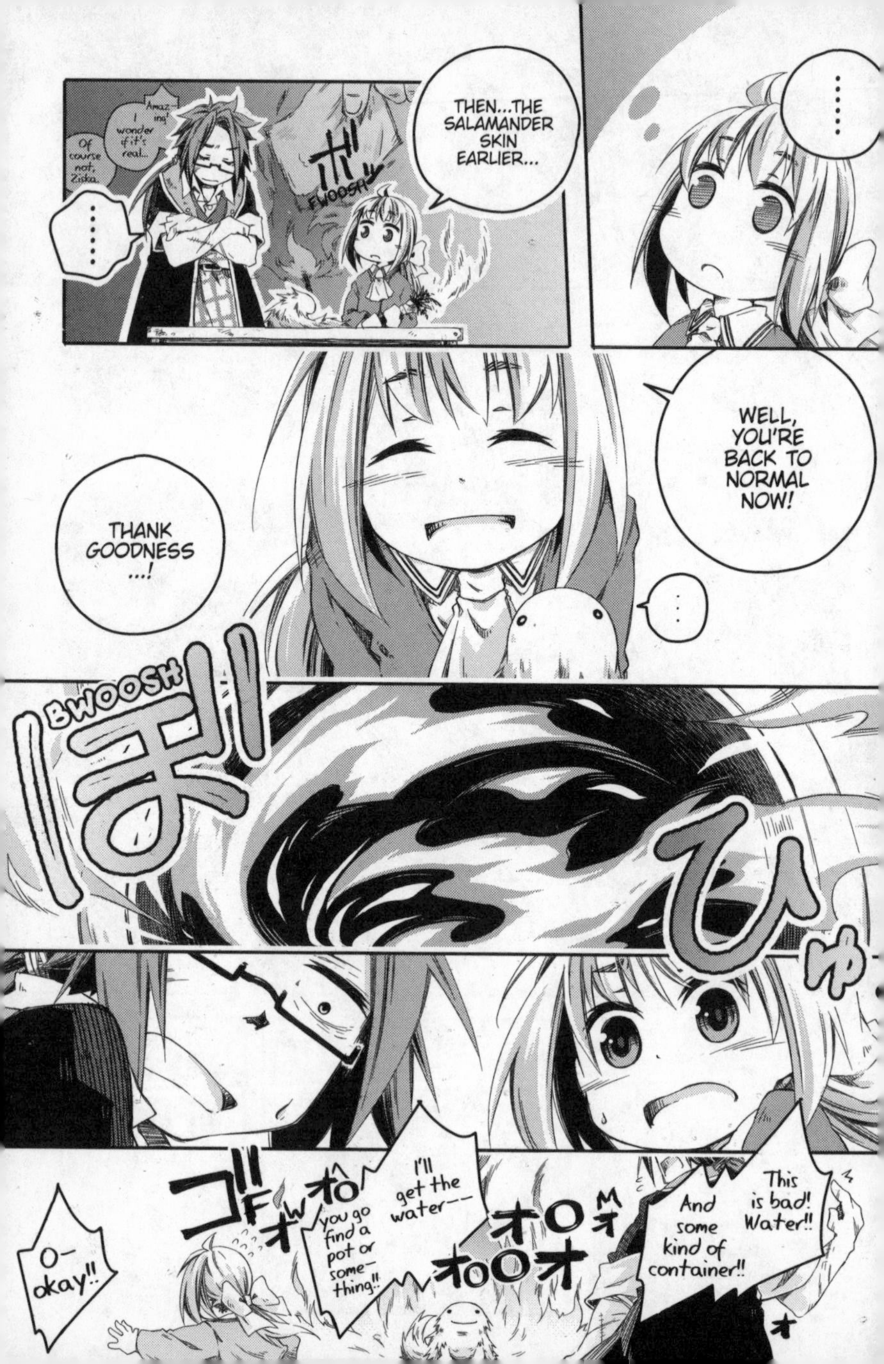
……
THEN…THE SALAMANDER SKIN EARLIER…
ボ FWOOSH
Amazing!
I wonder if it's real…
Of course not, Ziska.
……
WELL, YOU'RE BACK TO NORMAL NOW!
THANK GOODNESS …!
…
BWOOSH
ぼ
ひゅ
This is bad! Water!!
And some kind of container!!
オオオ MOO
I'll get the water--
you go find a pot or some-thing!!
ゴオオ FWOO
O-okay!!

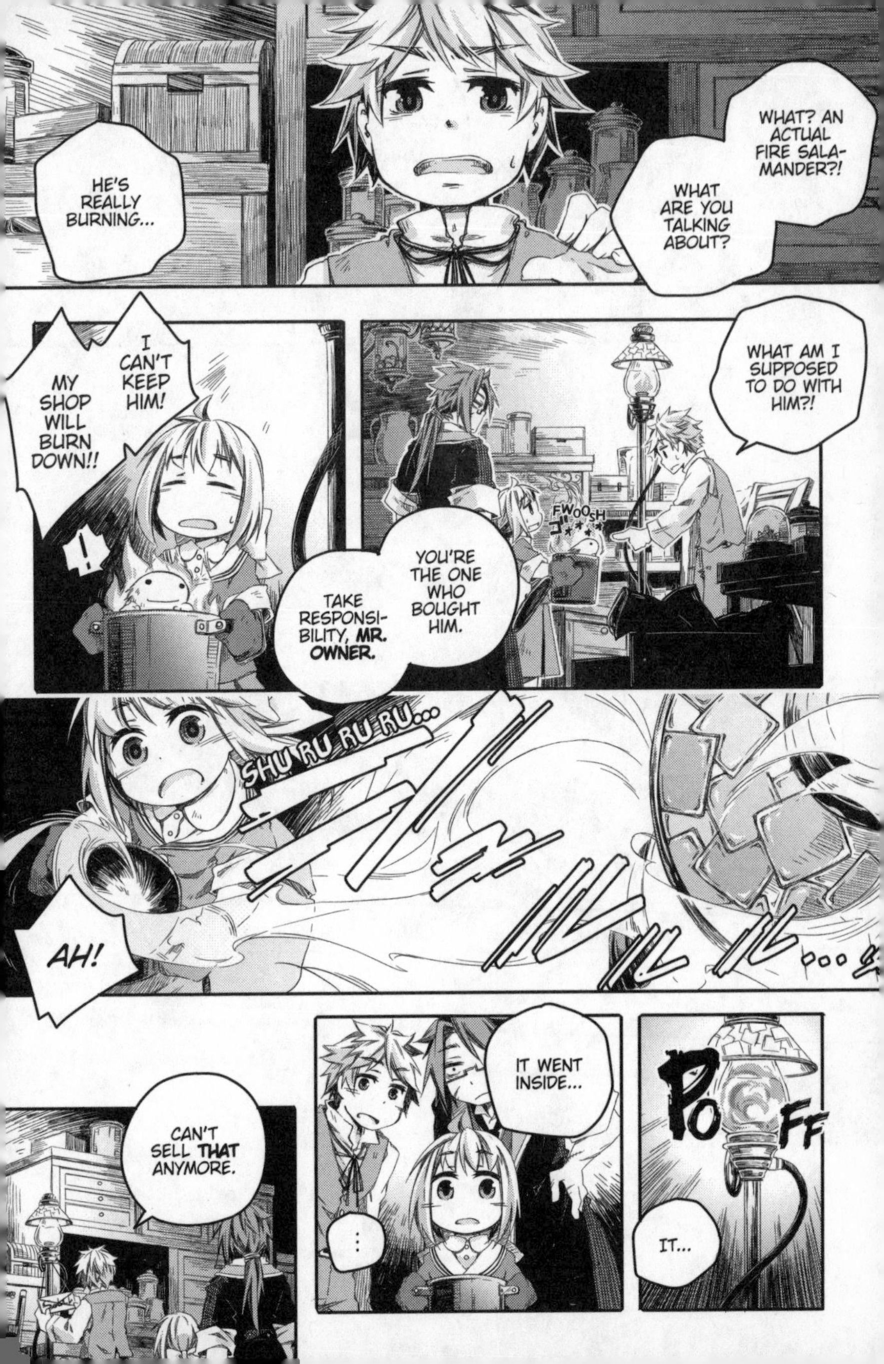
WHAT? AN ACTUAL FIRE SALAMANDER?!
WHAT ARE YOU TALKING ABOUT?
HE'S REALLY BURNING...
WHAT AM I SUPPOSED TO DO WITH HIM?!
FWOOSH
YOU'RE THE ONE WHO BOUGHT HIM.
TAKE RESPONSIBILITY, **MR. OWNER.**
I CAN'T KEEP HIM!
MY SHOP WILL BURN DOWN!!
!
SHU RU RU RU...
AH!
POFF
IT...
IT WENT INSIDE...
...
CAN'T SELL **THAT** ANYMORE.

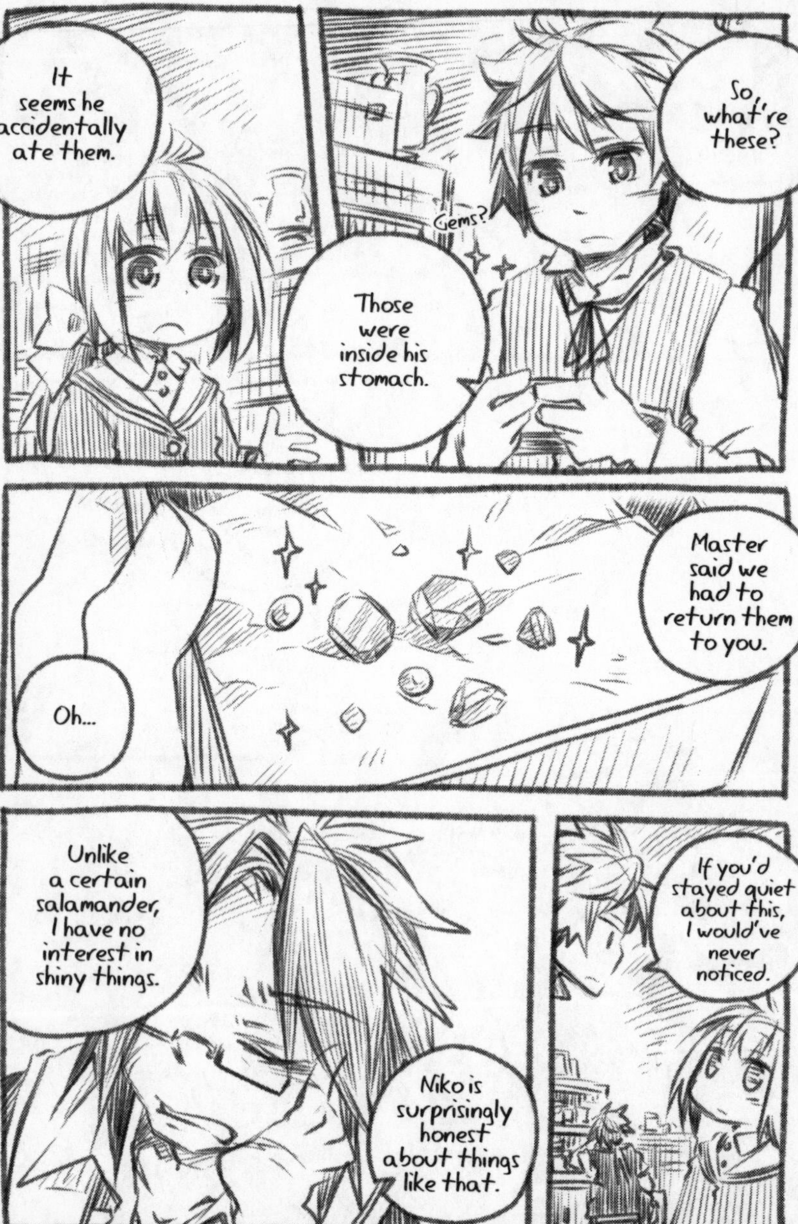
So, what're these?
Gems?
Those were inside his stomach.
It seems he accidentally ate them.
Master said we had to return them to you.
Oh...
If you'd stayed quiet about this, I would've never noticed.
Unlike a certain salamander, I have no interest in shiny things.
Niko is surprisingly honest about things like that.

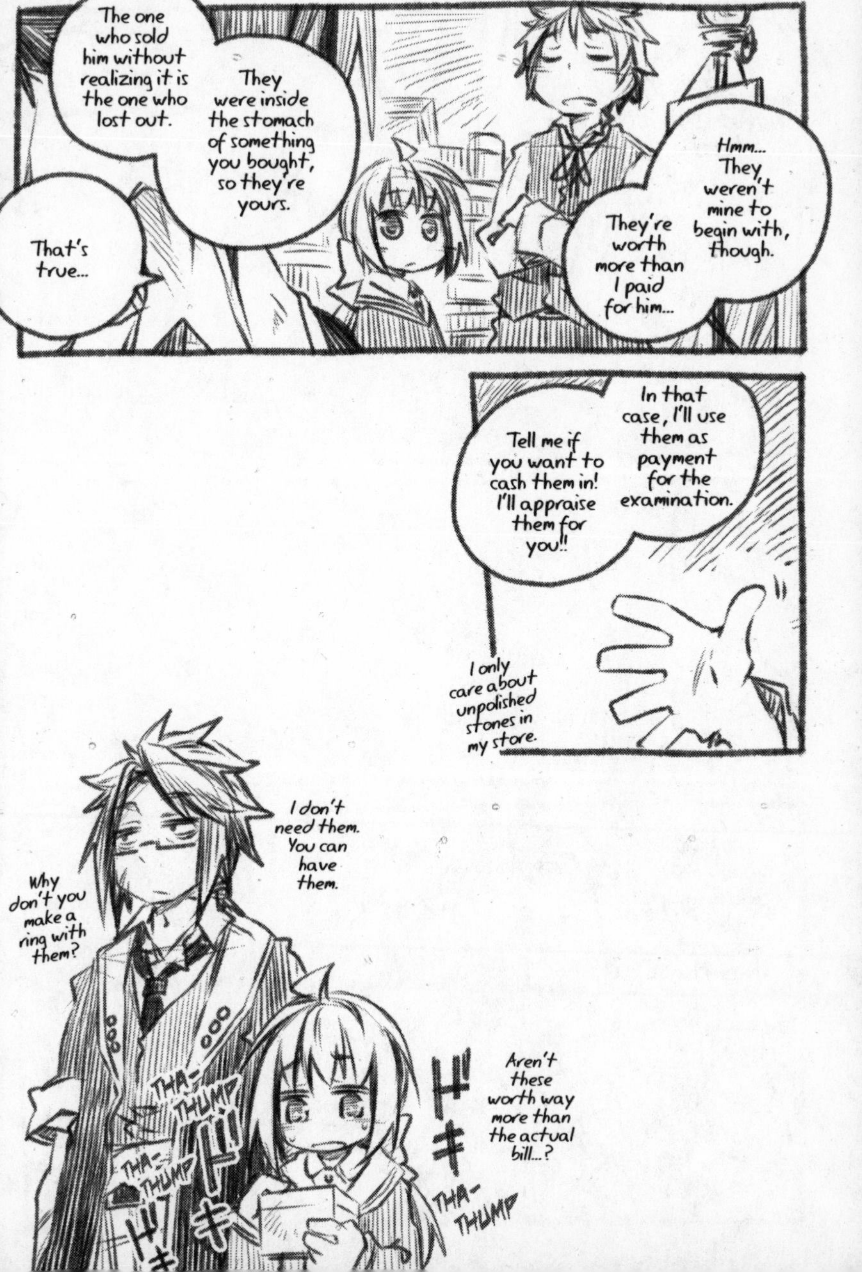
Hmm... They weren't mine to begin with, though.
They're worth more than I paid for him...
They were inside the stomach of something you bought, so they're yours.
The one who sold him without realizing it is the one who lost out.
That's true...
In that case, I'll use them as payment for the examination.
Tell me if you want to cash them in! I'll appraise them for you!!
I only care about unpolished stones in my store.
I don't need them. You can have them.
Why don't you make a ring with them?
Aren't these worth way more than the actual bill...?
THA-THUMP
THA-THUMP
THA-THUMP

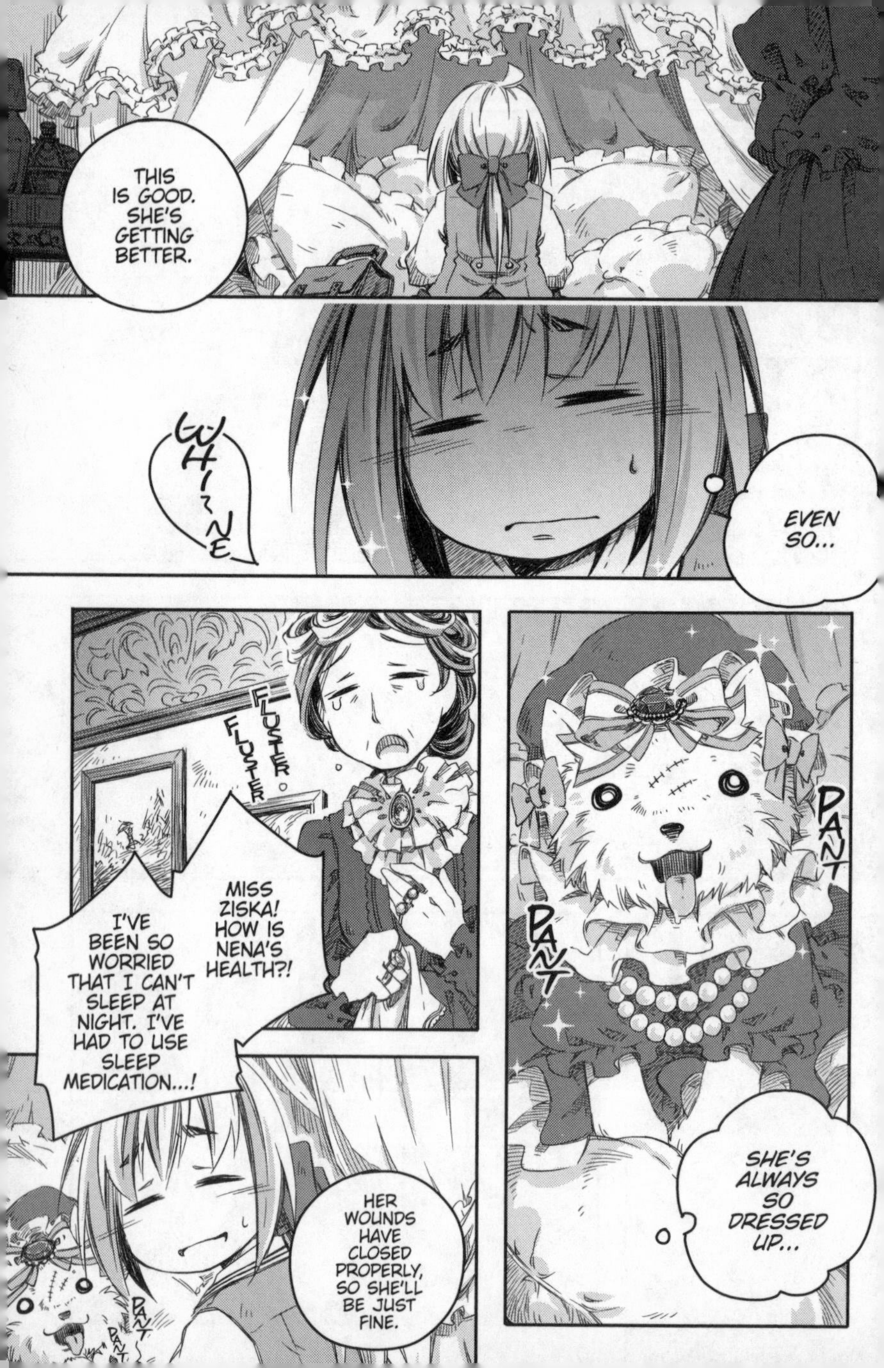
THIS IS GOOD. SHE'S GETTING BETTER.
EVEN SO...
WHI~NE
PANT
PANT
SHE'S ALWAYS SO DRESSED UP...
FLUSTER FLUSTER
MISS ZISKA! HOW IS NENA'S HEALTH?!
I'VE BEEN SO WORRIED THAT I CAN'T SLEEP AT NIGHT. I'VE HAD TO USE SLEEP MEDICATION...!
HER WOUNDS HAVE CLOSED PROPERLY, SO SHE'LL BE JUST FINE.
PANT PANT

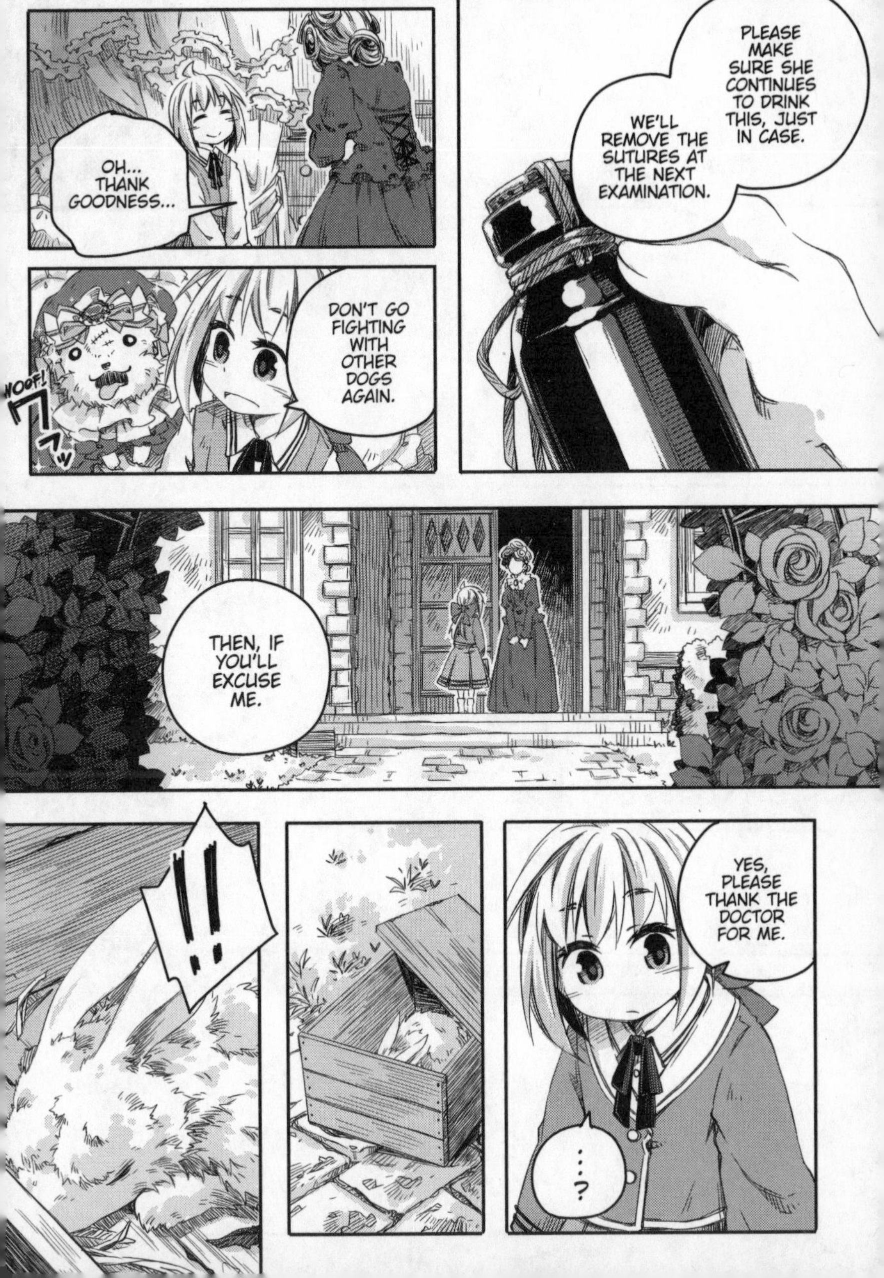
PLEASE MAKE SURE SHE CONTINUES TO DRINK THIS, JUST IN CASE.
WE'LL REMOVE THE SUTURES AT THE NEXT EXAMINATION.
OH... THANK GOODNESS...
DON'T GO FIGHTING WITH OTHER DOGS AGAIN.
WOOF!
THEN, IF YOU'LL EXCUSE ME.
YES, PLEASE THANK THE DOCTOR FOR ME.
...?
!!

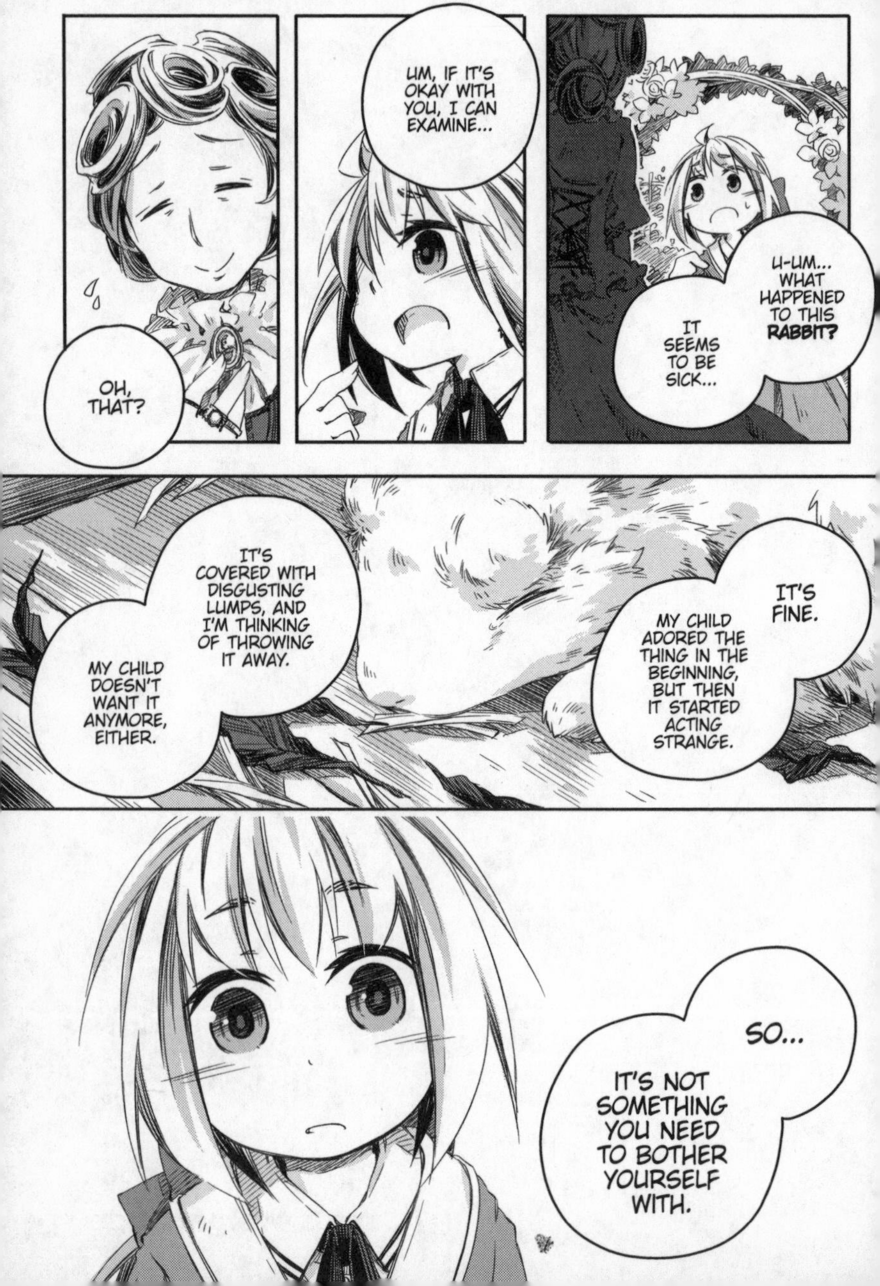
U-UM... WHAT HAPPENED TO THIS **RABBIT?**
IT SEEMS TO BE SICK...
UM, IF IT'S OKAY WITH YOU, I CAN EXAMINE...
OH, THAT?
IT'S FINE.
MY CHILD ADORED THE THING IN THE BEGINNING, BUT THEN IT STARTED ACTING STRANGE.
IT'S COVERED WITH DISGUSTING LUMPS, AND I'M THINKING OF THROWING IT AWAY.
MY CHILD DOESN'T WANT IT ANYMORE, EITHER.
SO...
IT'S NOT SOMETHING YOU NEED TO BOTHER YOURSELF WITH.

[Case 3: Wolpertinger]

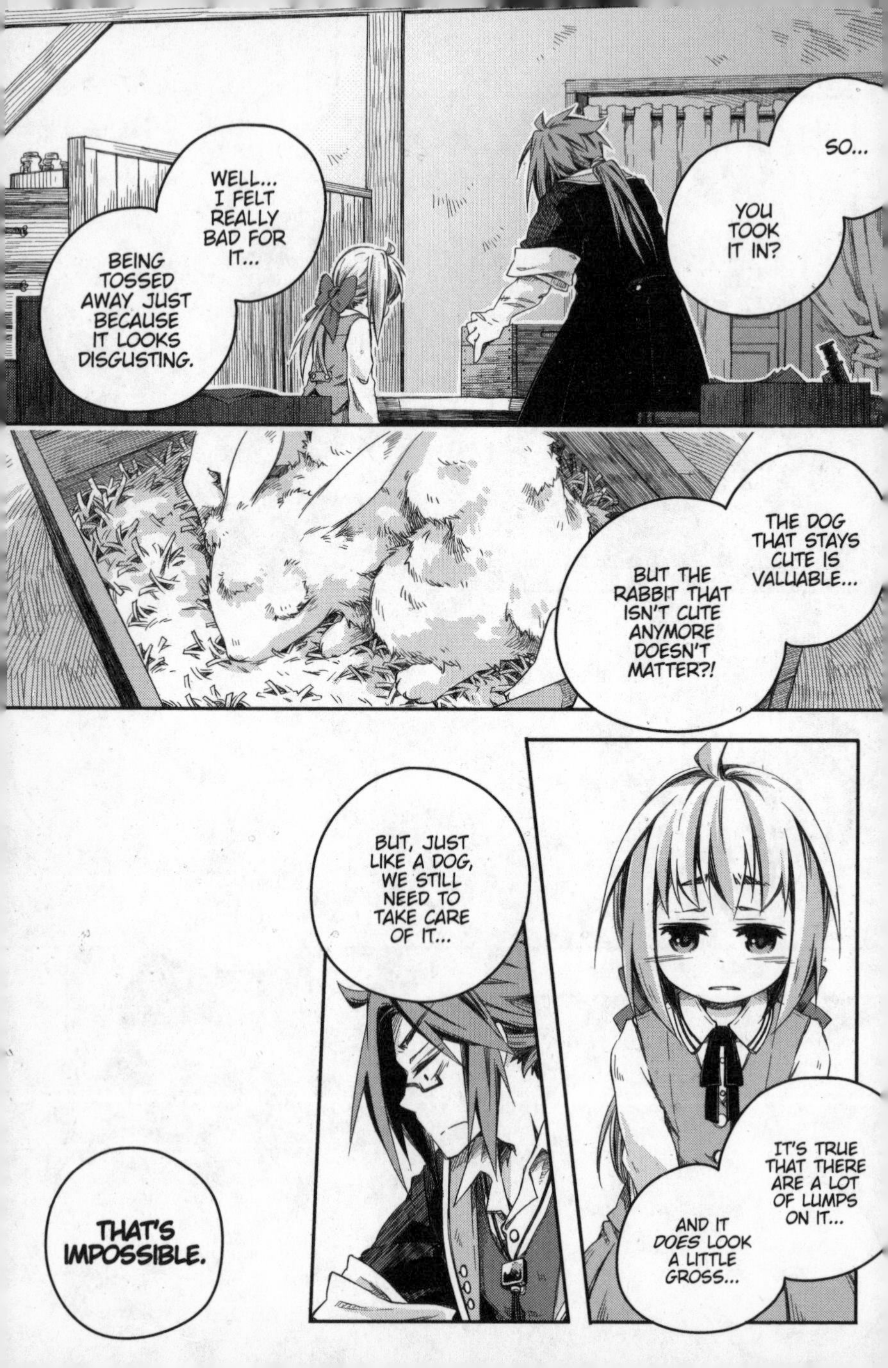
SO...
YOU TOOK IT IN?
WELL... I FELT REALLY BAD FOR IT...
BEING TOSSED AWAY JUST BECAUSE IT LOOKS DISGUSTING.
THE DOG THAT STAYS CUTE IS VALUABLE...
BUT THE RABBIT THAT ISN'T CUTE ANYMORE DOESN'T MATTER?!
IT'S TRUE THAT THERE ARE A LOT OF LUMPS ON IT...
AND IT DOES LOOK A LITTLE GROSS...
BUT, JUST LIKE A DOG, WE STILL NEED TO TAKE CARE OF IT...
THAT'S IMPOSSIBLE.

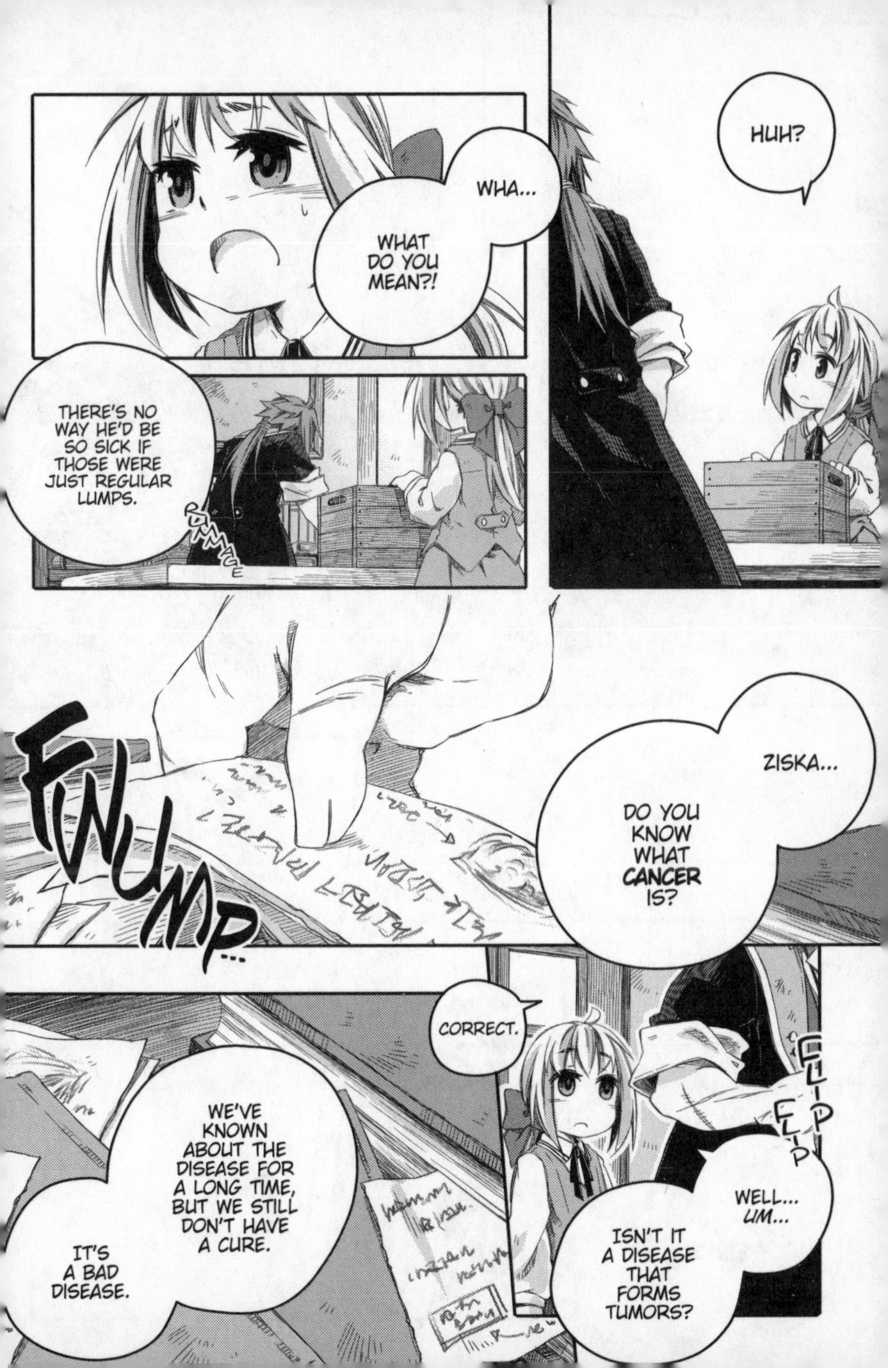
HUH?
WHA... WHAT DO YOU MEAN?!
THERE'S NO WAY HE'D BE SO SICK IF THOSE WERE JUST REGULAR LUMPS.
RUMMAGE
ZISKA... DO YOU KNOW WHAT **CANCER** IS?
FWUMP...
FLIP FLIP
WELL... UM...
ISN'T IT A DISEASE THAT FORMS TUMORS?
CORRECT.
WE'VE KNOWN ABOUT THE DISEASE FOR A LONG TIME, BUT WE STILL DON'T HAVE A CURE.
IT'S A BAD DISEASE.

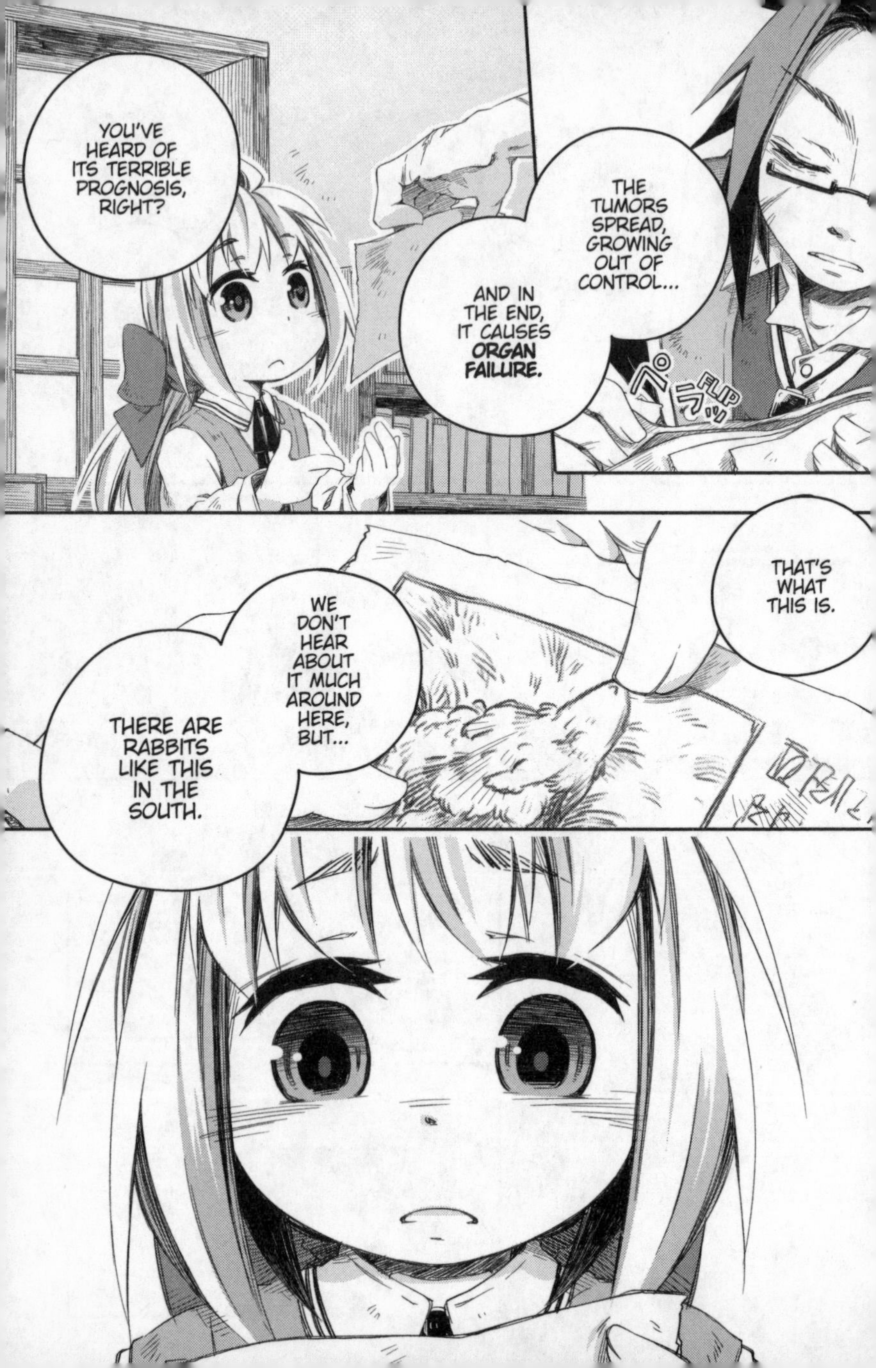
THE TUMORS SPREAD, GROWING OUT OF CONTROL...
AND IN THE END, IT CAUSES **ORGAN FAILURE.**
FLIP
YOU'VE HEARD OF ITS TERRIBLE PROGNOSIS, RIGHT?
THAT'S WHAT THIS IS.
WE DON'T HEAR ABOUT IT MUCH AROUND HERE, BUT...
THERE ARE RABBITS LIKE THIS IN THE SOUTH.

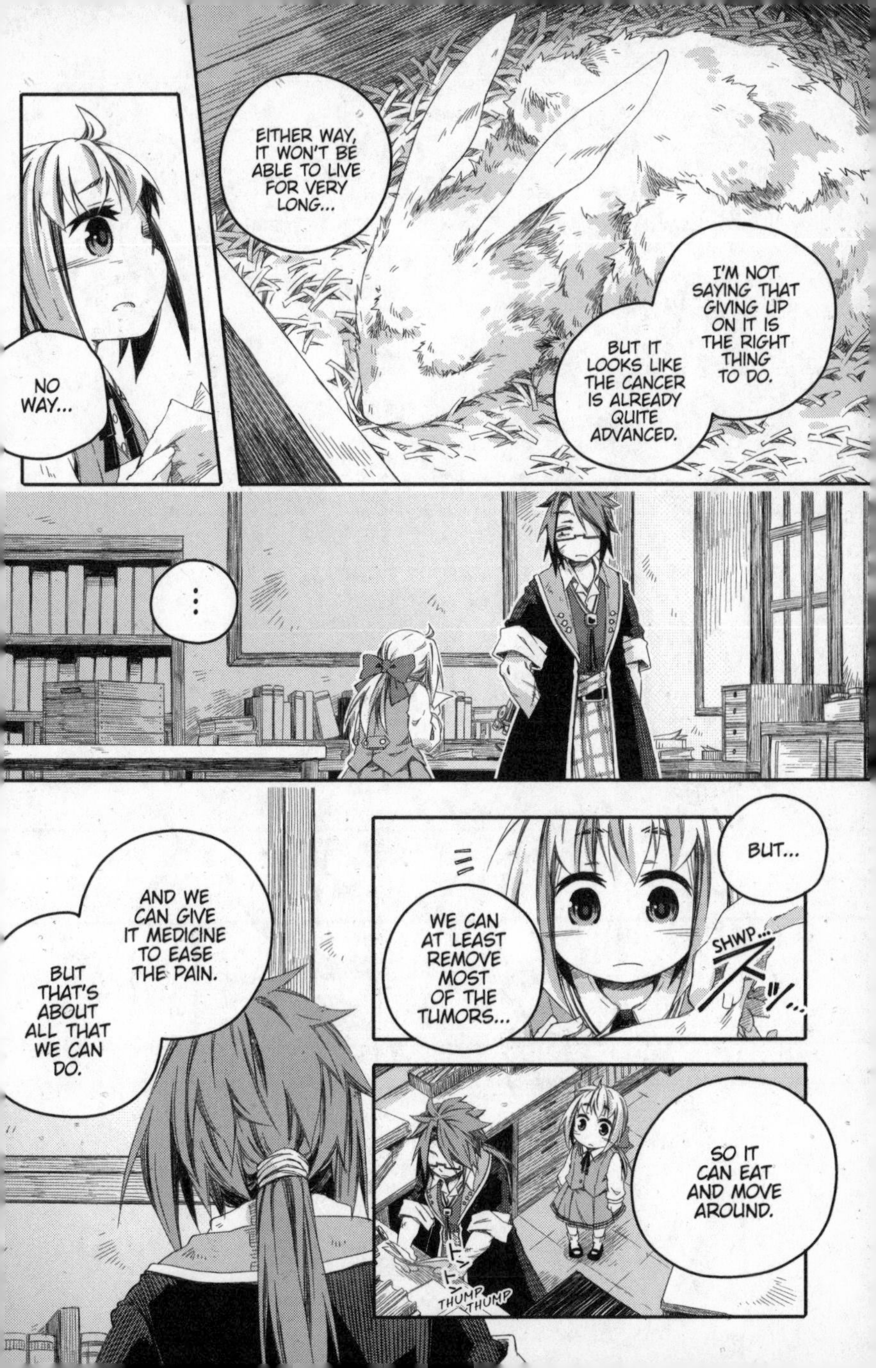
I'M NOT SAYING THAT GIVING UP ON IT IS THE RIGHT THING TO DO.
BUT IT LOOKS LIKE THE CANCER IS ALREADY QUITE ADVANCED.
EITHER WAY, IT WON'T BE ABLE TO LIVE FOR VERY LONG...
NO WAY...
...
BUT...
WE CAN AT LEAST REMOVE MOST OF THE TUMORS...
SHWP...
SO IT CAN EAT AND MOVE AROUND.
THUMP THUMP
AND WE CAN GIVE IT MEDICINE TO EASE THE PAIN.
BUT THAT'S ABOUT ALL THAT WE CAN DO.

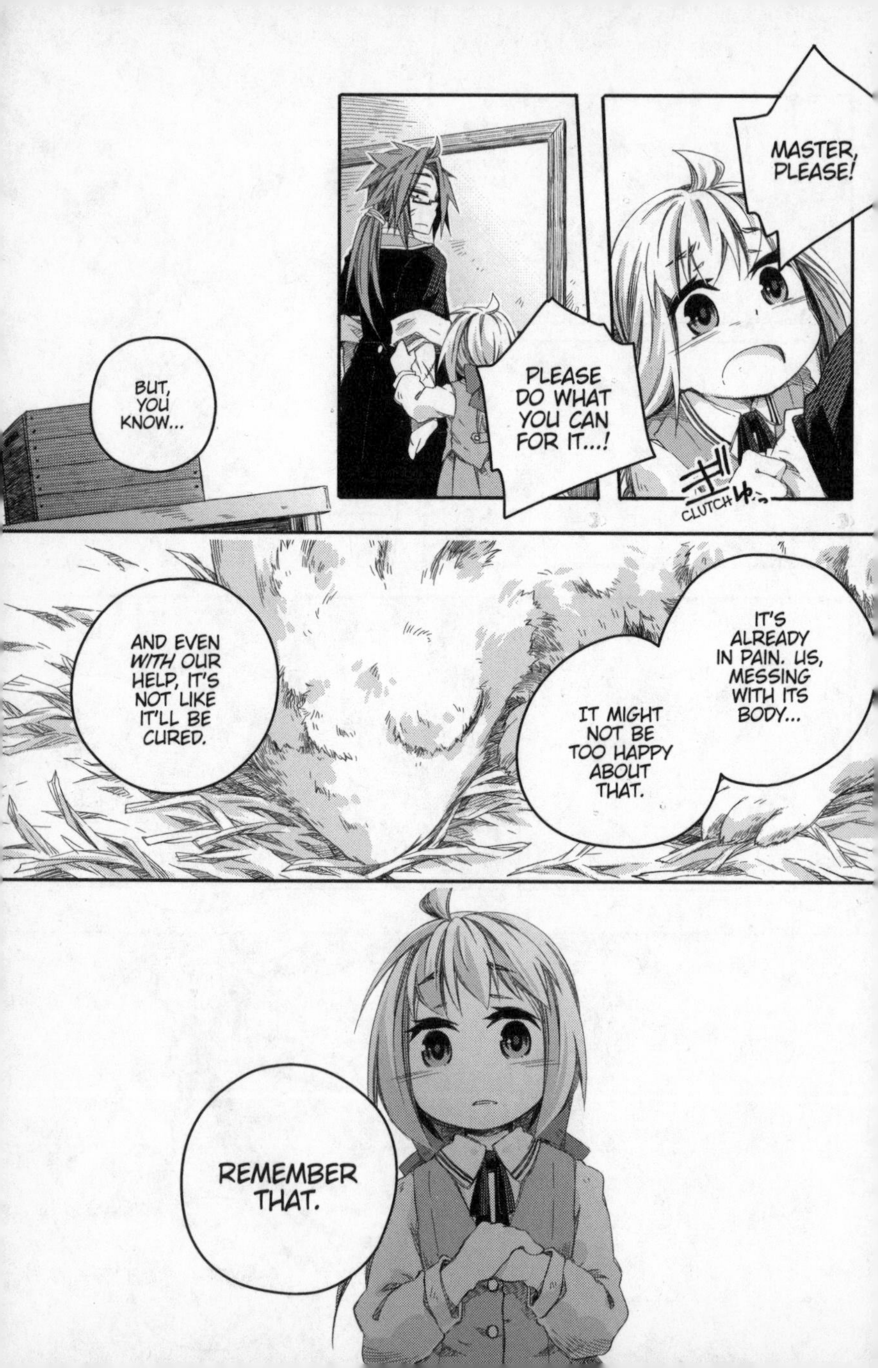
MASTER, PLEASE!
PLEASE DO WHAT YOU CAN FOR IT...!
CLUTCH
BUT, YOU KNOW...
IT'S ALREADY IN PAIN. US, MESSING WITH ITS BODY...
IT MIGHT NOT BE TOO HAPPY ABOUT THAT.
AND EVEN *WITH* OUR HELP, IT'S NOT LIKE IT'LL BE CURED.
REMEMBER THAT.

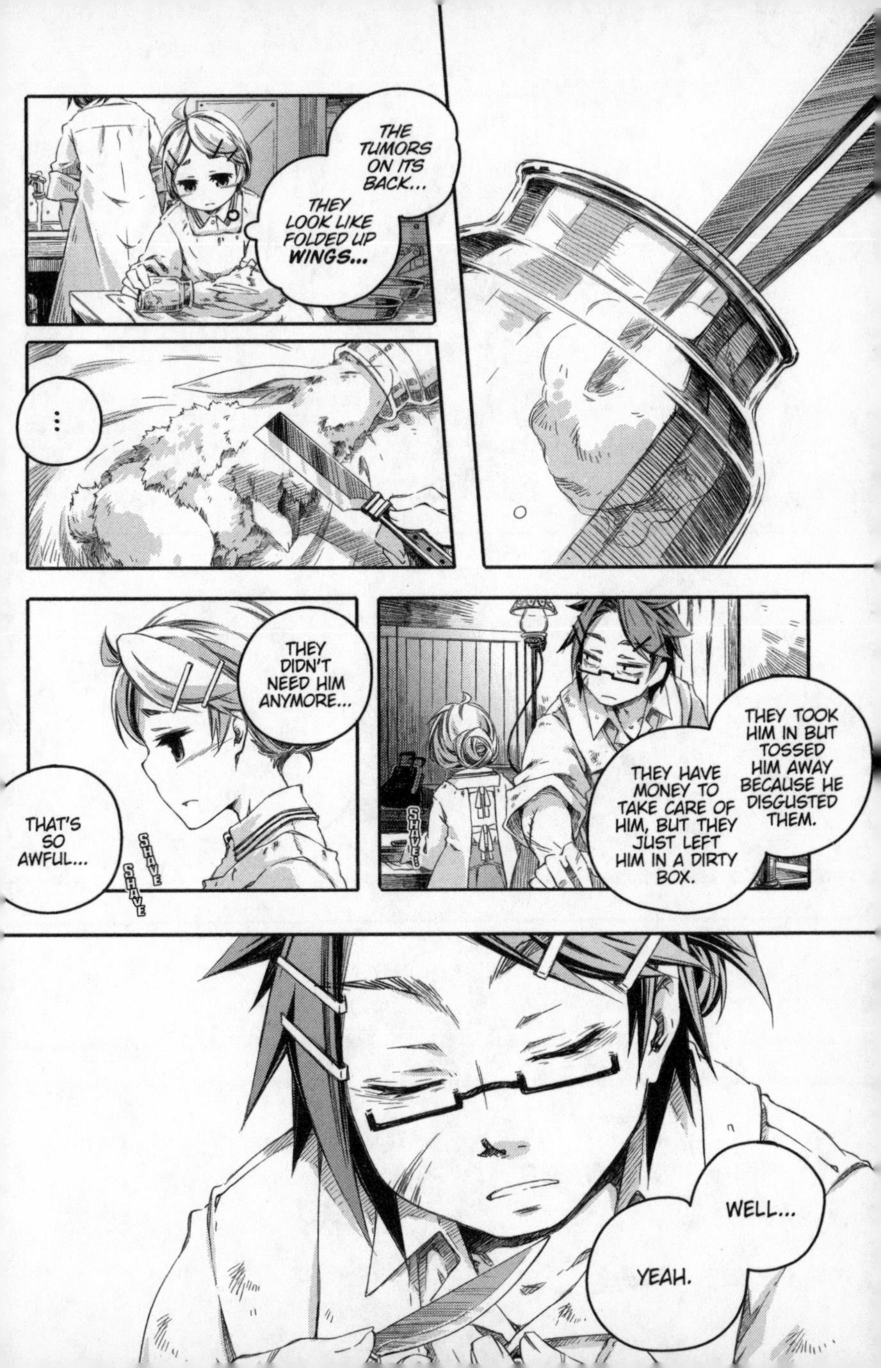

THE TUMORS ON ITS BACK...
THEY LOOK LIKE FOLDED UP WINGS...
...
THEY TOOK HIM IN BUT TOSSED HIM AWAY BECAUSE HE DISGUSTED THEM.
THEY HAVE MONEY TO TAKE CARE OF HIM, BUT THEY JUST LEFT HIM IN A DIRTY BOX.
SHAVE
THEY DIDN'T NEED HIM ANYMORE...
THAT'S SO AWFUL...
SHAVE
SHAVE
WELL...
YEAH.

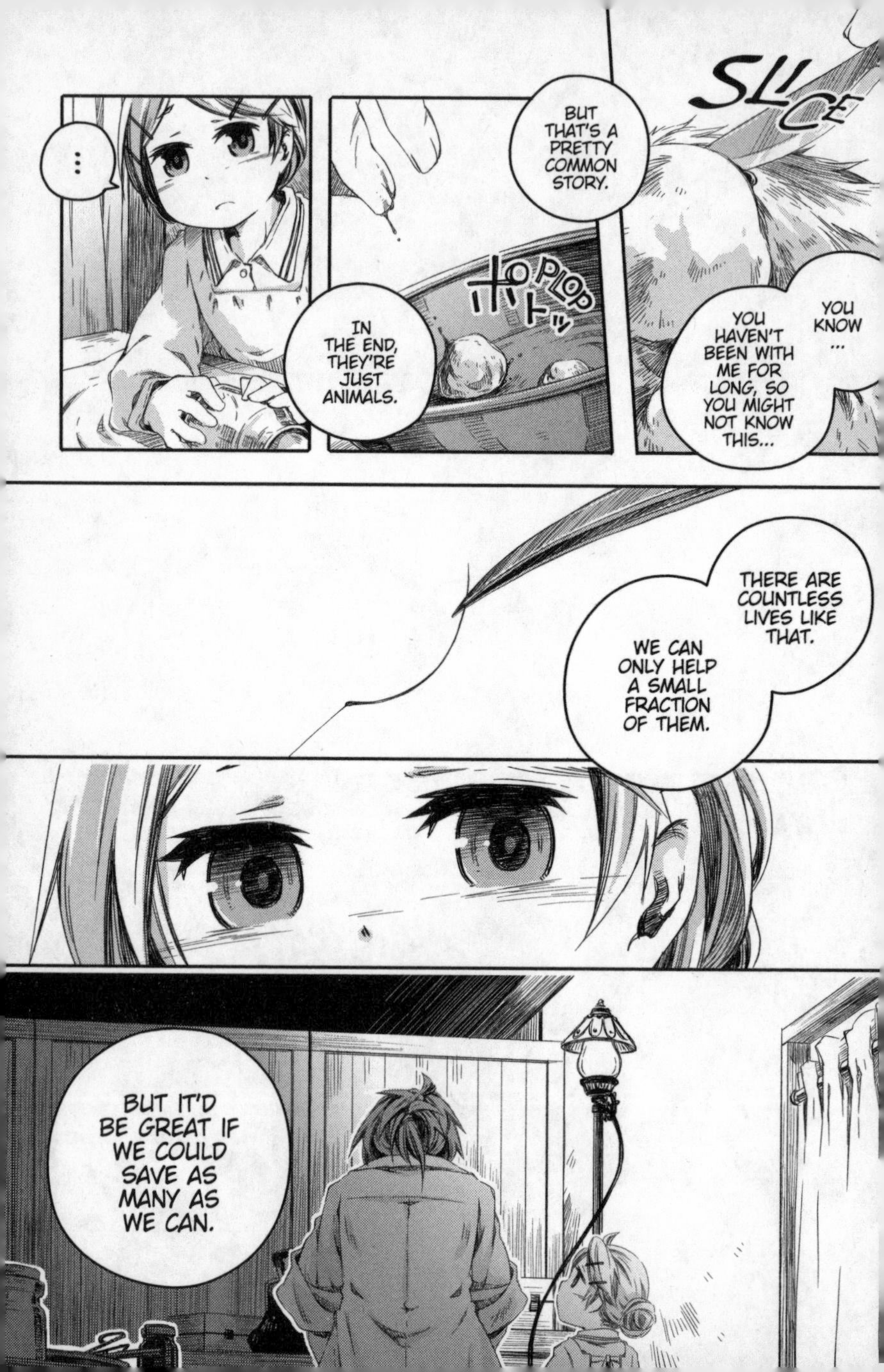
SLICE
YOU KNOW ...
YOU HAVEN'T BEEN WITH ME FOR LONG, SO YOU MIGHT NOT KNOW THIS...
BUT THAT'S A PRETTY COMMON STORY.
PLOP
IN THE END, THEY'RE JUST ANIMALS.
...
THERE ARE COUNTLESS LIVES LIKE THAT.
WE CAN ONLY HELP A SMALL FRACTION OF THEM.
BUT IT'D BE GREAT IF WE COULD SAVE AS MANY AS WE CAN.

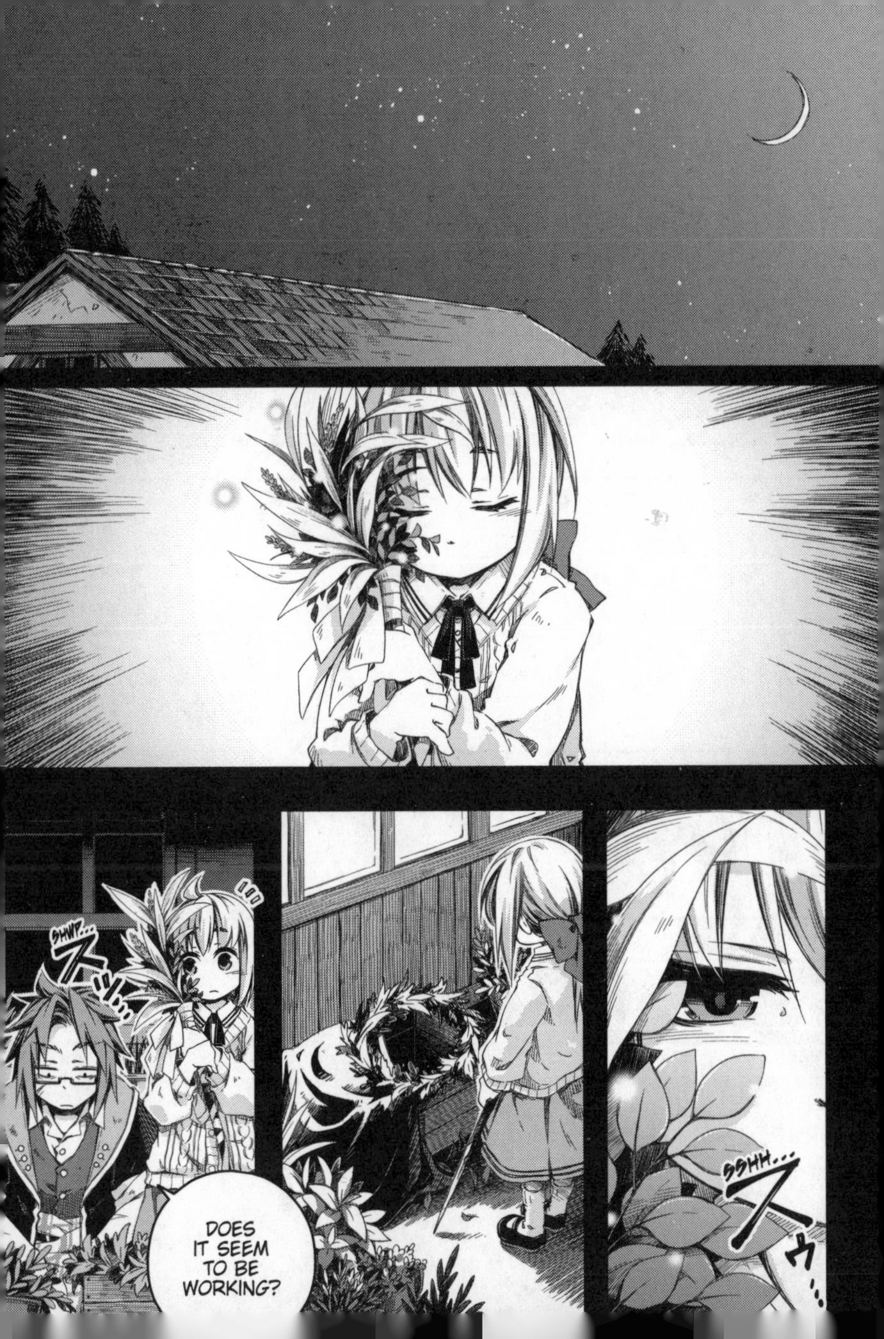
SSHH...
SHWP...
DOES IT SEEM TO BE WORKING?

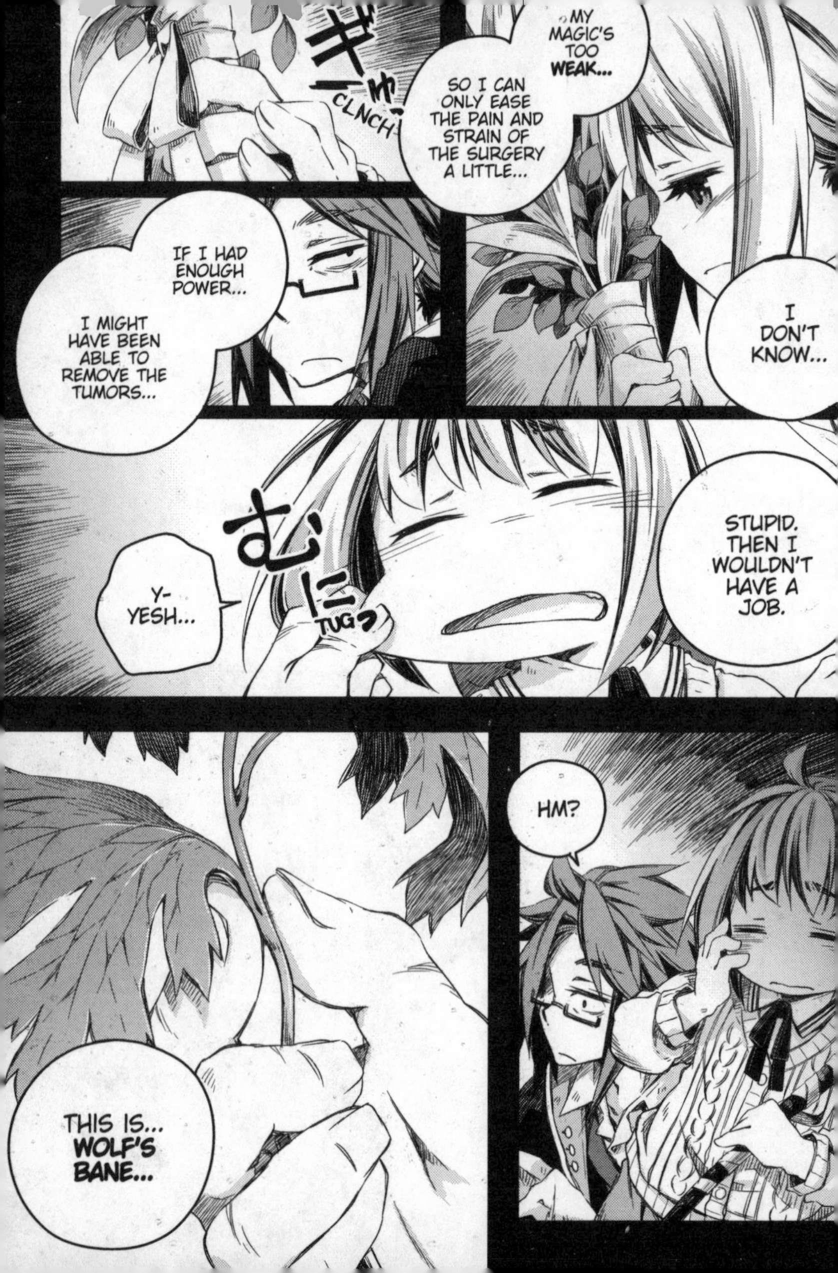
MY MAGIC'S TOO WEAK...
SO I CAN ONLY EASE THE PAIN AND STRAIN OF THE SURGERY A LITTLE...
I DON'T KNOW...
ギュ CLNCH
IF I HAD ENOUGH POWER...
I MIGHT HAVE BEEN ABLE TO REMOVE THE TUMORS...
STUPID. THEN I WOULDN'T HAVE A JOB.
むに TUG
Y-YESH...
HM?
THIS IS... WOLF'S BANE...

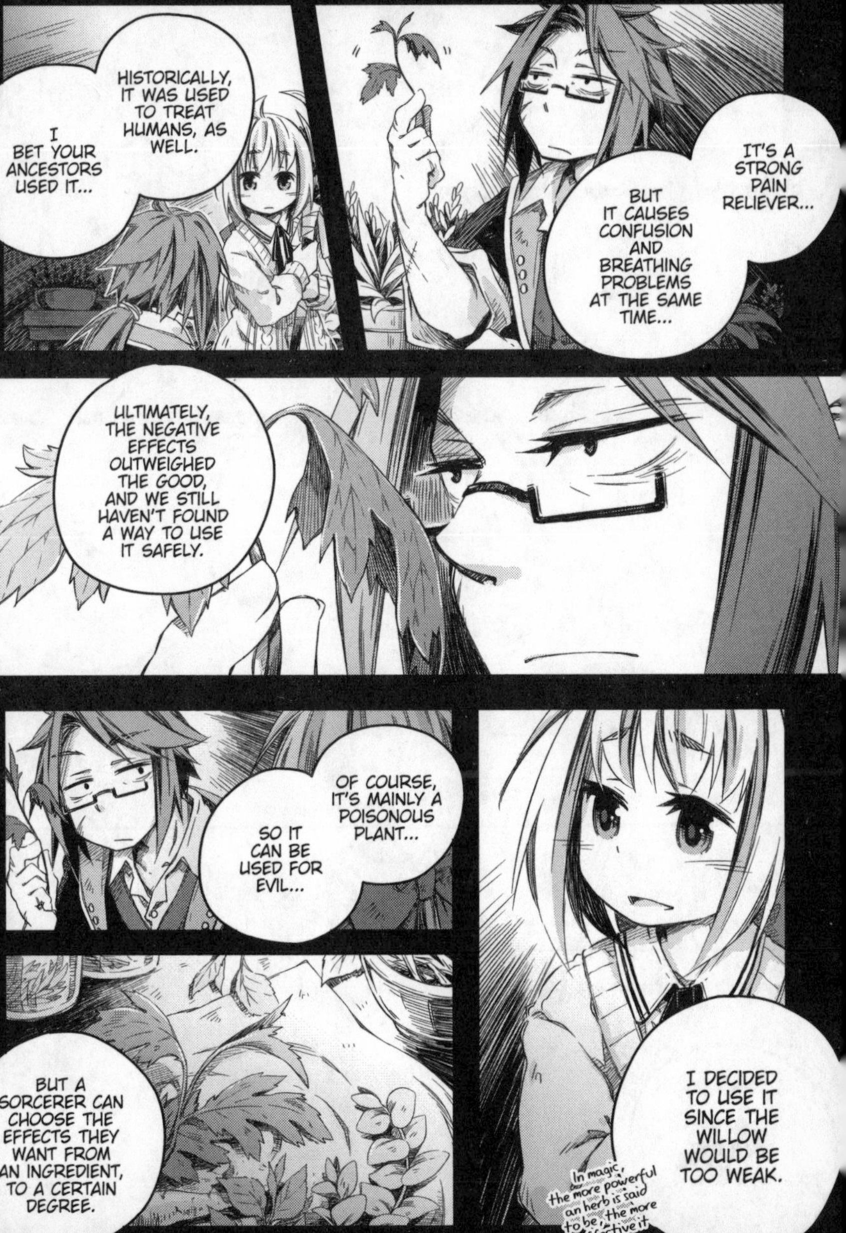
IT'S A STRONG PAIN RELIEVER...
BUT IT CAUSES CONFUSION AND BREATHING PROBLEMS AT THE SAME TIME...
HISTORICALLY, IT WAS USED TO TREAT HUMANS, AS WELL.
I BET YOUR ANCESTORS USED IT...
ULTIMATELY, THE NEGATIVE EFFECTS OUTWEIGHED THE GOOD, AND WE STILL HAVEN'T FOUND A WAY TO USE IT SAFELY.
I DECIDED TO USE IT SINCE THE WILLOW WOULD BE TOO WEAK.
In magic, the more powerful an herb is said to be, the more effective it can be.
OF COURSE, IT'S MAINLY A POISONOUS PLANT...
SO IT CAN BE USED FOR EVIL...
BUT A SORCERER CAN CHOOSE THE EFFECTS THEY WANT FROM AN INGREDIENT, TO A CERTAIN DEGREE.

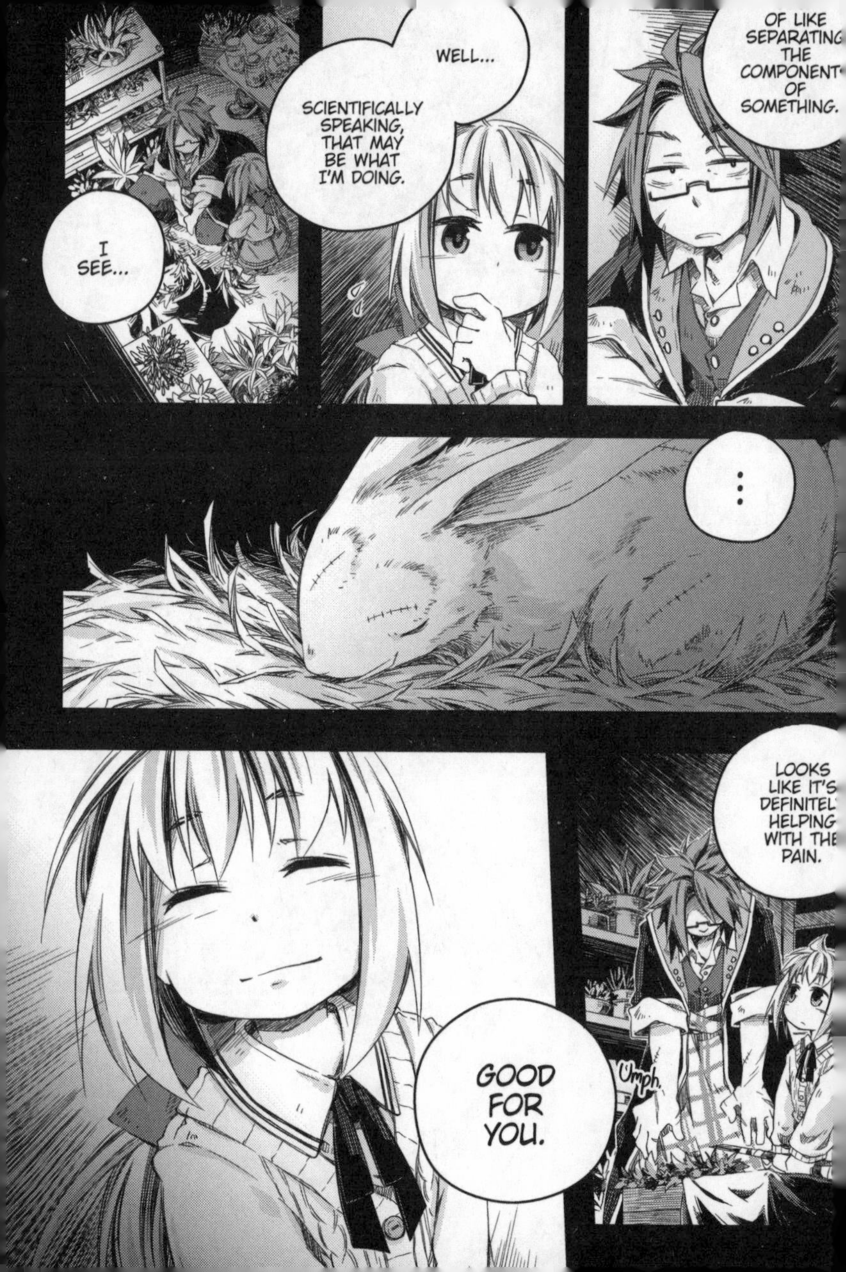
OF LIKE SEPARATING THE COMPONENT OF SOMETHING.
WELL...
SCIENTIFICALLY SPEAKING, THAT MAY BE WHAT I'M DOING.
I SEE...
...
LOOKS LIKE IT'S DEFINITEL HELPING WITH THE PAIN.
Umph.
GOOD FOR YOU.

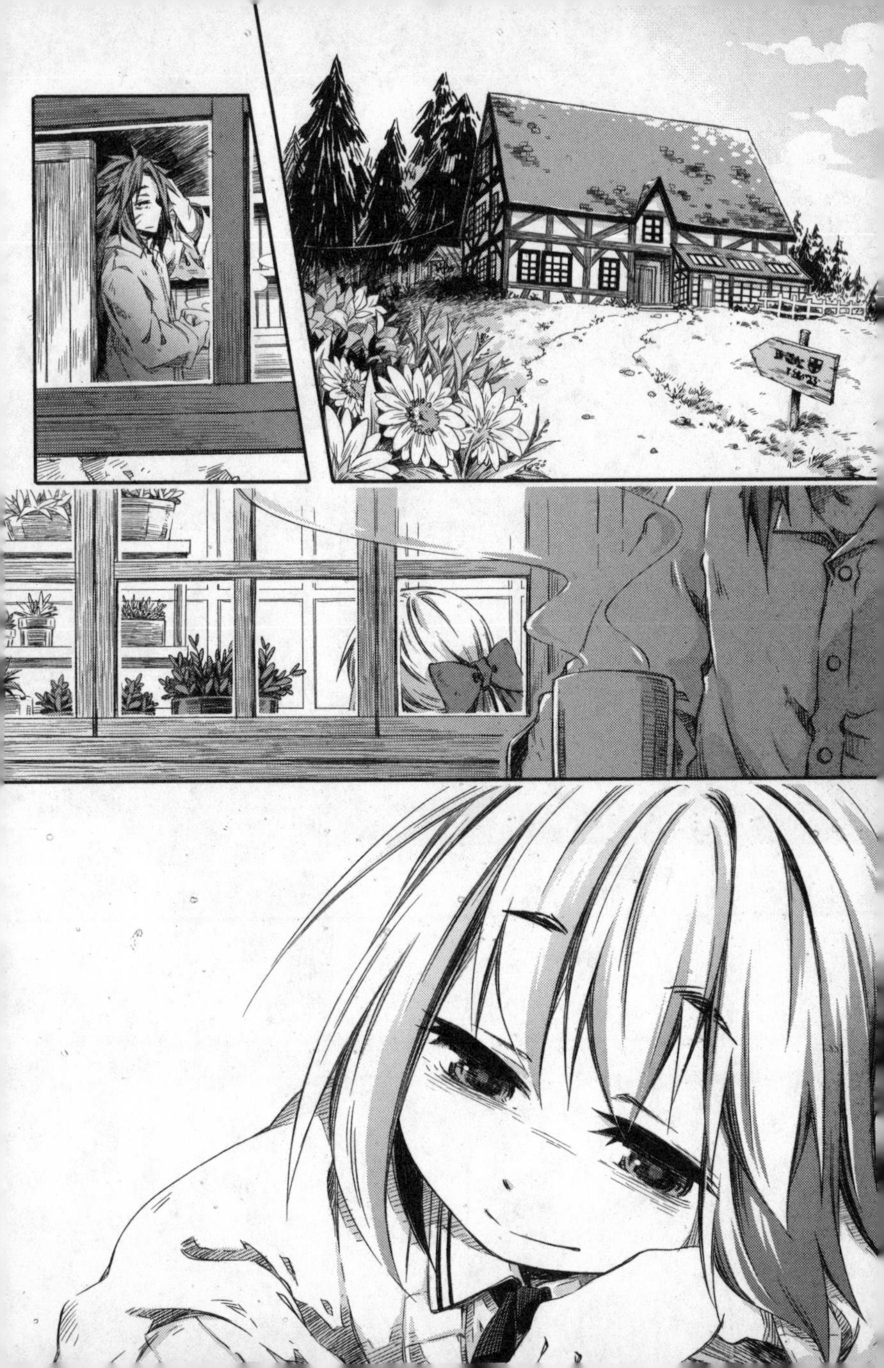

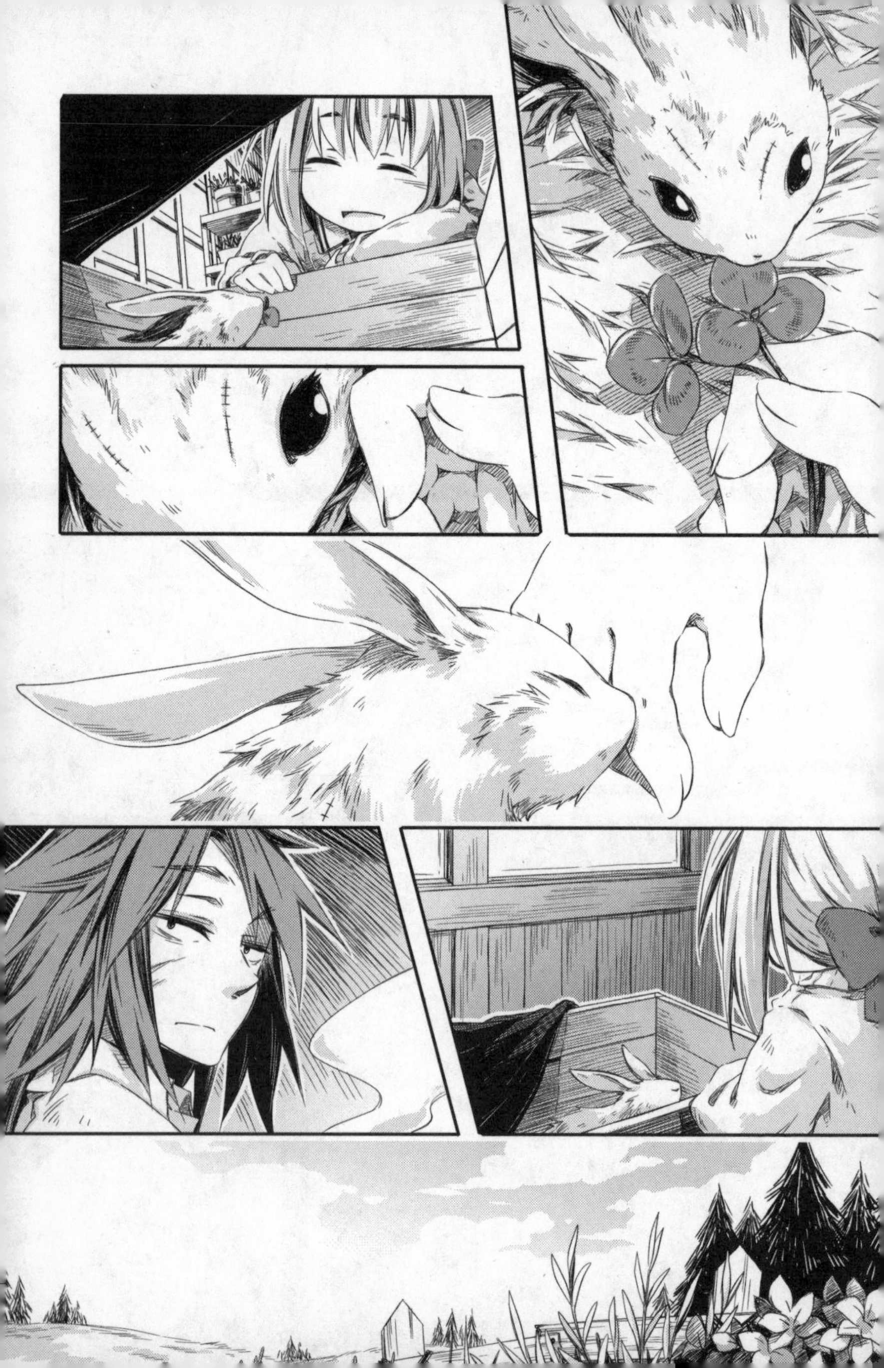

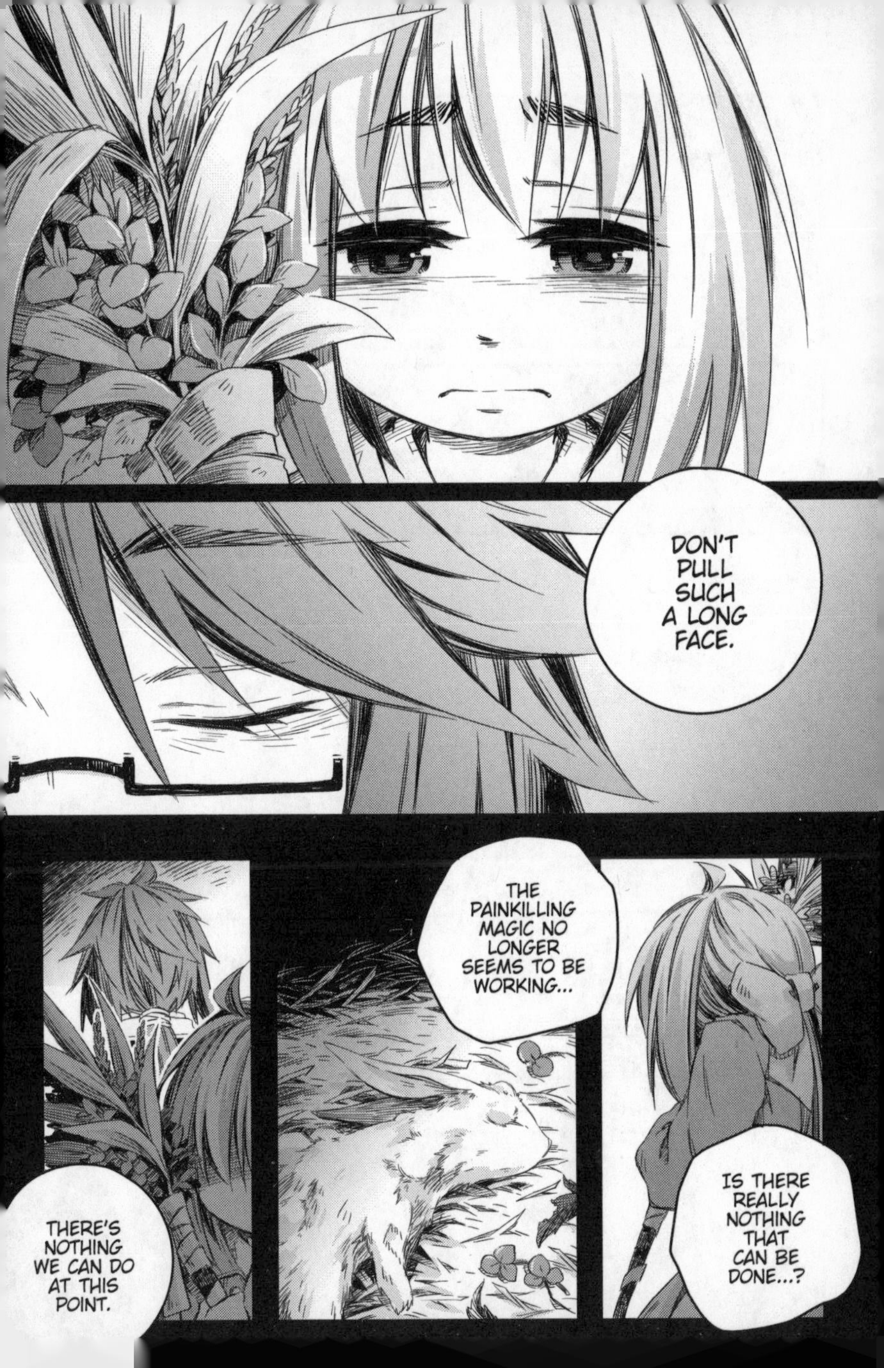
DON'T PULL SUCH A LONG FACE.
IS THERE REALLY NOTHING THAT CAN BE DONE...?
THE PAINKILLING MAGIC NO LONGER SEEMS TO BE WORKING...
THERE'S NOTHING WE CAN DO AT THIS POINT.

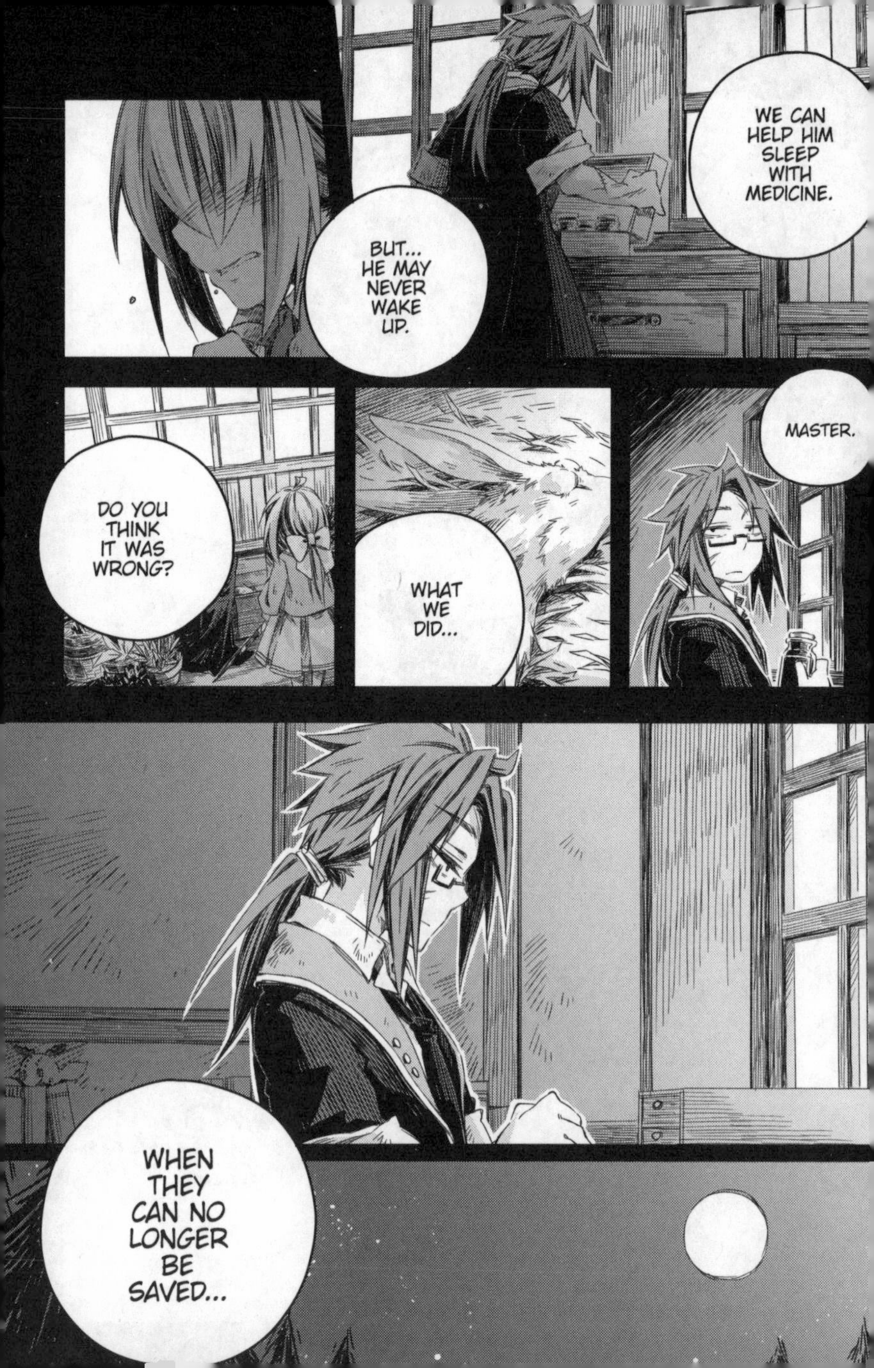
WE CAN HELP HIM SLEEP WITH MEDICINE.
BUT... HE MAY NEVER WAKE UP.
MASTER.
WHAT WE DID...
DO YOU THINK IT WAS WRONG?
WHEN THEY CAN NO LONGER BE SAVED...

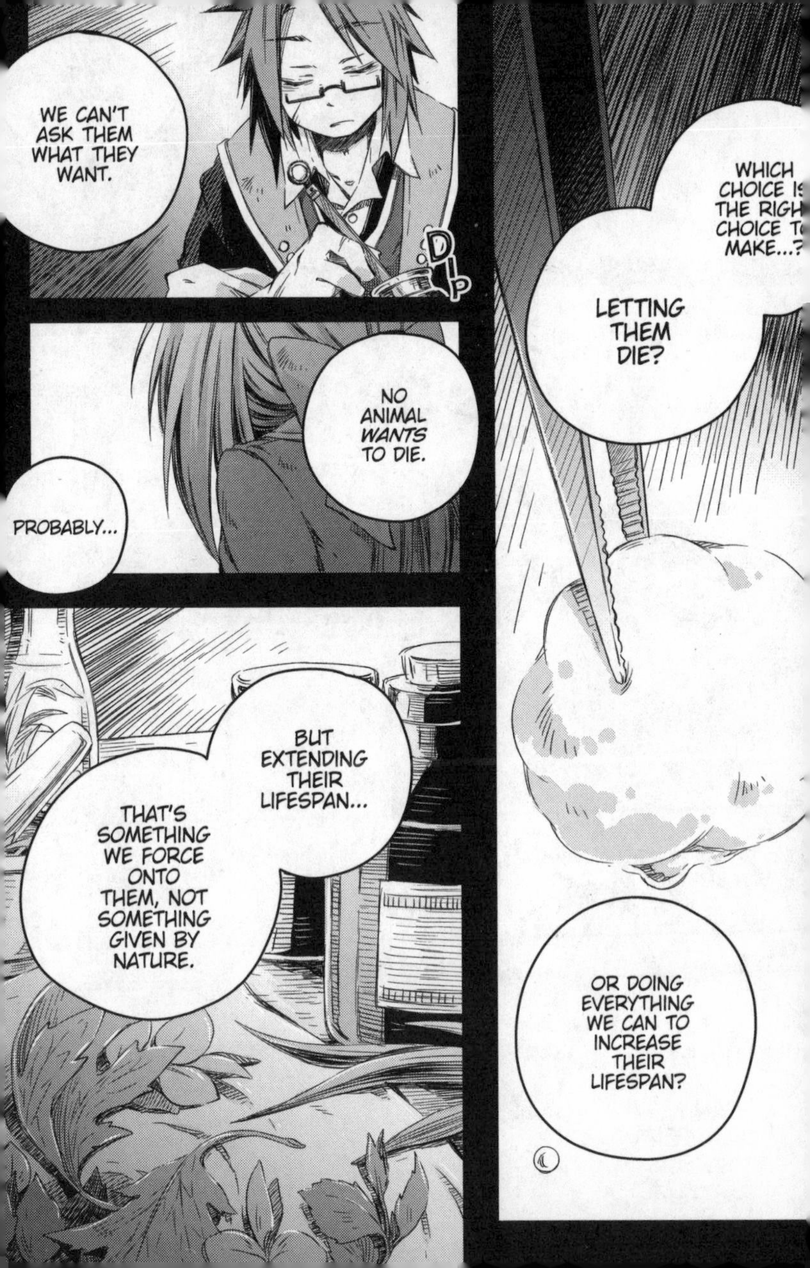
WHICH CHOICE I THE RIGH CHOICE T MAKE...?
LETTING THEM DIE?
OR DOING EVERYTHING WE CAN TO INCREASE THEIR LIFESPAN?
WE CAN'T ASK THEM WHAT THEY WANT.
DIP
NO ANIMAL *WANTS* TO DIE.
PROBABLY...
BUT EXTENDING THEIR LIFESPAN...
THAT'S SOMETHING WE FORCE ONTO THEM, NOT SOMETHING GIVEN BY NATURE.

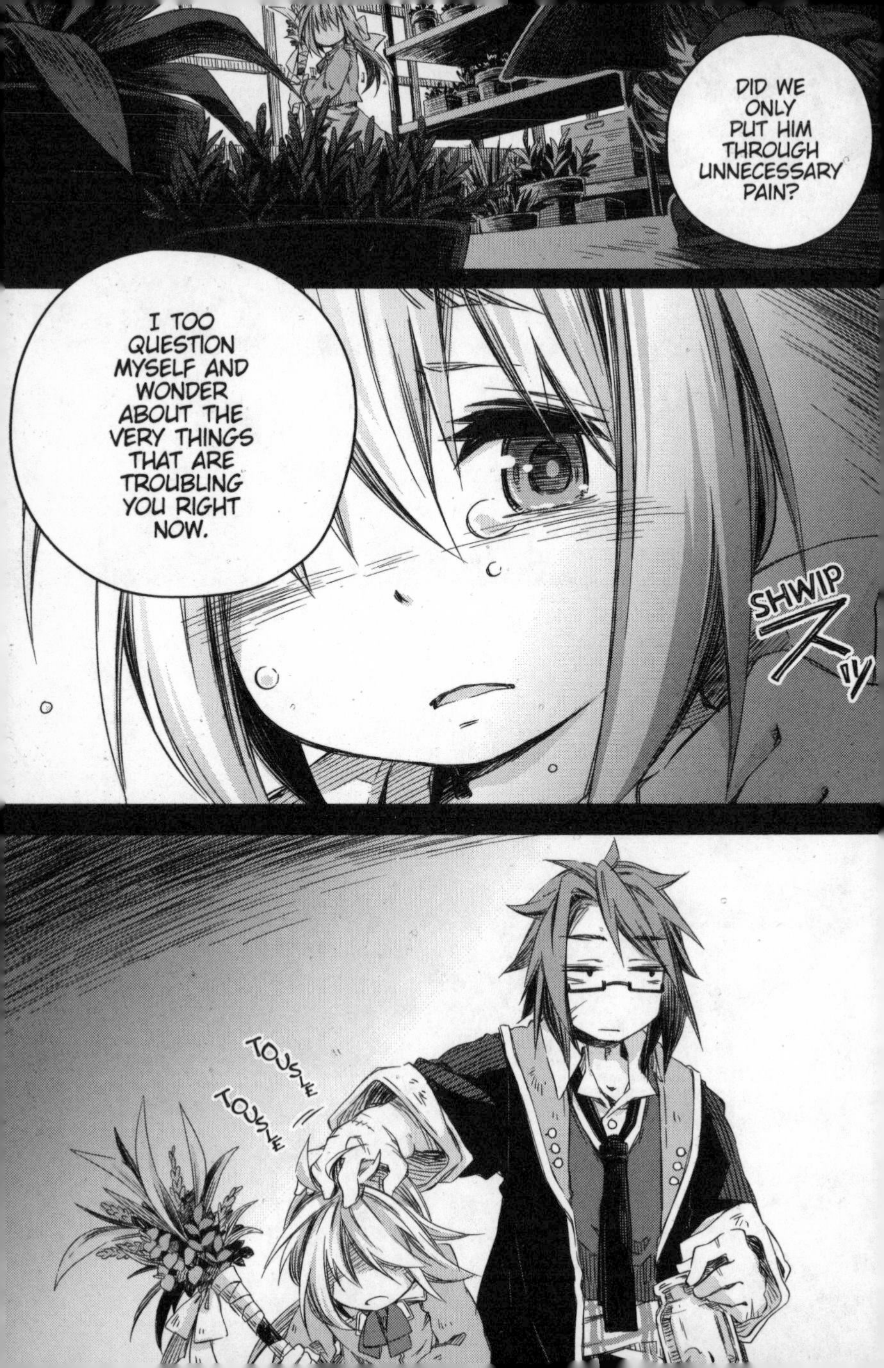
DID WE ONLY PUT HIM THROUGH UNNECESSARY PAIN?
I TOO QUESTION MYSELF AND WONDER ABOUT THE VERY THINGS THAT ARE TROUBLING YOU RIGHT NOW.
SHWIP
TOUSLE
TOUSLE

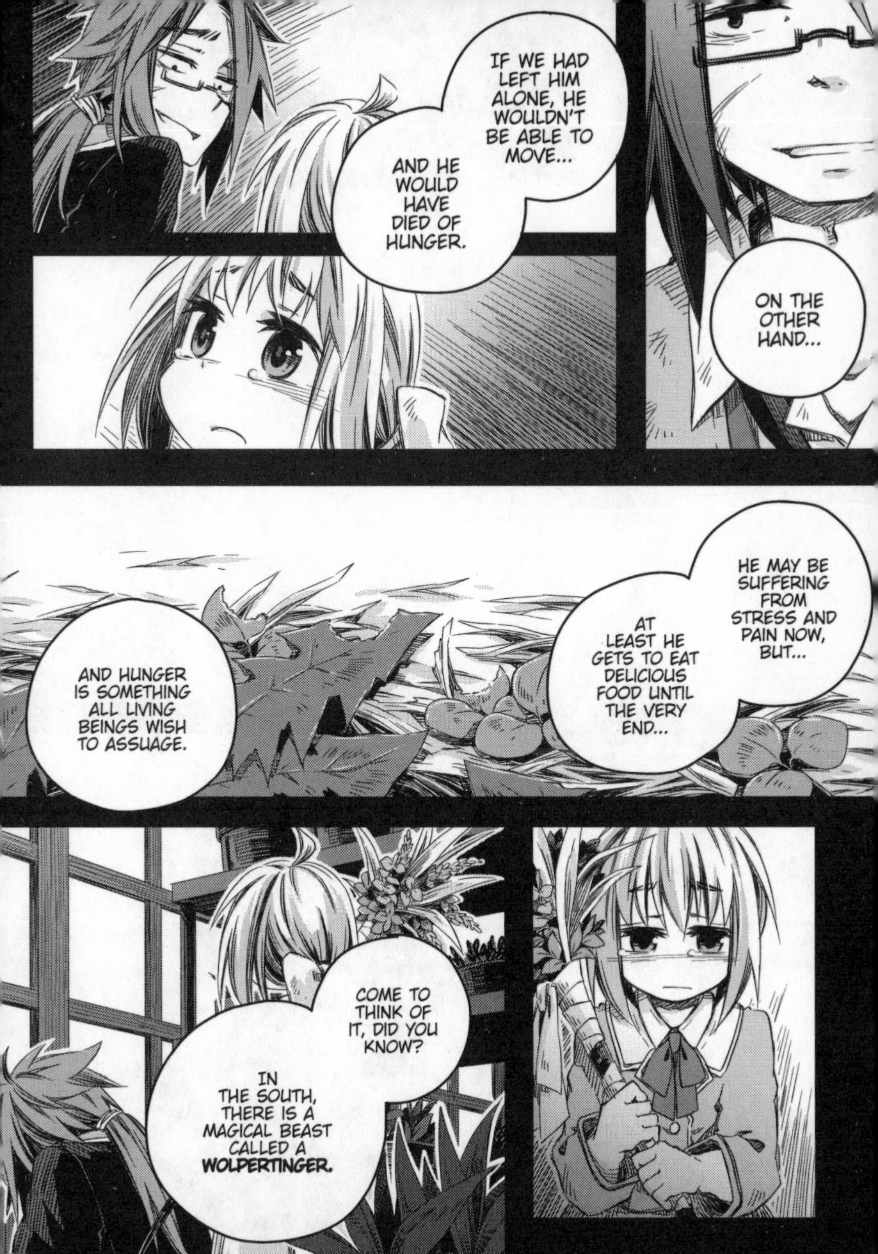
ON THE OTHER HAND...
IF WE HAD LEFT HIM ALONE, HE WOULDN'T BE ABLE TO MOVE...
AND HE WOULD HAVE DIED OF HUNGER.
HE MAY BE SUFFERING FROM STRESS AND PAIN NOW, BUT...
AT LEAST HE GETS TO EAT DELICIOUS FOOD UNTIL THE VERY END...
AND HUNGER IS SOMETHING ALL LIVING BEINGS WISH TO ASSUAGE.
COME TO THINK OF IT, DID YOU KNOW?
IN THE SOUTH, THERE IS A MAGICAL BEAST CALLED A **WOLPERTINGER.**

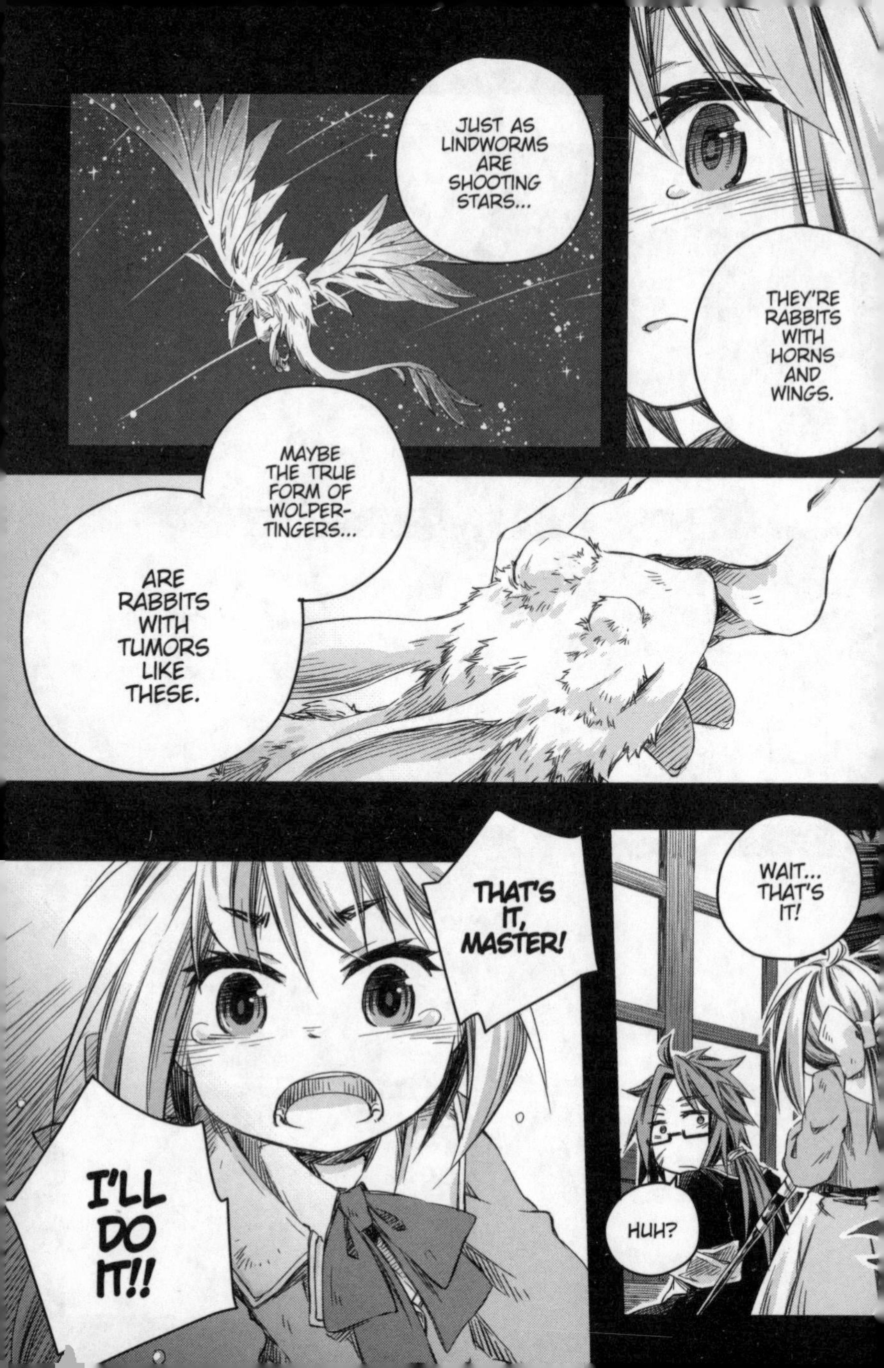
THEY'RE RABBITS WITH HORNS AND WINGS.
JUST AS LINDWORMS ARE SHOOTING STARS...
MAYBE THE TRUE FORM OF WOLPER-TINGERS...
ARE RABBITS WITH TUMORS LIKE THESE.
WAIT... THAT'S IT!
HUH?
THAT'S IT, MASTER!
I'LL DO IT!!

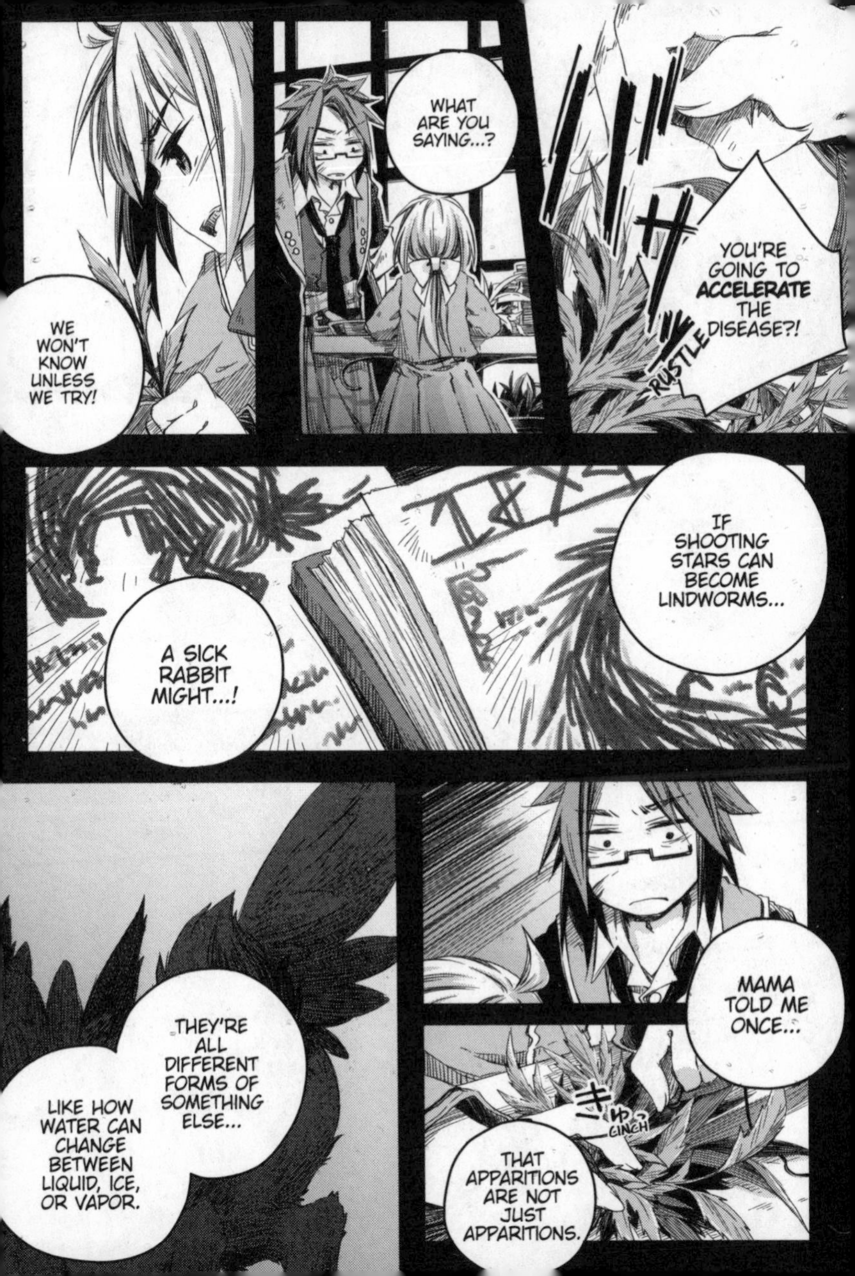
YOU'RE GOING TO ACCELERATE THE DISEASE?!
RUSTLE
WHAT ARE YOU SAYING...?
WE WON'T KNOW UNLESS WE TRY!
IF SHOOTING STARS CAN BECOME LINDWORMS...
A SICK RABBIT MIGHT...!
MAMA TOLD ME ONCE...
GINCH
THAT APPARITIONS ARE NOT JUST APPARITIONS.
THEY'RE ALL DIFFERENT FORMS OF SOMETHING ELSE...
LIKE HOW WATER CAN CHANGE BETWEEN LIQUID, ICE, OR VAPOR.

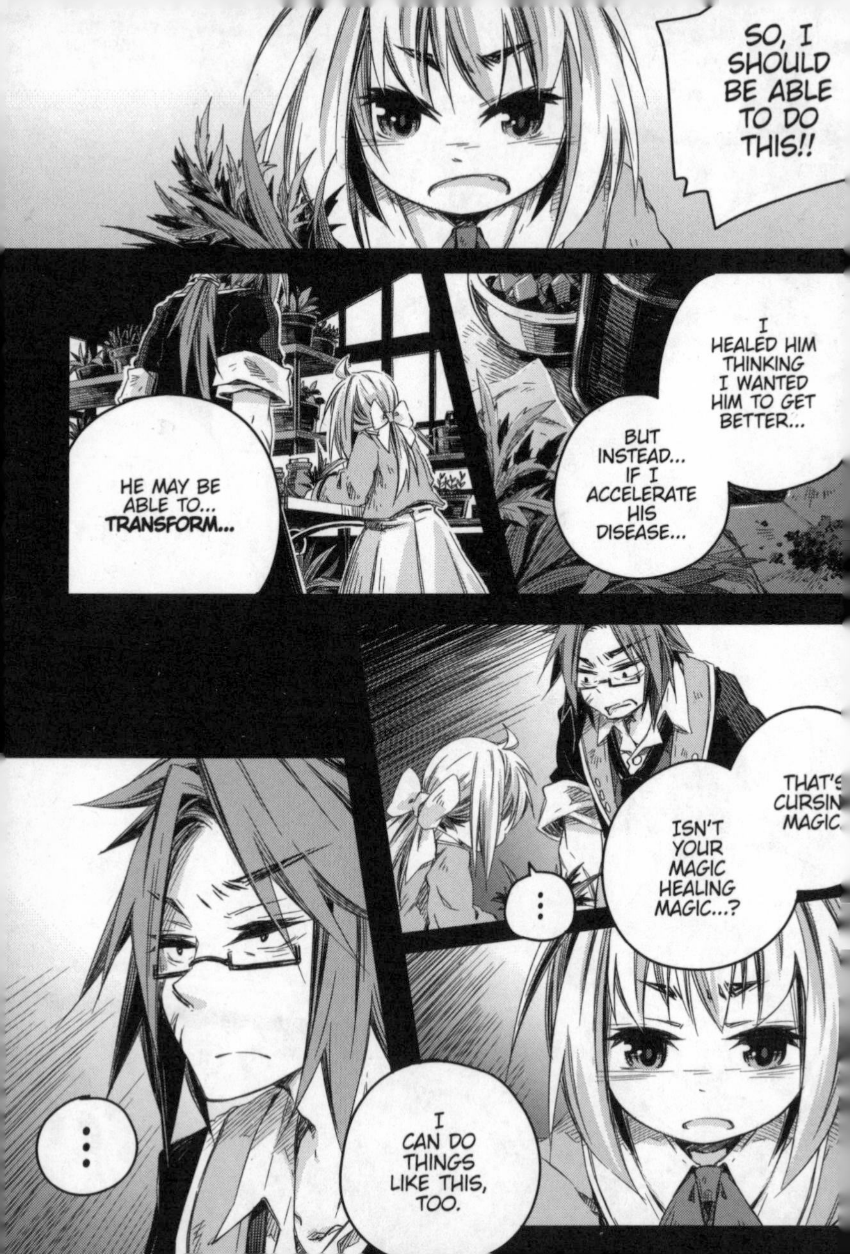
SO, I SHOULD BE ABLE TO DO THIS!!
I HEALED HIM THINKING I WANTED HIM TO GET BETTER...
BUT INSTEAD... IF I ACCELERATE HIS DISEASE...
HE MAY BE ABLE TO... **TRANSFORM...**
THAT'S CURSIN MAGIC.
ISN'T YOUR MAGIC HEALING MAGIC...?
...
I CAN DO THINGS LIKE THIS, TOO.
...

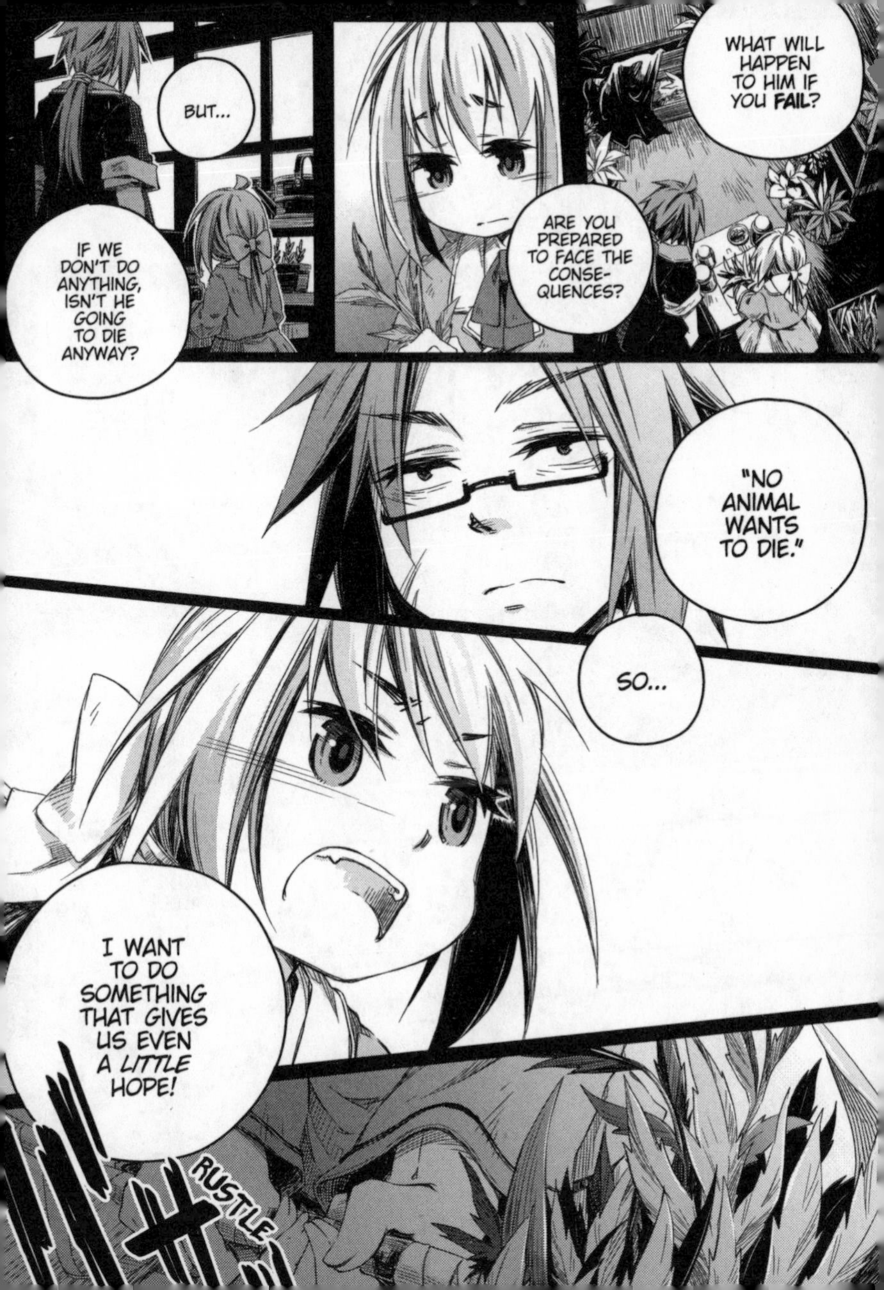
WHAT WILL HAPPEN TO HIM IF YOU **FAIL**?
ARE YOU PREPARED TO FACE THE CONSE-QUENCES?
BUT...
IF WE DON'T DO ANYTHING, ISN'T HE GOING TO DIE ANYWAY?
"NO ANIMAL WANTS TO DIE."
SO...
I WANT TO DO SOMETHING THAT GIVES US EVEN A *LITTLE* HOPE!
RUSTLE

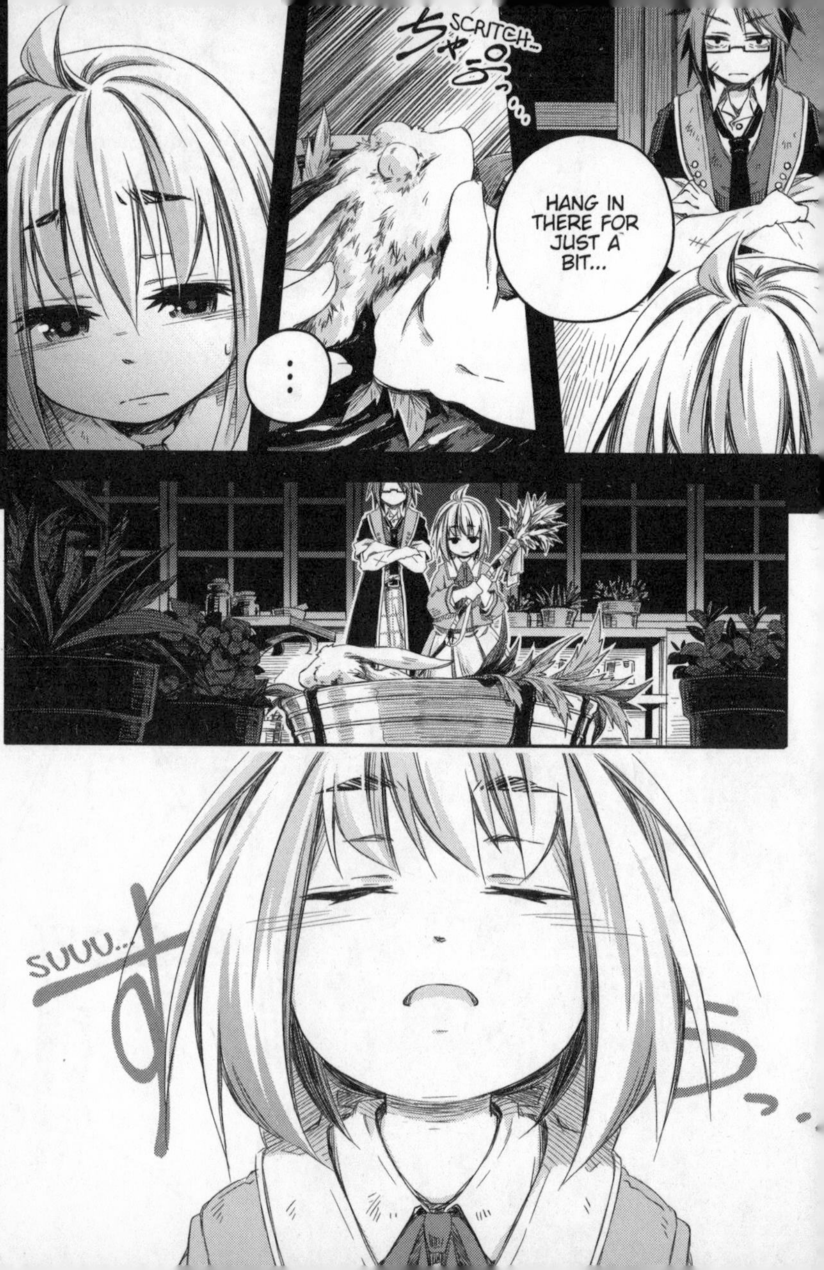
HANG IN THERE FOR JUST A BIT...
SCRITCH...
...
SUUU...

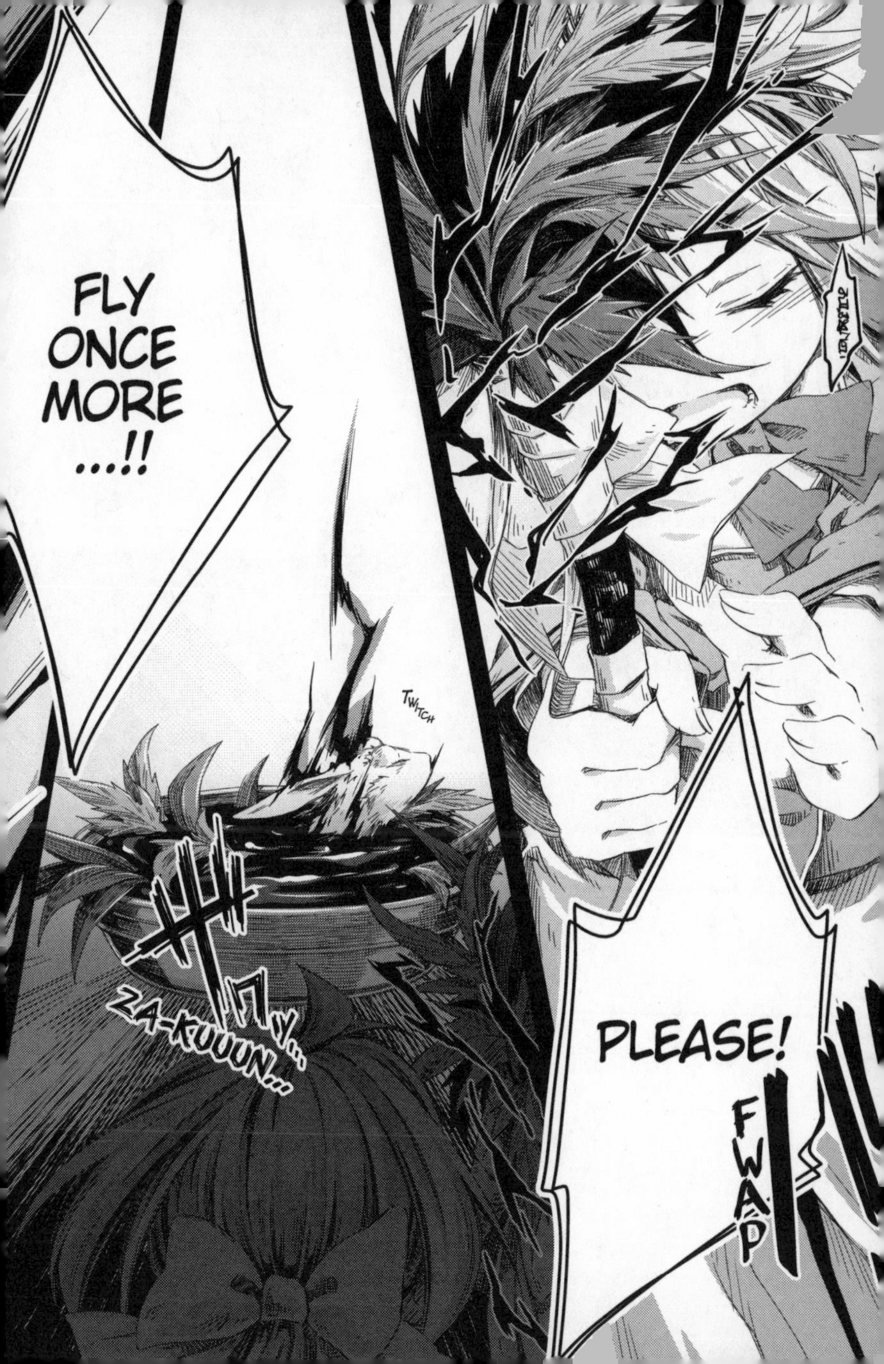
PLEASE!
FWAP
FLY ONCE MORE ...!!
TWITCH
ZA-KUUUN...

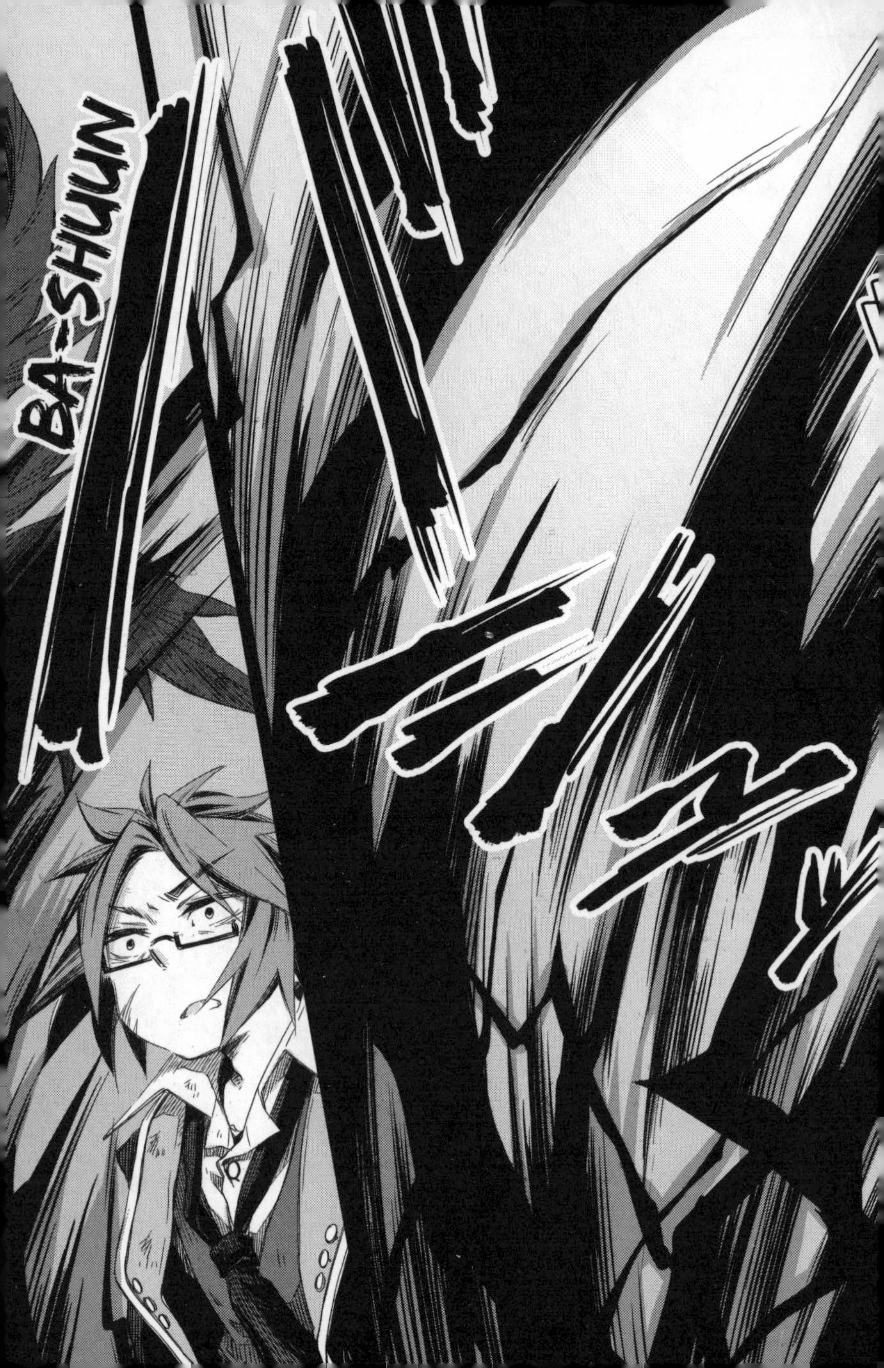
BA-SHUUN

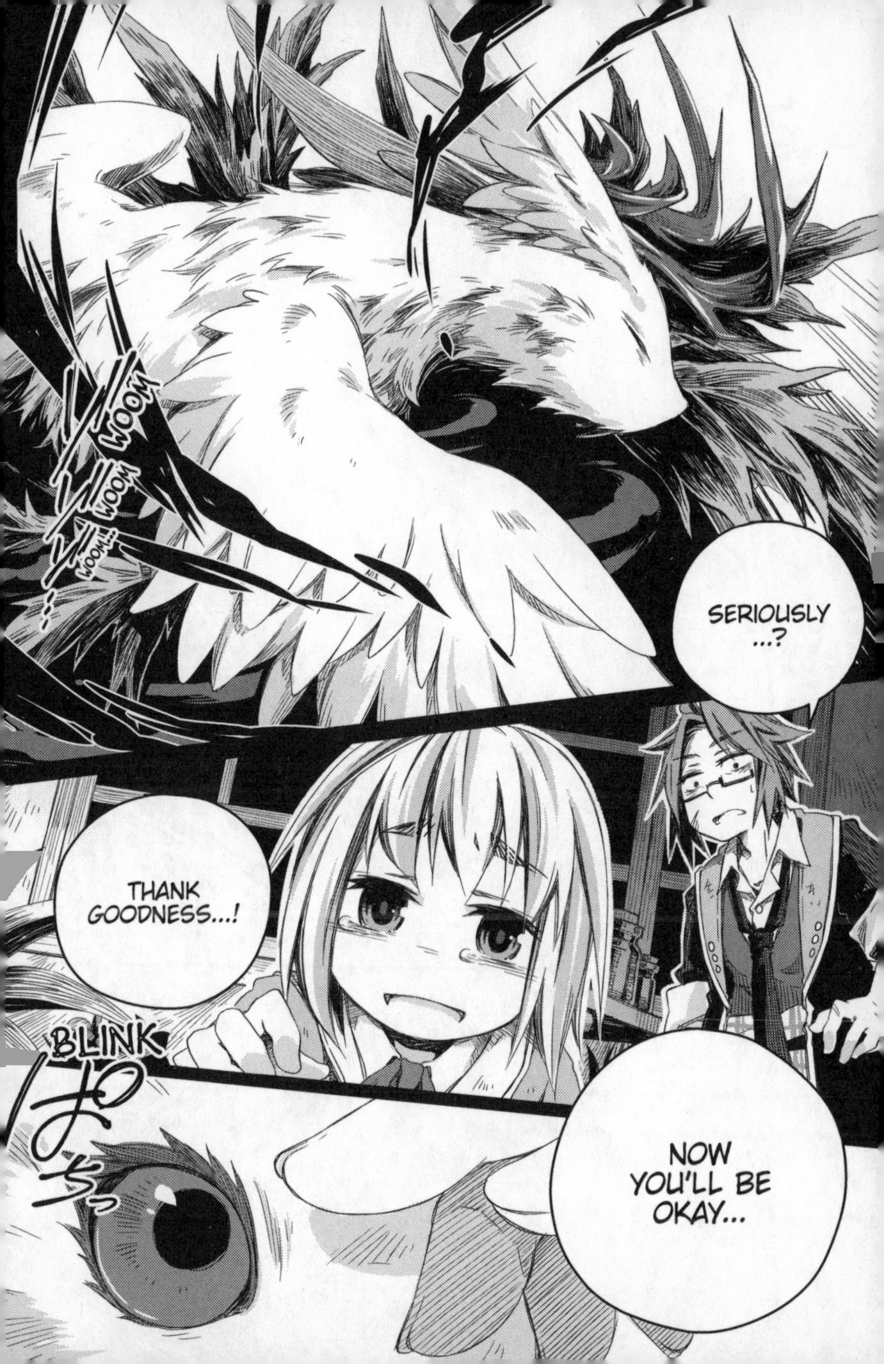
...WOOM!! WOOM WOOM
SERIOUSLY ...?
THANK GOODNESS...!
NOW YOU'LL BE OKAY...
BLINK

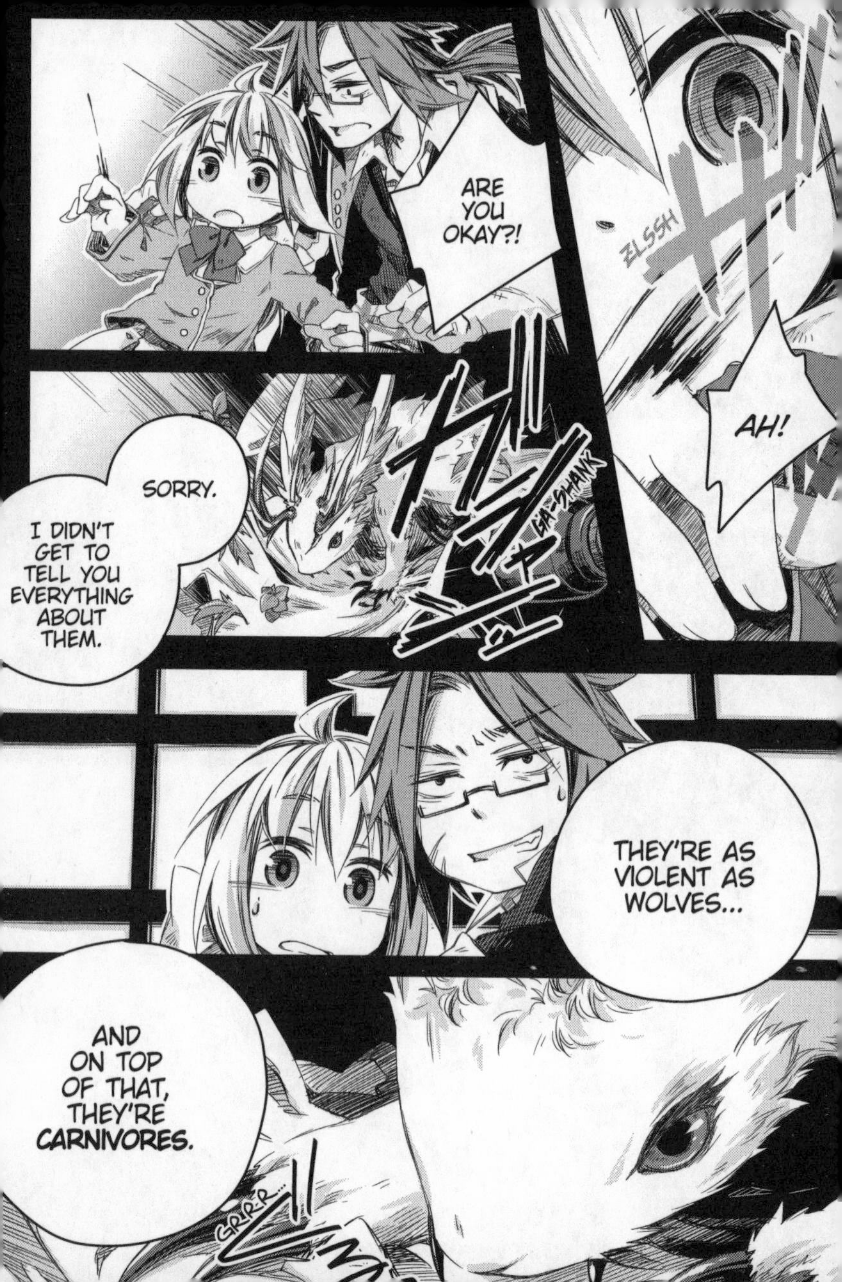
ELSSH
AH!
ARE YOU OKAY?!
GA-SHANK
SORRY.
I DIDN'T GET TO TELL YOU EVERYTHING ABOUT THEM.
THEY'RE AS VIOLENT AS WOLVES...
AND ON TOP OF THAT, THEY'RE **CARNIVORES.**
GRRR...

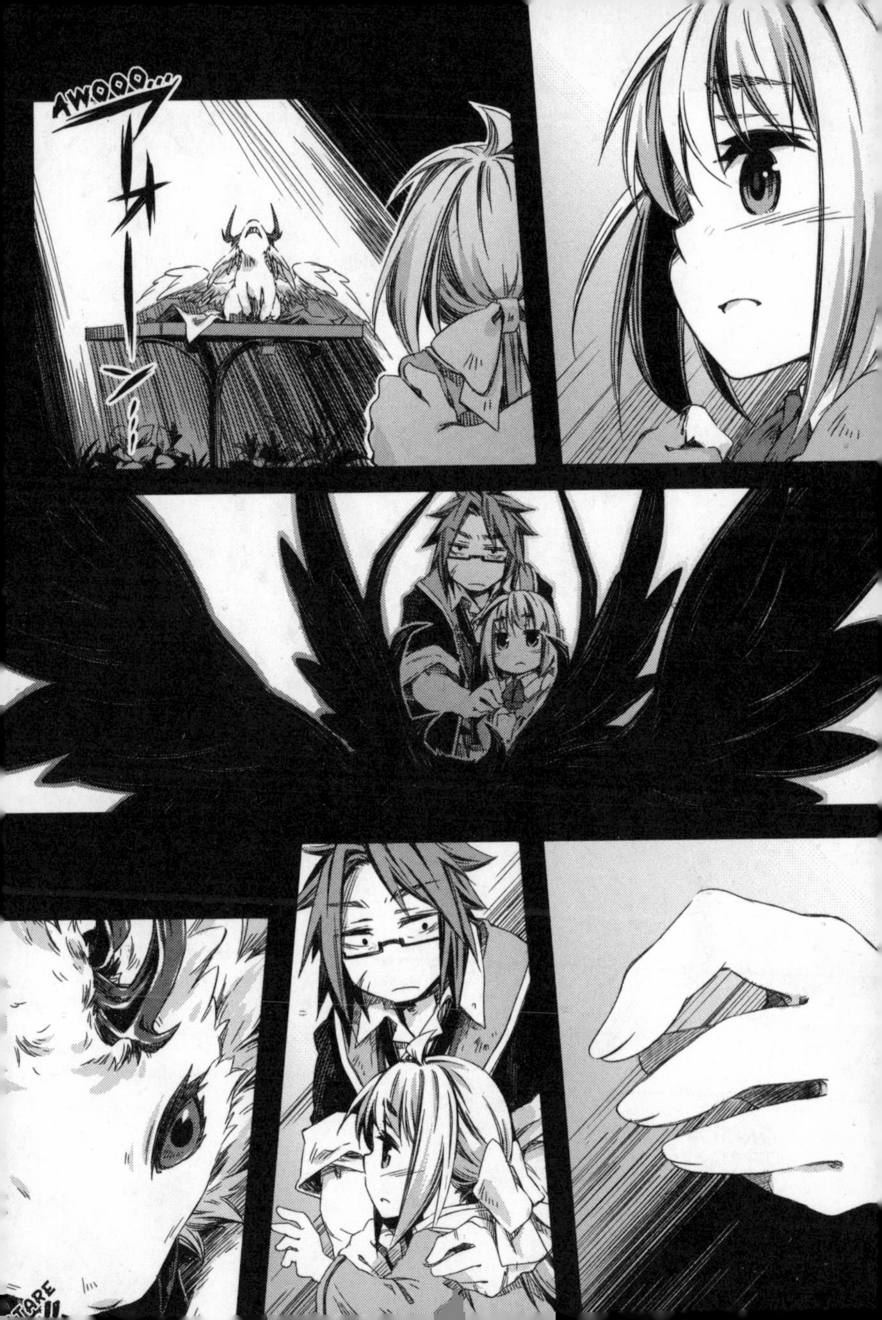
AWOOO...
アオーーン…
TARE

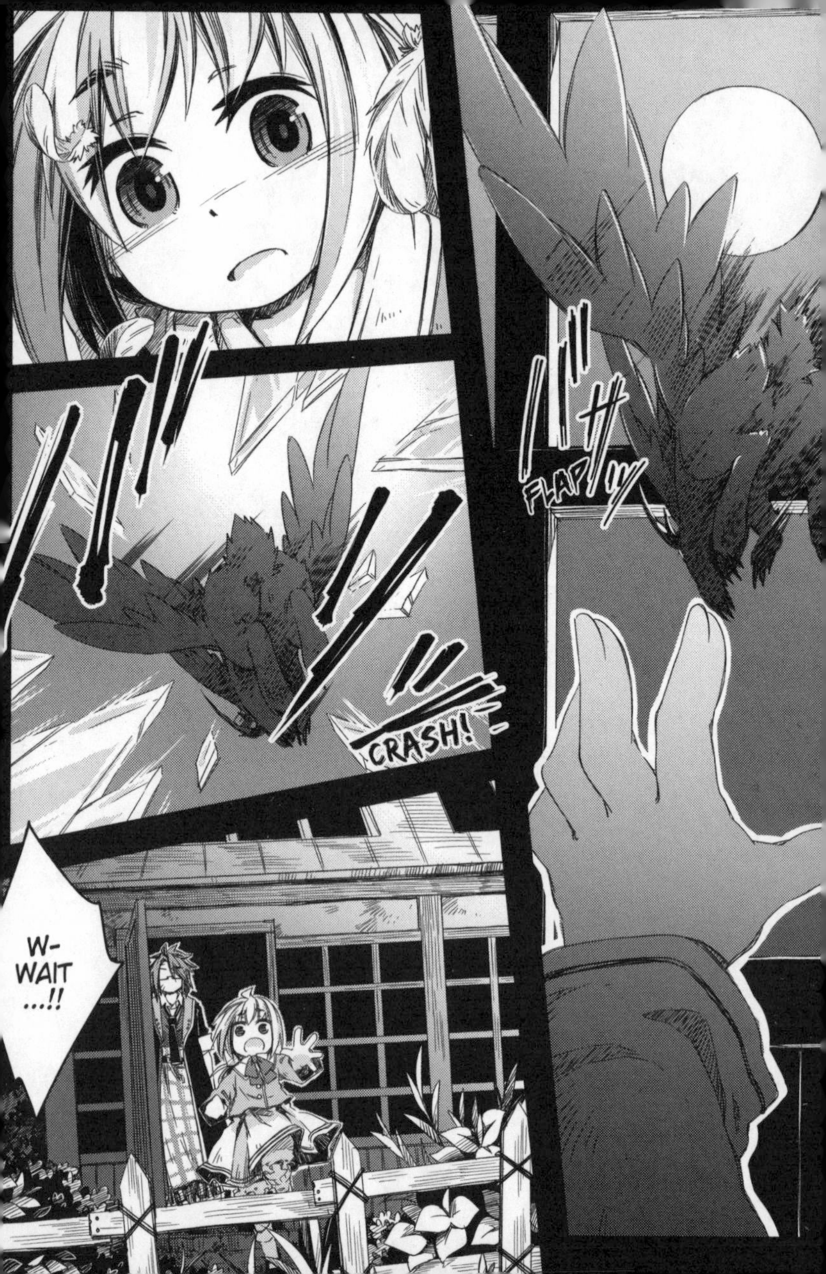
FLAP
CRASH!
W-WAIT ...!!

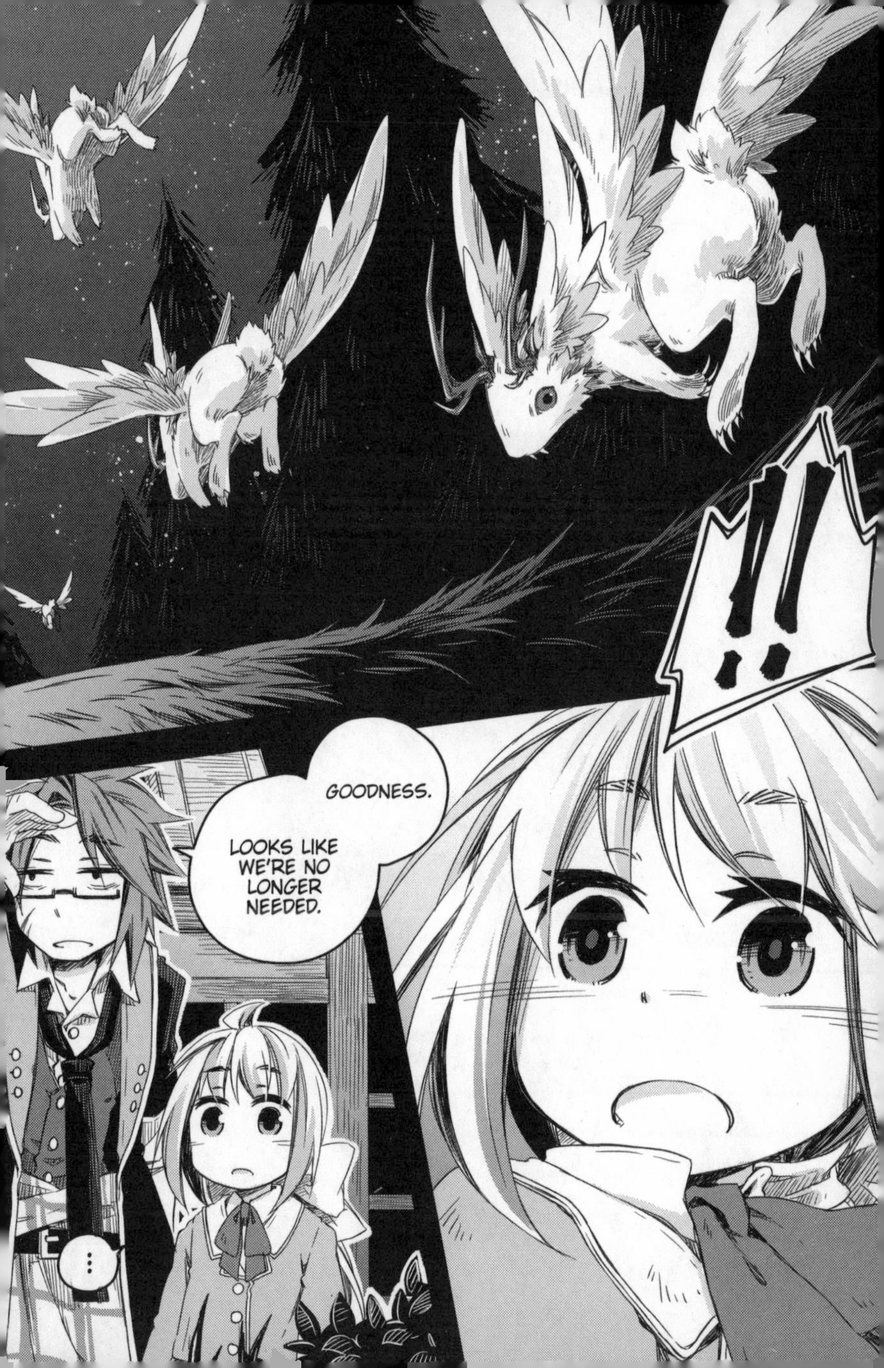
!!
GOODNESS.
LOOKS LIKE WE'RE NO LONGER NEEDED.
...

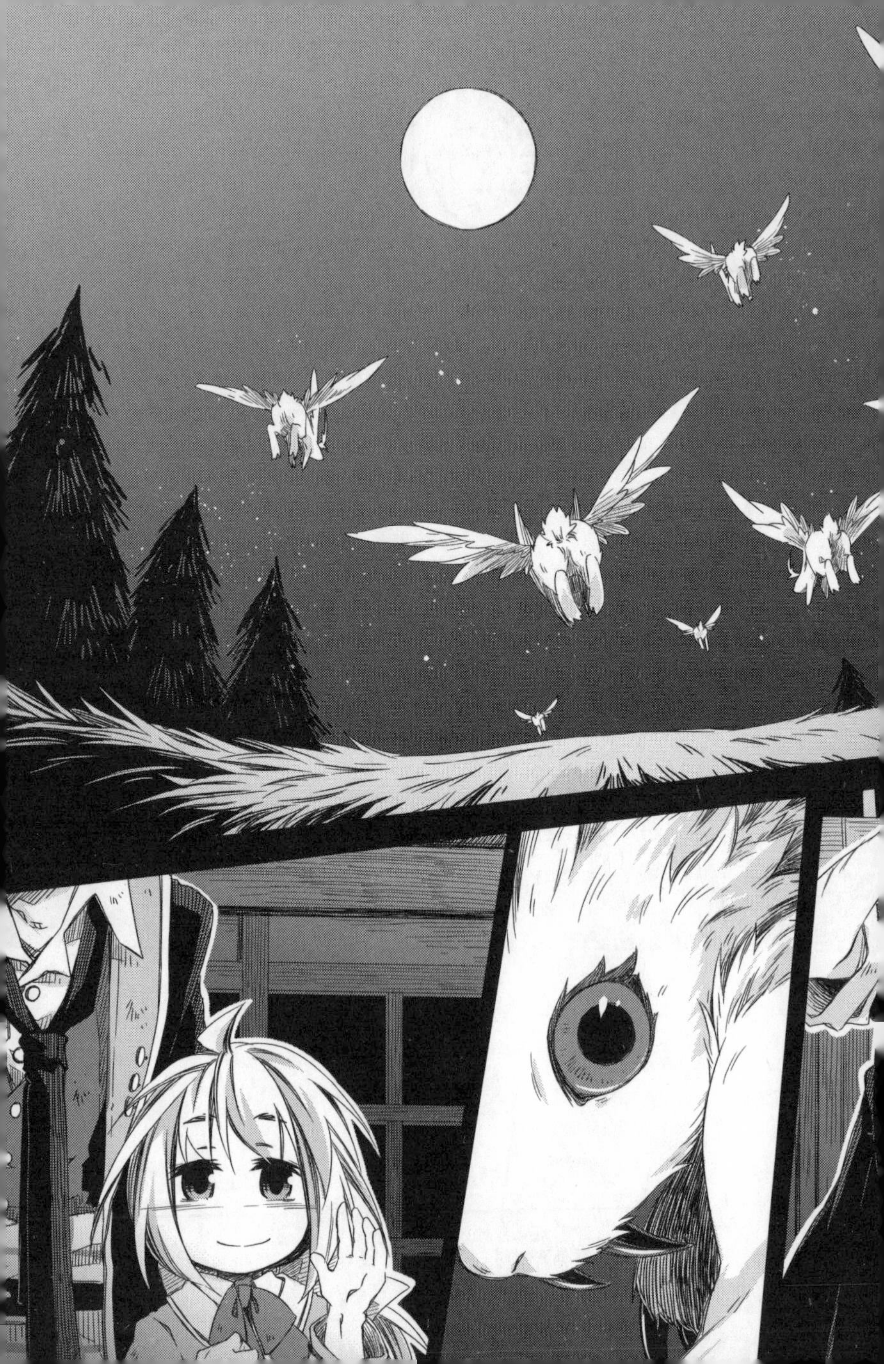

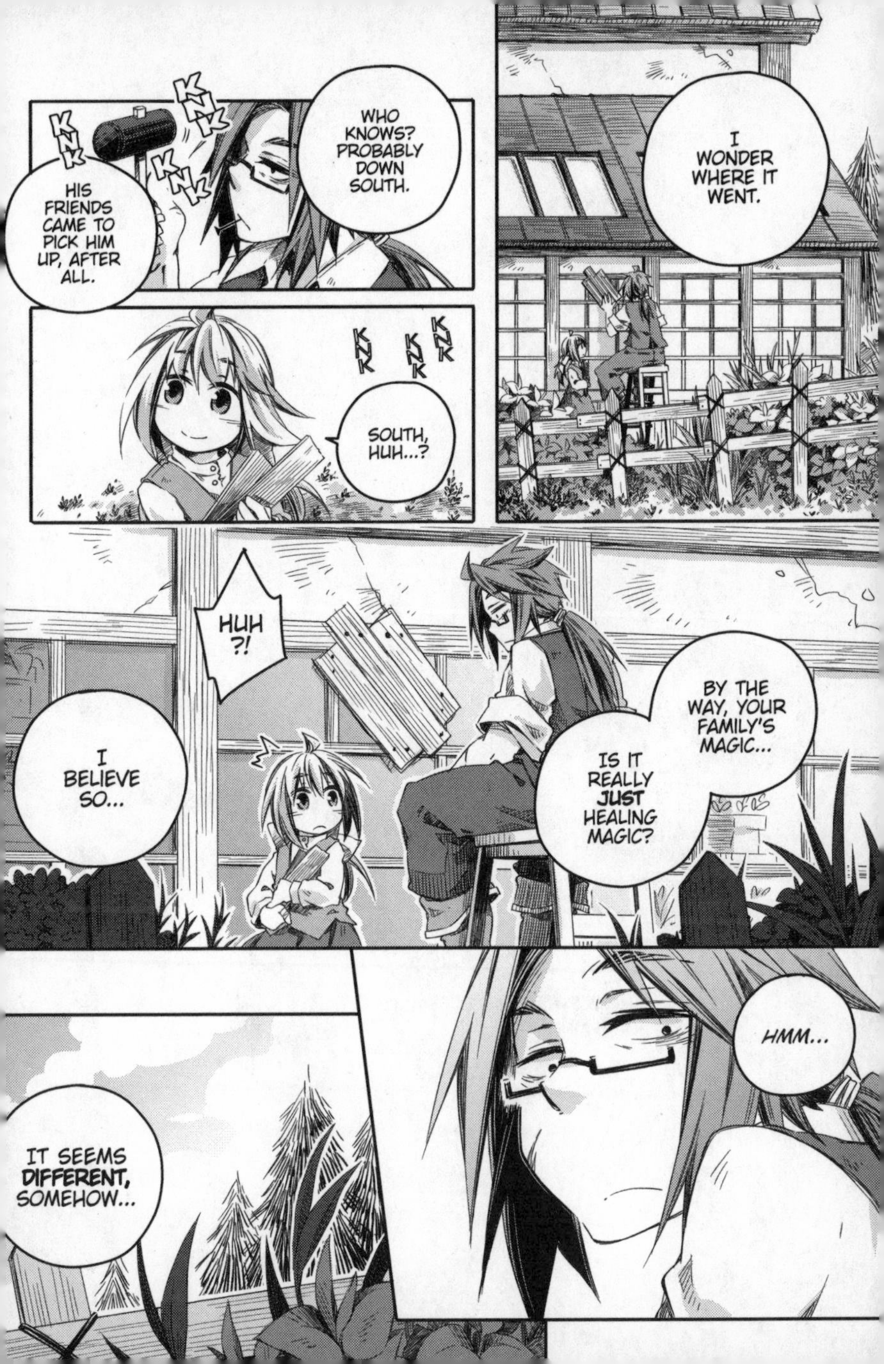
I WONDER WHERE IT WENT.
KNK KNK
WHO KNOWS? PROBABLY DOWN SOUTH.
KNK
HIS FRIENDS CAME TO PICK HIM UP, AFTER ALL.
KNK KNK KNK
SOUTH, HUH...?
BY THE WAY, YOUR FAMILY'S MAGIC...
IS IT REALLY **JUST** HEALING MAGIC?
HUH?!
I BELIEVE SO...
HMM...
IT SEEMS **DIFFERENT,** SOMEHOW...

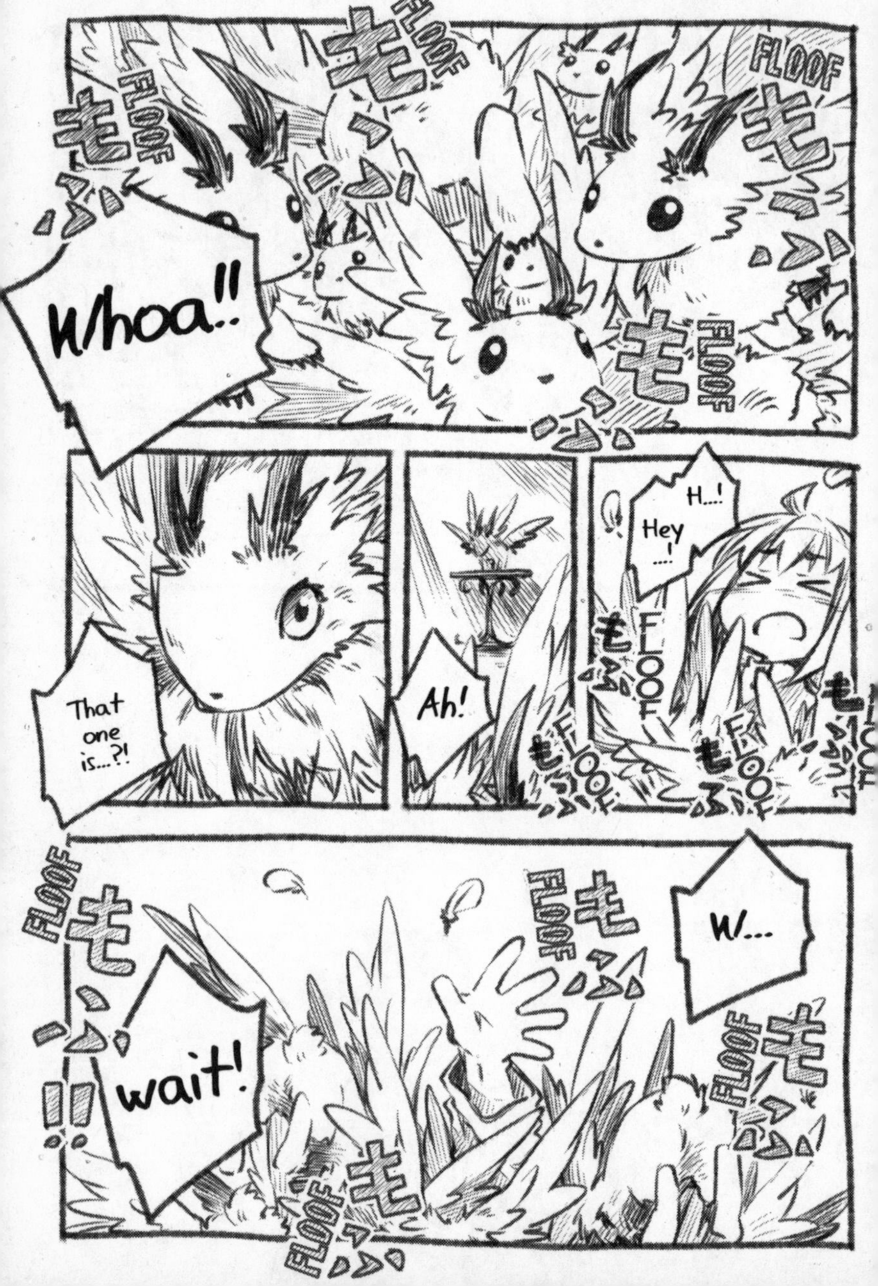
FLOOF
FLOOF
FLOOF
FLOOF
Whoa!!
H...!
Hey...!
FLOOF
FLOOF
FLOOF
FLOOF
Ah!
That one is...?!
W...
FLOOF
FLOOF
FLOOF
wait!
FLOOF

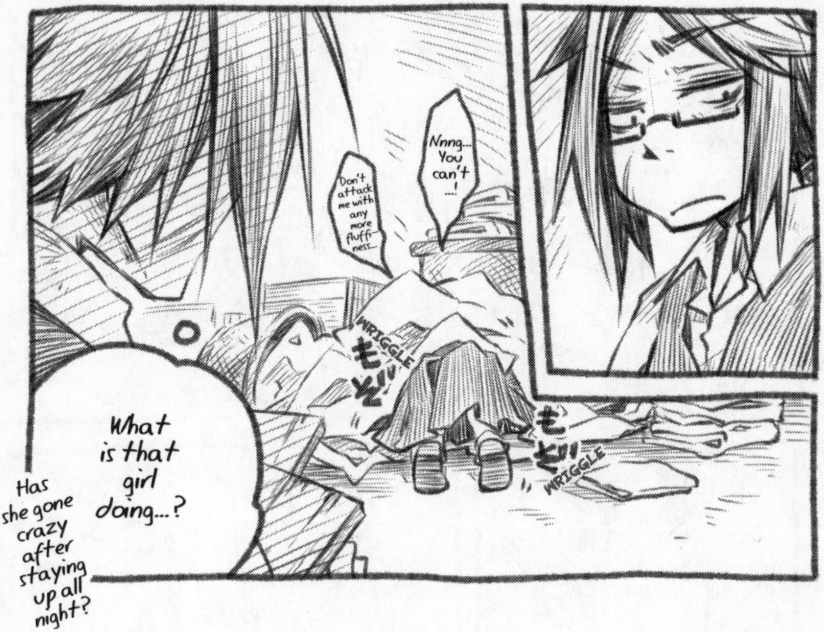
Nnng... You can't...!
Don't attack me with any more fluffiness...
WRIGGLE
WRIGGLE
What is that girl doing...?
Has she gone crazy after staying up all night?

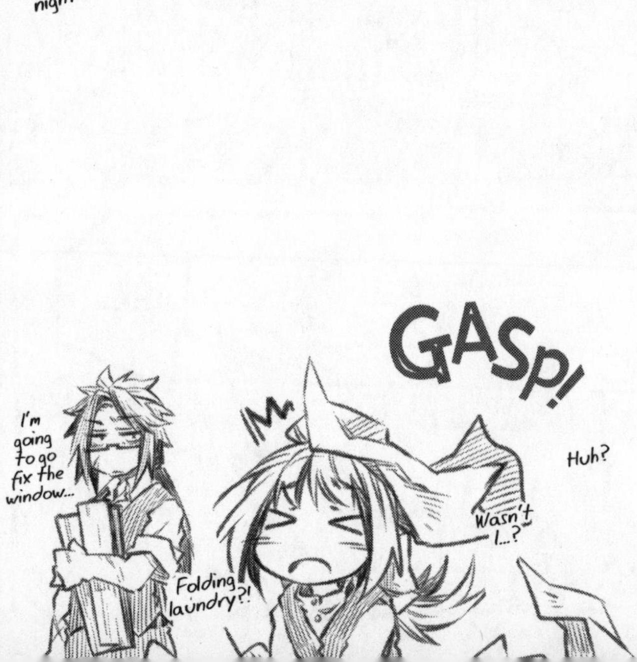
GASP!
Huh?
Wasn't I...?
I'm going to go fix the window...
Folding laundry?!

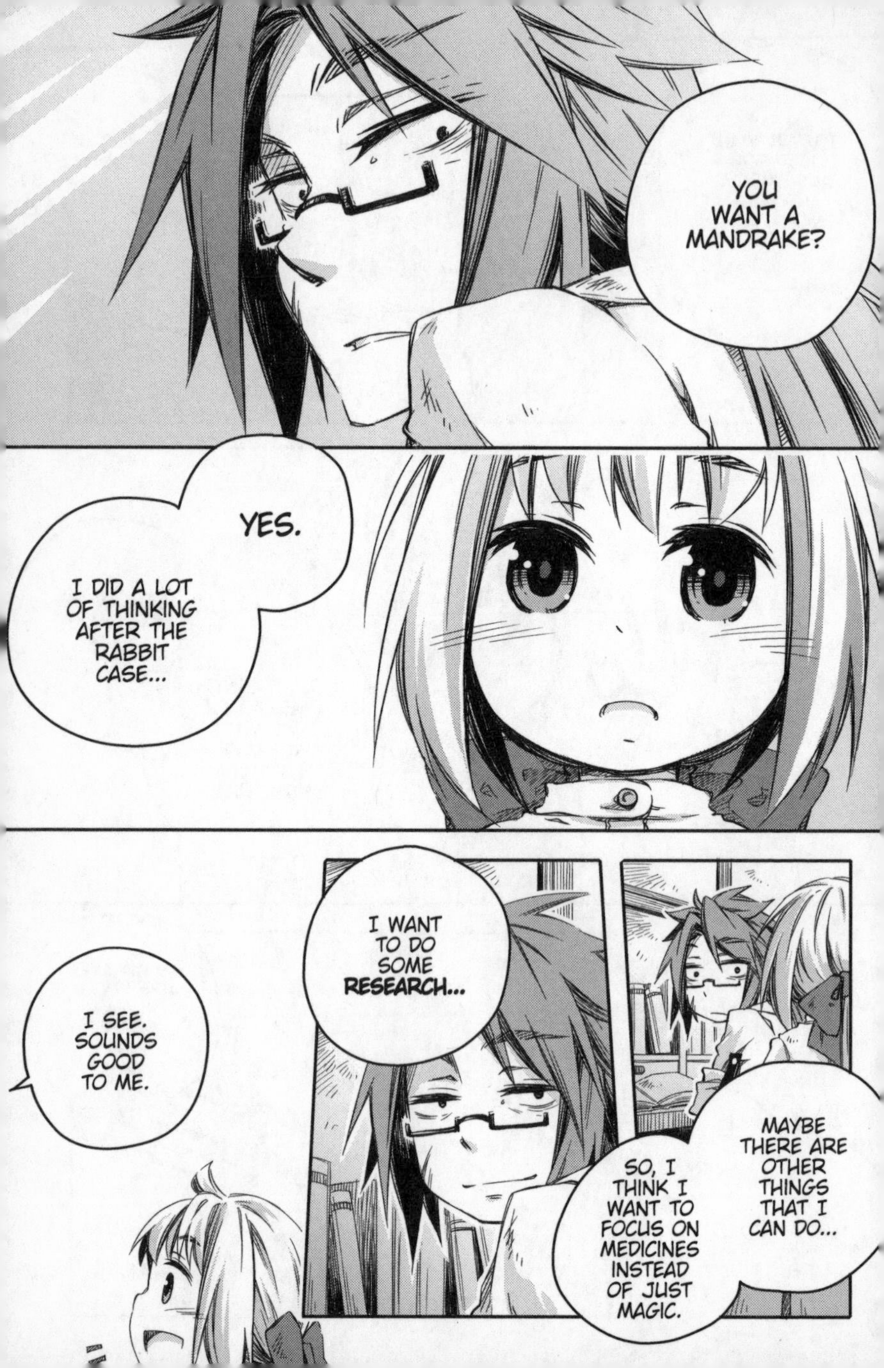
YOU WANT A MANDRAKE?
YES.
I DID A LOT OF THINKING AFTER THE RABBIT CASE...
MAYBE THERE ARE OTHER THINGS THAT I CAN DO...
SO, I THINK I WANT TO FOCUS ON MEDICINES INSTEAD OF JUST MAGIC.
I WANT TO DO SOME **RESEARCH...**
I SEE. SOUNDS GOOD TO ME.

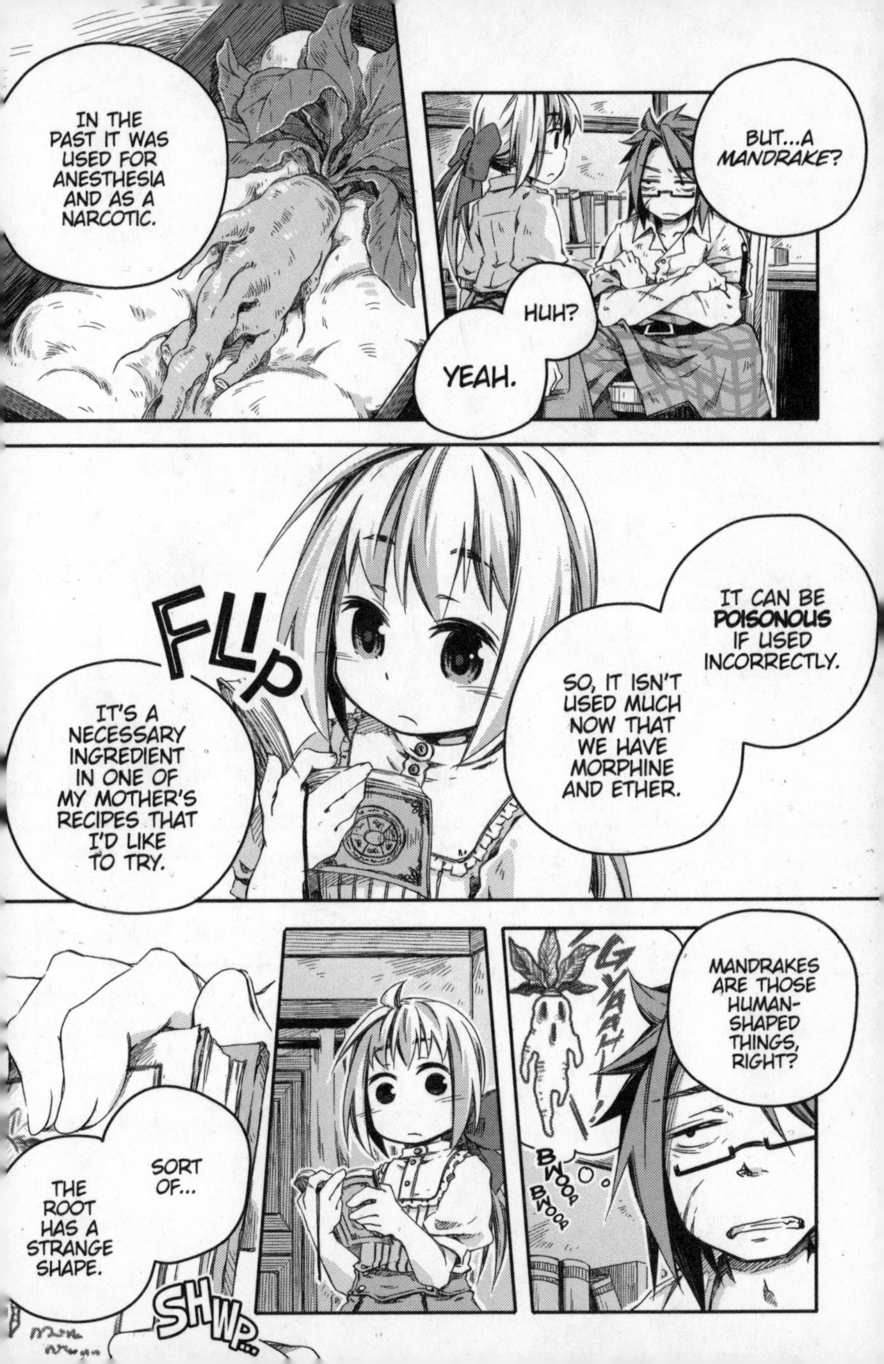
BUT...A MANDRAKE?
HUH?
YEAH.
IN THE PAST IT WAS USED FOR ANESTHESIA AND AS A NARCOTIC.
IT CAN BE POISONOUS IF USED INCORRECTLY.
SO, IT ISN'T USED MUCH NOW THAT WE HAVE MORPHINE AND ETHER.
FLIP
IT'S A NECESSARY INGREDIENT IN ONE OF MY MOTHER'S RECIPES THAT I'D LIKE TO TRY.
MANDRAKES ARE THOSE HUMAN-SHAPED THINGS, RIGHT?
BWOOA BWOOA
SORT OF...
THE ROOT HAS A STRANGE SHAPE.
SHWP...

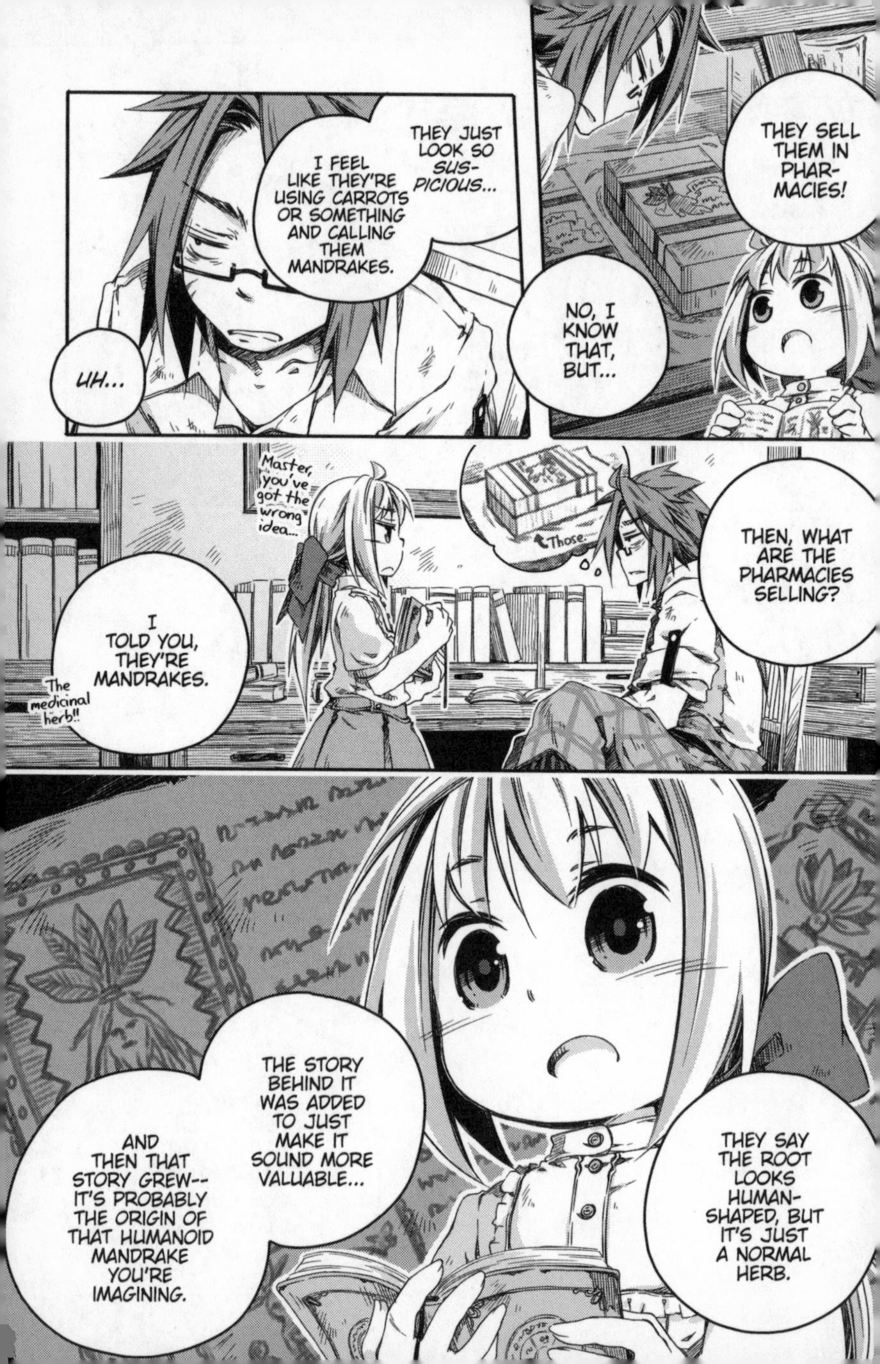
THEY SELL THEM IN PHARMACIES!
NO, I KNOW THAT, BUT...
THEY JUST LOOK SO SUSPICIOUS...
I FEEL LIKE THEY'RE USING CARROTS OR SOMETHING AND CALLING THEM MANDRAKES.
UH...
THEN, WHAT ARE THE PHARMACIES SELLING?
Those.
Master, you've got the wrong idea...
I TOLD YOU, THEY'RE MANDRAKES.
The medicinal herb!!
THEY SAY THE ROOT LOOKS HUMAN-SHAPED, BUT IT'S JUST A NORMAL HERB.
THE STORY BEHIND IT WAS ADDED TO JUST MAKE IT SOUND MORE VALUABLE...
AND THEN THAT STORY GREW-- IT'S PROBABLY THE ORIGIN OF THAT HUMANOID MANDRAKE YOU'RE IMAGINING.

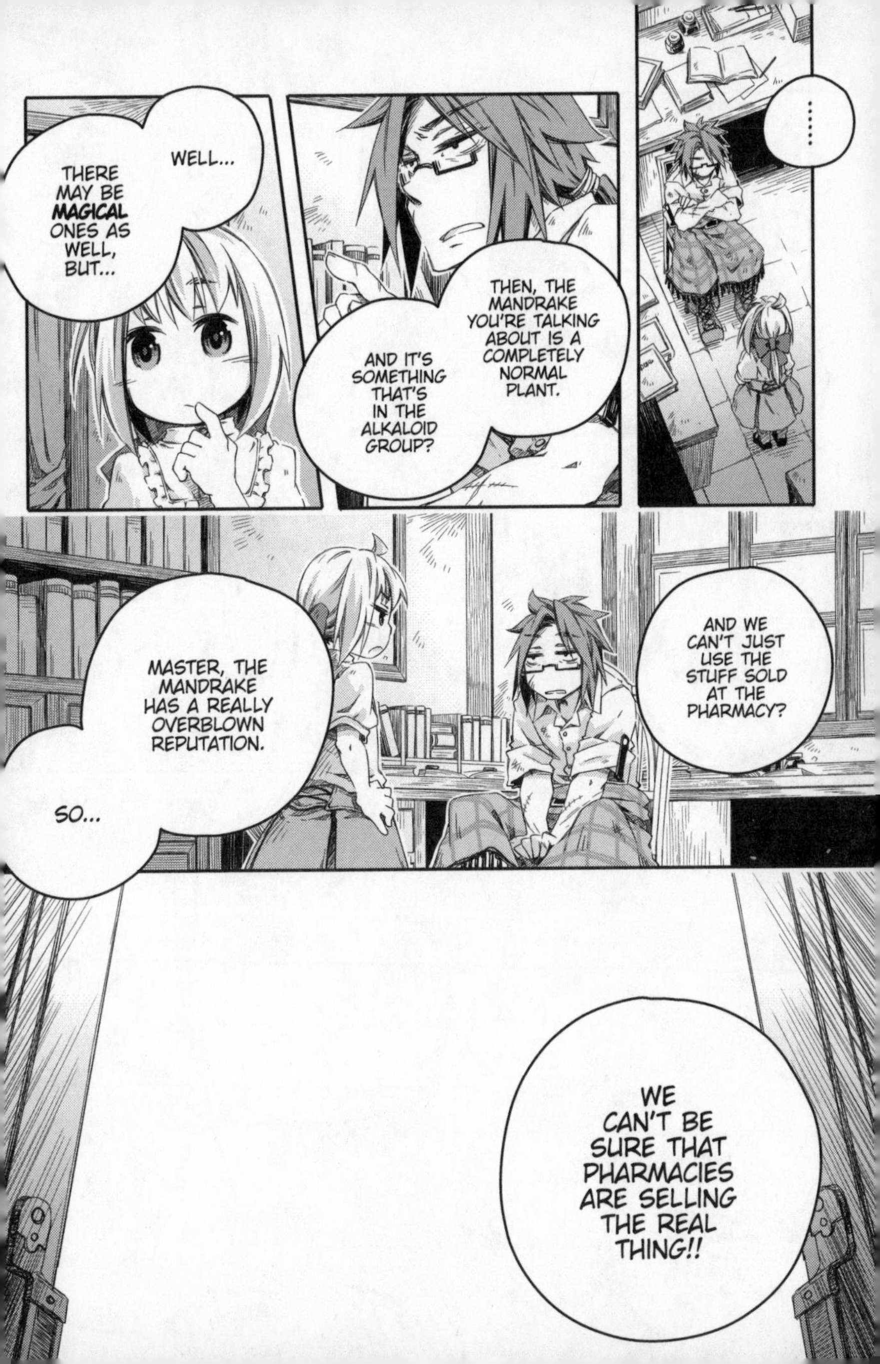
......
THEN, THE MANDRAKE YOU'RE TALKING ABOUT IS A COMPLETELY NORMAL PLANT.
AND IT'S SOMETHING THAT'S IN THE ALKALOID GROUP?
WELL...
THERE MAY BE **MAGICAL** ONES AS WELL, BUT...
AND WE CAN'T JUST USE THE STUFF SOLD AT THE PHARMACY?
MASTER, THE MANDRAKE HAS A REALLY OVERBLOWN REPUTATION.
SO...
WE CAN'T BE SURE THAT PHARMACIES ARE SELLING THE REAL THING!!

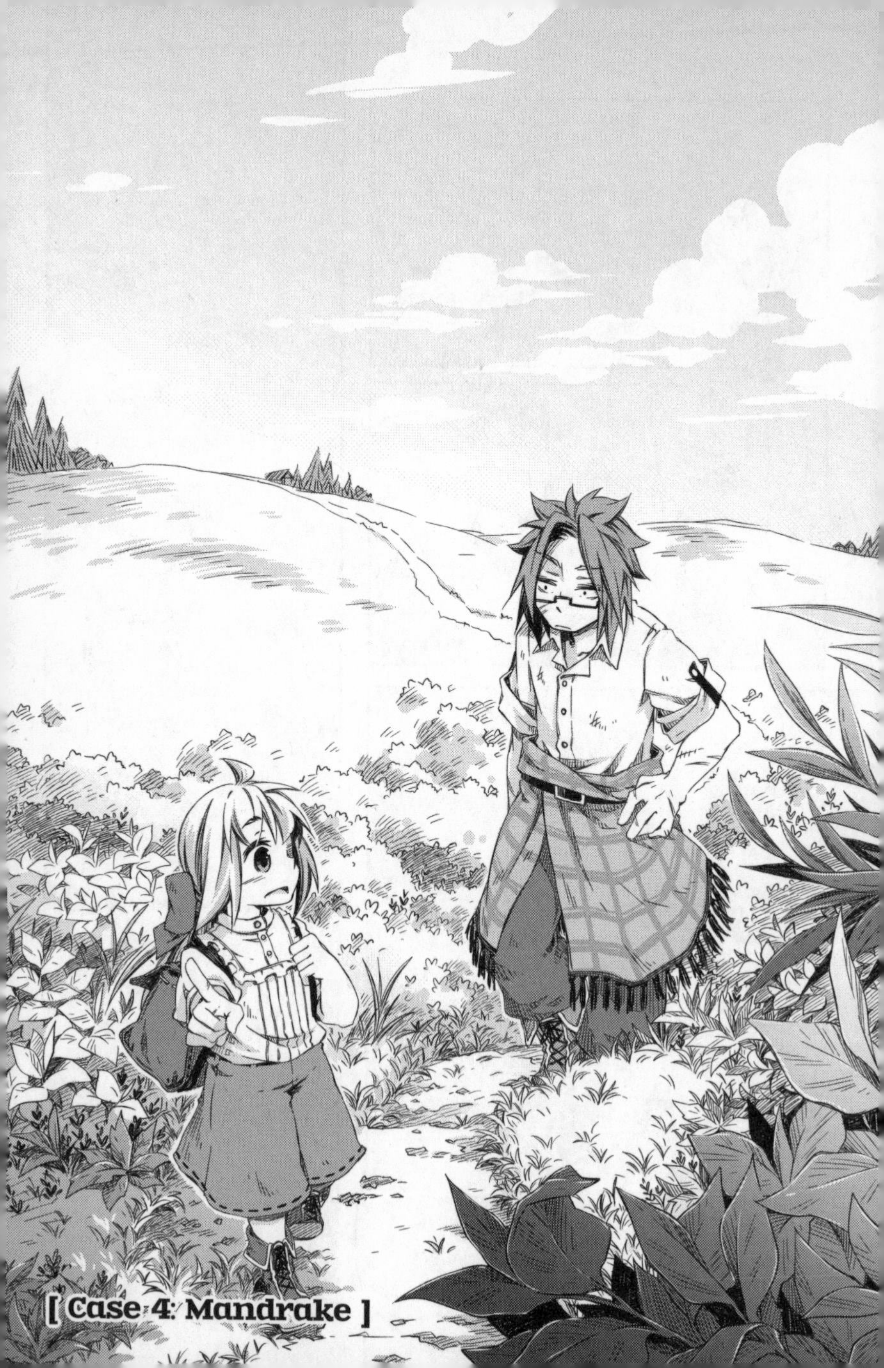
[Case 4: Mandrake]

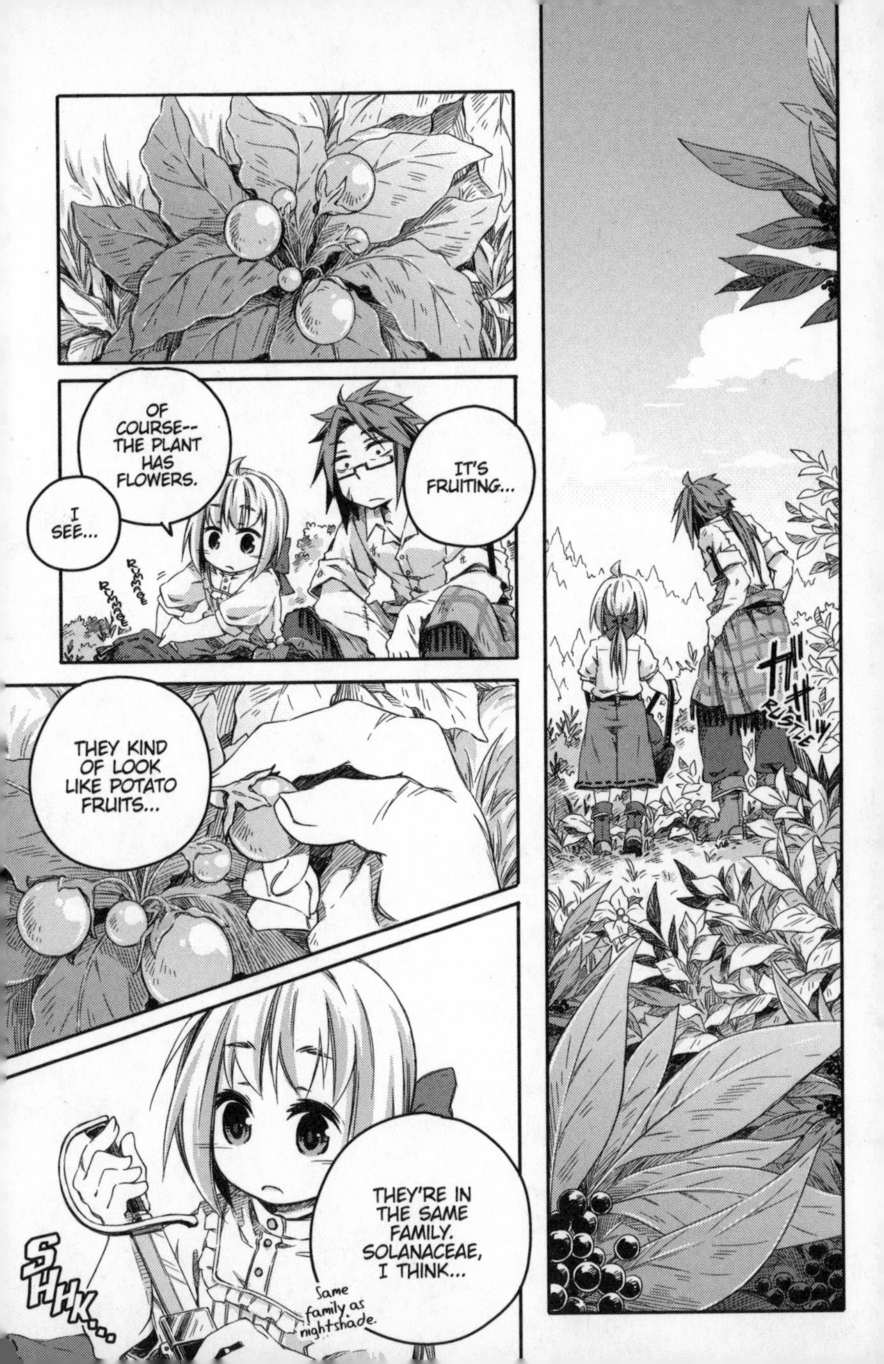
RUSTLE
IT'S FRUITING...
OF COURSE-- THE PLANT HAS FLOWERS.
I SEE...
RUMMAGE RUMMAGE
THEY KIND OF LOOK LIKE POTATO FRUITS...
THEY'RE IN THE SAME FAMILY. SOLANACEAE, I THINK...
Same family as nightshade.
SHHK...

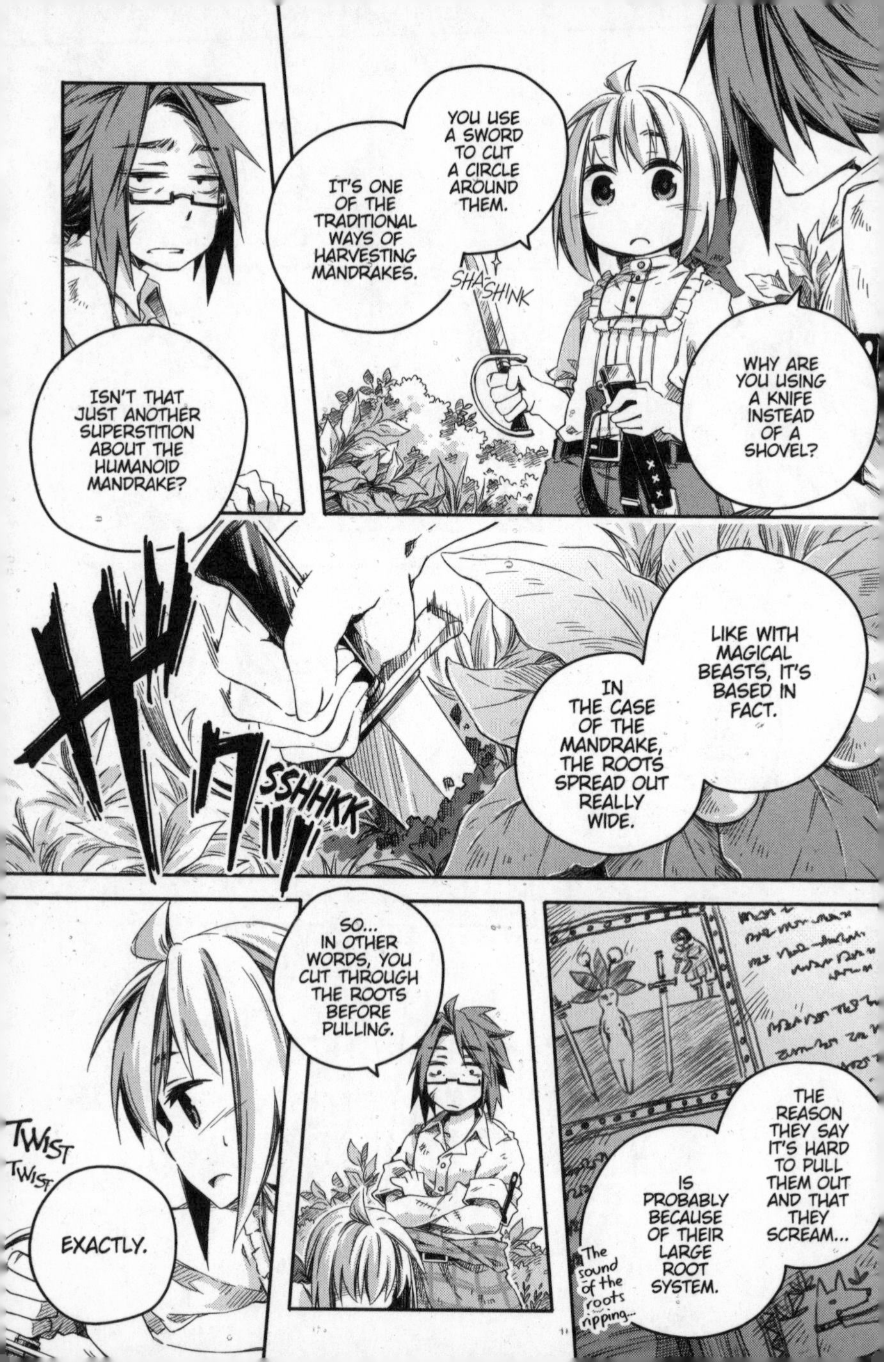
WHY ARE YOU USING A KNIFE INSTEAD OF A SHOVEL?
YOU USE A SWORD TO CUT A CIRCLE AROUND THEM.
IT'S ONE OF THE TRADITIONAL WAYS OF HARVESTING MANDRAKES.
SHA-SHINK
ISN'T THAT JUST ANOTHER SUPERSTITION ABOUT THE HUMANOID MANDRAKE?
LIKE WITH MAGICAL BEASTS, IT'S BASED IN FACT.
IN THE CASE OF THE MANDRAKE, THE ROOTS SPREAD OUT REALLY WIDE.
SSHHKK
THE REASON THEY SAY IT'S HARD TO PULL THEM OUT AND THAT THEY SCREAM...
IS PROBABLY BECAUSE OF THEIR LARGE ROOT SYSTEM.
The sound of the roots ripping...
SO... IN OTHER WORDS, YOU CUT THROUGH THE ROOTS BEFORE PULLING.
TWIST
TWIST
EXACTLY.

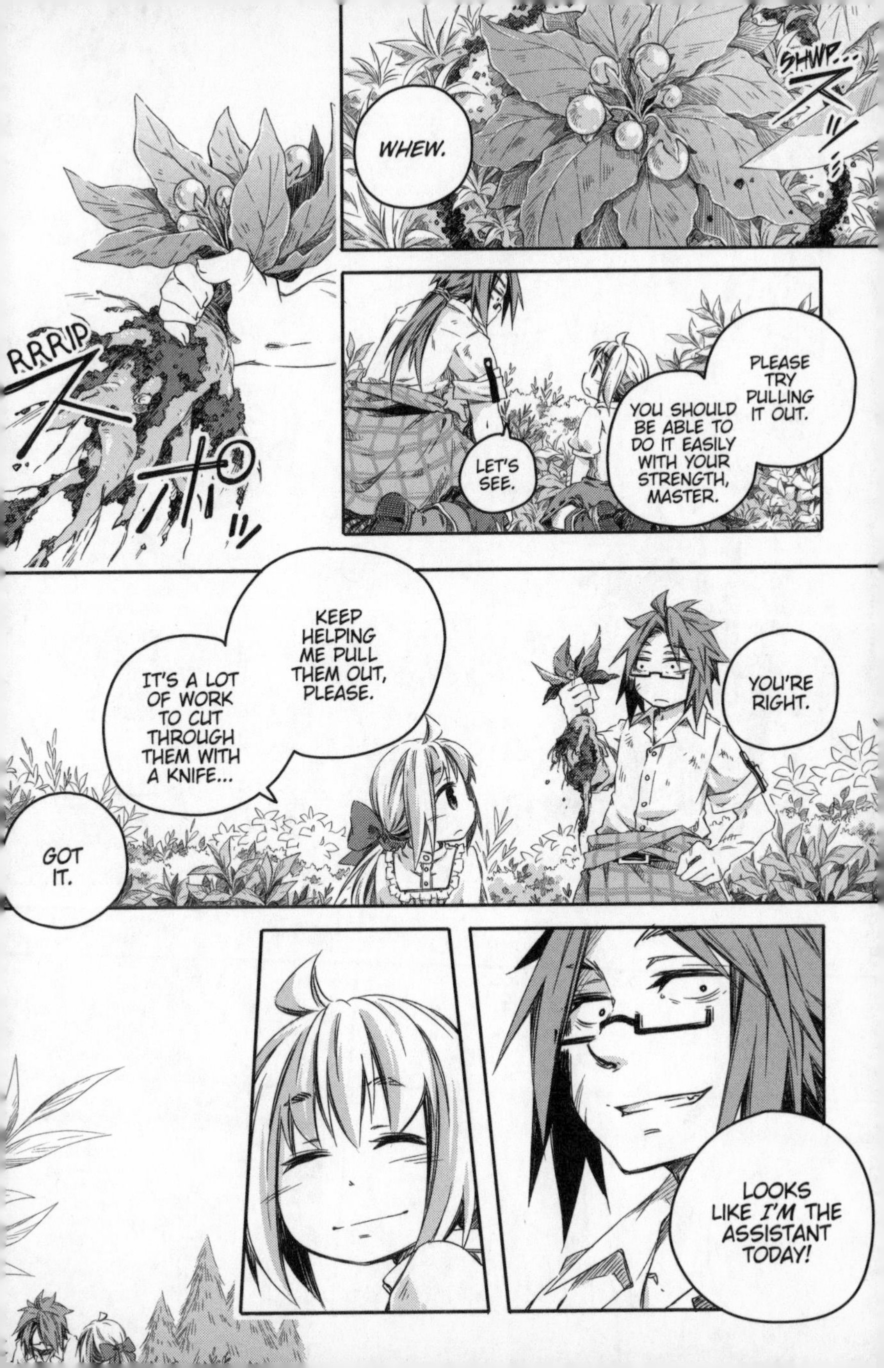
SHWP...
WHEW.
PLEASE TRY PULLING IT OUT.
YOU SHOULD BE ABLE TO DO IT EASILY WITH YOUR STRENGTH, MASTER.
LET'S SEE.
RRRIP
YOU'RE RIGHT.
KEEP HELPING ME PULL THEM OUT, PLEASE.
IT'S A LOT OF WORK TO CUT THROUGH THEM WITH A KNIFE...
GOT IT.
LOOKS LIKE *I'M* THE ASSISTANT TODAY!

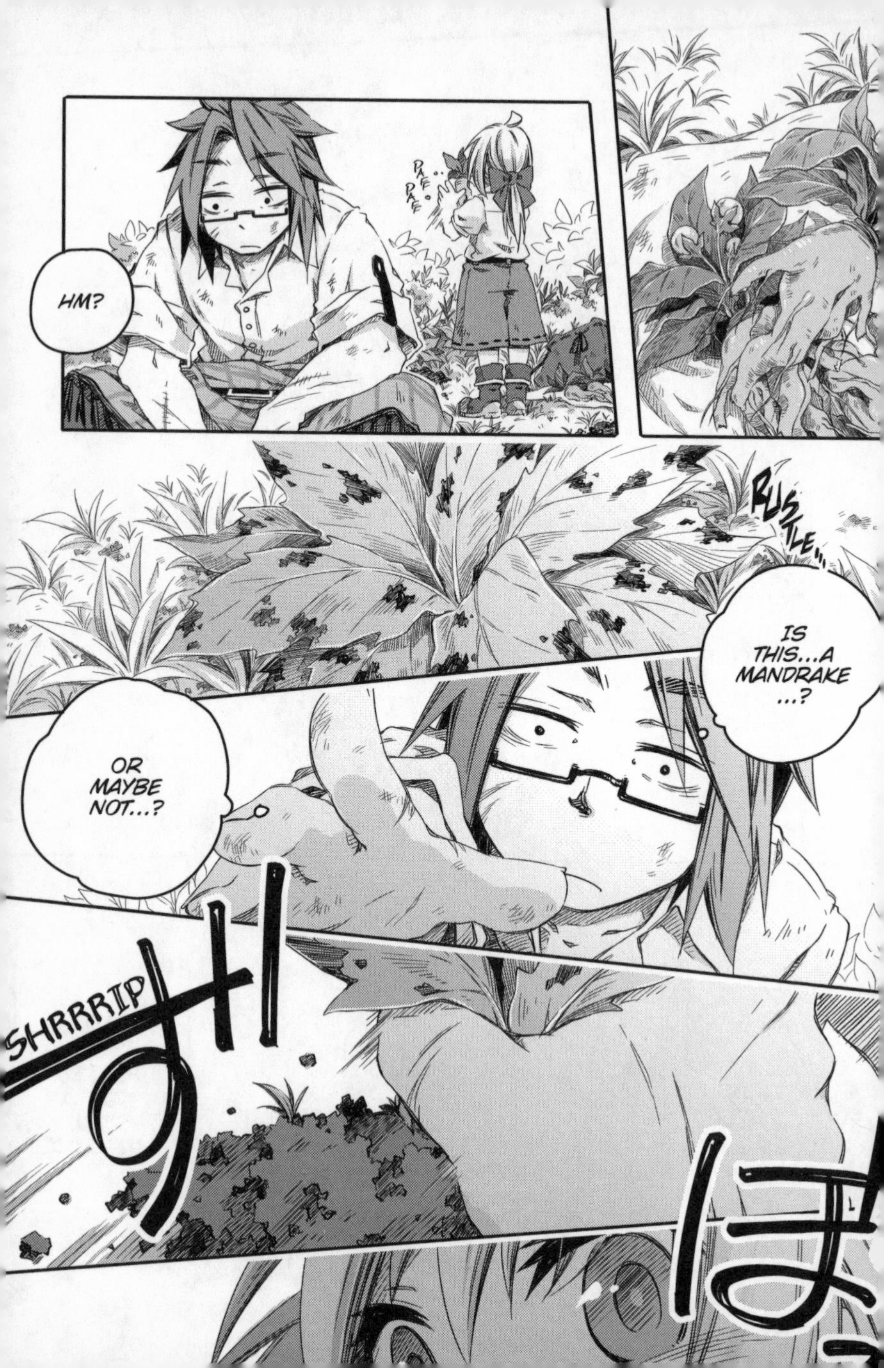
PAE PAE...
HM?
RUSTLE...
IS THIS...A MANDRAKE...?
OR MAYBE NOT...?
SHRRRIP
すり
ぽ

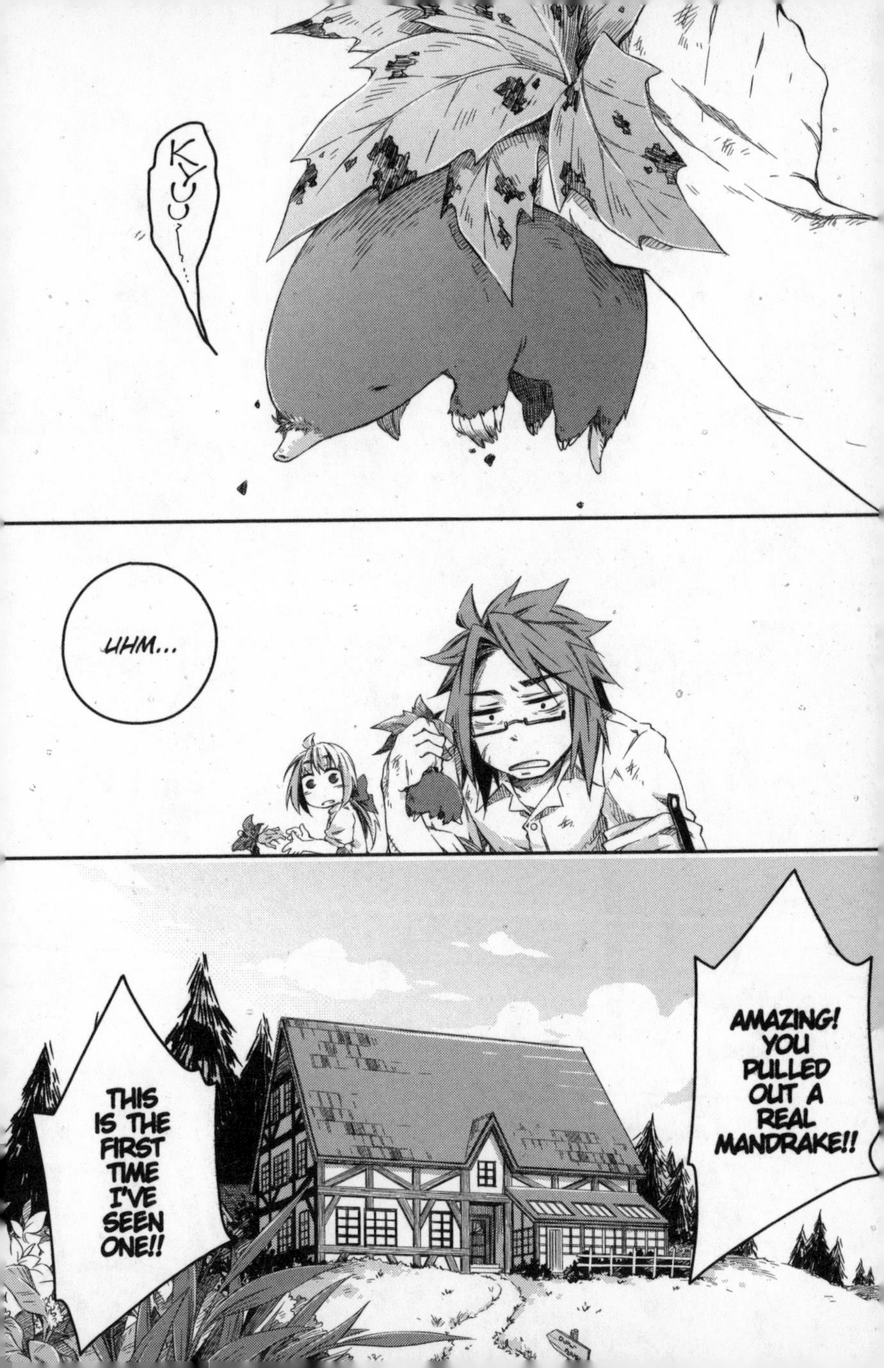
KYUU~...
UHM...
AMAZING! YOU PULLED OUT A REAL MANDRAKE!!
THIS IS THE FIRST TIME I'VE SEEN ONE!!

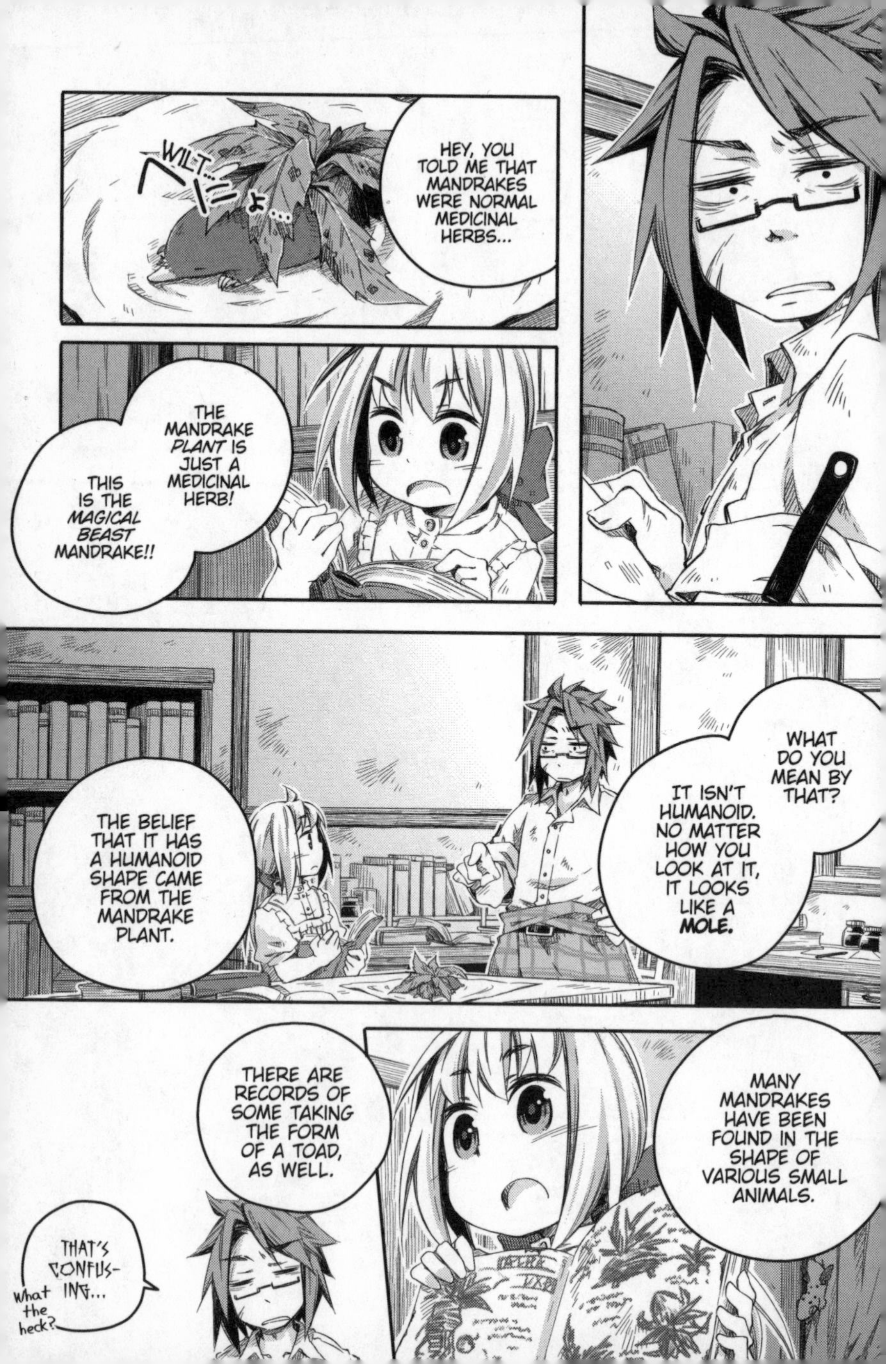
HEY, YOU TOLD ME THAT MANDRAKES WERE NORMAL MEDICINAL HERBS...
WILT...
THE MANDRAKE PLANT IS JUST A MEDICINAL HERB!
THIS IS THE MAGICAL BEAST MANDRAKE!!
WHAT DO YOU MEAN BY THAT?
IT ISN'T HUMANOID. NO MATTER HOW YOU LOOK AT IT, IT LOOKS LIKE A MOLE.
THE BELIEF THAT IT HAS A HUMANOID SHAPE CAME FROM THE MANDRAKE PLANT.
MANY MANDRAKES HAVE BEEN FOUND IN THE SHAPE OF VARIOUS SMALL ANIMALS.
THERE ARE RECORDS OF SOME TAKING THE FORM OF A TOAD, AS WELL.
THAT'S CONFUS-ING...
What the heck?

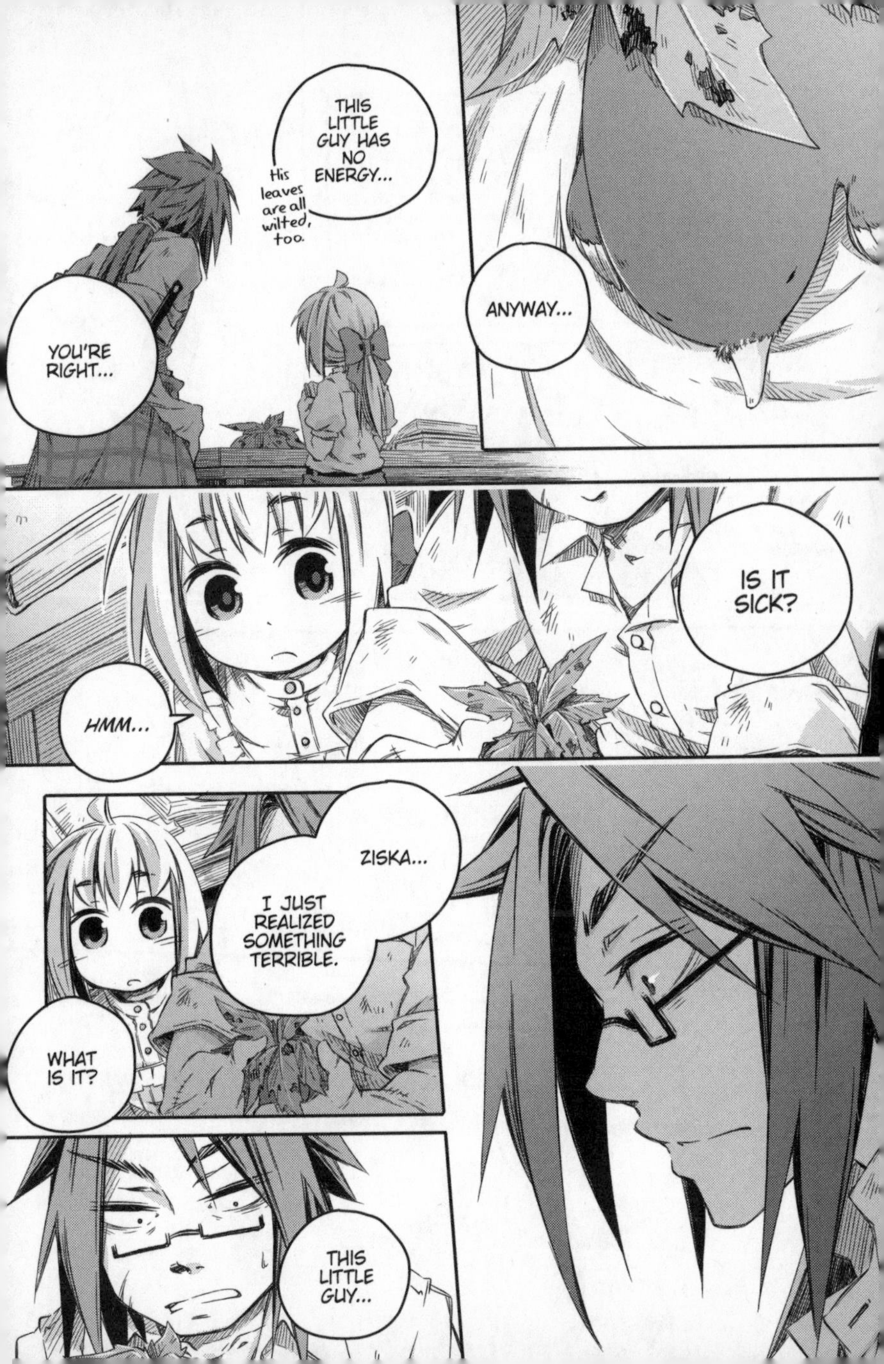
ANYWAY...
THIS LITTLE GUY HAS NO ENERGY...
His leaves are all wilted, too.
YOU'RE RIGHT...
IS IT SICK?
HMM...
ZISKA...
I JUST REALIZED SOMETHING TERRIBLE.
WHAT IS IT?
THIS LITTLE GUY...

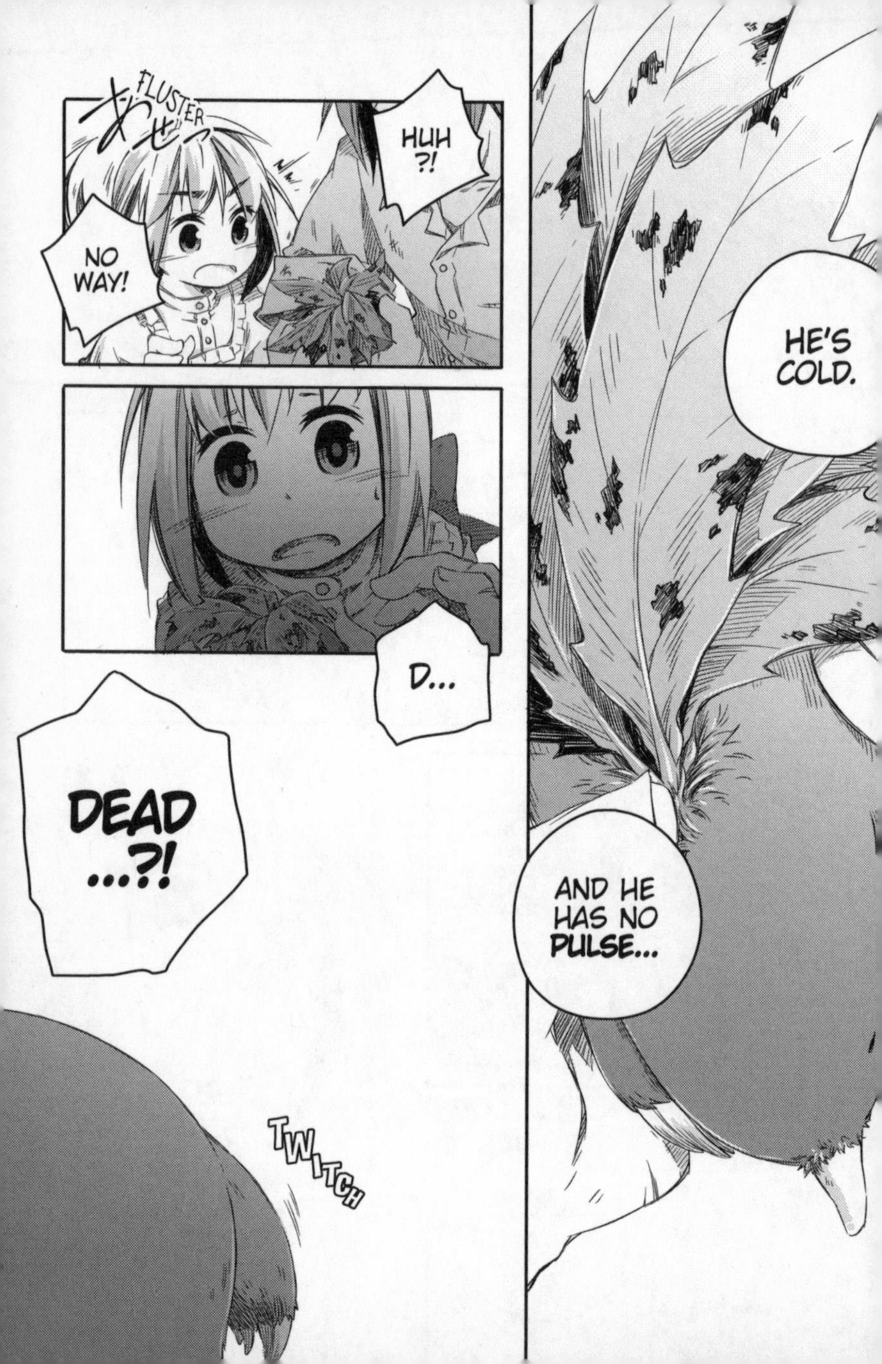
HE'S COLD.
AND HE HAS NO PULSE...
HUH ?!
FLUSTER
おせっ
NO WAY!
D...
DEAD ...?!
TWITCH

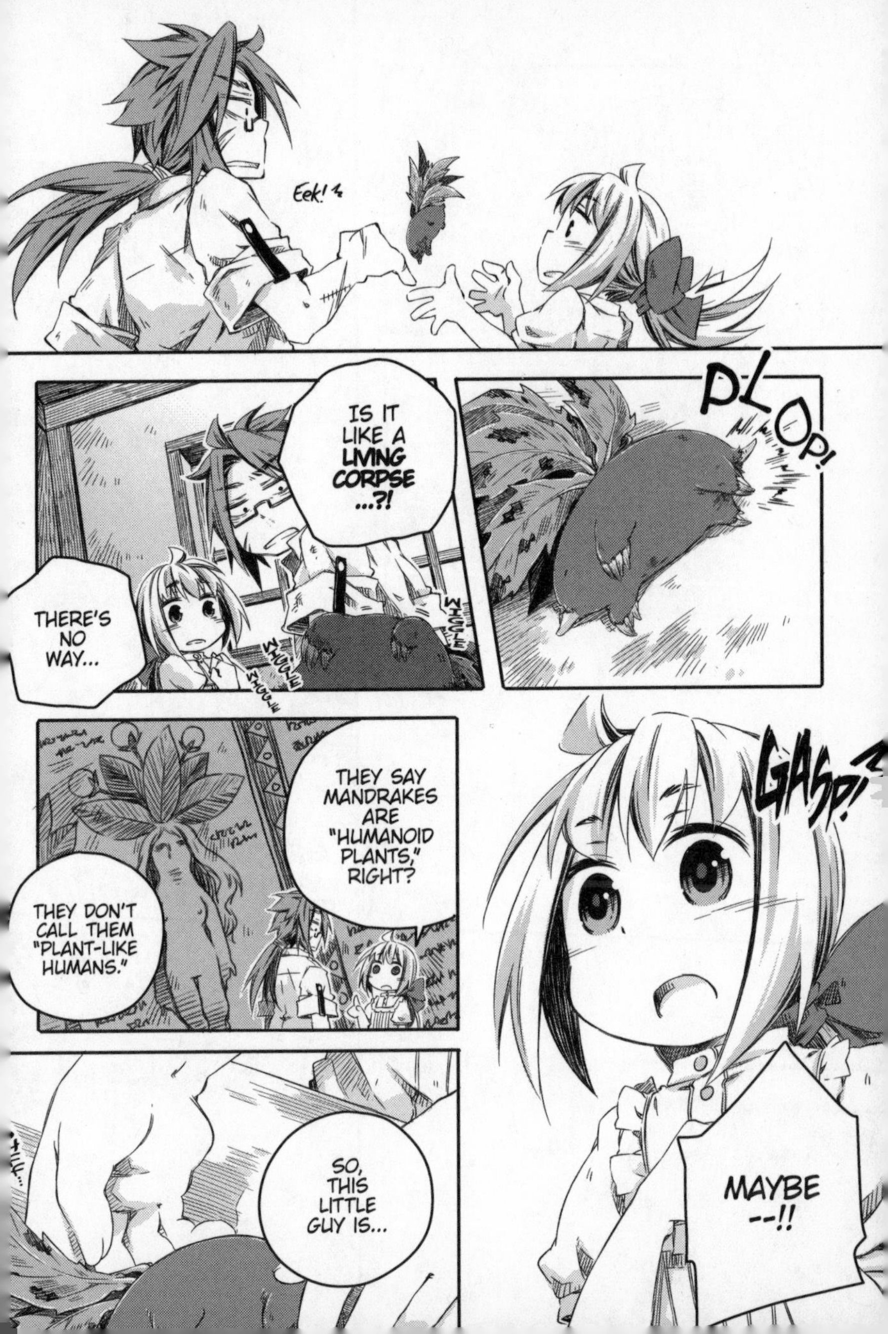
Eek!
PLOP!
IS IT LIKE A LIVING CORPSE ...?!
WIGGLE
WIGGLE
WIGGLE
THERE'S NO WAY...
GASP!
MAYBE --!!
THEY SAY MANDRAKES ARE "HUMANOID PLANTS," RIGHT?
THEY DON'T CALL THEM "PLANT-LIKE HUMANS."
SO, THIS LITTLE GUY IS...

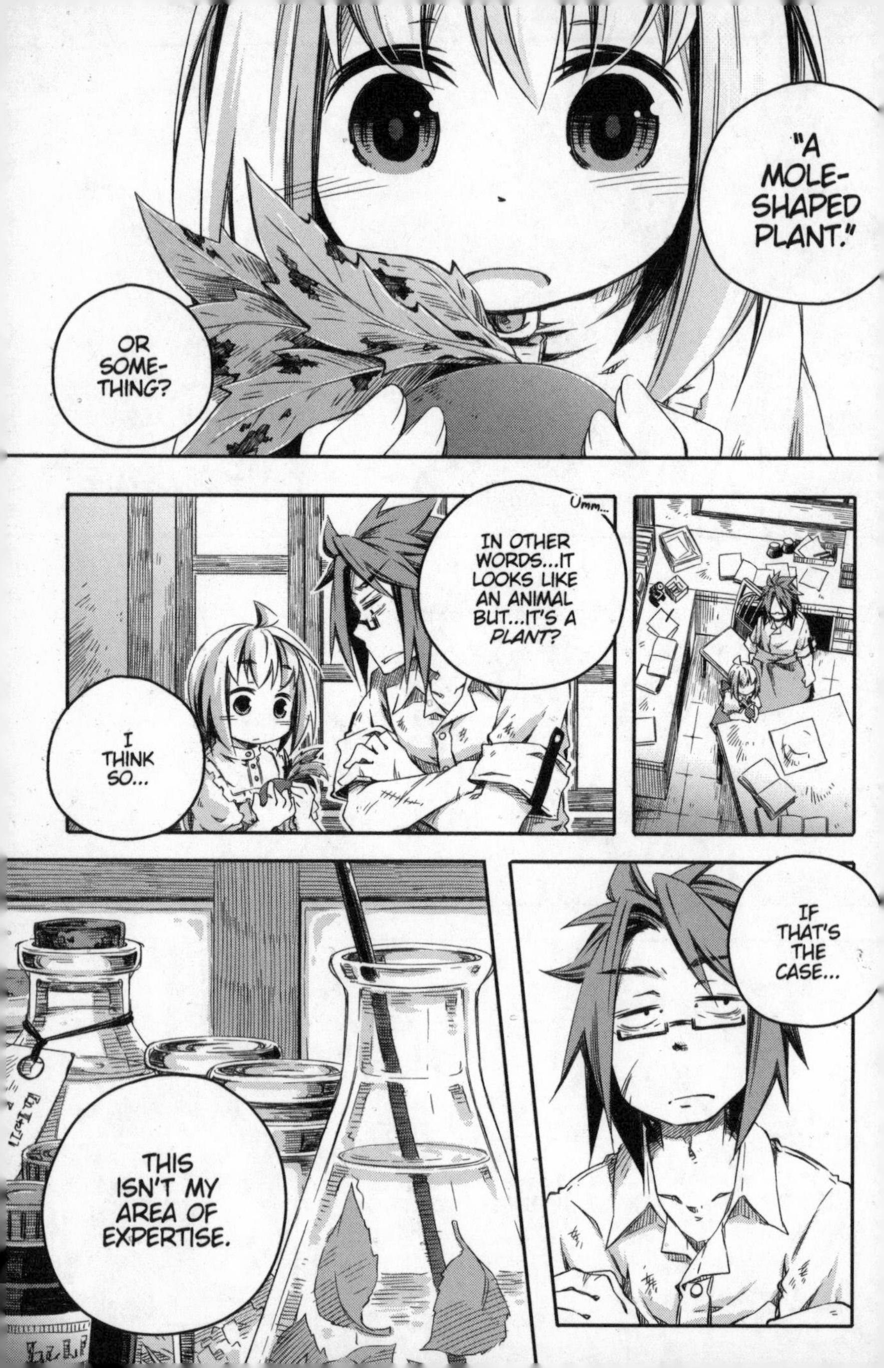
"A MOLE-SHAPED PLANT."
OR SOMETHING?
Umm...
IN OTHER WORDS...IT LOOKS LIKE AN ANIMAL BUT...IT'S A *PLANT*?
I THINK SO...
IF THAT'S THE CASE...
THIS ISN'T MY AREA OF EXPERTISE.

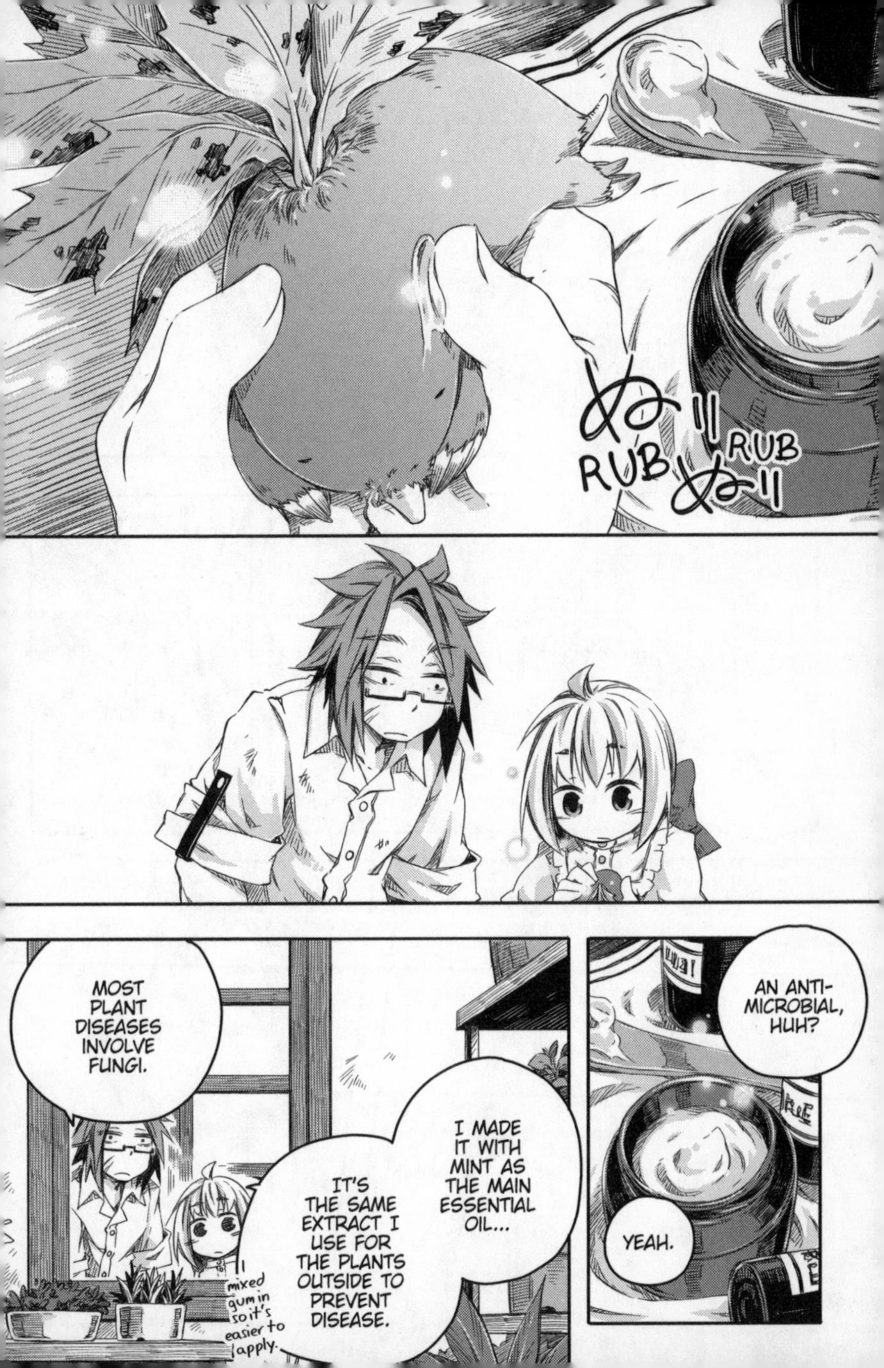
ぬ
RUB
RUB
ぬ
AN ANTI-MICROBIAL, HUH?
YEAH.
MOST PLANT DISEASES INVOLVE FUNGI.
I MADE IT WITH MINT AS THE MAIN ESSENTIAL OIL...
IT'S THE SAME EXTRACT I USE FOR THE PLANTS OUTSIDE TO PREVENT DISEASE.
I mixed gum in so it's easier to apply.

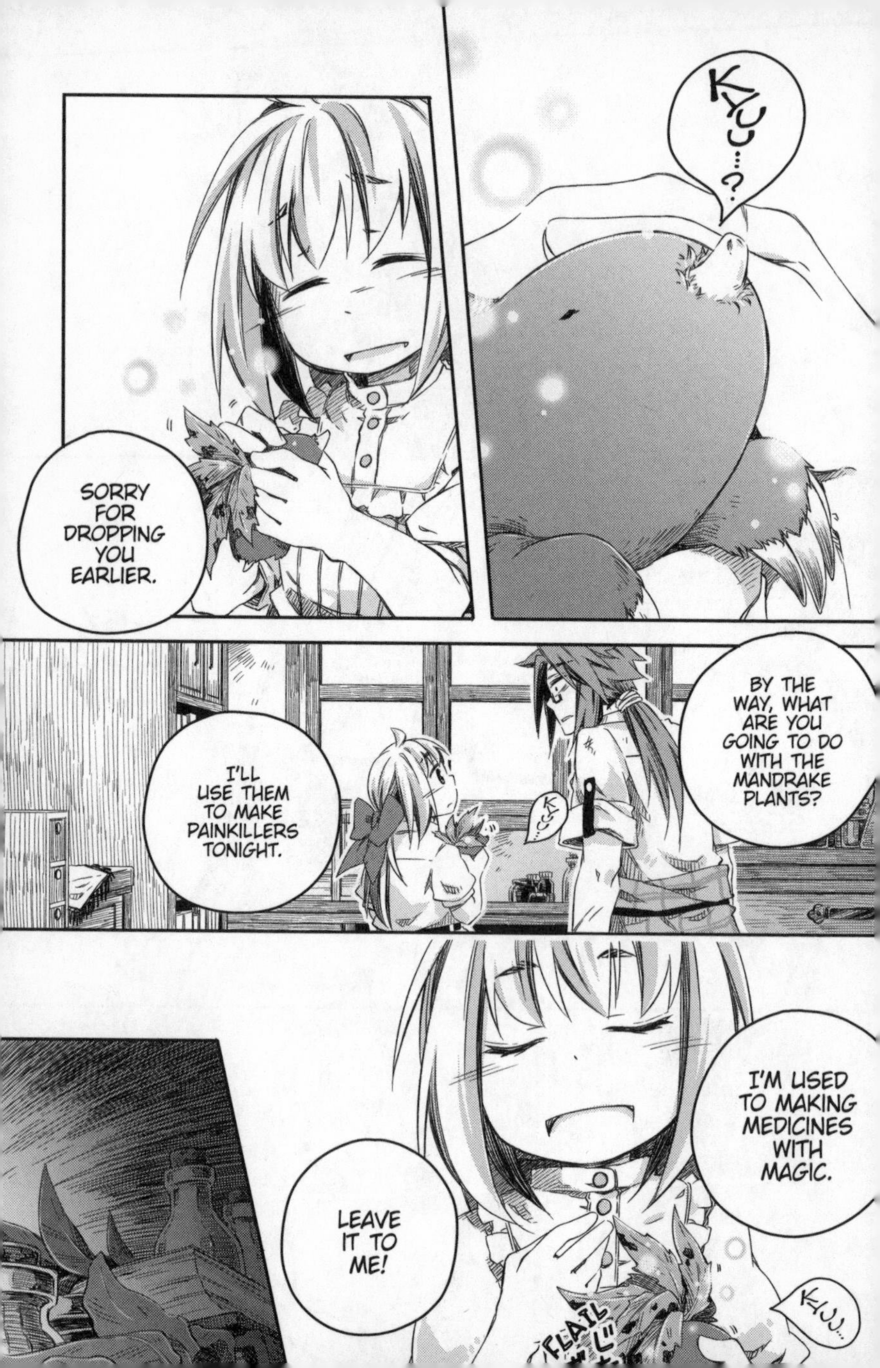
KYUU...?
SORRY FOR DROPPING YOU EARLIER.
BY THE WAY, WHAT ARE YOU GOING TO DO WITH THE MANDRAKE PLANTS?
KYUU...
I'LL USE THEM TO MAKE PAINKILLERS TONIGHT.
I'M USED TO MAKING MEDICINES WITH MAGIC.
LEAVE IT TO ME!
KYUU...
FLAIL

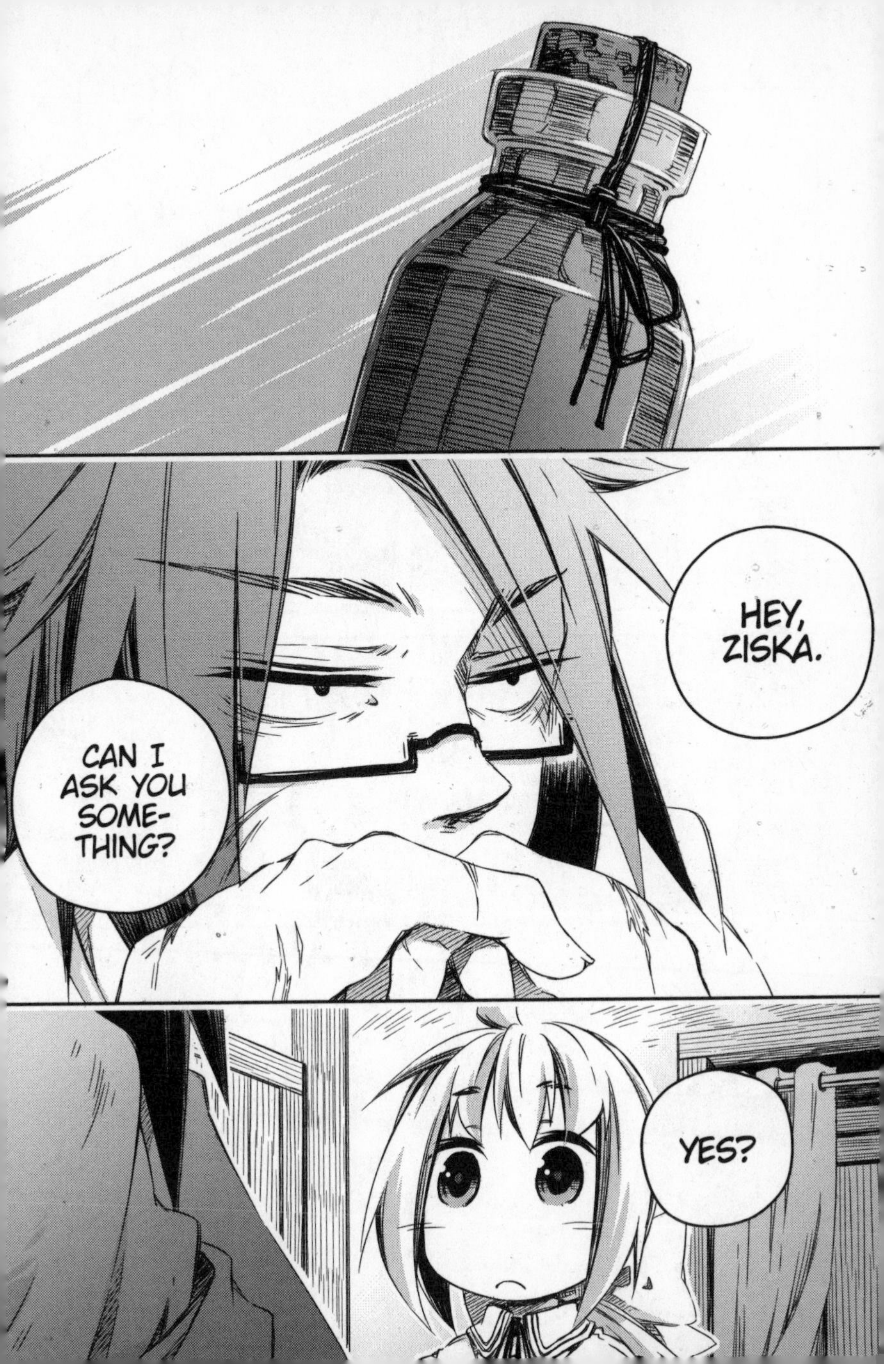
HEY, ZISKA.
CAN I ASK YOU SOME-THING?
YES?

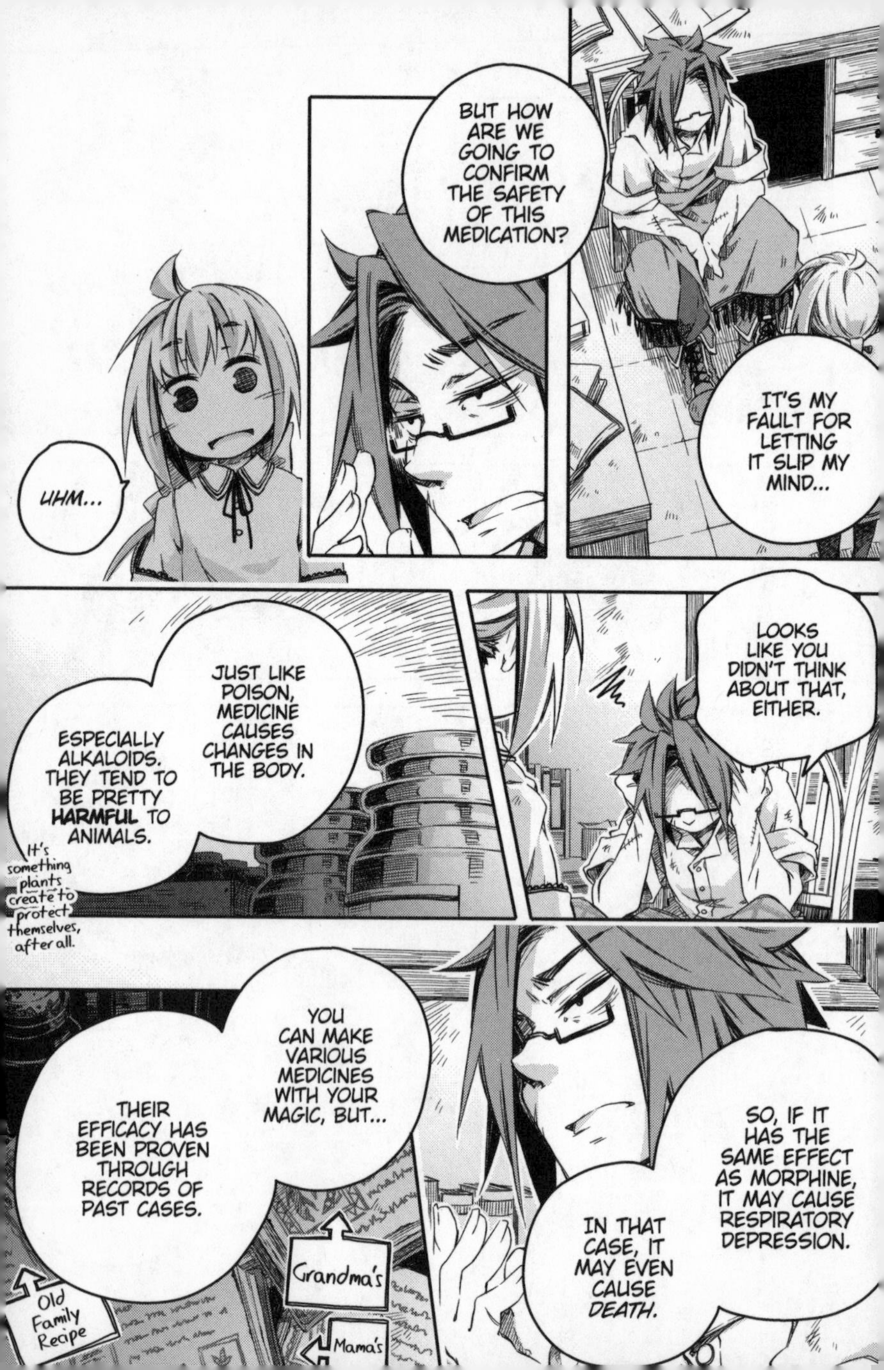
IT'S MY FAULT FOR LETTING IT SLIP MY MIND...
BUT HOW ARE WE GOING TO CONFIRM THE SAFETY OF THIS MEDICATION?
UHM...
LOOKS LIKE YOU DIDN'T THINK ABOUT THAT, EITHER.
JUST LIKE POISON, MEDICINE CAUSES CHANGES IN THE BODY.
ESPECIALLY ALKALOIDS. THEY TEND TO BE PRETTY **HARMFUL** TO ANIMALS.
It's something plants create to protect themselves, after all.
SO, IF IT HAS THE SAME EFFECT AS MORPHINE, IT MAY CAUSE RESPIRATORY DEPRESSION.
IN THAT CASE, IT MAY EVEN CAUSE DEATH.
YOU CAN MAKE VARIOUS MEDICINES WITH YOUR MAGIC, BUT...
THEIR EFFICACY HAS BEEN PROVEN THROUGH RECORDS OF PAST CASES.
Grandma's
Mama's
Old Family Recipe

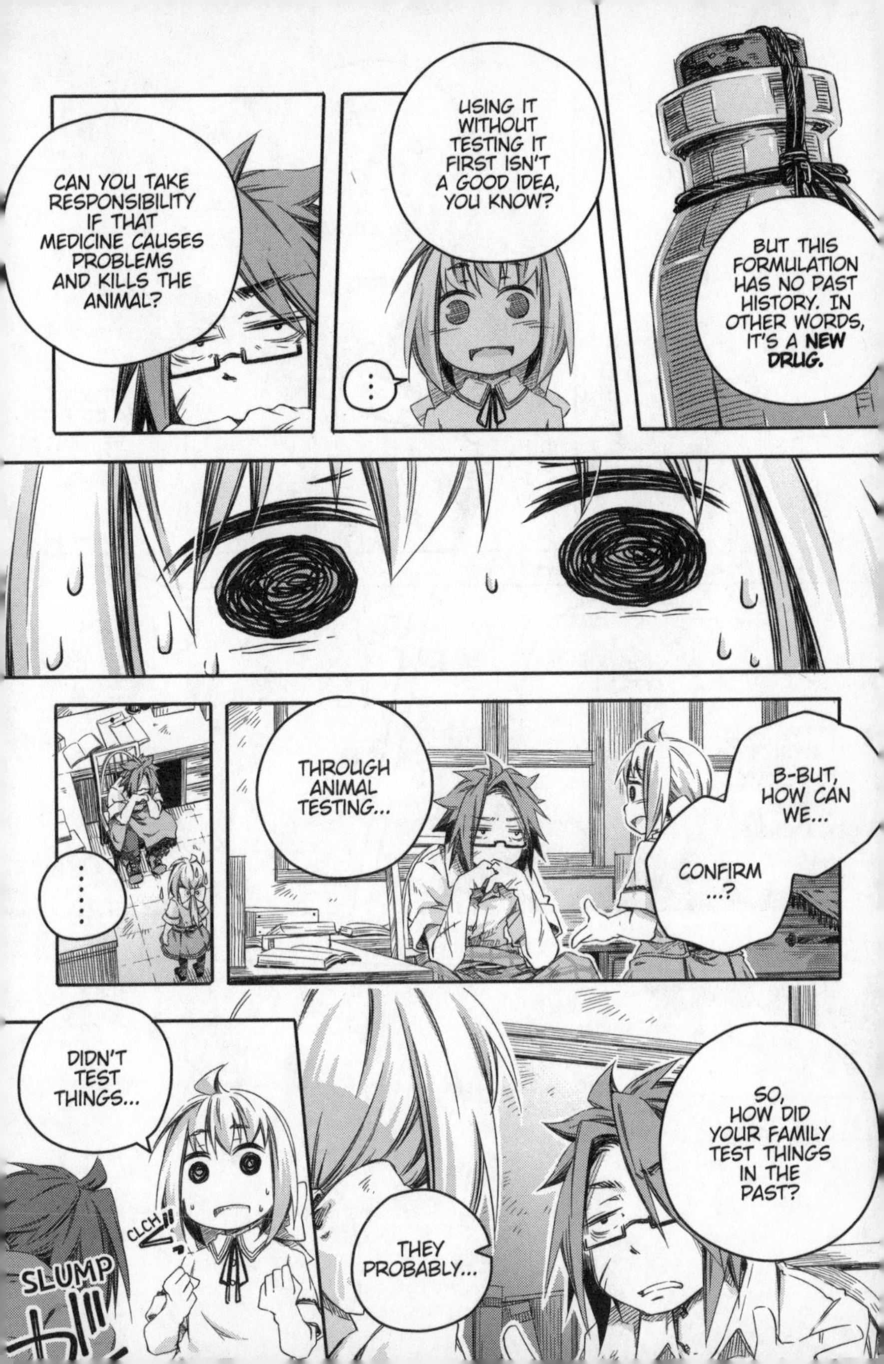
BUT THIS FORMULATION HAS NO PAST HISTORY. IN OTHER WORDS, IT'S A **NEW DRUG.**
USING IT WITHOUT TESTING IT FIRST ISN'T A GOOD IDEA, YOU KNOW?
...
CAN YOU TAKE RESPONSIBILITY IF THAT MEDICINE CAUSES PROBLEMS AND KILLS THE ANIMAL?
B-BUT, HOW CAN WE...
CONFIRM ...?
THROUGH ANIMAL TESTING...
......
SO, HOW DID YOUR FAMILY TEST THINGS IN THE PAST?
THEY PROBABLY...
DIDN'T TEST THINGS...
CLCH
SLUMP

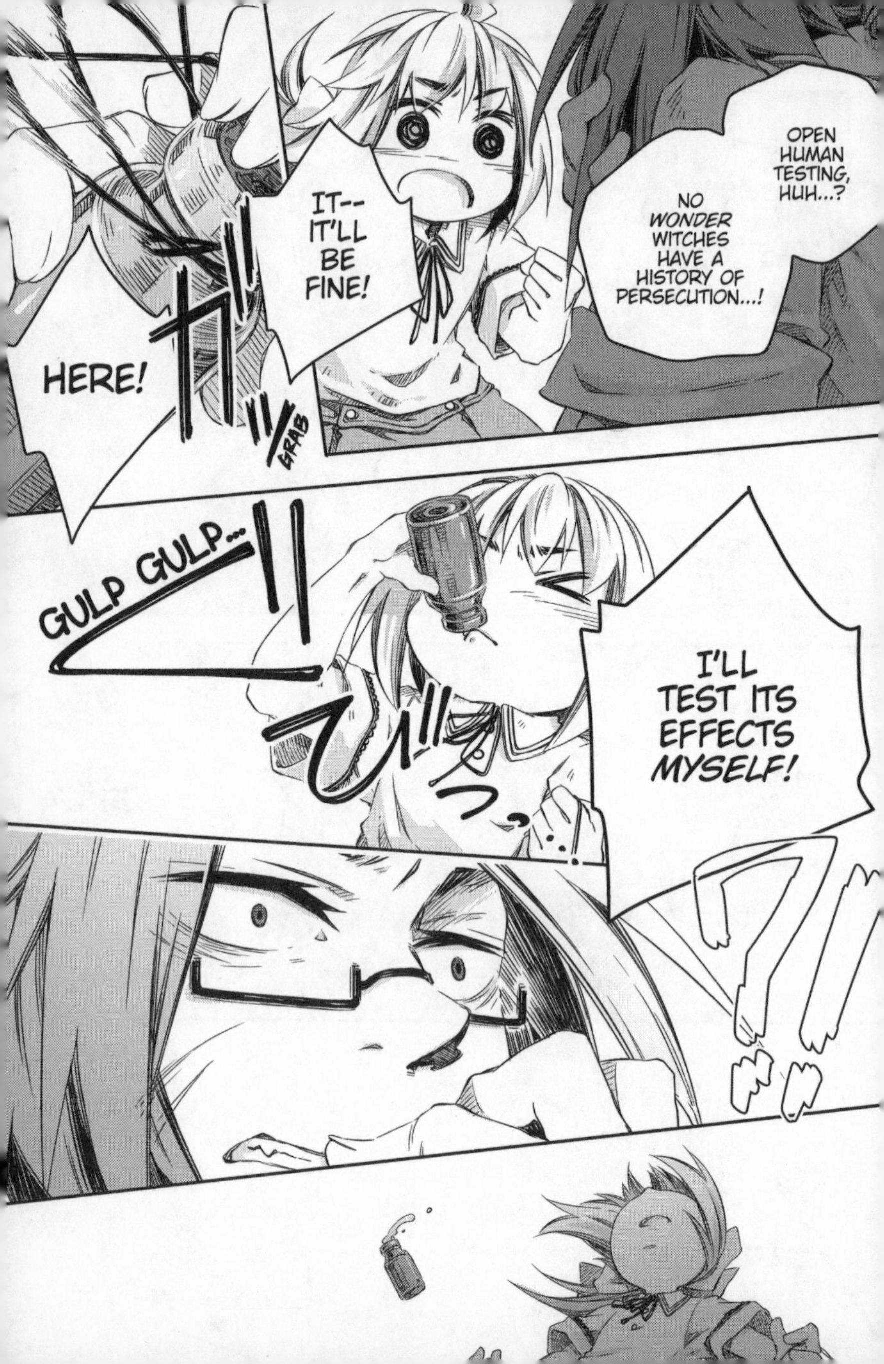

OPEN HUMAN TESTING, HUH...?
NO *WONDER* WITCHES HAVE A HISTORY OF PERSECUTION...!
IT-- IT'LL BE FINE!
HERE!
GRAB
I'LL TEST ITS EFFECTS *MYSELF*!
GULP GULP...

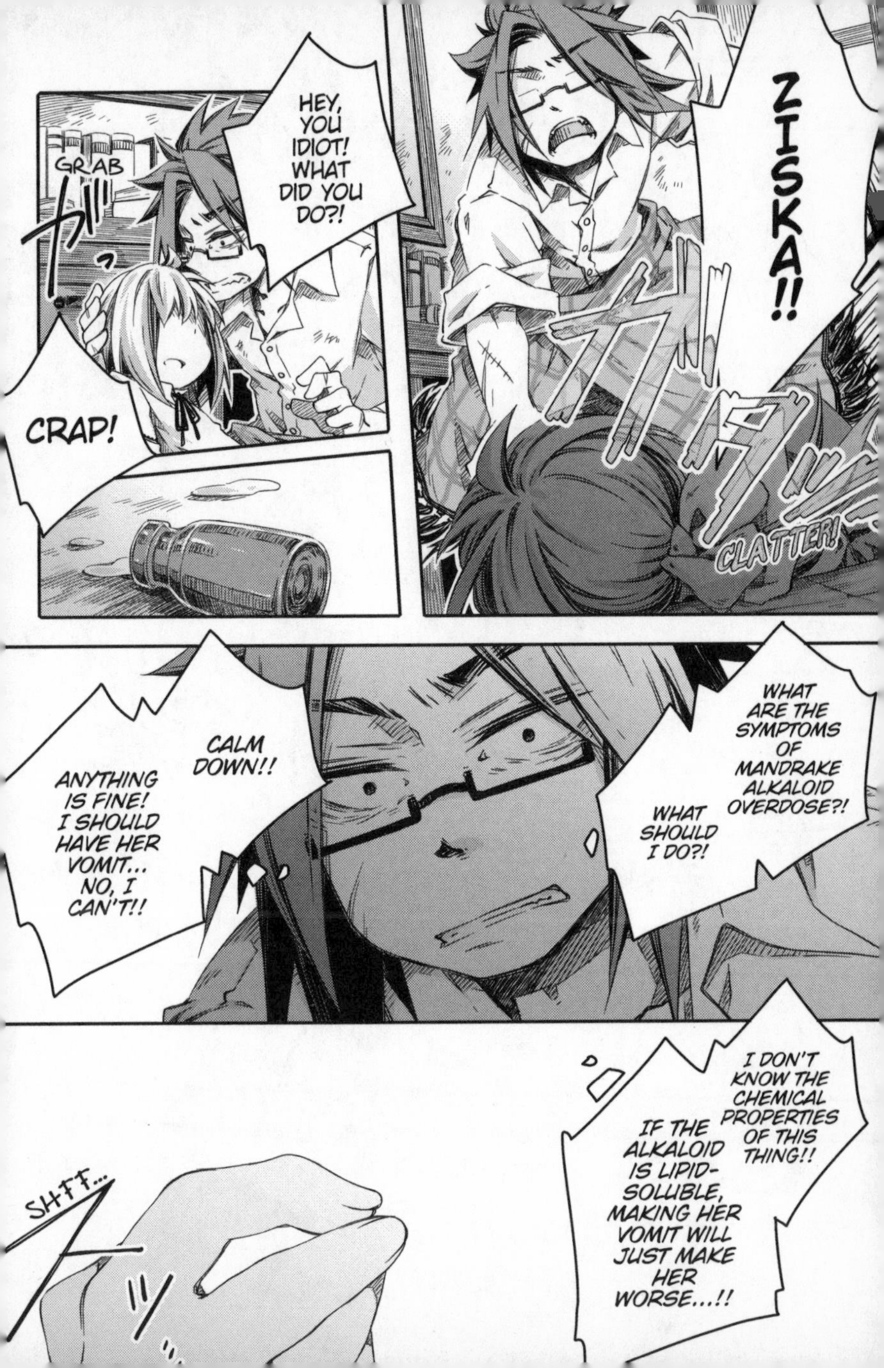
ZISKA!!
CLATTER!
HEY, YOU IDIOT! WHAT DID YOU DO?!
GRAB
CRAP!
WHAT ARE THE SYMPTOMS OF MANDRAKE ALKALOID OVERDOSE?!
WHAT SHOULD I DO?!
CALM DOWN!!
ANYTHING IS FINE! I SHOULD HAVE HER VOMIT... NO, I CAN'T!!
I DON'T KNOW THE CHEMICAL PROPERTIES OF THIS THING!!
IF THE ALKALOID IS LIPID-SOLUBLE, MAKING HER VOMIT WILL JUST MAKE HER WORSE...!!
SHFF...

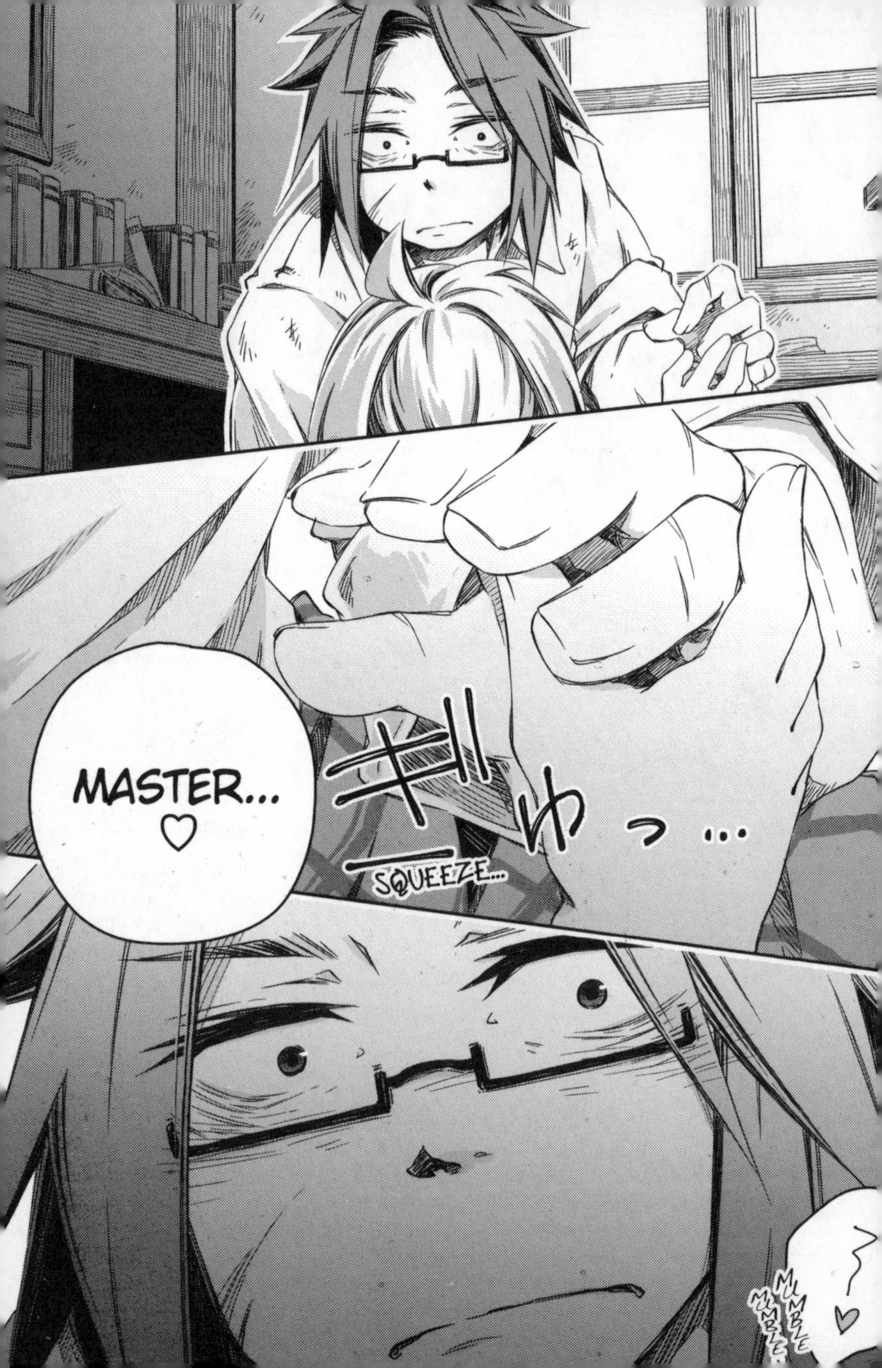
ぎゅっ...
SQUEEZE...
MASTER... ♡
MUMBLE MUMBLE
〜♡

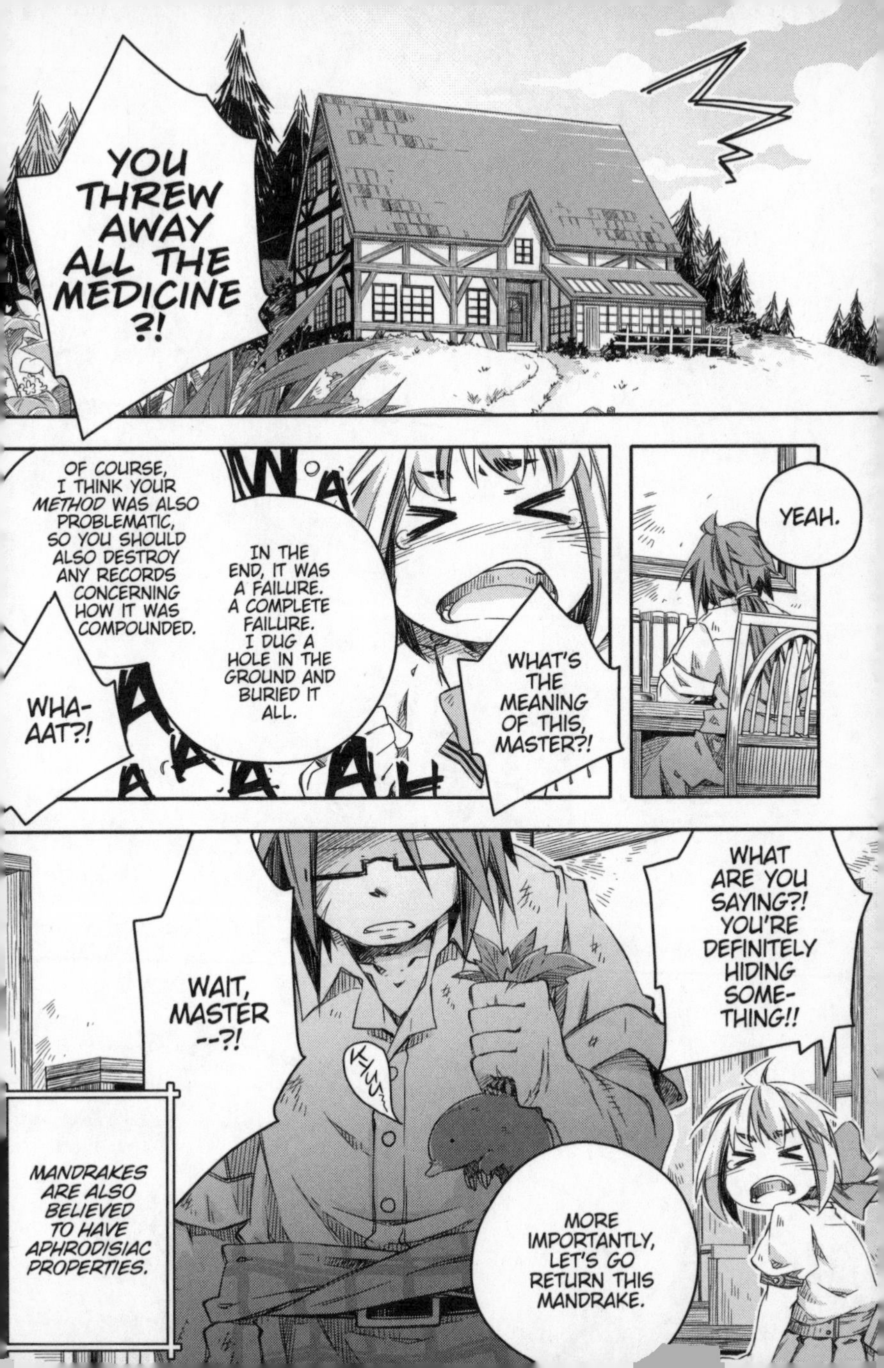
YOU THREW AWAY ALL THE MEDICINE ?!
YEAH.
WHAT'S THE MEANING OF THIS, MASTER?!
IN THE END, IT WAS A FAILURE. A COMPLETE FAILURE. I DUG A HOLE IN THE GROUND AND BURIED IT ALL.
OF COURSE, I THINK YOUR *METHOD* WAS ALSO PROBLEMATIC, SO YOU SHOULD ALSO DESTROY ANY RECORDS CONCERNING HOW IT WAS COMPOUNDED.
WHA-AAT?!
WHAT ARE YOU SAYING?! YOU'RE DEFINITELY HIDING SOME-THING!!
MORE IMPORTANTLY, LET'S GO RETURN THIS MANDRAKE.
WAIT, MASTER --?!
MANDRAKES ARE ALSO BELIEVED TO HAVE APHRODISIAC PROPERTIES.

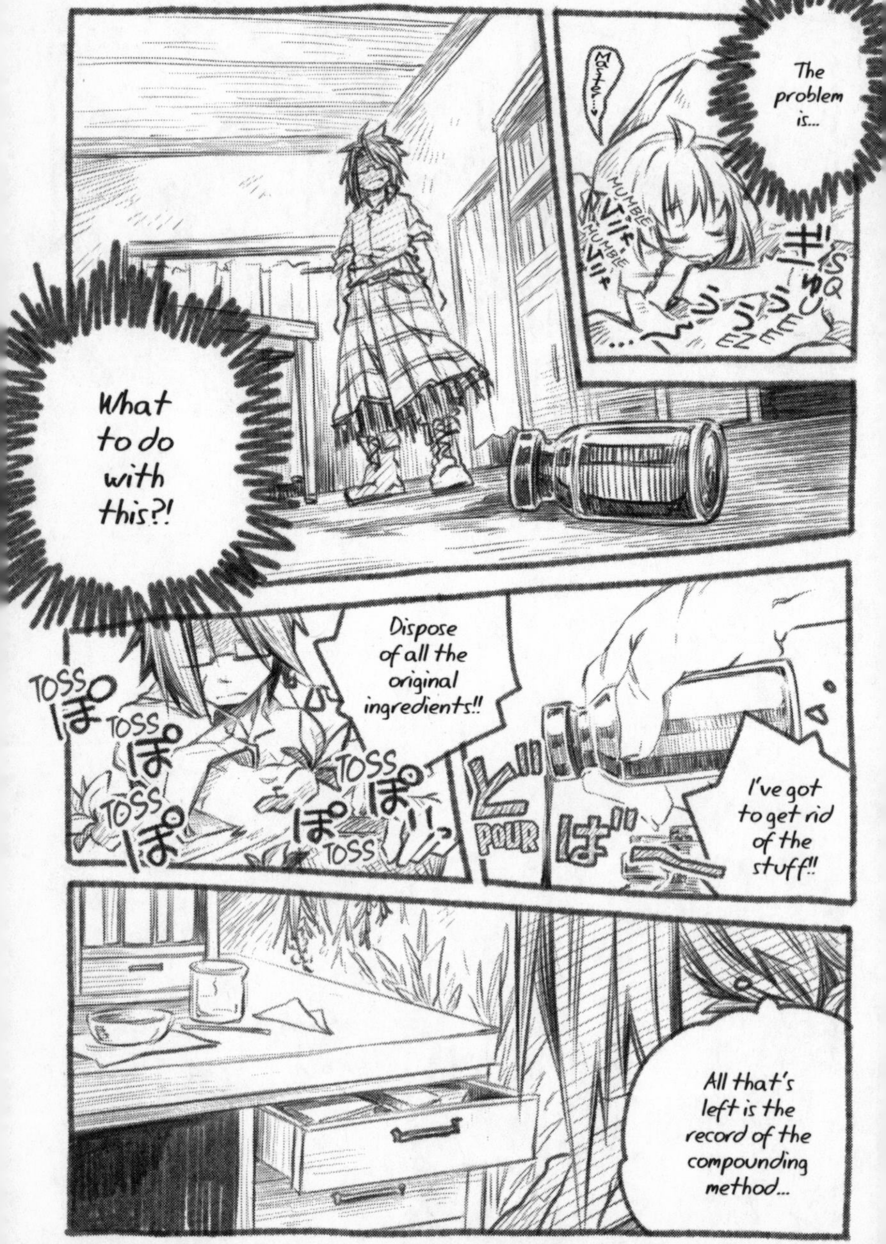
The problem is...
Master...
MUMBLE MUMBLE
SQUEEZE
What to do with this?!
I've got to get rid of the stuff!!
POUR
Dispose of all the original ingredients!!
TOSS TOSS TOSS TOSS TOSS
All that's left is the record of the compounding method...

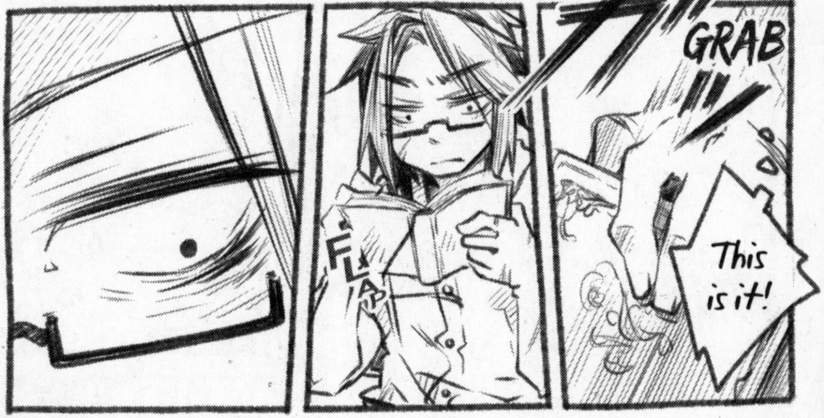
GRAB
This is it!
FLAP

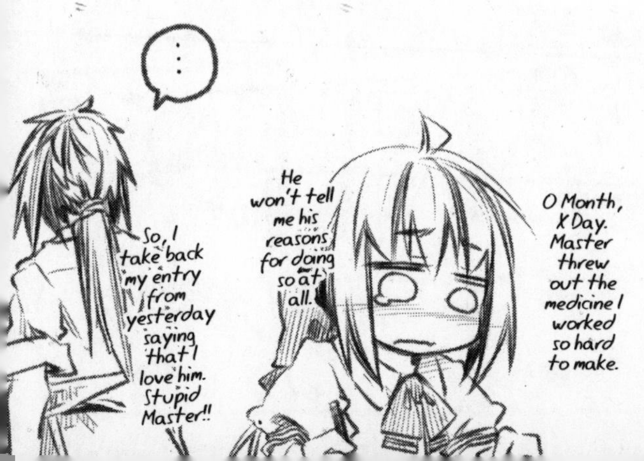
O Month, X Day. Master threw out the medicine I worked so hard to make.
He won't tell me his reasons for doing so at all.
...
So, I take back my entry from yesterday saying that I love him. Stupid Master!!

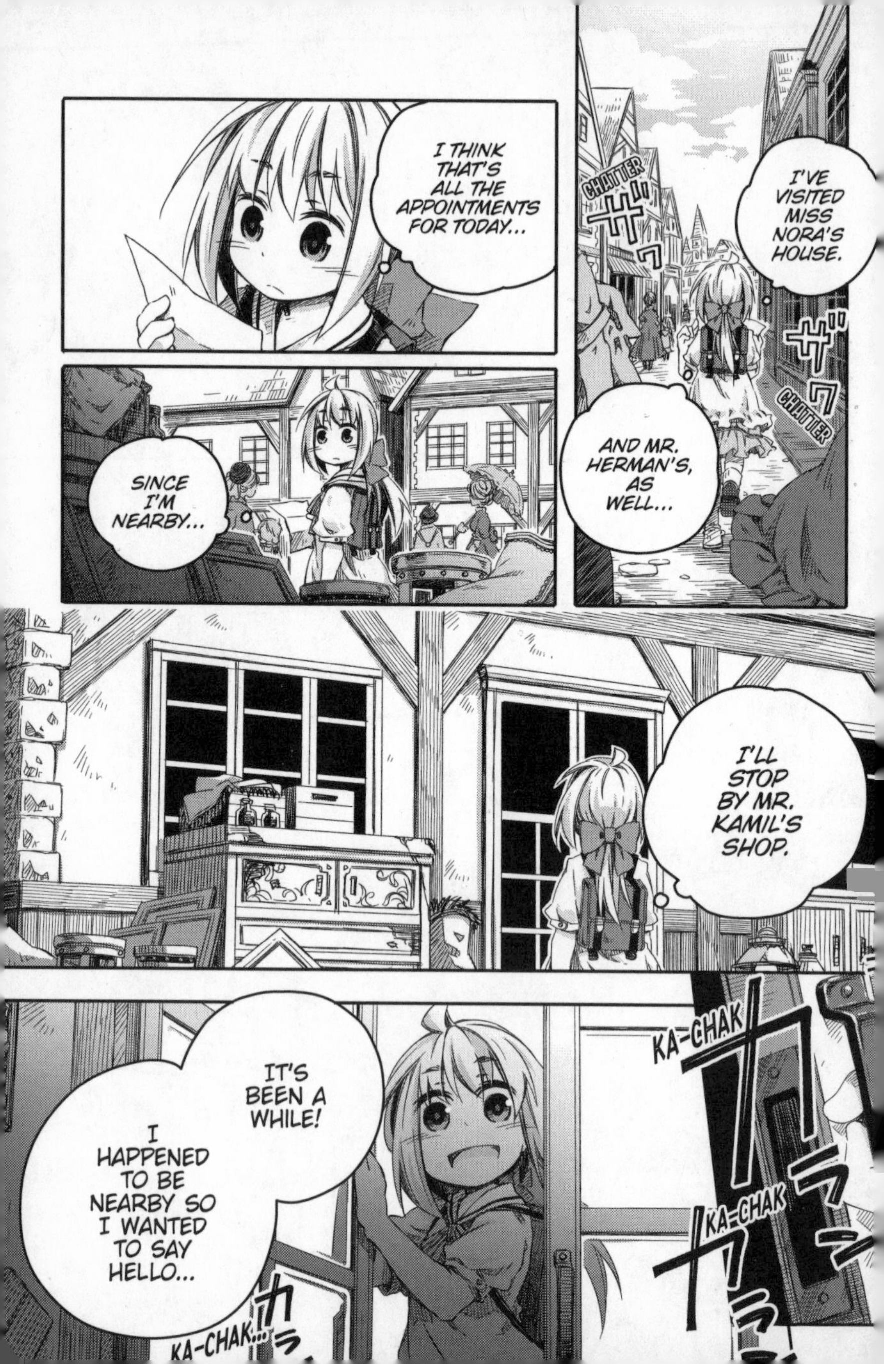
CHATTER
I'VE VISITED MISS NORA'S HOUSE.
CHATTER
AND MR. HERMAN'S, AS WELL...
I THINK THAT'S ALL THE APPOINTMENTS FOR TODAY...
SINCE I'M NEARBY...
I'LL STOP BY MR. KAMIL'S SHOP.
KA-CHAK
KA-CHAK
IT'S BEEN A WHILE!
I HAPPENED TO BE NEARBY SO I WANTED TO SAY HELLO...
KA-CHAK...

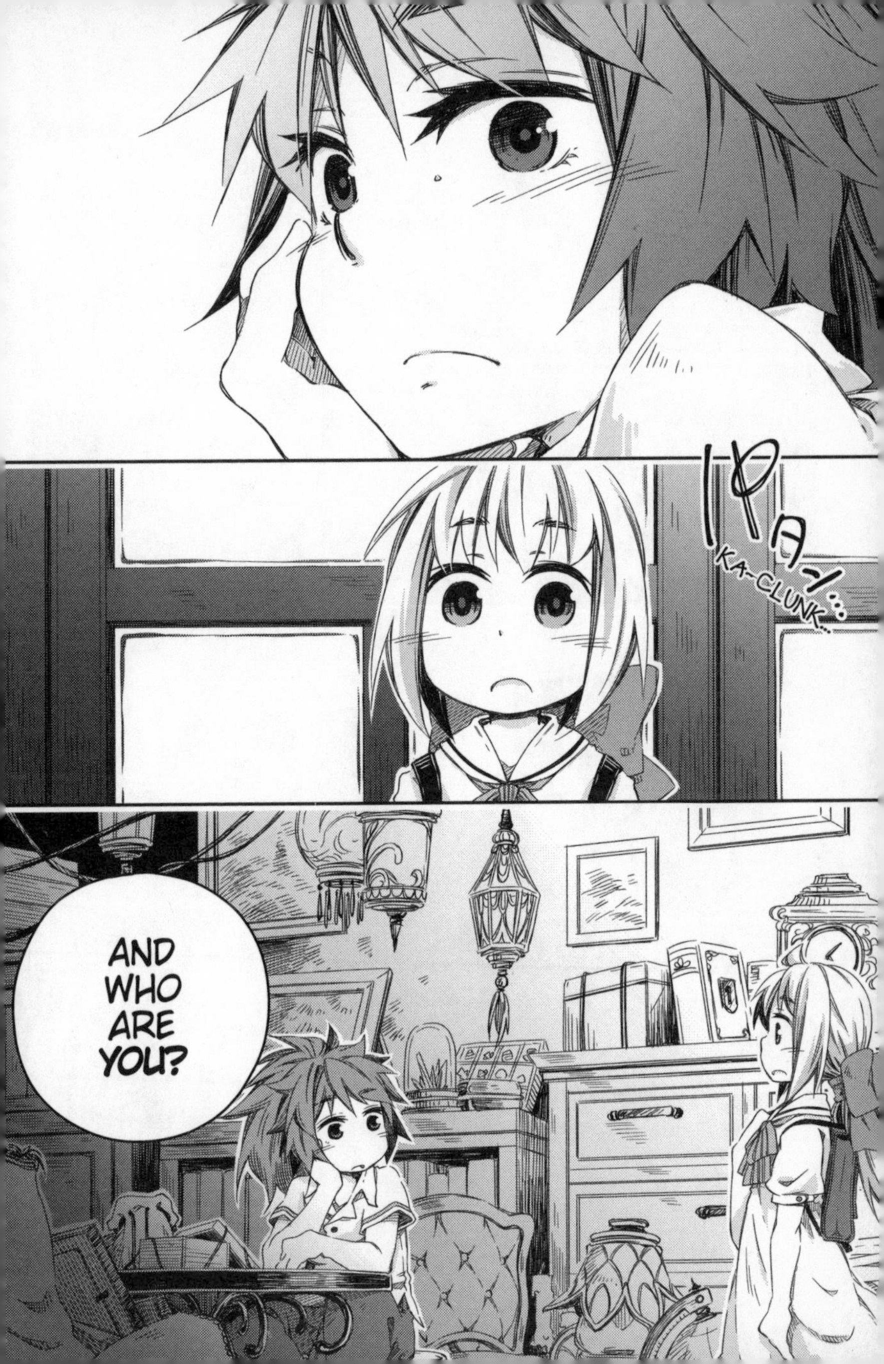
パタン…
KA-CLUNK...
AND WHO ARE YOU?

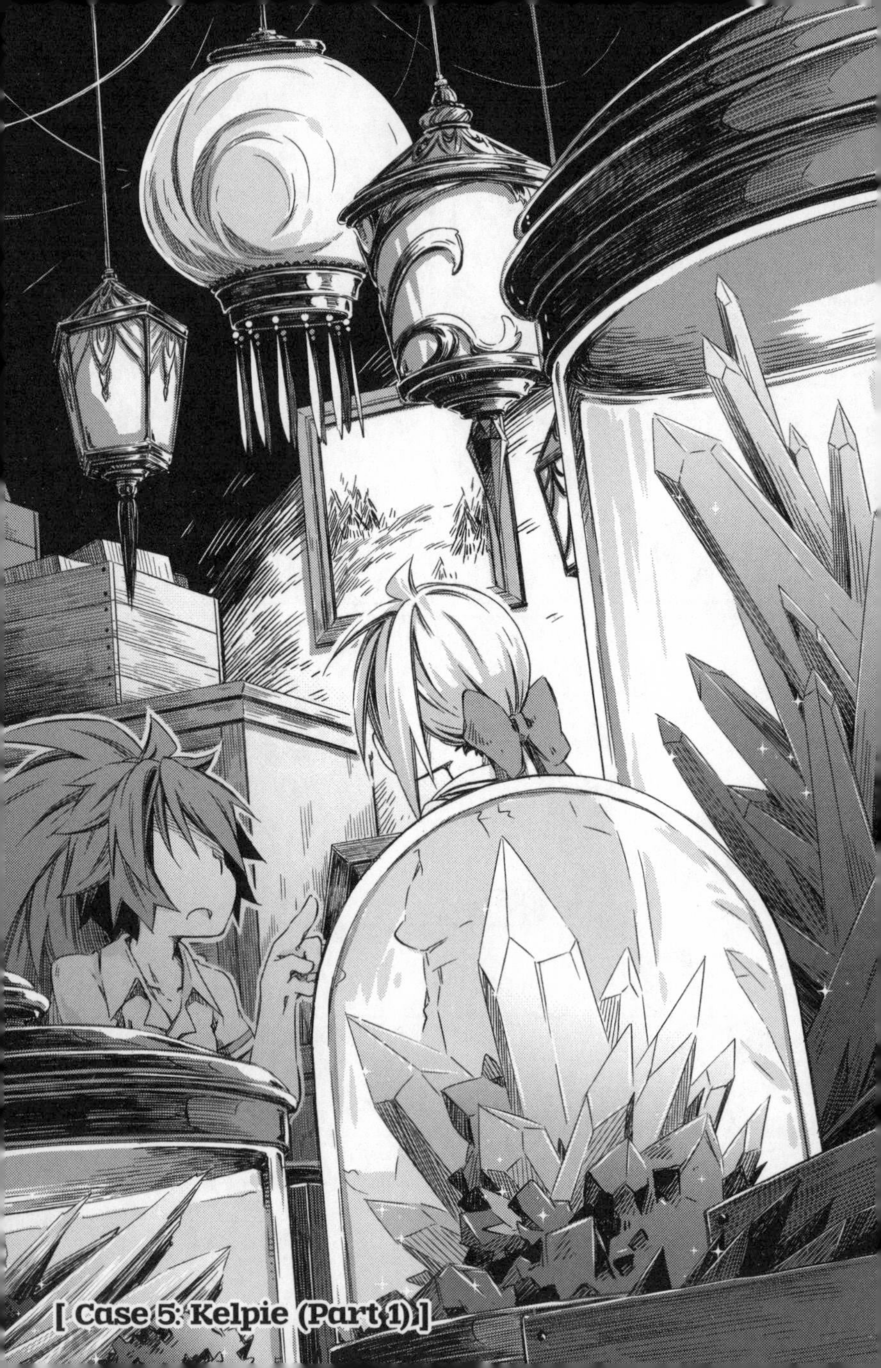
[Case 5: Kelpie (Part 1)]

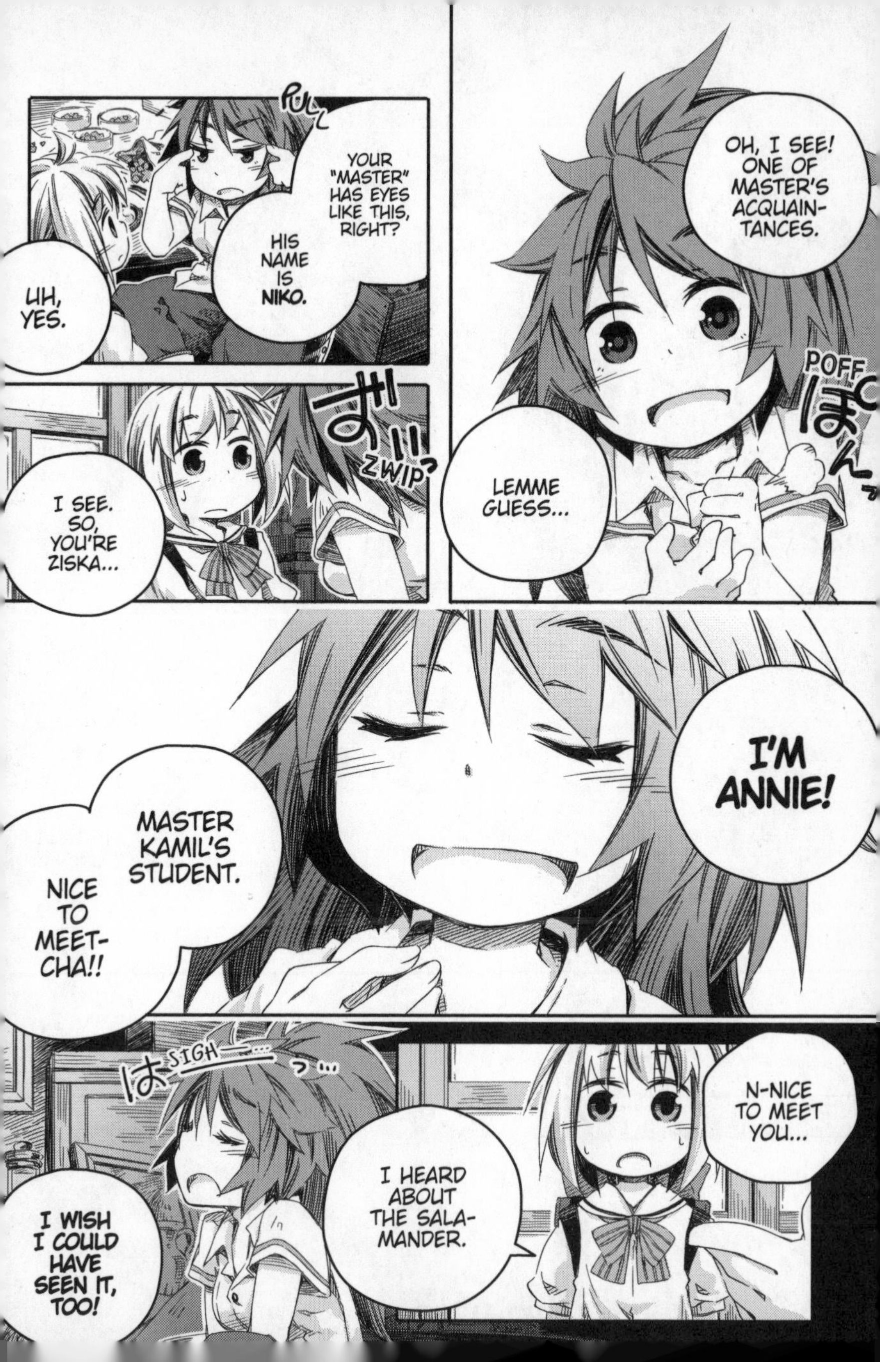
OH, I SEE! ONE OF MASTER'S ACQUAIN-TANCES.
POFF
ぽんっ
LEMME GUESS...
PULL
YOUR "MASTER" HAS EYES LIKE THIS, RIGHT?
HIS NAME IS NIKO.
UH, YES.
ずい
ZWIP
I SEE. SO, YOU'RE ZISKA...
I'M ANNIE!
MASTER KAMIL'S STUDENT.
NICE TO MEET-CHA!!
N-NICE TO MEET YOU...
I HEARD ABOUT THE SALA-MANDER.
は——っ…
SIGH
I WISH I COULD HAVE SEEN IT, TOO!

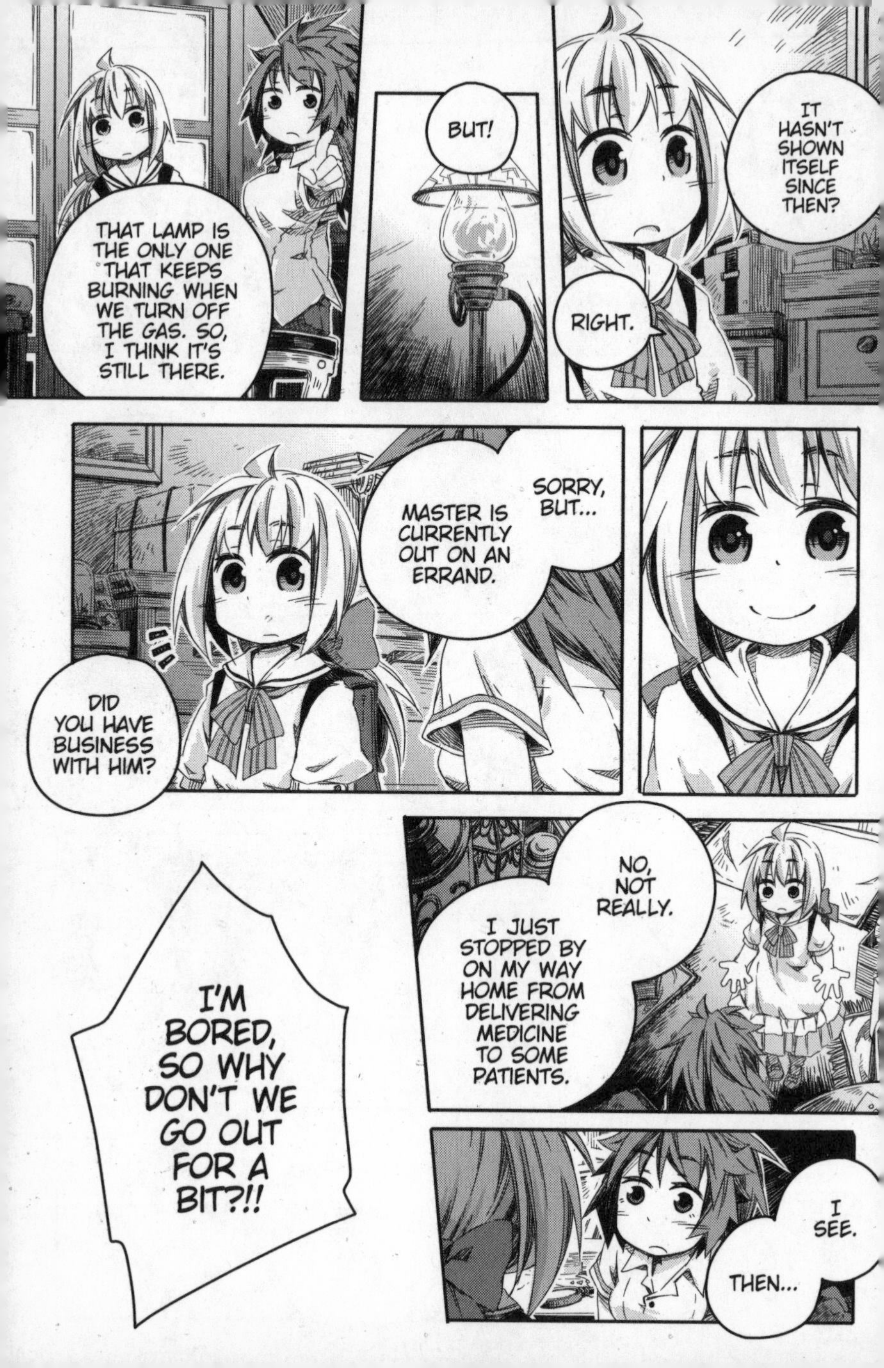

IT HASN'T SHOWN ITSELF SINCE THEN?
RIGHT.
BUT!
THAT LAMP IS THE ONLY ONE THAT KEEPS BURNING WHEN WE TURN OFF THE GAS. SO, I THINK IT'S STILL THERE.
SORRY, BUT...
MASTER IS CURRENTLY OUT ON AN ERRAND.
DID YOU HAVE BUSINESS WITH HIM?
NO, NOT REALLY.
I JUST STOPPED BY ON MY WAY HOME FROM DELIVERING MEDICINE TO SOME PATIENTS.
I SEE.
THEN...
I'M BORED, SO WHY DON'T WE GO OUT FOR A BIT?!!

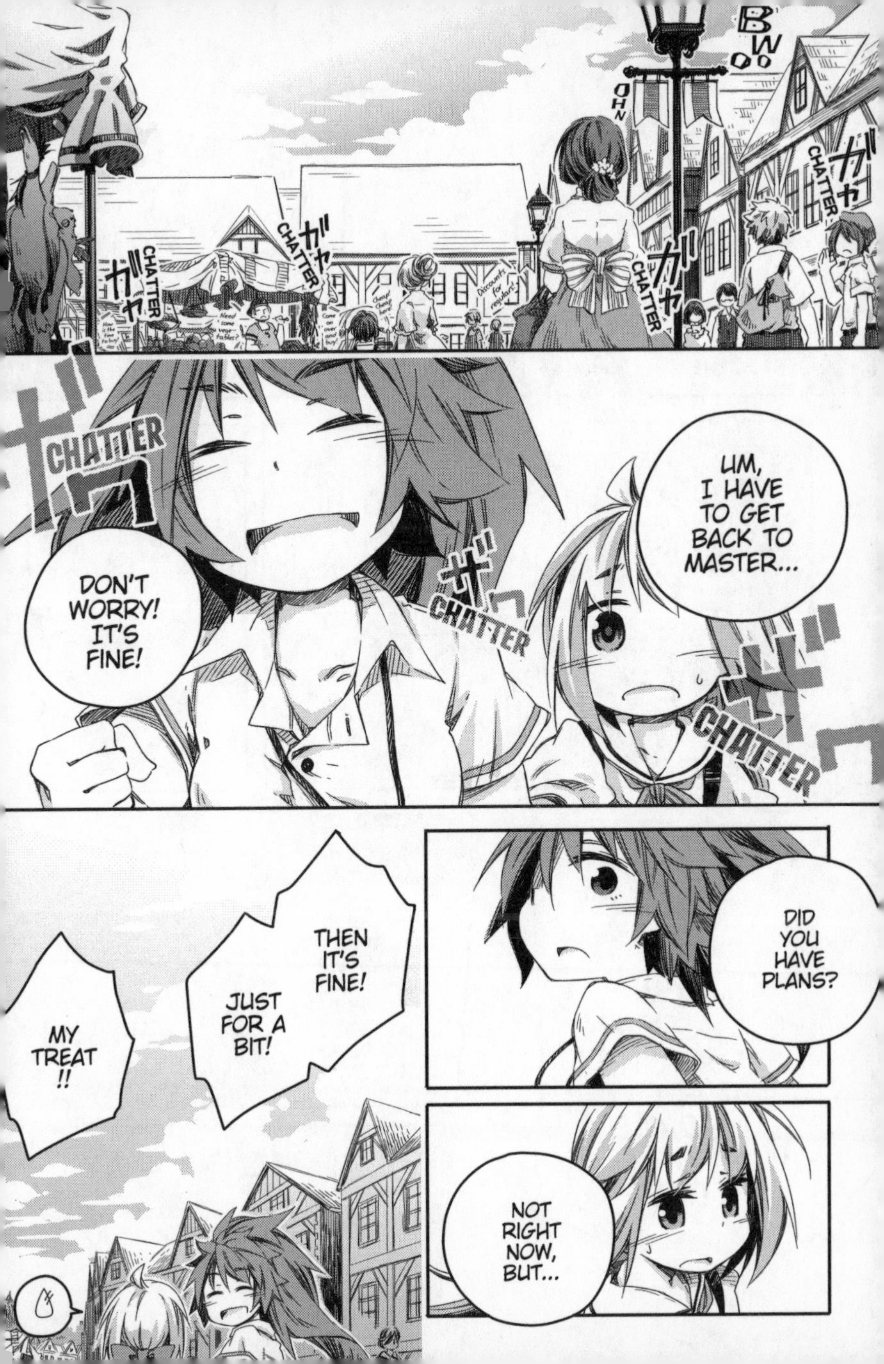
BWOOOHN
ガヤ CHATTER
ガヤ CHATTER
Discounts for regulars!
Cheap! Cheap here!
Come on over and buy!
ガヤ CHATTER
Need some vegetables?
ガヤ CHATTER
Now is the time to buy!
UM, I HAVE TO GET BACK TO MASTER...
ザワ CHATTER
ザワ CHATTER
DON'T WORRY! IT'S FINE!
ザワ CHATTER
DID YOU HAVE PLANS?
NOT RIGHT NOW, BUT...
THEN IT'S FINE!
JUST FOR A BIT!
MY TREAT!!

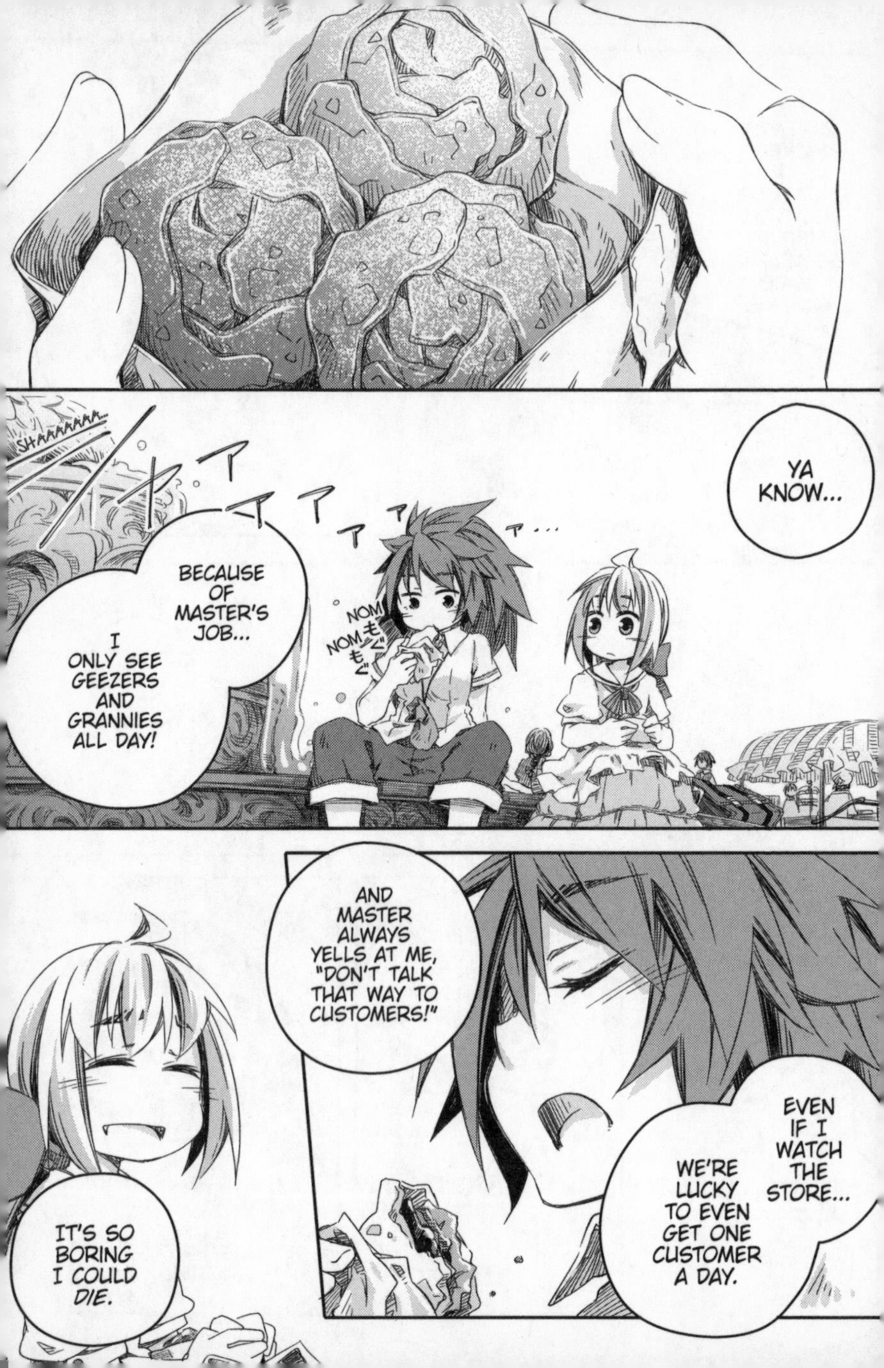
YA KNOW...
SHAAAAAAA...
BECAUSE OF MASTER'S JOB...
I ONLY SEE GEEZERS AND GRANNIES ALL DAY!
NOM もぐ NOM もぐ
AND MASTER ALWAYS YELLS AT ME, "DON'T TALK THAT WAY TO CUSTOMERS!"
EVEN IF I WATCH THE STORE...
WE'RE LUCKY TO EVEN GET ONE CUSTOMER A DAY.
IT'S SO BORING I COULD DIE.

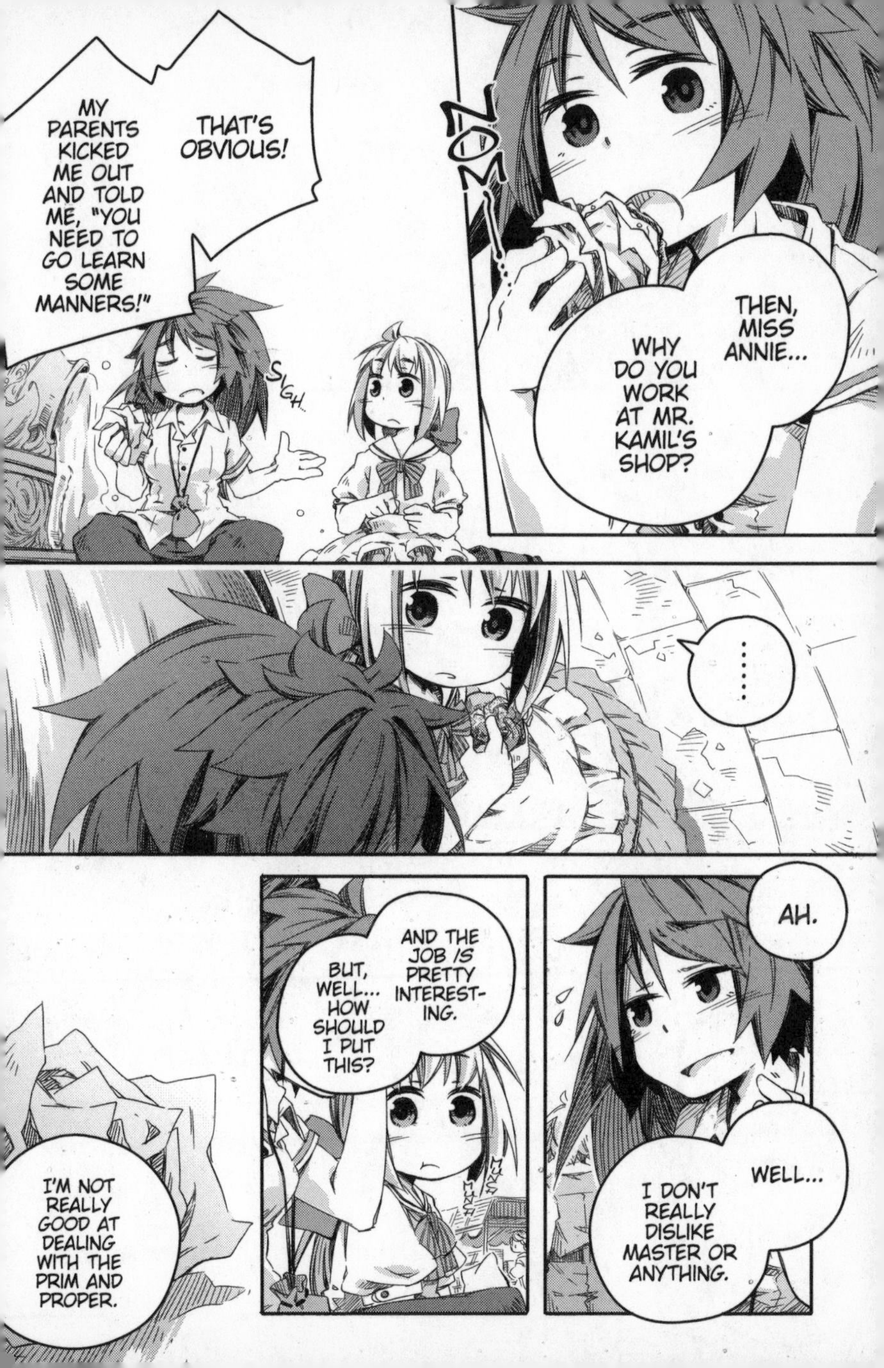
NOM
THEN, MISS ANNIE...
WHY DO YOU WORK AT MR. KAMIL'S SHOP?
THAT'S OBVIOUS!
MY PARENTS KICKED ME OUT AND TOLD ME, "YOU NEED TO GO LEARN SOME MANNERS!"
SIGH...
......
AH.
WELL...
I DON'T REALLY DISLIKE MASTER OR ANYTHING.
AND THE JOB IS PRETTY INTERESTING.
BUT, WELL... HOW SHOULD I PUT THIS?
MUNCH MUNCH
I'M NOT REALLY GOOD AT DEALING WITH THE PRIM AND PROPER.

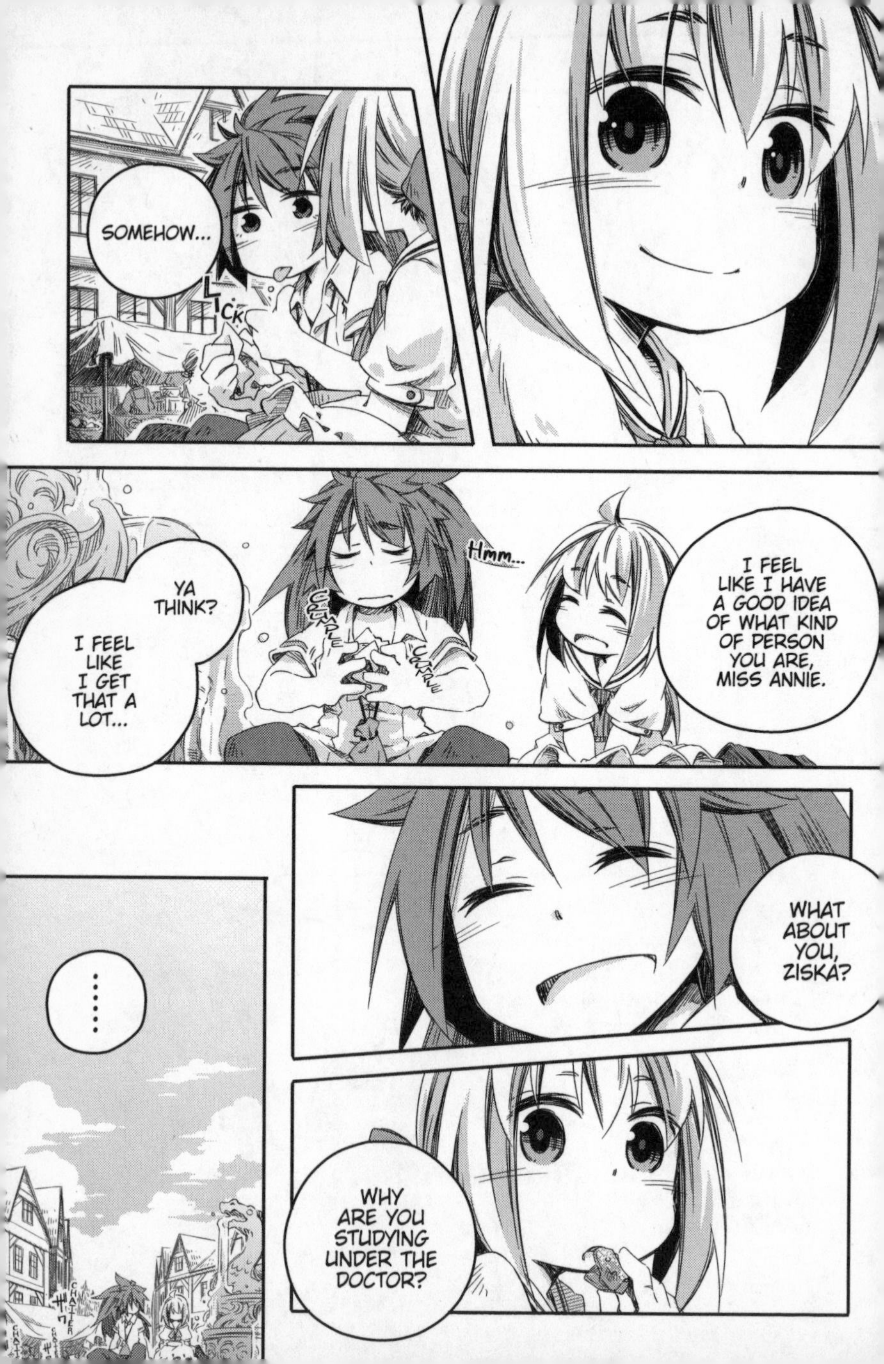
SOMEHOW...
LICK
I FEEL LIKE I HAVE A GOOD IDEA OF WHAT KIND OF PERSON YOU ARE, MISS ANNIE.
Hmm...
CRUMPLE
CRUMPLE
YA THINK?
I FEEL LIKE I GET THAT A LOT...
WHAT ABOUT YOU, ZISKA?
WHY ARE YOU STUDYING UNDER THE DOCTOR?
......

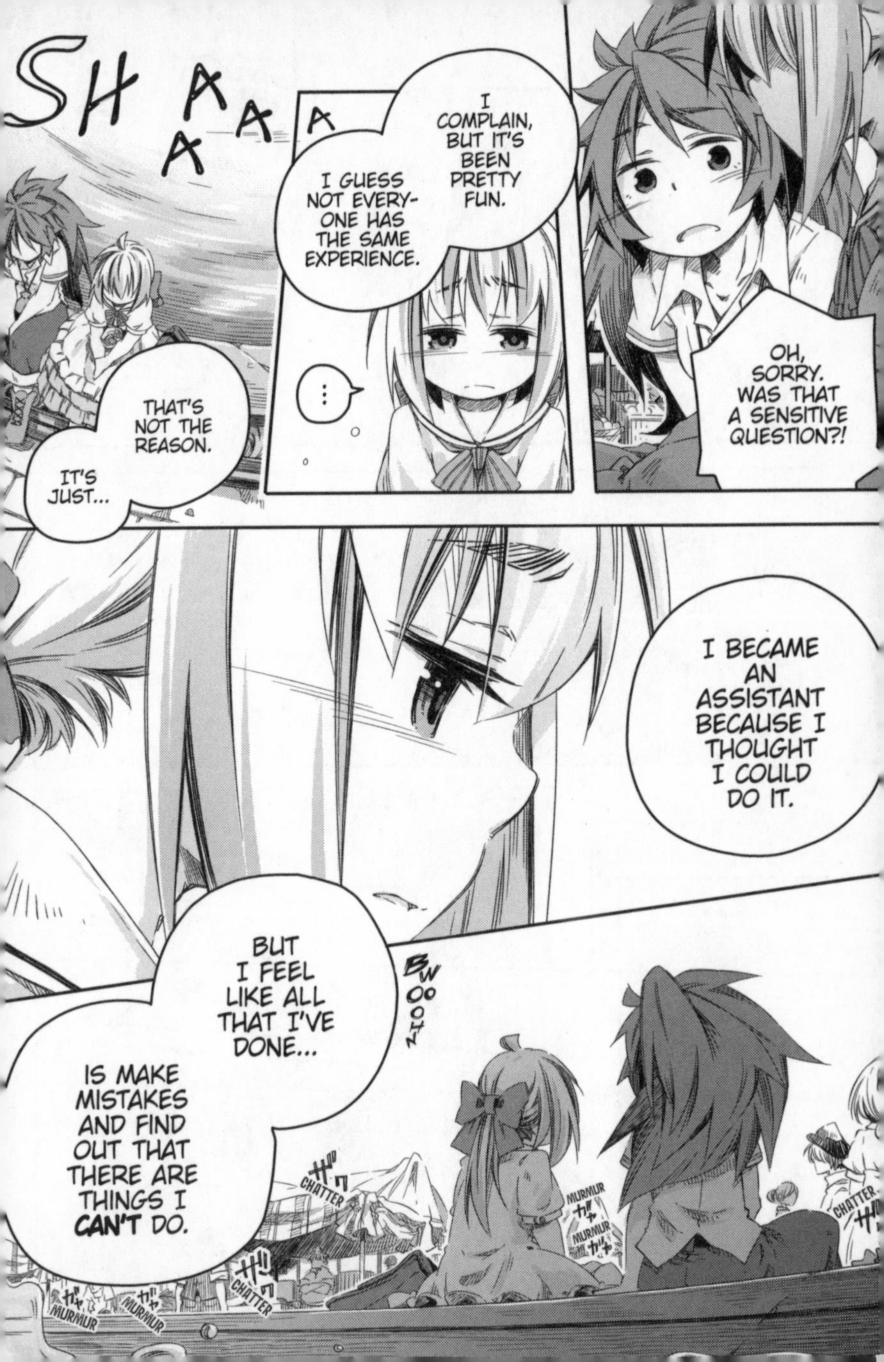
OH, SORRY. WAS THAT A SENSITIVE QUESTION?!
I COMPLAIN, BUT IT'S BEEN PRETTY FUN.
I GUESS NOT EVERY-ONE HAS THE SAME EXPERIENCE.
...
SHAAAAA
THAT'S NOT THE REASON.
IT'S JUST...
I BECAME AN ASSISTANT BECAUSE I THOUGHT I COULD DO IT.
CHATTER
MURMUR
MURMUR
BWOOOHN
BUT I FEEL LIKE ALL THAT I'VE DONE...
IS MAKE MISTAKES AND FIND OUT THAT THERE ARE THINGS I **CAN'T** DO.
CHATTER
CHATTER
MURMUR
MURMUR

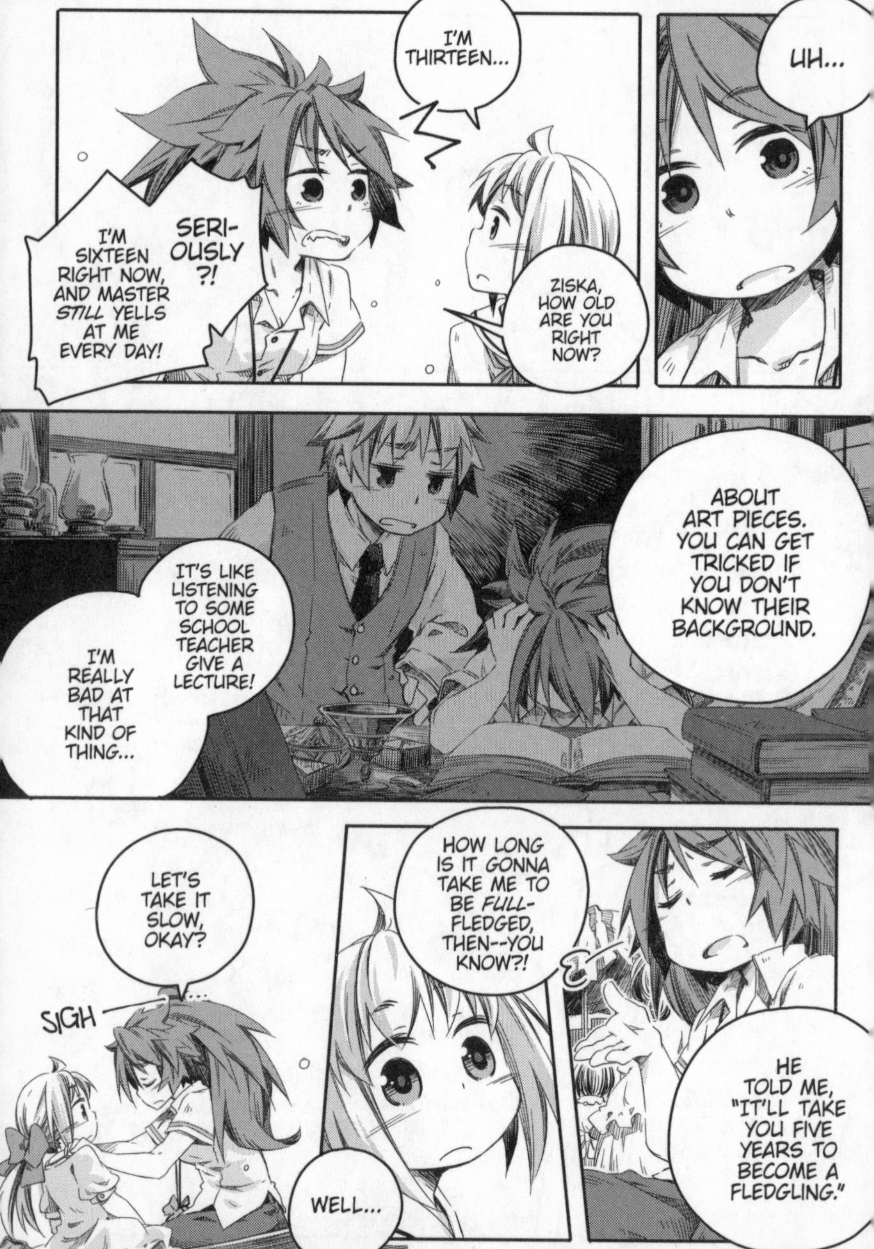
UH...
I'M THIRTEEN...
ZISKA, HOW OLD ARE YOU RIGHT NOW?
SERIOUSLY?!
I'M SIXTEEN RIGHT NOW, AND MASTER *STILL* YELLS AT ME EVERY DAY!
ABOUT ART PIECES. YOU CAN GET TRICKED IF YOU DON'T KNOW THEIR BACKGROUND.
IT'S LIKE LISTENING TO SOME SCHOOL TEACHER GIVE A LECTURE!
I'M REALLY BAD AT THAT KIND OF THING...
HOW LONG IS IT GONNA TAKE ME TO BE *FULL*-FLEDGED, THEN--YOU KNOW?!
HE TOLD ME, "IT'LL TAKE YOU FIVE YEARS TO BECOME A FLEDGLING."
WELL...
LET'S TAKE IT SLOW, OKAY?
SIGH

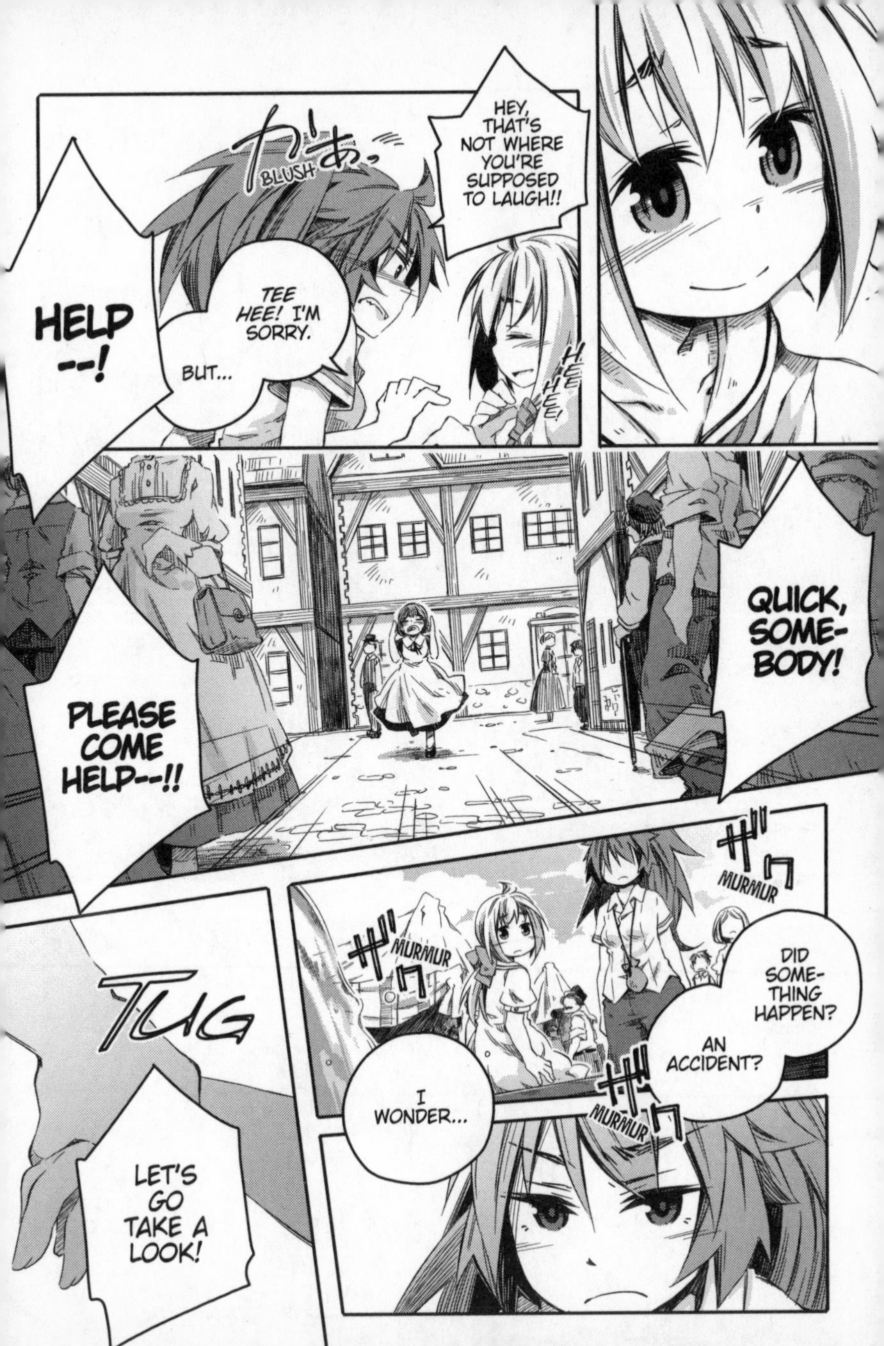
HEY, THAT'S NOT WHERE YOU'RE SUPPOSED TO LAUGH!!
BLUSH
TEE HEE! I'M SORRY.
BUT...
HEHEHE!
HELP --!
QUICK, SOME-BODY!
PLEASE COME HELP--!!
MURMUR
DID SOME-THING HAPPEN?
AN ACCIDENT?
MURMUR
MURMUR
I WONDER...
TUG
LET'S GO TAKE A LOOK!

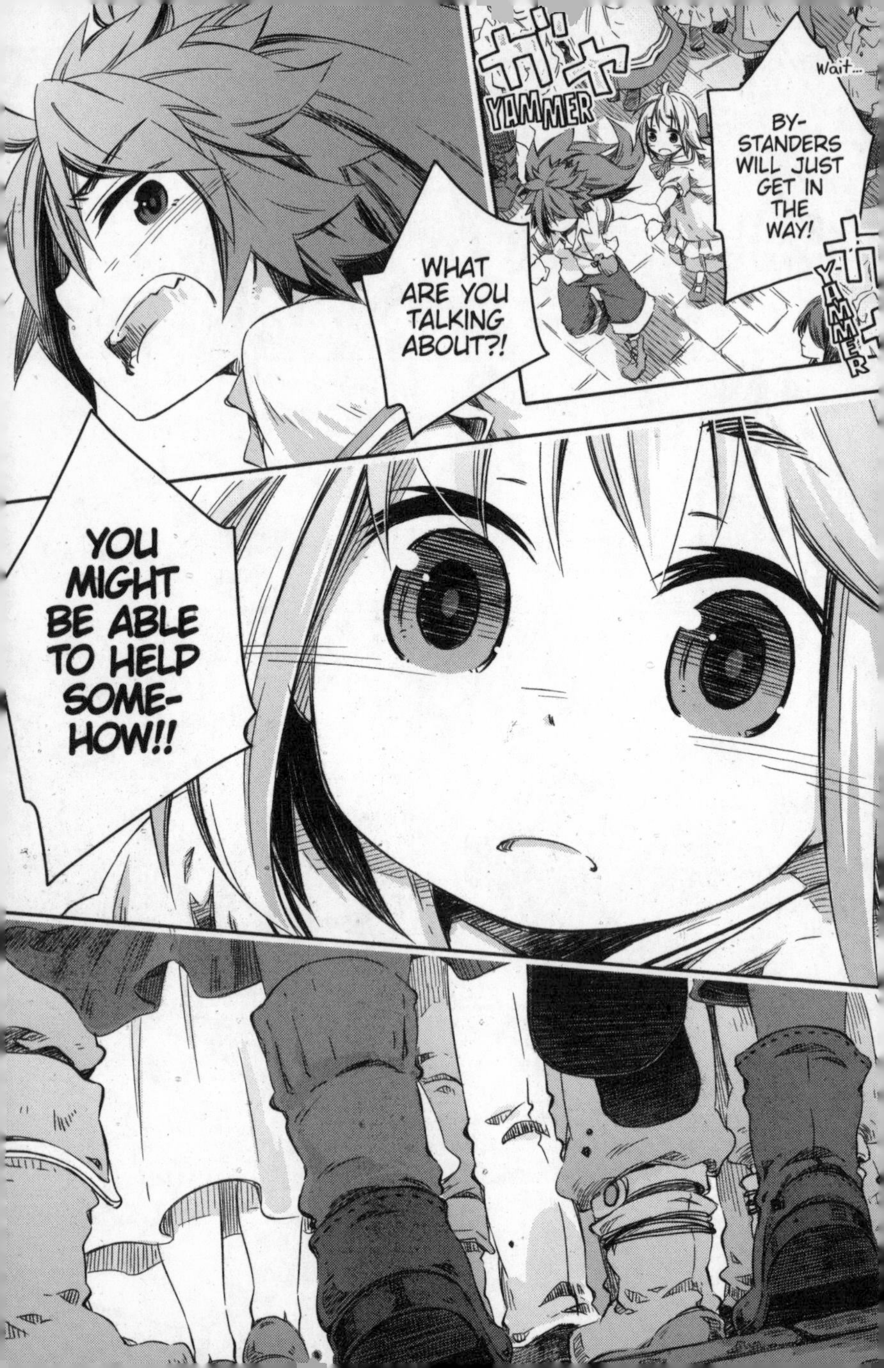

Wait...
BY-STANDERS WILL JUST GET IN THE WAY!
YAMMER
YAMMER
WHAT ARE YOU TALKING ABOUT?!
YOU MIGHT BE ABLE TO HELP SOME-HOW!!

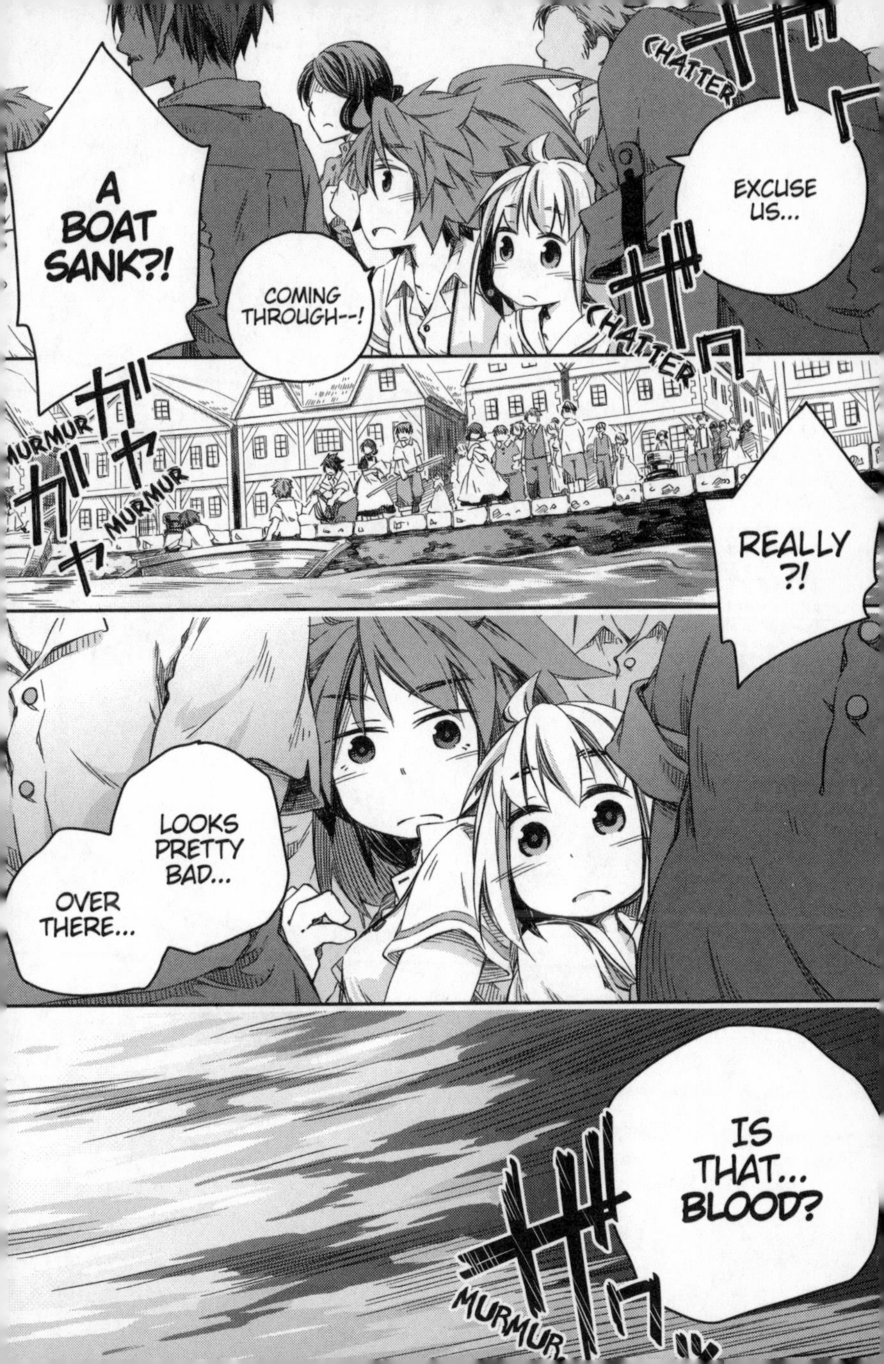
CHATTER
EXCUSE US...
CHATTER
COMING THROUGH--!
A BOAT SANK?!
REALLY ?!
MURMUR
MURMUR
LOOKS PRETTY BAD...
OVER THERE...
IS THAT... BLOOD?
MURMUR

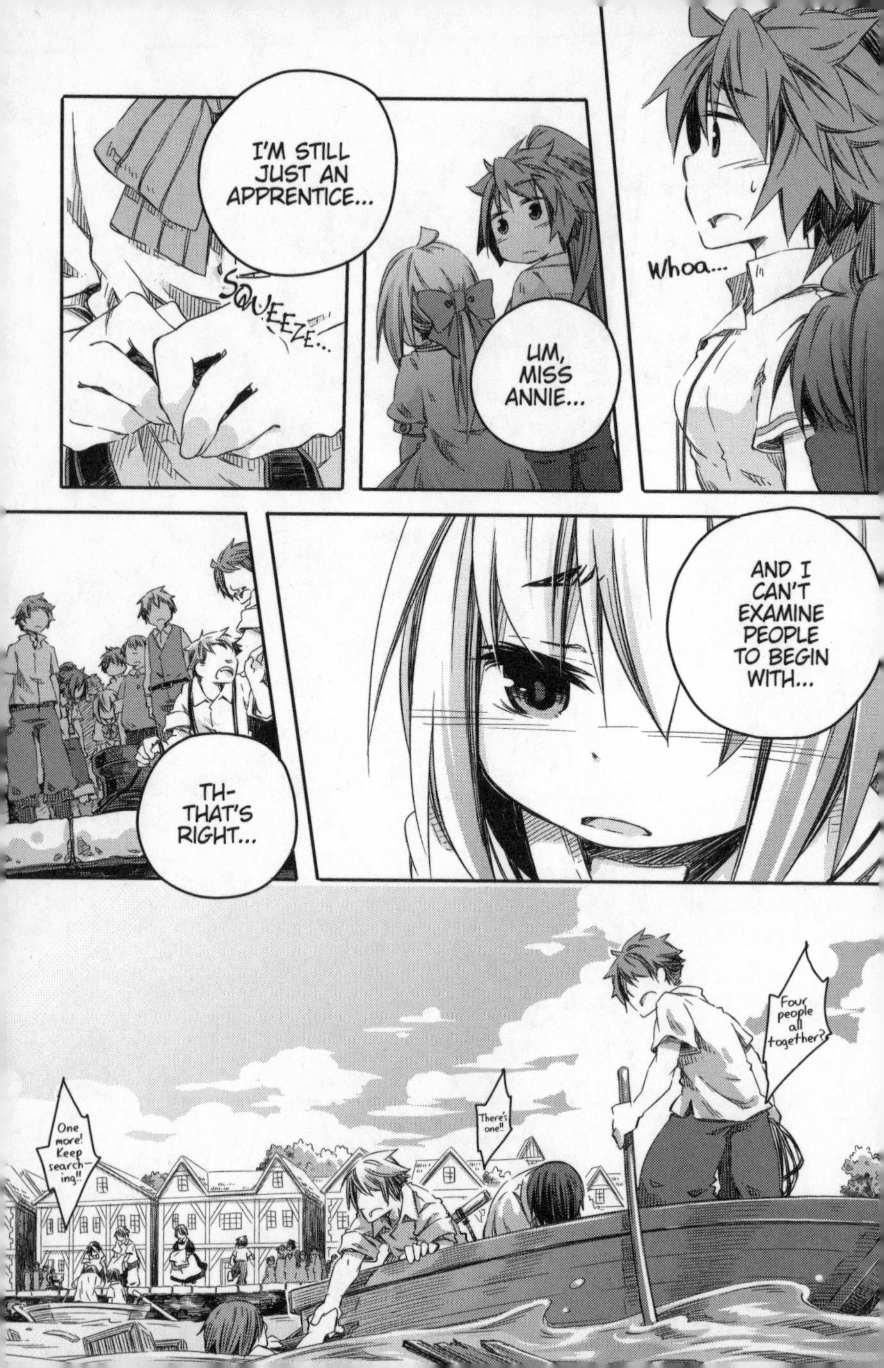
Whoa...
UM, MISS ANNIE...
I'M STILL JUST AN APPRENTICE...
SQUEEZE...
AND I CAN'T EXAMINE PEOPLE TO BEGIN WITH...
TH- THAT'S RIGHT...
Four people all together?
There's one!!
One more! Keep search-ing!!

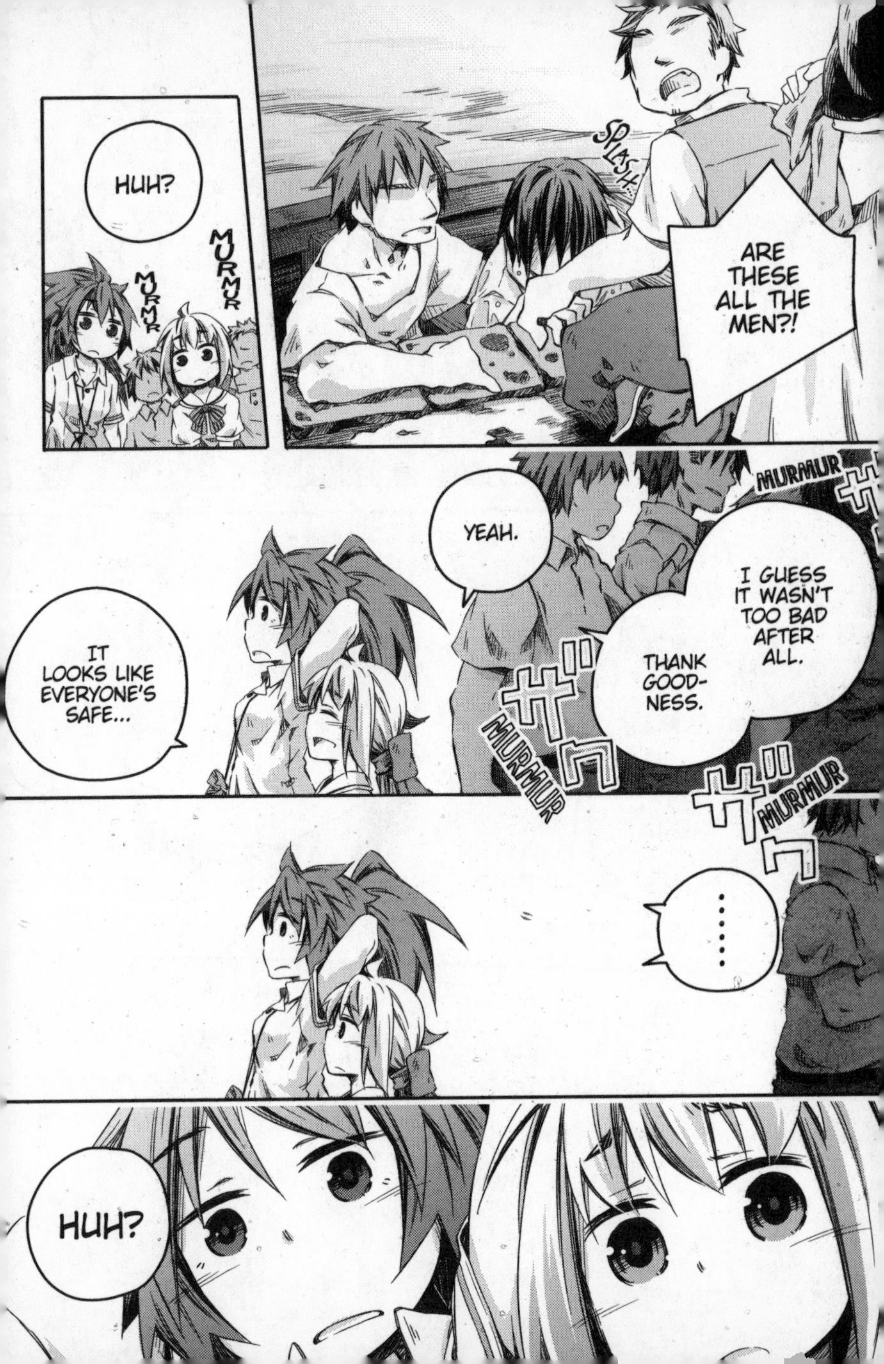
SPLASH...
ARE THESE ALL THE MEN?!
HUH?
MURMUR
MURMUR
MURMUR
I GUESS IT WASN'T TOO BAD AFTER ALL.
THANK GOODNESS.
YEAH.
IT LOOKS LIKE EVERYONE'S SAFE...
MURMUR
MURMUR
......
HUH?

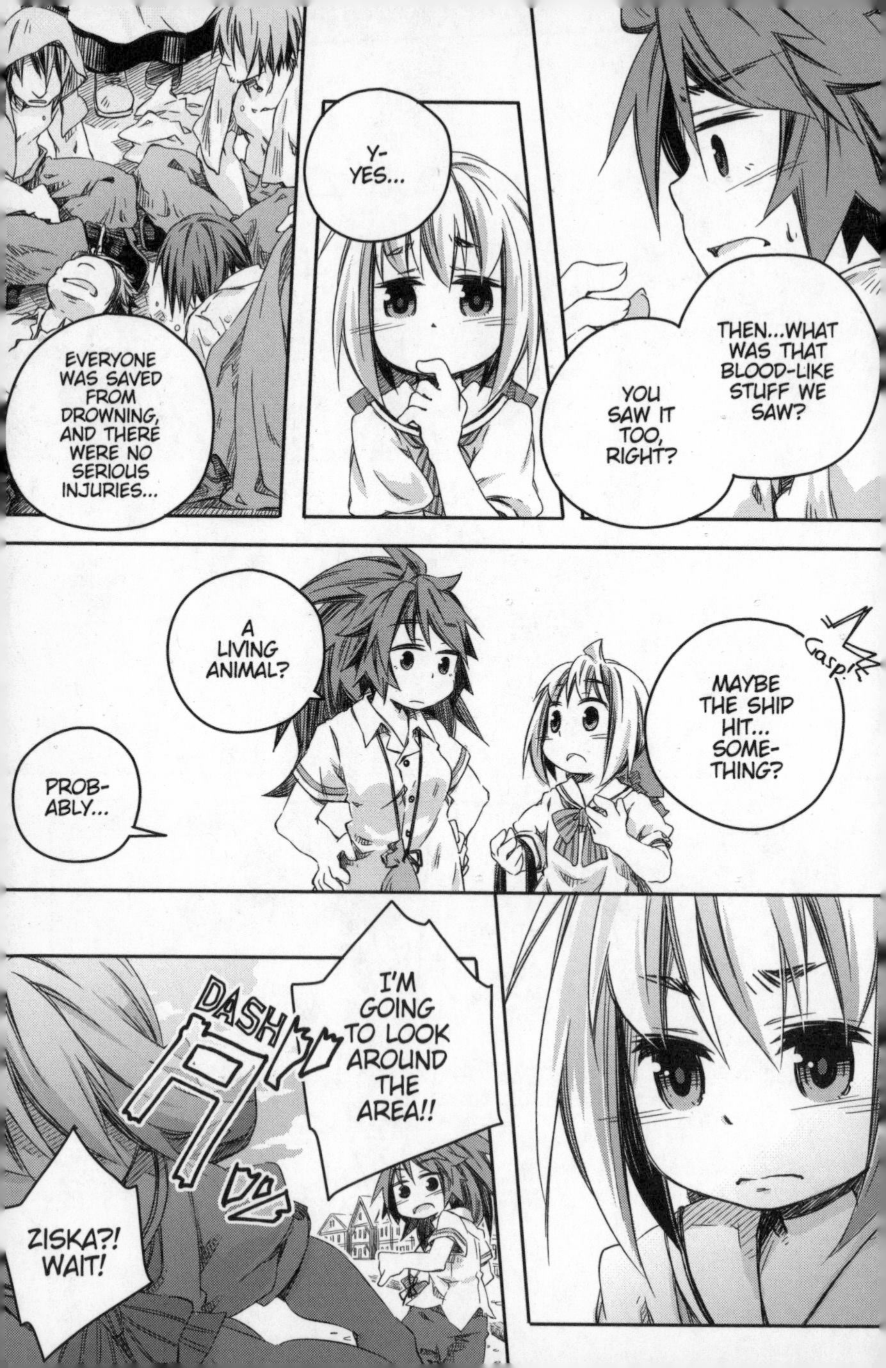
THEN...WHAT WAS THAT BLOOD-LIKE STUFF WE SAW?
YOU SAW IT TOO, RIGHT?
Y- YES...
EVERYONE WAS SAVED FROM DROWNING, AND THERE WERE NO SERIOUS INJURIES...
Gasp!!
MAYBE THE SHIP HIT... SOME-THING?
A LIVING ANIMAL?
PROB-ABLY...
I'M GOING TO LOOK AROUND THE AREA!!
DASH
ZISKA?! WAIT!

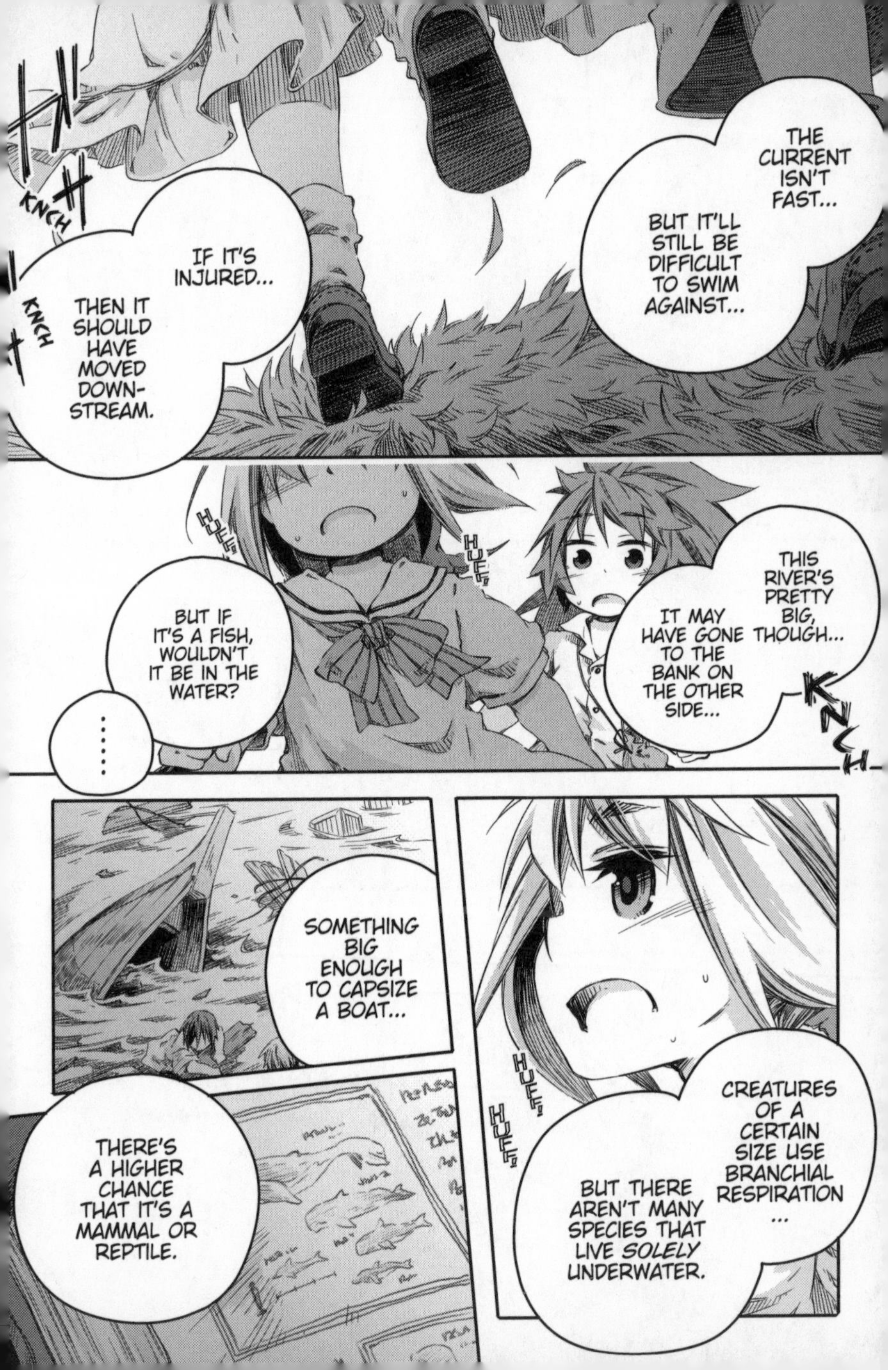
KNCH
KNCH
THE CURRENT ISN'T FAST...
BUT IT'LL STILL BE DIFFICULT TO SWIM AGAINST...
IF IT'S INJURED...
THEN IT SHOULD HAVE MOVED DOWN-STREAM.
THIS RIVER'S PRETTY BIG, THOUGH...
IT MAY HAVE GONE TO THE BANK ON THE OTHER SIDE...
KNCH
HUFF
HUFF
BUT IF IT'S A FISH, WOULDN'T IT BE IN THE WATER?
......
HUFF
HUFF
CREATURES OF A CERTAIN SIZE USE BRANCHIAL RESPIRATION...
BUT THERE AREN'T MANY SPECIES THAT LIVE *SOLELY* UNDERWATER.
SOMETHING BIG ENOUGH TO CAPSIZE A BOAT...
THERE'S A HIGHER CHANCE THAT IT'S A MAMMAL OR REPTILE.

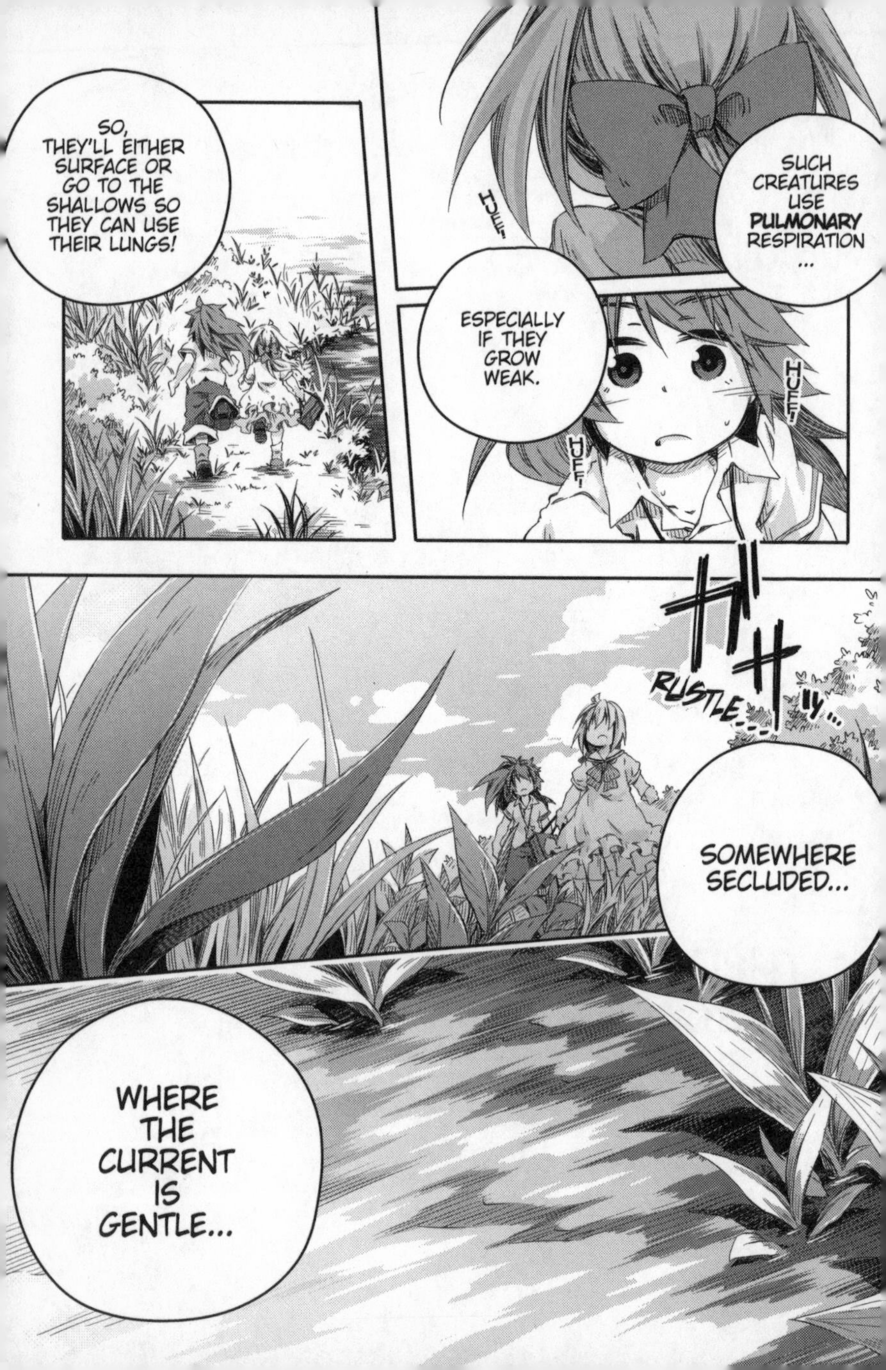
SUCH CREATURES USE **PULMONARY** RESPIRATION ...
HUFF!
ESPECIALLY IF THEY GROW WEAK.
HUFF!
HUFF!
SO, THEY'LL EITHER SURFACE OR GO TO THE SHALLOWS SO THEY CAN USE THEIR LUNGS!
RUSTLE...
SOMEWHERE SECLUDED...
WHERE THE CURRENT IS GENTLE...

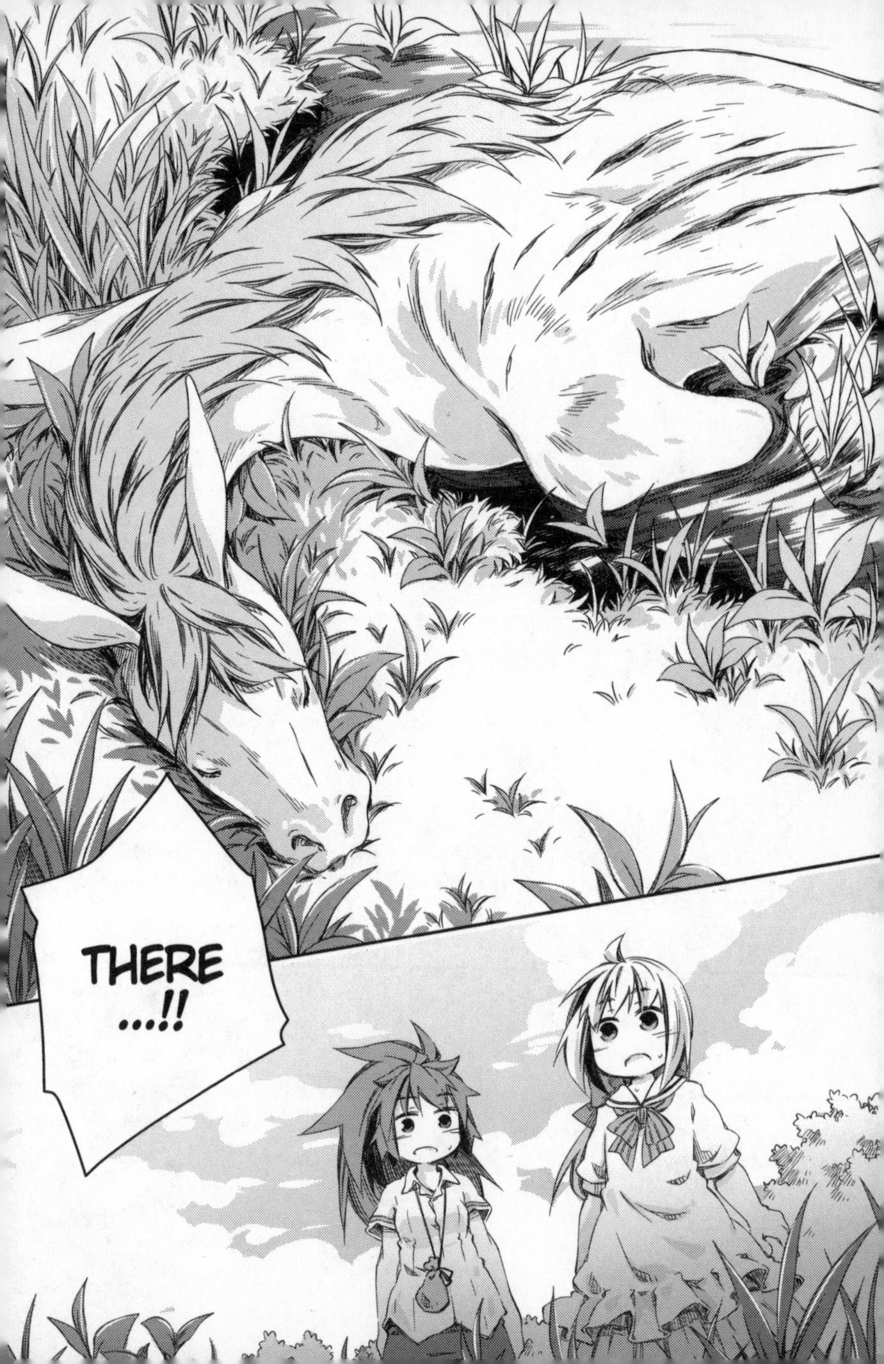
THERE ...!!

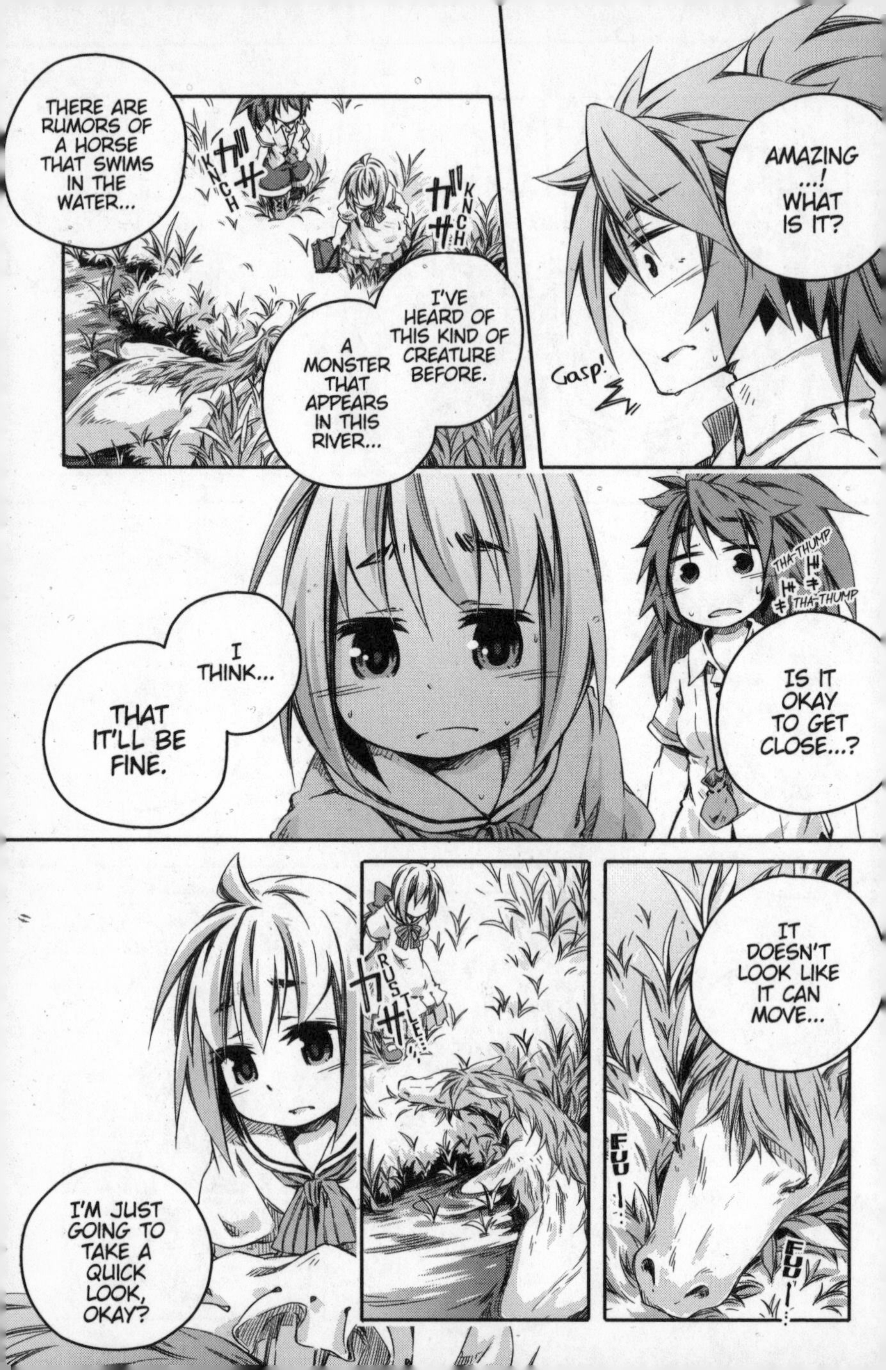
AMAZING...! WHAT IS IT?
Gasp!
KNCH
KNCH
I'VE HEARD OF THIS KIND OF CREATURE BEFORE.
A MONSTER THAT APPEARS IN THIS RIVER...
THERE ARE RUMORS OF A HORSE THAT SWIMS IN THE WATER...
THA-THUMP
THA-THUMP
IS IT OKAY TO GET CLOSE...?
I THINK...
THAT IT'LL BE FINE.
IT DOESN'T LOOK LIKE IT CAN MOVE...
FUU...!
FUU...!
RUSTLE...
I'M JUST GOING TO TAKE A QUICK LOOK, OKAY?

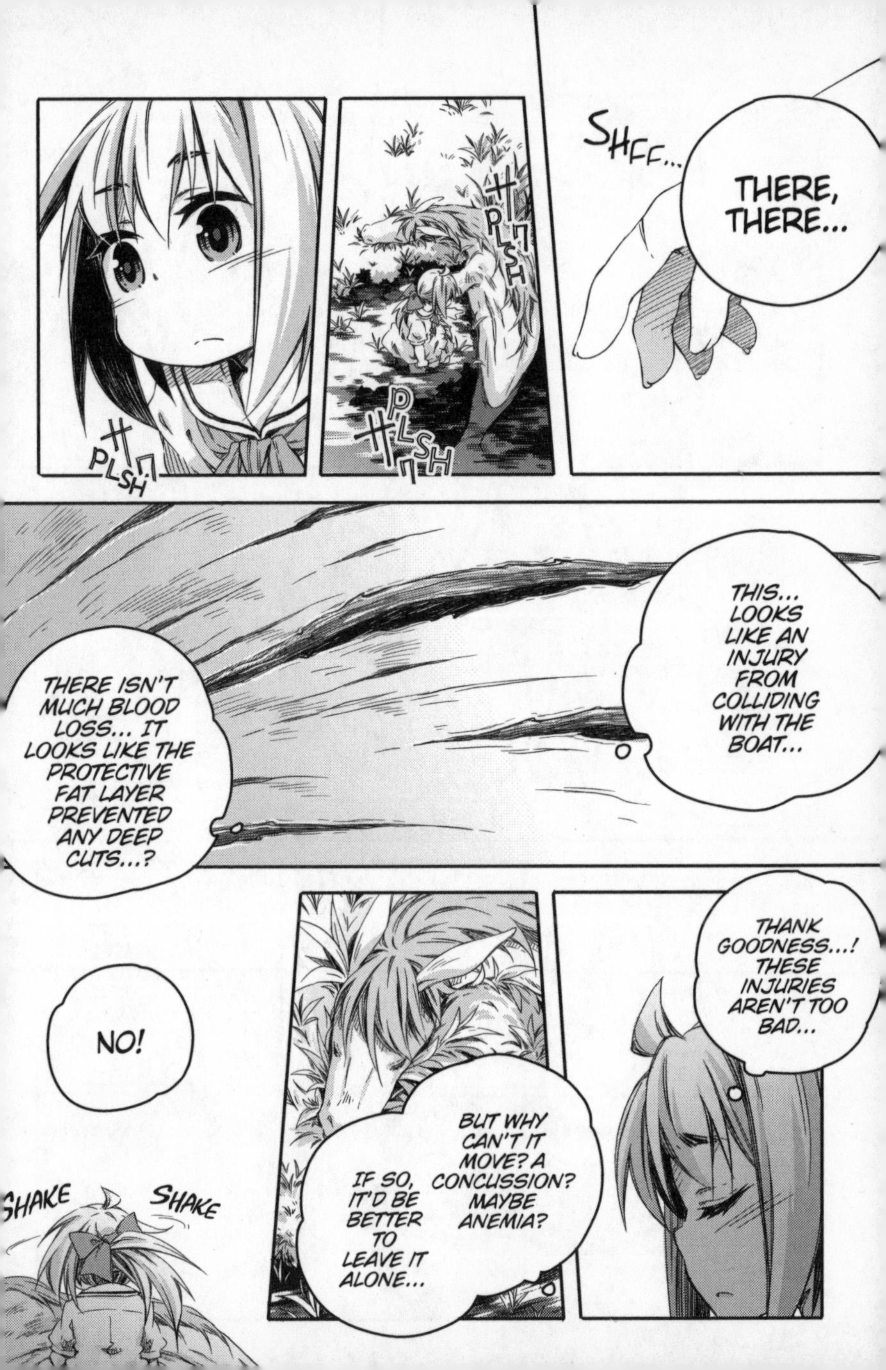
SHFF...
THERE, THERE...
PLSH
PLSH
PLSH
THIS... LOOKS LIKE AN INJURY FROM COLLIDING WITH THE BOAT...
THERE ISN'T MUCH BLOOD LOSS... IT LOOKS LIKE THE PROTECTIVE FAT LAYER PREVENTED ANY DEEP CUTS...?
THANK GOODNESS...! THESE INJURIES AREN'T TOO BAD...
BUT WHY CAN'T IT MOVE? A CONCUSSION? MAYBE ANEMIA?
IF SO, IT'D BE BETTER TO LEAVE IT ALONE...
NO!
SHAKE
SHAKE

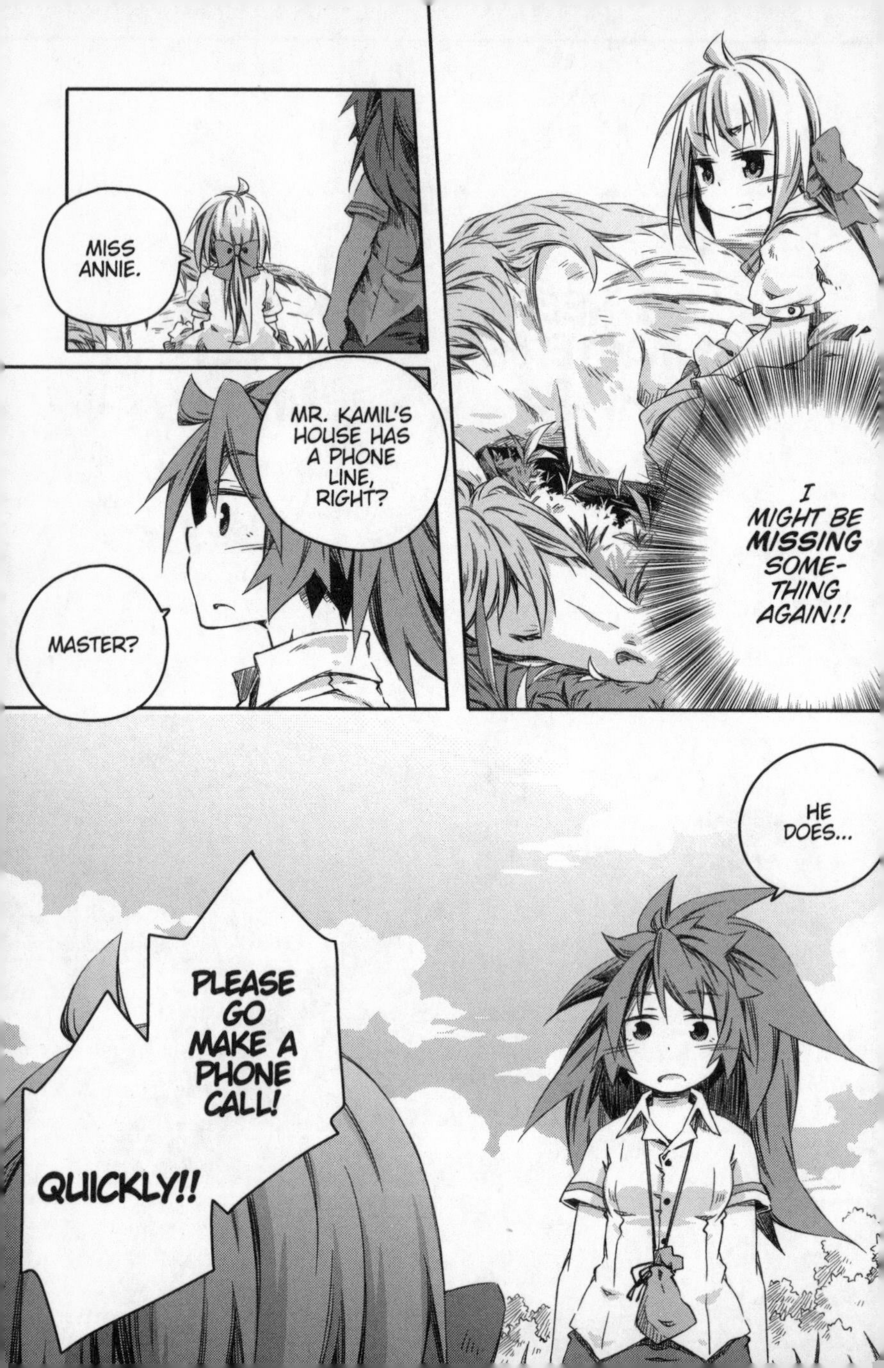
I MIGHT BE MISSING SOMETHING AGAIN!!
MISS ANNIE.
MR. KAMIL'S HOUSE HAS A PHONE LINE, RIGHT?
MASTER?
HE DOES...
PLEASE GO MAKE A PHONE CALL!
QUICKLY!!

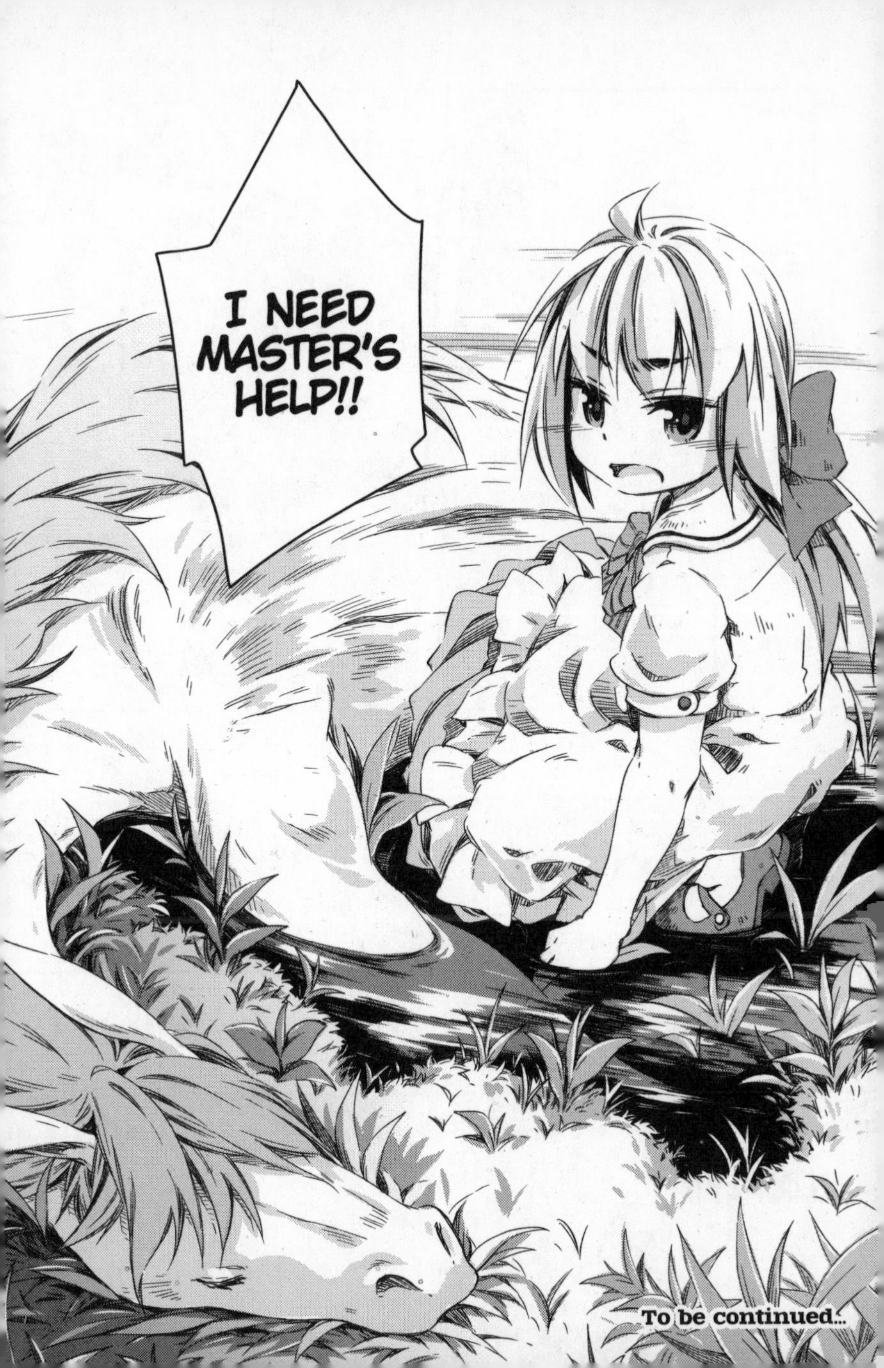
I NEED MASTER'S HELP!!
To be continued...